The Prophets and the
Rise of Judaism

PLATE I

An Assyrian king of the ninth or eighth century receiving the homage of a conquered enemy. From a fresco discovered by M. Thureau-Dangin, in the palace of Tell Ahmar (*Syria*, XI, 1930. Pl. XXIII)

THE PROPHETS
AND THE
RISE OF JUDAISM

By

ADOLPHE LODS

Professor at the Sorbonne

Author of **Israel from its Beginnings to the Middle
of the Eighth Century**

Translated by

S. H. HOOKE

*Davidson Professor of Old Testament
Studies, University of London*

GREENWOOD PRESS, PUBLISHERS
WESTPORT, CONNECTICUT

The Library of Congress cataloged this book as follows:

Lods, Adolphe, 1867–1948.
    The prophets and the rise of Judaism. Translated by
S. H. Hooke. Westport, Conn., Greenwood Press [1971]

    xxiv, 378 p. illus. 23 cm. $15.00

    Translation of Les prophètes d'Israël et les débuts des judaïsme.
    Reprint of the 1937 ed.
    Bibliography: p. 357–368.

    1. Judaism—History—Ancient period. 2. Prophets.   I. Title.

BM165.L613 1971   296′.09   77–109772
ISBN 0–8371–4262–8   MARC

Library of Congress   72 [4]

Originally published in 1937 by E. P. Dutton & Company,
New York

Reprinted in 1971 by Greenwood Press, Inc.,
51 Riverside Avenue, Westport, Conn. 06880

Library of Congress catalog card number 77-109772
ISBN 0-8371-4262-8

Printed in the United States of America

10 9 8 7 6 5 4 3 2

CONTENTS

PAGE

FOREWORD. By Henri Berr xi

INTRODUCTION

   I. Purpose and Plan of the Book. 1

  II. The Sources 2
     1. Epigraphy and Archæology, 2.—2. Literary Sources, 5.

PART I

THE ERA OF CONFLICT (760–586): ISRAEL AND JUDAH AT WAR WITH ASSYRIA AND BABYLONIA. THE STRUGGLE OF THE PROPHETS WITH THE NATIONAL RELIGION

BOOK I

THE POLITICAL STRUGGLE

CHAPTER

   I. THE ASSYRIAN CONQUEST. END OF THE KINGDOM OF ISRAEL 17

  II. END OF THE KINGDOM OF JUDAH . . . 28
     I. The Assyrian Power at its Height. Reigns of Hezekiah, Manasseh, and Amon (circ. 720–638), 28.—II. The Decline of Assyria. Judah's Last Period of Greatness: Josiah (circ. 637–609), 40.—III. The Egyptian Conquest. The Neo-Babylonian Empire. Last years of the Kingdom of Judah (609–586), 43.

BOOK II

THE RELIGIOUS CONFLICT. THE PROPHETS IN CONFLICT WITH THE NATIONAL RELIGION

   I. GENERAL CHARACTERISTICS OF THE PROPHETIC MOVEMENT 51
     I. The Phenomena of Inspiration among the Great Prophets, 51.—II. Spiritual Content of the Message of the Great

v

CONTENTS

Prophets, 59.—III. Origins of the various Elements of the Prophetic Message : (1) Certainty of the imminent downfall of the Nation, 62 ; (2) The Prophets and Civilization, 63 ; (3) The Prophets and the Cult, 66 ; (4) The Prophets' Vision of the Future, 69 ; (5) Ethical Monotheism, 72.—IV. The Main Lines of Development of the Prophetic Movement, 76.

II. THE PROPHETS OF ISRAEL IN THE EIGHTH CENTURY   79
I. Amos : (1) The Life of the Prophet, 79 ; (2) The Mission of Amos, 83.—II. Hosea, 87.

III. THE PROPHETIC MOVEMENT IN THE KINGDOM OF JUDAH IN THE EIGHTH CENTURY . .   99
I. Isaiah : (1) The Career of the Prophet, 99 ; (2) The Personality of Isaiah, 108.—II. Micah, 111.—III. Hezekiah's Reform, 114.—IV. The Spread of Prophetic Ideas, 116.

IV. RELIGIOUS LIFE IN THE KINGDOM OF JUDAH IN THE SEVENTH CENTURY   122
I. Period of Syncretism. Reigns of Manasseh and Amon. Josiah's Minority, 122.—II. Revival of Prophetic Opposition. Zephaniah. Beginning of Jeremiah's Career, 130.

V. JOSIAH'S REFORM   134
I. Customary Law and the Torah before the Reform, 134.—II. Josiah's Reform. Discussion of the Account in the Book of Kings, 137.—III. The Torah of Josiah, 142.—Appendix : Identity of the Code discovered in the reign of Josiah. Date of its Composition : (1) Josiah's Reform and Deuteronomy, 143 ; (2) Date of the Redaction of the Code of Josiah, 146.—IV. Nature of the Reform under Josiah, 149.—V. Consequences of Josiah's Reform, 153.

VI. THE LAST YEARS OF THE KINGDOM OF JUDAH .   155
I. End of the Reign of Josiah. Jeremiah's estimate of the Reform. Revival of national Jahwism : Nahum, 155.—II. Religious Life under the last four Kings of Judah, 158.—III. Work and Personality of Jeremiah, 167.

PART II

THE BEGINNINGS OF JUDAISM

BOOK I

THE HISTORICAL BACKGROUND

I. THE EXILE   173
I. The Jews split into three Groups. Their Political and Economic Condition, 173.—II. Rise and Fall of the Neo-Babylonian Empire, 180.

CONTENTS vii

CHAPTER   PAGE

II. THE JEWS UNDER PERSIAN DOMINATION . . 184
I. The Reign of Cyrus. The Return of the first body of
Exiles to Judah. Cambyses, 184.—Appendix: The List
of the Jews who returned from Exile in Ezra ii and
Nehemiah vii, 190.—II. Darius I (521–486). Rebuilding of
the Temple, 193.—III. Gradual Decay of the Persian
Empire, 194.

III. THE JEWS UNDER GREEK DOMINATION . . 200

BOOK II

RELIGION. DEVELOPMENT IN ISRAEL OF A NEW RELIGIOUS TYPE. JUDAISM   205

I. THE RELIGIOUS ATTITUDE OF THE MASSES AT
THE TIME OF THE EXILE 207

II. THE TRANSFORMATION OF PROPHECY DURING
THE EXILE 211
I. Ezekiel : (1) The Prophet and the Exiles before 586, 211 ;
(2) Ezekiel and the Exiles after 586, 217 ; (3) The
Personality of Ezekiel, 227.—II. Habakkuk, 232.—III.
The Prophets of the Close of the Exile : Isaiah, xiii–xiv ;
Isaiah xxi, Second Isaiah, 236.—IV. The Development of
Prophecy during the Exile, 249.

III. THE RITUALIST MOVEMENT AT THE TIME OF THE
EXILE 251
I. The Torah of Ezekiel, 251 : (1) The Idea of Holiness,
253 ; (2) The Importance of Ritual, 257 ; (3) The Idea of
Atonement, 258.—II. The Holiness Code, 262.

IV. THE FIRST CENTURY OF THE RESTORATION.
GRADUAL DISAPPEARANCE OF PROPHECY . 265
I. The Return, 265.—II. Haggai and Zechariah. Re-
building of the Temple, 268.—III. From the Rebuilding
of the Temple to that of the Walls, Isaiah lvi–lxvi,
Malachi, 272.

V. COMPLETION OF THE REDACTION OF THE
PRIESTLY LEGISLATION. ITS ADOPTION BY
THE JUDAISM OF THE SECOND CENTURY OF
THE RESTORATION 281
I. The Priestly Redaction and Sacred History, 281.—II.
Further Ritual Legislation of the Restoration Period. The
Priestly Code, 285.—III. Value and Purpose of Ritual
according to the Priestly Legislation, 290.—Appendix :
Nature and Function of Sacrifice according to the Priestly
Code, 293.—IV. Nehemiah and Ezra, 296.—V. The Jewish
Colony at Elephantine, 304.—VI. Completion of the
Pentateuch. The Samaritan Schism, 312.

CONTENTS

BOOK III

RELIGION (*concl.*). GENERAL CHARACTERISTICS OF RELIGIOUS LIFE IN EARLY JUDAISM

I. RELIGIOUS THOUGHT. GROWTH OF SYSTEMATIC THEOLOGY 321

I. The Doctrine of God, 322.—II. The Doctrine of Retribution, 325.—III. Eschatology, 331.

II. RELIGIOUS THOUGHT (*concl.*). DISCUSSION OF THE PREVALENT DOCTRINES 334

I. Ruth and Jonah, 334.—II. The Book of Job, 335.—III. Ecclesiastes, 341.

III. PIETY 346

BIBLIOGRAPHY 357

INDEX 369

LIST OF ILLUSTRATIONS

PLATE   PAGE

I. An Assyrian King of the Ninth or Eighth Century receiving the Homage of a Conquered Enemy. From a Fresco discovered by M. Thureau-Dangin, in the Palace of Tell Ahmar. (*Syria*, xi, 1930, pl. xxiii) . . . . *Frontispiece*

II. Sennacherib Receives the Surrender of the City of Lachish (2 Kings xviii, 13–17). Bas-relief in the British Museum 28

III. Esarhaddon Holding Conquered Princes by a Leash (from Ricciotti, *Storia d'Israele*, Societa Editrice internationale, i, 463) 30
Sargon II puts out the Eyes of a Conquered Enemy (from **XLV**, 4th ed., p. 599) 30

IV. Banquet of Asshurbanipal and his Queen. Bas-relief in the British Museum 122

V. Deportation of a Conquered People. Bas-relief from the Palace of Asshurbanipal at Nineveh. (In the Louvre, no. 65) 130

VI. Ezekiel and the Vision of the Valley of Dry Bones. The Prophet is successively represented as being carried by the hair into the Valley, commanding the bones to assemble, and entreating the Spirit to restore them to life. From a Mural Painting in the Synagogue of Dura on the Euphrates, a.d. 245 (from a photograph kindly furnished by M. du Mesnil du Buisson) 212

VII. 1. A Papyrus from Elephantine Rolled up and Sealed (after Ricciotti, *Storia d'Israele*, ii, p. 186) . 304
2. Papyrus from Elephantine : Abstract of the Letter from the Satrap Bagohi (from Sachau, **CCXXXVII**, Berlin, Reimer, 1908) 304

VIII. Synagogue of Capernaum. 1. Present State (photo, 1927). 2. Reconstruction (after Benzinger, *Heb. Arch.*, 3rd ed., fig. 425, p. 340) 316

FIGURES IN THE TEXT

FIG.   PAGE

1. Assyrian horsemen of the ninth or eighth century, after a
   mural painting discovered by M. Thureau-Dangin in the
   palace of Tell Ahmar (*Syria*, xi (1930), fig. 7, p. 126)   .   19

2. Coin of Artaxerxes II (after Ricciotti, *Storia d'Israele*, ii,
   p. 163, S. E. I., Turin)   198

3. Coin of Artaxerxes III (after Ricciotti, *Storia d'Israele*, ii,
   p. 35, S. E. I., Turin)   198

4. Coins of Alexander the Great (after Ricciotti, *Storia d'Israele*,
   ii, p. 51, S. E. I., Turin)   201

5. Chnum, the ram-god of Elephantine (after Ricciotti, *Storia
   d'Israele*, ii, p. 198, S. E. I., Turin)   310

FOREWORD

THE CONSTITUENT ELEMENTS OF JUDAISM
PROPHETIC INSPIRATION AND LEGALISM

IT may seem a platitude to say that the importance of historical events is not necessarily in proportion to the space which they occupy on the earth's surface. But it is a platitude which is no less true of the small Jewish people than of the equally small Greek people. Hence it will not be a matter of surprise that, since we have devoted six volumes to Hellenism, we should also have thought it fit to devote three to Judaism and six in all to the origins of Christianity. In the words of Renouvier quoted in the Foreword to Israel, *" the attitude of spirit "of that body of nomad Bedouins, the Hebrews, " produced those extraordinary religious phenomena which still exercise a potent influence among us, after four thousand years." [1]*

We have divided the volume which had been assigned to the subject of From the Prophets to Jesus *into two. In the present volume A. Lods has carried the history of Israel which, in his book* Israel *he had traced up to the middle of the eighth century, from Amos to Judas Maccabæus. These six centuries of political and religious conflict provide him with a varied and intricate subject-matter. In the companion volume C. Guignebert, dealing with the conditions obtaining in Palestine and the Jewish world in general at the beginning of the Christian era, will carry on the history of Israel and at the same time provide a necessary introduction to his book* Jesus.

Readers of Lods' first volume, Israel, *will find in the present volume the same qualities which made the first so valuable. There is here the same ample scholarship which is never allowed to obscure the balance and clarity of his discussion, a similar analysis of difficult passages and conflicting interpretations, always resulting in a convincing explanation, or, as in many cases, a cautious suspension of judgment. [2] Readers may be*

---

[1] A. Lods, *Israel*, p. xx, n. 3
[2] See, for example, pp. 142, 158, 232-3, 237-8, 244-6, etc.

assured that they can find no safer guide through the maze of facts and ideas characteristic of this period.

As in the case of Israel, *the present volume is linked up with the preceding ones which dealt with the place of the Eastern Empires in the evolution of humanity.*[1] *Assyria, and Babylonia Egypt, Persia, the Hellenistic world reappear here in their relations with Israel and Judah. Palestine, as we know, is the meeting-place of nations.*[2] *On this stage was unrolled the destiny of a little country, " the battlefield and the prey of its powerful neighbours," [3] in the stormy period whem empires followed or overthrew one another, when the march of civilization was accompanied by internecine warfare, savage reprisals, destruction of cities, and the transportation of entire populations.*

First of all Assyria inflicted sanguinary defeats upon the two kingdoms, the allies of Egypt, as from time to time they attacked or revolted against the " empire of spoliation " (p. 157).[4] *It dismembered Israel, and, in 734, began the policy of deportation ; twelve years later it annexed Israel and carried away the whole population.*[5] *The Israelite colonists, settled in Mesopotamia and Media were replaced by various elements, Syrians, Chaldeans, Elamites, and Arabs. In 701 the tentacles of the empire fastened on a portion of Judah, and 200,150 men, women, and children were carried away captive by Sennacherib (p. 33). The result of the resistance of Hezekiah was " diminished territory, decimation of the population, a ravaged country, and an impoverished treasury " (p. 36). From this time onward the King of Judah was one of the numerous vassals who experienced, voluntarily or involuntarily, the " Assyrian peace ". During his long reign Manasseh remained in abject submission to the masters of the world (p. 38).*

Nevertheless, it was a precarious peace. Egypt and Chaldea revolted and regained their freedom : the invasion of the barbarian Scythians swept over Asia ; the Assyrian Empire rapidly declined : Nineveh, " the bloody city," fell (p. 43).

---

[1] Vols. VI, VIII, XV, XXIV.

[2] See Lods, *op. cit.*, pp. 16 *ff. Cf.* XXVIII, pt. II, p. 41.

[3] *Ibid.*

[4] *Cf.* Lods, *op. cit.*, p. 386, and VIII, pp. 62, 283. Lods strikingly brings out the difference between the character and methods of the Assyrians and the Egyptians (pp. 18-20).

[5] 27,790 captives were carried away from Samaria (p. 24).

About 622, during the reign of Josiah, Judah gradually recovered its independence and its domination over the ancient kingdom of Israel. But from 609 onward, " the series of disasters begins again " (p. 43). Egypt, which had become the ally of Assyria in order to ward off the barbarian inroads, slew Josiah at Megiddo, and subjugated Judah.

The downfall of the kingdom of Judah was completed by the Neo-babylonian or Chaldean empire. Nebuchadnezzar, on the occasion of his first capture of Jerusalem, according to one account carried away 3,023 captives, according to another 10,000 (597). Nevertheless, he allowed the country to retain its independence. After a short respite a coalition brought about by Egypt, in which Judah took part, led to the resumption of the siege by the Chaldeans. Jerusalem was taken, sacked, and laid waste (586). After numerous executions a body of 832 captives (?) joined those who had been deported in 597. Only the country folk and the poor were left in the land. But, as the result of several rebellions, many of the Jews fled to Egypt, and in 581 745 more were deported to Babylon. " The political existence of Israel had come to an end." (p. 50).

Lods points out, however, that in spite of everything the population which clung to the soil in a state of comparative destitution must have represented three-fourths of the population of Judah (p. 174). Only the pick of them had been deported. Hence some allowance must be made for exaggeration in the prophetic picture of the Exile. The deportation was not merely intended to weaken the conquered country, but to strengthen that of the conquerors. In order to make the best use of this picked body of immigrants they were carefully handled. " The Jewish colonies of Babylonia quickly became prosperous " (p. 179). They regarded themselves as the true Israel, " the nucleus of the future people of Jahweh."

Forty-three years later Cyrus took Babylon, and the rule of the Persians, " a people hitherto almost unknown " (p. 236), caused the brutality of Semitic domination to be replaced by a generosity which must have surprised even its beneficiaries. When the captives were granted permission to return to their own country " many remained in Babylon because, according to the testimony of Josephus, they did not wish to abandon their property." These contented themselves with furnishing assistance towards the restoration of the city and the rebuilding of the Temple for those whose faith had induced them to return to the " barren rock on which their altar stood " (p. 266).

At first life was hard for those who had returned ; but, under the Persian empire, they enjoyed comparative peace and were able gradually to restore order. Finally, under Greek rule, in spite of the opposition of the Ptolemies and the Seleucids, they seem to have acquired a large degree of liberty and frequently even the goodwill of their masters.[1] " Having accepted the fact of Gentile rule they watched with indifference or even with a secret satisfaction the spectacle of the empires destroying each other " (pp. 200-1).

During this long period of history the ceaseless shifting of populations and the changes of empire were a constant cause of racial intermixture and of religious contamination, in short, of syncretism. By means of exile and emigration Israel began to be dispersed among the nations, influencing them and being influenced by them. Canaan, Assyria, Persia, Greece, the wisdom of the East, in turn contributed elements to its religion, some of which were assimilated, others rejected.[2] Hence it is not true to say that Israel was immune to the influence of its conquerors. But in the inmost depths of Israel's consciousness something remained hidden, or rather was created by the challenge to her faith of a destiny that seemed overwhelming, which became a ferment in the subsequent course of history. This is clearly brought out by Lods, and it is the central purpose of this volume, just as it was the aim of the previous one, to set forth the earliest manifestations of the genius of Israel.

In this study of the prophetic activity in Israel our colleague has depicted one of the most fascinating and most hopeful periods in the history of religion. By reason of his careful psychological observation, and, above all by that sympathetic insight essential to the true historian, he has been able to elicit the inner meaning

---

[1] " One of the characteristics of the Achæmenids was that they found a place in their government for moral considerations. With few exceptions their use of power was marked by generosity," G. Radet, *Alexander the Great*, p. 84. " The imperial policy of Alexander was characterized by tolerance as the foundation of international justice . . ." *ibid.*, p. 12. *Cf.* Huart, vol. XXIV, p. xii, and Jouguet, vol. XV, p. ix.

[2] *Cf.* A. Causse, *Israel and the Vision of Humanity*, pp. 28 *ff.*, and Kreglinger. *The Religion of Israel*, pp. 245 *ff.*

of the passages which he discusses, and of the facts which he establishes. He is familiar with the hidden springs from which the religion of Israel flows in its stirring course, inextricably intermingled with the history of a small but sensitive people, passionate, prone to extremes of ecstasy and despair. He lays bare the interplay of the forces which from time to time accelerate or divert the stream of spiritual experience. Keeping strictly within the limits of history, he nevertheless provides the devotee of religious speculation with suggestive material. He makes clear that necessity of understanding *which, as we have shown elsewhere,[1] is inherent in all religions, and which beset the people of Jahweh, but especially from the time of Moses, in a very different way from that which among other peoples produced pantheons and nature-myths. Although it may not be true to say that the desert was " monotheist ", it can be said that it produced strong and proud personalities ; such men created a god after their own image and sought, not to understand the universe, but to explain the heights and depths of their national destiny by the purposes of this God. What Renouvier called egoism was rather an egocentric individual and national consciousness which, as the drama of their history unrolled itself, disclosed the development of a moral consciousness and the advent of a universalistic monotheism. The instruments of this process were the* great prophets *who " are interlinked with one another " and are the bearers of a common revelation.*

Already, in the preceding volume, the nebi'im *have appeared on the stage, those ecstatics who embodied at the same time the cult of Jahweh, a religious fervour, and the ideal of a simplicity derived from the tradition of the desert sojourn which was opposed to an urban civilization. In many respects the protagonists of this volume resemble the earlier* nebi'im *and even the still more ancient exponents of* mana *(p. 52). They share " the general ancient Semitic conception of inspiration ; for them it is the inrush of an outside force into a human personality " (p. 53). They are subject to the experience of ecstasy [2] ; in the vision which accompanies the ecstasy the*

---

[1] See the Foreword to Vol XI.

[2] The existence among them has been established of " various conditions which modern psychiatrists have diagnosed in their patients : active and passive ecstasy, insensibility to pain, glossolaly, oral, visual, and sensory hallucinations, illusions of the senses, and occasionally

prophet receives the intimation of his vocation,[1] and in the ecstasy he acquires his inspiration.[2] He experiences a division of consciousness ; while one self ranges afar in time or space, the other self may question the experiences of the former and be shaken by its revelations (p. 237). By a reflex action of the ecstatic experience the vision which overwhelms him is translated into suitable acts and gestures, and the prophet often enacts in anticipation the events which he foresees : in this way " he introduces future events into the realm of reality " (p. 53). Because he is " in constant touch with the unseen " he combines with his power to foresee events a certain power to control them.[3]

But the principal difference between the great prophets and the common run of professional ecstatics, members of orders, oracle-mongers, diviners, and soothsayers, lay in the fact that independently and wholly disinterestedly they spoke and acted in fulfilment of their mission. *They no longer sought inspiration by physical means, " mass suggestion, music, dances, sleeping in a sanctuary, intoxicating drinks " (p. 58), but had recourse only to prayer. The ecstatic phenomena which they exhibit are to be found equally, as Lods points out, in Paul, Mahomet, Luther, or Pascal. To the personality of the ecstatic correspond the ecstatic experiences which embody his emotions and ideas (p. 57).*

In short, the characteristic mark of the great prophets is their conviction that they are the interpreters and the instruments of God, the righteous God who reveals himself to them and is revealed by them.[4] Jahweh is no longer thought of as the blind guardian

even hypnosis and auto-suggestion " (p. 56). On pp. 51-9 there is an interesting discussion of " pneumatic phenomena ". Such phenomena are particularly common in periods of religious excitement, when they are deliberately stimulated : this may be observed in the eleventh, ninth, the latter half of the eighth, and the beginning of the sixth centuries.

[1] See p. 100 ; " in his first vision Isaiah's mind received, in an objective form, some of the thoughts and tendencies which had, no doubt, long been taking shape in the sub-conscious depths of his personality." *Cf.* for Ezekiel, p. 215.

[2] See pp. 100-1, 214-17. " Of all the prophets of Israel it is Ezekiel in whom pneumatic phenomena manifest themselves in their most acute form, bordering at times on a pathological state " : he experiences alternations of exaltation and despair, apathy and silence, possibly even attacks of aphasia (pp. 215-16).

[3] See pp. 51-3, 108-9, 215-17. *Cf.* the character of prediction in the names which they give to their children, pp. 51, 87, 91, 108.

[4] See p. 126.

of a nation ; he tends to become the sole God of the human race. In this way the servants of Jahweh solved the problems presented to them by the premonition of the dangers which threatened Israel, and by the actual experience of the misfortunes which overwhelmed her : " *to the primitive mentality the strongest gods are always the best* " *(p. 127) ; to the interpreters of a righteous God the trials of Israel are the just* retribution *of her fundamental apostasy.*[1]

Such are the general characteristics of the psychology of the great prophets. But while they possess many traits in common and all contribute to a radical transformation of religious experience, their personalities are entirely distinct, and the contribution of each corresponds to their individual temperament (p. 61). Lods is at his best in differentiating the individual shades of character which distinguish these fascinating personalities.

Amos was a shepherd, an " *educated shepherd,*" *a* " *lonely puritan* ", *disgusted by the social inequalities,* " *the exploitation of the poor by the powerful,*" *the excesses of wealth and luxury, who maintained the worthlessness of civilization apart from moral purity. In his view God had turned away from Israel because of her sins.*

Hosea would seem to have been a priest or a well-to-do farmer. While Amos is characterized by a sensitive conscience Hosea is " *a burning and passionate soul* " *(p. 90). The former* " *expanded* " *religious experience, the latter* " *deepened* " *it. Possibly psychoanalysis might explain the experience of the latter as a sublimation, arising from his asceticism, of that* " *pure love which for him constitutes the essence of religion* " [2] *Israel had been faithless and ungrateful to her God : deprived of her army, her king, and her cult, her only hope lay in her devotion to her God. Hosea's* " *courageous idealism* " *and affectionate loyalty saw in repentance the ground of the future restoration of the people of Jahweh.*

Isaiah was " *a man of high rank* " *(p. 101), an eloquent orator, a far-seeing statesman, more involved in the course of events than Amos or Hosea. He was especially impressed by the*

---

[1] See pp. 61, 84, 147, 218 *f.* Cf. pp. 232 *f.* for the struggle of Habakkuk.

[2] Ḥesed is practically equivalent to the Latin *pietas.* See pp. 89 *ff.*

greatness of God, and felt himself abased before the " tremendous majesty ", the holiness [1] *of Jahweh, and the guilty pride of his people. But the righteousness of God is tempered by mercy : a remnant of Israel will be saved by " faith ".* [2]

Micah, as a representative of the country folk, stands out in contrast to the aristocratic Isaiah, and his " democratic " tendencies suggest affinities with Amos (pp. 111-14).

After the lapse of three-quarters of a century of Assyrian domination, a period during which Judah had fallen under the sway of foreign influences, the voice of the great prophets, long silent, was heard again in Zephaniah and Jeremiah. The former undoubtedly belonged to the royal family, while Jeremiah was the son of a priest. On behalf of the national religion both prophets protested against polytheism and syncretism. Both announced the approach of worse disasters, not only to Judah but to the surrounding nations. When Josiah's reform, by which Judah had hoped to recover the favour of her God, was followed by fresh disasters, in the midst of the general dismay Jeremiah advised his people to bow to the chastisement, and urged the exiles to patient submission.

To outward seeming a " great fighter ", fiery and passionate in his vindication of Jahweh, Jeremiah was actually a man of " a gentle and retiring disposition ". Lods gives us a penetrating analysis of his character and emphasizes his originality. Jeremiah's humanity appears in his outbursts of pity for the victims of Jahweh's chastisement, however they may have deserved it (p. 168). He has moments of revulsion from the task laid upon him by the divine revelation, of proclaiming violence and destruction. At times he falls into despair, confesses it and triumphs over it. " His self-revelations are characterized by an inimitable spontaneity. He may justly be called the first author of Confessions " (p. 169). No prophet had " a clearer vision of the religion of the spirit " (p. 171). The new covenant between Jahweh and his people would be written in their hearts.

The personality of Ezekiel is depicted with equal vividness ; " it is of the profoundest interest for the psychologist and the historian by reason of the contrasts which it presents " (p. 227).

---

[1] " That which is holy, divine, unapproachable by man " : in itself the word has no moral connotation (p. 109).

[2] See p. 110, " the wealth of content which Isaiah imparted to this term, a term which was to have such an extraordinary history."

*He, too, as priest and prophet, in the midst of the exiles
announces the destruction of Jerusalem ; but, when his prediction
is fulfilled, he preaches hope to the " bewildered sufferers " ;
he assumes the role of a " shepherd ", a spiritual guide. After
the prophets of woe come the prophets of hope. Because he was
a priest, and even more attached than his predecessors to the
national religious tradition, Ezekiel declared that the holy God
had chosen a Land and a People : " Israel is the sole people
of a universal God " (p. 231). He carried even farther than
Jeremiah a tendency emphasized by Lods, and attributed a
religious value to the individual life, arriving at the conception of individual retribution. This theory, which only
established itself in the face of obstructions and objections
towards the second century, with the help of the belief, hitherto
unknown in Israel, in the sanctions of a future life, is " here and
there shot through with the gleams of an evangelical hope "
(p. 222). Nor is this all ; even before the consummation of a
general repentance, he regards it as a condition of the conversion
of Israel that God shall forgive for the sake of his holy name ;
we are face to face with the conception of the divine grace
(p. 224). As prophet and " dogmatist ", dreamer and realist,
giving forth a poetry that is both powerful, obscure, and fantastic
(p. 225), Ezekiel is a link between the past and the future.*

*The author of Second Isaiah is also a lyric poet, and at the
same time an apologist with a profound philosophy of History.
He believes that Jahweh, the creator and controller of the
universe,[1] is destined to become the sole God of all nations : " I
am God, and beside me there is none other. To me every knee
shall bow, and every tongue shall swear by me " (p. 243). Israel
has a mission to fulfil ; as a martyr nation her destiny is to
suffer for the sins of the many, for the salvation of the nations
(p. 248). Scattered among them she will carry " the true
doctrine ", and after her martyrdom her exaltation will redound
to the glory of her God, the only God.*

*Here the thought of Israel reaches its highest point : in
Jesus the conception of vicarious suffering passes from the nation
to the individual (p. 249).*

The point is emphasized by Lods, that the evolution of

---

[1] " Scattered from Egypt to Babylonia the Jewish people became
conscious of the real extent of the world," p. 243. *Cf.* Causse, *op. cit.*,
p. 39.

prophecy reveals a wholly new religious ideal. Nothing in the ethical teaching of the East can be compared to, nor suffices to explain, " the heroic passion for righteousness of an Amos or a Jeremiah . . . or the depth of the religious conceptions of Second Isaiah " (p. 76). But, in the course of this evolution, a fusion of various conflicting elements was brought about.

Of these the first was the idea that true religion demanded that a man should " do justly, love mercy, and walk humbly with his God ", and hence that external religious practices were useless and even to be reprobated. Indeed, ritual in essence is merely the continuation of magic ; it is the persistence of activities directed either to the protection of man from invisible powers, or to obtain their favour, in short, to control them. Even if the ritual practices in question be regarded as the will of the god they still remain an indirect means of influencing him. But as soon as the moral law is made the basis of religion instead of the powers of the external world man himself becomes the servant of man, and that in the name of the will of God.[1]

But the opposition between the new conception of religion and the traditional cult, uncompromising at first, gradually diminished. We know that Jeremiah and Ezekiel were priests. Jahwism and the prophetic religion began to converge, and it is necessary to lay special stress on the peculiar character which was impressed upon the Jewish community as the result of this convergence.

For the prophets Jahweh was Israel's king. The monarchy, apparently always circumscribed among the Hebrews by the ancient Bedouin individualism,[2] was the object of the open hostility of the prophets, in that it stood for temporal ambition and " civilizing " tendencies.[3] To their way of thinking it could only be tolerated on the condition of obedience to the will of God as revealed by the inspired prophet (p. 119). They exercised a considerable influence upon the kings, upon Hezekiah, for instance, in the later period of the monarchy, and especially upon Josiah.

[1] See p. 120. It has been remarked that in China also thought was turning towards wisdom, and not towards science. But while, for Israel, the moral law was the expression of the divine will, for Chinese thinkers there existed a close link between nature and man, so that, for them, Civilization constitutes the order of the Universe, establishing " universal goodwill ". See vol. XXV, pt. ii, pp. vii *ff.*

[2] See Lods, *op. cit.*, p. 393.

[3] p. 118, and vol. XXVII, p. 412.

Israel was governed by custom, handed down from the fathers. In special instances this was supplemented by the torah, *the decision of the priestly legislator :* " *by its very nature the torah was oral, living, never complete : it was the ever-flowing spring of law in Israel* " (p. 135). *Since it reflected Hebrew thought and custom it could never be divorced from the teaching of the prophets. The first decalogue, which brought the prophetic ideals within the reach of the masses, was deeply permeated by it. Deuteronomy in its earliest form, dating from the seventh century, was an attempt to* " *rationalize* " *popular custom, and resulted in the reforms of Josiah. In conformity with the priestly view of religion the law henceforth set its seal upon the Temple and its ritual ; but at the same time it infused the ritual with* " *a very pure and exalted ethical and religious spirit* " (p. 153). *Hence the law gathered up the living word in order to give it a permanent written form. Thus Israel became the people of the* Book *and of the* Synagogue *where it was expounded.* Judaism *was born* (p. 154).

With Lods we follow the expansion of the Law, first of all during the period of the exile, when the priestly legislators revived the ancient " *half-magical* " *conception of holiness, in which ritual becomes at least equal in importance to righteousness, and the cultus becomes* " *nothing less than the most essential of all public services* ".[1] " *Ecstatic* " *phenomena, no doubt, did not disappear immediately, but inspiration gradually grew weaker. Haggai and Zechariah, in a* " *somewhat dull mixture of ritual and morality* " (p. 273), *clung to the hope of the Kingdom of God. The rugged personality known as Malachi is not so much a genuine prophet as a forerunner of the scribes and rabbinists, the interpreters of the Torah* (p. 278-9).

After the exile the reconstituted Jewish community presented the appearance of a Church rather than of a State.[2] The forms of the religion grew rigid as the result of an intense intellectual labour such as no ancient religion had hitherto known, and the " *Priestly Writer* " *described the institution of these forms by God. Sacred history was nothing more than* " *legislation clothed with an historical garb* ". *Various laws were added, and the whole constituted the Priestly Code which organized the entire category of sacred places, persons, acts, and times. The Code ascribed to a high priest supremacy over the civil power* (p. 286-7).

[1] pp. 257, 259, 264.　　　[2] p. 206 ; cf. pp. 259, 265.

Jerusalem, under Nehemiah, an official of the Persian court, and Ezra, a priestly scribe, saw the rebirth of a purely Jewish community, rigidly legal, hostile to every sign of syncretism, and to the intermarriage with Gentiles which prevailed in other Jewish communities.[1]

Side by side with the editing of the Law there developed a type of teaching mainly derived from the prophets. To Jahweh, sole God, creator of heaven and earth,[2] were ascribed infinite power, wisdom, and holiness (p. 322). The two most essential elements of the prophetic legacy were the assertion of divine righteousness and of the religious value of the individual (p. 328). But the spirit of the religion was no longer the same ; there was something utilitarian in the attitude of the scribes ; righteousness became the result of self-interest rather than of love as the mainspring of religion. Moreover, reward was conceived of as purely terrestrial. The promises of Jahweh had been made to the nation, and the coming of the day of Jahweh no longer meant chastisement but deliverance. To the question of the time and character of the Day an answer will be given in the sequel to this volume, which will describe the growth of eschatology in Judaism.

But the rigidity of the ritual framework, which had grown up round the " religious values " created by the prophets, was not able to stifle completely, during the centuries of early Judaism, either the exercise of reflection or the expression of emotion. In his admirable study of the book of Job and of Ecclesiastes Lods reveals the inward unrest of the scribal thinkers and poets : " A protest of the moral consciousness, an implied and veiled appeal, in the face of the moral problems of the universe, to the God who rules the world " (p. 340) or, on the other hand, since all is vanity, " a serene and sincere delight in the simple joys of daily life " (p. 344).

It is in the Psalms that Lods finds the reflection of the religious ideals of those circles which were sustained by a simpler faith. Here we see a religious life characterized by an interest in moral considerations and entire trust in God. If the psalmist

[1] On the Jewish colony at Elephantine and on the conflict between the South and the North, between Jerusalem and Samaria, see pp. 304 ff and vol. XXVIII, b. See also vol. XV, pp. 114, 314, 436.

[2] Or rather the one who has established the order of heaven and earth : see pp. 322 f.

*is troubled by the problem of the prosperity of the wicked and the
suffering of the righteous, his trust in God accepts these things as
the trial of faith and prepares the way for the subsequent solution
of the problem : the difficulties of a theodicy are to be resolved
by the doctrine of the immortality of the soul.*

*We have seen the rise of Judaism, with its two factors of
inspiration and legalism, and its two tendencies, a narrow
nationalism and a passionate universalism. With the help of
the two valuable studies which Lods has given us we are now in a
position to estimate the total significance of the influence which
the genius of this small people has exercised upon the history of
the world.*

*It has been pointed out above that, turning away from the
world of external phenomena, from the rich diversity of nature,
the thought of Israel has been characterized by an essentially
human interest, tending to the development of a moral insight.
Working upwards from man to his creator, from the chosen people
to the God who set his choice upon them, Israel arrived at an
ethical monotheism.*

*Life takes on a meaning from morality. In the daring logic
of her prophets Israel finds the significance of her own destiny
and that of the individual in the will of a God who rewards and
punishes righteously. " In the words of Darmesteter, by their
faith in righteousness the prophets made it an active factor in
history."*

*Believing that the meaning and order of life was moral,
Israel remained fundamentally indifferent to material progress,
careless of the arts which raised the standard of living, and of the
fleeting pleasure of the moment.[1] The only art natural to Israel
was the lyric art of poetry and music. The prophetic spirit
was one of abnegation, of practical asceticism. It also displayed
a naïve socialism : the prophets looked towards the recovery of
a lost equality, the regaining of the lost paradise of the desert.[2]*

*The prophets were opposed to the monarchy and to civil
organization. But the religious tradition found its fruition in the
Law. But a Law which established the sanctity of ritual—in
which the conception of magical potency survived—which
canalized the very utterances of inspiration, involved the existence*

[1] See pp. 62, 66, 84, 149 *f.*
[2] See Kreglinger, *op. cit.*, pp. 187, 190, 193, 197 *f.*, 239.

of an authority to formulate it, to control and interpret its application. As the power of the king declines that of the priest and the teacher increases. Thus there arose the ideal of a city of priests, of a theocratic State. Elsewhere the king was the god, here God was King.

Israel stands out in contrast to the empires, to their greed of power and pleasure. Nevertheless, its quick intelligence, its passionate emotional life, yielded at times to the lure, not of the imperialistic ambitions, but of the civilization of the peoples, with whom, voluntarily or involuntarily, it chanced to mingle. In spite of opposition Israel was initiated by Canaan, Egypt, Assyria, Chaldea, Persia, Greece, and finally Rome, into those modes of life and thought so distasteful to the anawim *and the prophets. The great Dispersion affected Israel in divers ways. The Old Testament philosophy of history was an optimistic one ; the kingdom of God might be realized in many ways. The messianic idea, liberally interpreted, became a theory of progress ; and it is only an apparent paradox to maintain, as has been done, that the prophets " join hands " with the Encyclopædists.*

HENRI BERR.

FROM THE PROPHETS TO JESUS

THE PROPHETS OF ISRAEL AND THE BEGINNINGS OF JUDAISM

INTRODUCTION

I

PURPOSE AND PLAN OF THE BOOK

IN an earlier volume of this series the history of the Hebrew tribes was traced out from their nomad state up to the period when, having settled in Palestine and absorbed the current civilization of the ancient East they became an agricultural people, divided by the political situation into two kingdoms, but closely bound together by the link of a common national religion, the worship of Jahweh, a religion which, ever since its institution by Moses, had formed the rallying point of the nation.

In the first volume of the present work the attempt will be made to describe the expansion of this strongly exclusivist religion until it embraced, in principle, the whole of mankind, and the process by which the nation of Israel, hitherto resembling in all essentials the other nations of the ancient world, emerged as a totally new community, the Jewish people ; a community which exhibited the characteristics both of a racial group and a Church, yet without being entirely the one or the other.

In the first part of this book will be set forth the two main historical facts underlying these religious, political, and social

1   B

changes : first, the rise of the great Asiatic empires of Assyria and Babylon, which brought about the fall of the two Israelite kingdoms ; second, the appearance, in these two insignificant states, of a succession of prophets who openly opposed the narrow national Jahwism of their times, and set before their contemporaries the ideal of a purer life, a broader and more exalted religious attitude, culminating in a universalist ethical monotheism.

In the second part we shall see how a compromise between the old state of things and the principles introduced by the new prophets led to the growth of that novel type of politico-religious organization which we know as Judaism, whose fortunes we shall trace up to the Maccabean period.

A second volume will be devoted to the elements at work in the Jewish world up to the time when it gave birth to Christianity, and the official religion took on its rabbinical character.[1]

II

The Sources

In this section of the Introduction we shall make a rapid survey of the documents whence we derive our information concerning the first two periods to be dealt with, namely, from the middle of the eighth century to the Babylonian exile (760–586), and from the Exile to the Maccabean period (686–168). It is necessary to take the sources for both these periods together, since several of the relevant documents pertain to both periods.

1. *Epigraphy and Archæology.*

There are only two Hebrew inscriptions of any length coming from Israelite sources : the inscription from the Siloam tunnel, describing the details of the boring of this subterranean aqueduct, a daring undertaking for this period, which was undoubtedly carried out by the orders of Hezekiah [2] about the end of the eighth century, to provide Jerusalem

---

[1] Vol. 28*b*, *From the Prophets to Jesus : II, The Jewish World about the time of Jesus*, by Charles Guignebert.

[2] *Cf.* 2 Kings xx, 20 ; 2 Chr. xxxii, 30 ; Sir. xlviii, 17.

with water [1] ; and an agricultural calendar found at Gezer,[2] generally believed to date from the sixth century, but probably much older.[3] These two documents have only a secondary historical importance.

Among fragments of lesser importance mention may be made of thirteen stamped jar-handles discovered by Professor W. F. Albright at Tell el-Fûl (ancient Gibeah). These cover the period of the eighth and seventh centuries.[4] Also seals such as the seal of Jaazaniahu discovered by Professor Badé at En-Nasbeh ; if this Jaazaniah is the leader of a band of Jews mentioned in Jer. xl, 8, and 2 Kings xxv, 23, it would strengthen the identification of En-Nasbeh with the site of Mizpah.[5]

At Gezer were discovered two tablets in Accadian, in cuneiform script, containing contracts relating to the sale of land ; they were dated in the Assyrian manner by the eponym of the year.[6] From this Benzinger has inferred that cuneiform survived in Canaan from the Tell el-Amarna period as the official script for legal documents.[7] This theory is somewhat doubtful, since these two contracts, dating 649 and 647, belong to the reign of Manasseh, a time when the Assyrians were absolute masters of Palestine, and their prestige alone would have sufficed to give currency to their legal, just as it did to their religious customs.

The same can be said of the small limestone fragment bearing Assyrian characters which Mr. Crowfoot found at Samaria,[8] and which seems to belong to the reign of Sargon.[9]

The monuments found in Egypt only contain information concerning the internal condition of Egypt, and are few and much mutilated : in general the period of Egyptian history

---

[1] See **II**, 193–5 ; Kautsch, **ZDPV**, iv (1881), 102 *ff.*, 260 *ff.*, v, 205 *ff.* ; Guthe, **ZDPV**, iv, 250 *ff.* ; **ZDMG**, 1882, 725 *ff.* ; Driver, *Notes*, 2nd ed., ix *f.* ; **LIV**, i, 439 ; **LXXXI**, i, 590–4.

[2] Macalister, *Excavation of Gezer*, ii, 24 *ff.* ; pl. 127 ; Dalman, **ZDPV**, xxix (1906), 92–4 ; H. Vincent, **RB**, 1909, p. 111 ; Marti, **ZATW**, 1909, 222.

[3] Mark Lidzbarski, *Ephemeris*, iii, 36 *ff.* ; **PEF, QS**, 1909, 26 ; Dussaud, **SY**, 1924, 147 ; H. Gressmann, **XXVII**, ii, 169.

[4] Dhorme, **RES**, 1934, xxiv.

[5] Badè, **ZATW**, 1933, 150 *ff.* ; Dhorme, **RES**, xxiii–xxiv.

[6] **PEF**, 1904, 229 *ff.* ; 1905, 206 *ff.*

[7] **I**, 177.

[8] **PEF, QS**, July, 1933, 130.

[9] Dhorme, **RES**, 1934, xxi–xxii.

from the eighth to the third century was one of decline. We may, however, mention the excavations made by an American expedition at Napata in Nubia,[1] the cradle of the Ethiopian dynasty (twenty-fifth) which ruled Egypt in the eighth and seventh centuries, and to which Tirhaqah, the ally of Hezekiah, belonged.[2]

Mention may also be made of the fact that Semites were certainly among the mercenaries of Psammeticus who scrawled their names upon the colossi of Ipsambul in the course of a campaign against Ethiopia.

But the soil of Egypt has yielded another group of documents of far greater importance for the history of Judaism, namely the archives, edited between 1901 and 1911, of the family of a certain Yedoniah settled at Elephantine, in the furthest south of Upper Egypt. These documents, mostly dated in the reigns of Xerxes, Artaxerxes I, and Darius II, have revealed to us the existence in this fortress of a Jewish military colony, already settled there before the conquest of Egypt by the Persians (525). They have thrown the most striking light on the organization, law, religious beliefs and practices of this community and, indirectly, upon the state of the Jewish Diaspora in the fifth century. We shall return to this subject later.[3]

From Mesopotamian epigraphy we derive much more extensive information. In the annals of their reigns the Assyrian and Babylonian kings give various accounts of their campaigns against Israel and Judah. These official documents, however, must be used with circumspection, since the royal scribes who edited them preserved a discreet silence concerning any events which did not redound to the glory of their masters, and occasionally they even transformed defeats into brilliant victories. On the other hand, these sources are full of detailed and accurate data. They enable us to relate the events which took place in Palestine to the intricate and disturbed political history of Asia Minor at that time. Furthermore, these documents, together with Assyrian, Babylonian, and Greek chronological lists, enable us to date with exactitude certain facts in the history of Israel and Judah. It was the Assyrian custom to give to each year the name of the king or of an important official. Lists

---

[1] **CLXV.**   [2] 2 Kings xix, 9 ; Isa. xxxvii, 9.   [3] Pp. 304–312.

of these " eponyms " were drawn up, and occasionally there were added to the names a reference to the important events of the year. We possess these lists for the years 893 to 666. Moreover, Ptolemy, who lived about A.D. 150, has preserved an accurate chronological list of the kings who reigned at Babylon from Nabonassar (747) to Alexander the Great. Since several Assyrian kings, between 747 and 666, were also kings of Babylon, they occur both in the " canon " of Ptolemy and in the Assyrian lists. Hence it is easy to arrive at a synchronism whose accuracy can be controlled mathematically by various astronomical data, especially by the mention, in a year which can be shown to be the year 763 B.C., of an eclipse of the sun which took place at that date, and which was almost total for the district of Nineveh. These precise data enable us occasionally to correct, to some extent, the confused and often contradictory chronological information of the books of Kings. The Israelites at this period merely dated events from the beginning of the reign of the contemporary king. Palestinian Jews did not possess an exact system of chronology until their adoption of the Seleucid era, which began in the year 312 B.C.

Certain cuneiform documents of a private nature are also of historical value : the archives of the business house of the son of Murahu, of Nippur, provide us with valuable information concerning the number, the occupations, the degree of prosperity, and, indirectly, the religious outlook of the Jews in Babylonia under Artaxerxes I and Darius II.[1]

2. *Literary Sources.*

For the period from 760 to 168, as for the preceding epochs, our chief sources of information concerning the history of the people of Israel are those literary sources, which, with one exception, the Story of Aḥiqar, are only known to us from the Hebrew Bible or the Greek translation of the Old Testament.

There are two historical works which give a continuous account of the history of Israel ; they are the books of Kings which carry the history up to 561, and the source upon which our books of Chronicles, Ezra, and Nehemiah are based, which

[1] See pp. 195-6.

takes the history to about the end of the fifth century. Both of these present numerous examples of the usual method of Israelite historians, which consisted in the literal reproduction of extracts from earlier sources.[1] This method of composition confers great value upon certain portions of these books (since some of the sources incorporated appear to be contemporary with the events which they relate), but it also involves the historian in the laborious task of a preliminary critical analysis in order to separate the incorporated sources from the text in which they are found, and to determine their date.

The book of *Kings,* probably edited shortly before the fall of Jerusalem (586), but worked over during the Babylonian exile, contains, in addition to numerous items of information, ultimately derived, no doubt, from the official annals, extremely valuable accounts of the religious policy of Ahaz (2 Kings xvi, 10–18) and Josiah (2 Kings xxii and xxiii), various stories concerning the prophet Isaiah, more or less influenced by popular legend, and three accounts, one of which is very valuable, of the struggle of Hezekiah against Sennacherib in 701 (2 Kings xviii–xx).

The great history of Judah, which in modern Bibles has been divided into four books—*1 and 2 Chronicles, Ezra, and Nehemiah*—was not edited until after 332, for the author mentions Darius III Codomanus, whom he designates Darius the Persian (Neh. xii, 22), evidently in distinction from the Greek Alexander. It may even have been edited later than 190, otherwise it is difficult to explain why Ben Sirach does not mention Ezra in his " praise of the fathers ". On the other hand, it must have been edited before 165, since the author of the apocalyptic book of Daniel seems to have read and misinterpreted his account of the reign of Jehoiakim.[2] For the period prior to the Exile, this late annalist usually reproduces the book of Kings verbatim ; some of his additions seem to be derived from reliable sources, but on the whole they are tendentious variations, throwing post-exilic institutions back into early times, and governed by the principle that all the pious kings were rewarded and all the wicked ones punished. In the section of his work which recounts the events which took

---

[1] *Cf.* **LVII,** 10–16.
[2] Dan. i, 1–3 ; *cf.* 2 Chron. xxxvi, 6–7.

place after the return from the Exile (Ezra and Nehemiah), the editor has preserved excerpts from completely reliable sources. This is generally acknowledged in the case of the autobiographical fragments of Nehemiah.[1]

He also gives extracts from, or summaries of, some portions of the memoirs of Ezra [2]; the authenticity of these has been recently challenged,[3] but there seems to be no reason for doubting it.[4] The authenticity of the official documents, of which the editor reproduces a large number, has of late been strongly called in question, but without good grounds as far as most of the documents are concerned. On the other hand, the sections composed by the editor himself are open to serious suspicion, since it is clear that in several cases he has completely misunderstood the meaning of his sources.

The *prophetic books* are our first-hand sources for the religious movement which developed in Israel from the middle of the eighth century under the leadership of the " great prophets ". These documents are, for the most part, either the work of the prophets whose names they bear, or of contemporaries who had recorded the revelations received by the *nabi*. Nevertheless, before making use of these sources, it is necessary to submit them to a careful critical examination, since the originals in the form in which they have come down to us have been worked over and have received various additions : disciples have occasionally added biographical details or stories concerning their masters (e.g. Amos vii, 10–17 ; Isaiah xxxvi–xxxix ; Jer. xxvi, xxxvi, etc.). Here and there copyists have inserted anonymous oracles or oracles taken from other prophets, either in order to relieve by the light of hopeful promises the gloomy horizon of the judgments of the early *nabis*, or merely to use up the blank spaces of a roll, and to make the collection of oracles as complete as possible : actually, the question of the authorship of the revelation which was being transmitted was only of minor importance, the essential thing was that the oracle should come from Jahweh. It was an age which had no interest in literary rights.

---

[1] Neh. i, 1–7, 5*a* (except for some additions); xi, 1–2 ; xii, 27–42 (much amplified); xiii, 4–31, and, in our opinion, xiii, 1–2, and x, 1, 31–8, 40.　　[2] Ez. vii–x ; Neh. viii–ix (amplified).
[3] **XXXIV.**　　[4] Pp. 299–300.

We have then the " words " of *Amos*, the shepherd-
prophet who flourished in the middle of the eighth century
(*circ.* 760),[1] and of his contemporary, *Hosea* (*circ.* 750–722).[2]
We possess a collection of the oracles of *Isaiah* (from 740 to
at least 701),[3] which became the nucleus of the book which
now goes by his name, but comprises barely a quarter of it
(15 chapters or so out of 66). *Micah* lived at the same period,
but only the first three chapters of the book which bears his
name can be claimed with any certainty as authentic. The
short books of *Zephaniah* (626–621) and *Nahum* (probably
circ. 612) have both been considerably worked over at a later
period. There is no doubt that *Jeremiah* (627 to about 586)
dictated to his amanuensis Baruch, about 604, the substance
of the revelations which he had received up to that time (see
c. xxxvi, especially v. 32) ; but this collection arranged by
the prophet himself, and no doubt completed later under his
supervision, has, in the form in which it has reached us, been
combined with a biography of the author, a reliable document
which was probably the work of the scribe Baruch ; furthermore, the book has received numerous later additions : a
comparison between the very divergent texts of the Hebrew
Bible and the Greek Old Testament shows how freely the
text of Jeremiah has been handled. On the other hand, the
book of *Ezekiel*, although the former view of its unity has
been abandoned, only seems to have been slightly worked
over [4] ; but its text has suffered greatly from the carelessness
of copyists. The book of *Habakkuk* seems to be a composite

[1] The book of Amos seems to be the work of the prophet himself,
except i, 2, 6–10 (unless at vv. 6 and 9 " Edom " is altered to " Aram "),
11–12 ; iv, 13 ; v, 8–9 ; ix, 5–6, 8–15, and the biographical fragment
about which no doubt exists, vii, 10–17.
[2] The book of Hosea is directly or (*c.* 1) indirectly the work of the
prophet, except for certain promises, e.g. ii, 1–3 ; xi, 10–11 ; xiv, 2 ; and
the mention of Judah or David in i, 7 ; iii, 5 ; iv, 15 ; vi, 11 ; x, 11.
[3] The most undoubtedly authentic are i ; ii, 5–22 ; iii, 1–4, 1 ;
v, 1–7, 8–29 ; vi ; vii ; viii, 1–20 ; ix, 7–10, 4 ; x, 5–34 in part ; xiv,
28–32 ; xvii, 1–11 ; viii ; xxii ; xxviii, 1–4, 7–22, 23–9 (?) ; xxix, 1–15 ;
xxx, 1–17 ; xxxi, 1–5.
[4] We cannot share the views of recent critics who deny the
authenticity of nearly half the book (Hölscher), still less of those who
deny it of the whole (Torrey), or who think that the prophet's activities
belong to quite a different period from that indicated by the book in its
present redaction (James Smith, Hernstrich, Oesterley and Robinson).
Cf. Kuhl, **TR,** 1933, 92–118 ; Otto Eissfeldt, *Einl. in das A.T.*,
Tübingen, Mohr, 1934, 412–427. See below, pp. 212–13.

work, of which the greater part must have been written during the Babylonian Exile, between 597 and 549. From the same period come several anonymous prophecies which have been added to the book of Isaiah, e.g. cc. xiii; xiv, 4*b*–21; xxi (*circ.* 459), and especially the great collection whose unknown author goes by the name of *Second Isaiah* (cc. xl–lv, *circ.* 550–538). Many inspired prophets arose about the time of the Restoration, i.e. during the century which followed the Return (538–432). We have some authentic information concerning their activities: the oracles of *Haggai* (520); those of Zechariah, comprising cc. i–viii of the book which bears his name (520–518); the anonymous prophecies, apparently the work of several authors, which have been added as an appendix to the book of Isaiah (cc. lvi–lxvi), whence the name of *Trito-Isaiah*, by which they are sometimes known; various predictions relating to foreign nations (Isaiah xix, 18–25, perhaps 525; *Obadiah*, and Isaiah xv–xvi, *circ.* 400); lastly, the book known as *Malachi*, where we find addresses characteristic of a preacher-prophet, who seems to have prepared the way for Nehemiah (445–432) and Ezra.

A few more recent fragments or short books enable us to follow the development from prophecy in the strict sense to apocalyptic: the book of *Joel*, a liturgy belonging to the rituals for averting the plague of locusts, has been enlarged into a picture of the " day of Jahweh " (after 445); Isaiah xxiv–xxvii, perhaps reflecting the conquests of Alexander (after 336); Zechariah ix–xiv, an apocalyptic collection which in its present form seems to belong to the third or second century B.C.

From the seventh to the fifth century was a period of intense legislative activity. The critical study of more than a century has shown that the text of the laws which have been preserved to us in the Hebrew Bible passed through the process of redaction in this period. The only exceptions, in our judgment, consist of the second Decalogue (Ex. xxxiv), which, in its original form, was contained in the work of the Jahwist (J., ninth–eighth cents.), and of the short collection called the Book of the Covenant (Ex. xx, xxii–xxiii, 19), which formed a part of the Elohist document (E., eighth cent.).

The *First Decalogue*, in the form in which it is found in

Deuteronomy (v, 1–21), is later than 622, since it shows abundant traces of the style and ideas of the Deuteronomic Code. In the form in which it appears in Exodus (xx, 2–17) it is still later, as is shown by an allusion to the Priestly account of the Creation.[1] But even if the " Ten Words " are freed from the glosses and explanations which have certainly been added later, the resultant text cannot be earlier than the seventh century : it is an attempt to codify the demands of Jahweh according to the great prophets.[2]

It is generally recognized that Deuteronomy is clearly related to the reform of the cult carried out by Josiah in 622–621, as the result, according to the narrative in the book of Kings, of the discovery of a law-book in the Temple (2 Kings xxii, 3–xxiii, 27). In recent years various divergent views have been propounded concerning the nature of this narrative. The historicity of the story of the " discovery " of a law-book in the reign of Josiah has been challenged.[3] Some scholars have maintained that the Deuteronomic Code was not the cause but the consequence of the reform, and that it was a codification of the decrees of Josiah, with the addition of idealistic provisions amplifying the measures of the king.[4] Other scholars, on the contrary, consider that the Deuteronomic Code, at least in its original form, was very early, going back to the beginnings of the monarchy,[5] even to a period prior to Solomon,[6] if not to the Mosaic age,[7] or even to Moses himself.[8] Some have attempted to demonstrate that it did not prescribe the centralization of the cult in a single sanctuary, a provision characteristic of the reform of Josiah.[9] It would appear that some of these conjectures are improbable, while others are certainly erroneous, and that we must adhere to the fundamental element of the point of view which has prevailed among scholars since the time of De Wette, namely that the narrative of the book of Kings,

---

[1] Ex. xx, 11 ; cf. Gen. i, 1–2, 4a.
[2] See LVII, 365–6.
[3] L. Seinecke, E. Havet, G. d'Eichthal, M. Vernes, L. Horst ; G. Maspero, K. Budde (VI, 109), K. Marti (XLVIII, 259–260).
[4] Havet, d'Eichthal, Vernes, L. Horst ; G. Hölscher, A. Loisy, F. Horst ; Kennett, Cook, Binns, Burkitt.
[5] Oestreicher, Welch.
[6] Klostermann.   [7] Max Löhr.
[8] E. Naville, Orr, Wiener, G. L. Robinson.
[9] Oestreicher, Welch.

apart from some later modifications, must be regarded as reliable, and that the law-book found in the Temple, whose discovery was the immediate cause of the reform, has been preserved in Deuteronomy. This code could not have been drawn up long before its discovery, and belongs, in any case, to the seventh century, for in regard to the use of images, standing stones, and the sacred pillar in the cult, it represents a more radical point of view than that of the eighth century prophets. Unfortunately it has not been possible to distinguish with certainty those elements in Deuteronomy of which the code of 622 consisted. It may be thought that several editions of the code, accompanied by various commentaries, were in circulation, and that the present book is the result of the combination of these different editions.[1]

At the end of the book of Ezekiel (ch. xl–xlviii) is an important outline of legislation intended for use after the return from exile. We are told that it was revealed in a vision to the prophet in 573.[2]

The redaction of the Levitical laws which form the principal contents of what is called the *Priestly Code* (P), the most recent stratum of the Hexateuch,[3] took place certainly at a later date than this. The code is not the work of a single author, but of a whole school of legislating priests. From this vast assemblage of texts it is still possible to pick out collections which at one time must have been independent. This can be divided into five groups :—

(*a*) P 1, the earliest portions of the code. The chief element in this group is the so-called *Holiness Code* (Lev. xvii–xxvi, excluding additions). Its distinctive features are the greater prominence given to civil and moral laws, the absence of technical terms dear to the priestly school, such as " sin-offerings ", " trespass-offerings ", the frequency of set phrases such as " I am the Lord thy God ", etc. This code bears so much resemblance to Ezekiel's outline of legislation that some critics have attributed it to the prophet of Tel Abib. It is, however, much more likely that the Holiness code was composed, or at least part of it, under the influence of Ezekiel (hence after 573), towards the end of the exile.

(*b*) P 2. The *Priestly Code* in the strict sense or *Priestly*

---

[1] *Cf.* pp. 143–153 below.   [2] See pp. 251–3 as to authenticity.
[3] See **LVII**, 15.

Narrative itself. The aim of this vast work, the principal element of the priestly section, was both historical and legislative, namely to tabulate in chronological order the origin of all the religious institutions of Israel, from the creation of the world (when the sabbath was instituted) to the death of Joshua.

(*c*) Po, a collection of laws regulating *Offerings*, now forming chapters i–vii of Leviticus, subsequently inserted in P 2 (mistakenly separating Ex. xxxix from Lev. viii) and certainly of later date ; it contains allusions to an altar of incense and daily burnt offerings. This collection is not homogeneous, but contains an amalgamation of two previous collections, Po 1 and Po 2.

(*d*) Pp, a group of laws about the clean and the unclean, the *Laws of Ritual Cleansing* (Lev. xi–xv). Also composed of different elements and showing traces of successive re-editing, this group was in the same way interposed at a later date between chapters x and xvi, which had previously been consecutive.

(*e*) P 3 includes the somewhat numerous and important elements added at later dates to the above-named collections ; for example, the law fixing the date of the Day of Atonement (Lev. xvi, 29–34*a*), those prescribing two daily burnt offerings, and those extending the rite of anointing to all the priests.

It is easy enough to fix the relative age of the different elements in the Priestly Code. To determine with certainty the exact period of their redaction is a task requiring much greater skill. It seems, however, most probable, in spite of Hoelscher's objections, that the book of Nehemiah (ch. viii and ix) has preserved for us an account of the ceremony at which Ezra solemnly introduced the priestly laws to the people of Jerusalem. At a date not earlier than 444, and more likely after 432, he read them before an assembly held at the Gate of the Waters, and they were adopted. It is clear from the account that the Priestly Code did not at that time include some of the more recent laws, for Ezra does not prescribe the Feast of Atonement, at least not at the date fixed by the text of Leviticus as we know it (xvi, 29).

A few *Poems*, dating certainly from the period of the exile or of the return, bear witness to the profound impression made upon the masses by the preaching of the prophets. Such are the national confession which appears in our Bible in the form of a *Song of Moses* (Deut. xxxii) and the *Lamentations* attributed in the Septuagint to Jeremiah, but in reality emanating from various authors. These were probably ritual laments intended for use at the annual fasts commemorating the fall of Jerusalem in 586 (*cf.* Zech. vii, 3–5 ; viii, 19).

There can be little doubt also that the greater part of the *Psalms* was liturgical, and that they were meant to be sung at the various ceremonies of the cult.[1] They closely resemble, and sometimes imitate, the hymns, prayers, and incantations which characterized Egyptian and Babylonian formularies. Unfortunately it is extremely difficult to assign dates to Hebrew psalms. Most of them seem to reflect the ideas and sentiments of the average pious Jew between the return from exile and the Maccabean insurrection (538–168). But there are some which were certainly written before the exile, and others which were composed during the period of the struggle between the Hasmonæans and the persecuting Seleucids.

As the *Song of Songs* contains Greek words, it must belong to the time when, after the conquests of Alexander, the Jews entered into permanent contact with the Hellenic world. These love songs, some of them probably intended for use during the seven days of rejoicing which accompanied a wedding, give us some idea of profane poetry among the Jews of the last centuries before the Christian era.

The Oriental sages had long been in the habit of expressing, either in the form of brief rhythmical maxims or in verse, precepts based on their own thoughts and experiences, and primarily intended, when collected together, to assist in the training of the royal scribes, their future successors. Much gnomic writing of this kind has been preserved for us in Egypt ; a few fragments and the *Wisdom of Ahiqar* prove that it flourished among the Assyrians. Since one of the eight collections of maxims composing the *Book of Proverbs* contains an adaptation of the Wisdom of the Egyptian scribe Amen-em-ope,[2] recently published, it is now proved that the scribes of Israel drew their inspiraton from these foreign sources. A good many of the maxims contains in the book of Proverbs may have been composed before the exile, in particular those dealing with the attitude to be observed

---

[1] *Cf.* pp. 346–8.   [2] **CVI, CXIV, CXX, XXXIX.**

with regard to the king. The collections were probably only arranged in their present form after the return, for divine retribution is represented as being exclusively individual [1]—a doctrine in conformity with that formulated by Ezekiel (iii, 16–21 ; xviii ; xxxiii, 1–20)—and independent of any sacrifices which the guilty may have offered.[2]

The poet of genius to whom we owe the *Book of Job* made use of a theme which belonged to the folklore of Israel (*cf.* Ez. xiv, 14–20), perhaps even to universal folklore. Job and his friends are, indeed, described as foreigners, " Orientals " or Edomites, and his story is reminiscent of an Indian legend, that of King Hariscandra who, as a result of the jealousy of a God or of the rivalry of magicians, is grievously tried and afflicted, but having patiently endured his trials recovers, by favour of the gods, all that he had lost.[3]

It was no doubt because of its clear statement of the problem of the suffering of the just that this popular story of Job appealed to the poet. He reproduced it partly at the beginning, partly at the end of his book (i, 1–2, 10 ; xlii, 11–16), and interpolated in dialogue form a discussion of the enigma which obsessed him. Several Babylonian and Egyptian works have been cited as possible sources, particularly those known as " the Babylonian poem of the just man afflicted " or " the Babylonian Job ",[4] and the Egyptian dialogue between the disillusioned man and his soul.[5] In point of fact the poet is indebted to them only for a few details. On closer acquaintance the " Babylonian Job " proves to be nothing more than a psalm of thankfulness

---

[1] According to Amen-em-ope, ch. 3 (end), 9, and 15 (end), on the contrary, the children may be punished instead of the fathers.

[2] Prov. xxi, 3, and, on the contrary, *Instructions to Merikere*, ll. 65–67 and 129 (**XXVII**, 35), and the Babylonian text quoted **XXVII**, 293, ll. 76–8.

[3] *Markandeya Purana*, ch. 7 and 8 (Engl. transl. by F. Eden Pargiter, *Bibliotheca Indica*, *The M.P.*, Calcutta, Asiatic Soc., 1904, pp. 32–58 ; R. C. Temple, *The Legends of the Punjab*, xxvi, 1886, vol. iii, Bombay–London, Trübner, pp. 53–88 ; Bouchet, *The Religious Ceremonies and Customs of the various Nations*, p. 283 ; Maine Stokes, *Indian Fairy Tales*, Calcutta, 1879, pp. 68–72. For the relation between the folk-story and the book of Job *cf.* Const. Schlottmann, *Das Buch Hiob*, 1851, pp. 16 *ff.*; Albrecht Weber, *Indisches Studien*, xv, pp. 415–17 ; Ad. Lods, **CCXVII**.

[4] **XIV**, 372 *ff.*; **XLIV**, ii, 247–252 ; **XLIII**, 195–8 ; **XXVII**, 273–281.

[5] *Cf.* **XXXIX**, 75–6, 81.

addressed to Marduk on recovery from an illness. The fact that the Hebrew thinker confines himself to rebellion against the doctrine of individual retribution, without even mentioning the idea that Job might have suffered from the sins of his fathers or the ill-will of an enemy, suggests that he lived long after Ezekiel's time. The text of the book has been altered for the worse, and the order of chapters xxvi, xxvii, xxxix, 31–xli, 6 completely upset. All kinds of amplifications have been added, some perhaps by the poet himself (xxviii ; xxxix, 13–18 ; xl, 10–xli, 25), others, such as Elihu's discourse (ch. xxxii–xxxvii), by pious emendators scandalized at the freethinking of the original.

The book of Ecclesiastes, sceptical, disillusioned, pessimistic, is still later than the poem of Job. The language is already reminiscent of the Hebrew of the Mishnah. The matter suggests that the author was not unfamiliar with the philosophic attitude of Hellenistic civilization. Is there, he asks, anything—riches, wisdom, justice—capable of making man permanently happy ?   In its original form this work was distinctly unorthodox ; its bolder passages were subjected to repeated emendations.

The " son of Sirach ", author of *Ecclesiasticus*, whether his name was Jesus,[1] or Simon son of Jesus,[2] returns to the traditional principles of Jewish wisdom as they appear in the book of Proverbs. He wrote probably at the beginning of the second century (190–170), since his grandson, who translated his work into Greek, arrived in Egypt in 132.

Finally there is *Jewish imaginative literature*, from which the student of manners and customs, no less than the student of ideas, can glean many items of historical interest, especially since the narrative, or *haggada*, generally tended to edify and instruct, as well as to entertain the reader.

The book of *Ruth* is a little idyll with no pretensions to historical accuracy, and was doubtless intended as a protest against the harshness with which the followers of Ezra unconditionally condemned marriage with foreigners (Ez. ix–x ; Neh. xiii, 23–7).   It would therefore seem to have been composed towards the end of the fifth century.

The curious story of Jonah is a satire, as generous as it is

---

[1] As in the Greek and Syriac texts.

[2] As in the Hebrew and Saadia.

witty, directed against the exclusiveness of certain Jews who were shocked at God's patience with heathen nations. It must have been written between 400 and 190.

Among the papyri which originally belonged to the family of Jedoniah, Jewish priest of Yahu (Yahweh), at Elephantine in Upper Egypt (end of the fifth century B.C.), considerable fragments of the *Romance of Ahiqar*, written in Aramaic, have been found. This book, which for long was so famous that it was translated into all the languages of the East, has been called the first example of international literature. Wonder-tale and moral teaching in the form of maxims and fables, figured in it side by side. It served as a model, on the one hand for the life of Æsop, and on the other for many Æsopian fables. It was probably of Assyrian origin, and the discovery made at Elephantine is an indication of the close contact which existed between fifth-century Judaism and the general literature of the East.

The same conclusion can be drawn with regard to the *Book of Tobit*, a Jewish composition dating apparently from before the time of the Maccabees and expressly intended as a continuation of the cycle of Ahiqar, for in it the illustrious vizier of the King of Assyria is introduced as the nephew of the old Tobit. The subject-matter of the book is a variant on a theme recurrent in international folklore, that of the grateful dead. It is interesting to see the way in which it has been adapted in the interests of Jewish monotheism. The book of Tobit also provides some interesting sidelights on primitive customs and practices prevalent in circles unaffected by the official religion.

Tales of a similar nature inserted in historical works already existing should be studied along with independent Haggadic books. Such are Gen. xiv; Jos. xxii, 9–34; 1 Sam. xvi, 1–13; xix, 18–24; 1 Kings xiii; 2 Kings i, 9–16.

PART I

THE ERA OF CONFLICT
(760–586)

ISRAEL AND JUDAH AT WAR WITH ASSYRIA AND BABYLONIA

THE PROPHETS OPPOSE THE NATIONAL RELIGION

BOOK I

THE POLITICAL STRUGGLE

CHAPTER I

THE ASSYRIAN CONQUEST. THE END OF THE KINGDOM OF ISRAEL

IN the first centuries of their existence the kingdoms of Israel and Judah had been a match for all their enemies. Once the oncoming tide of Assyrian victories reached their frontiers their immunity was at an end.

Assyria was a military state, organized throughout with a view to war. To each of its men-at-arms, no less than to its kings and its god Asshur, the spoils of war brought wealth and glory. War was literally its national industry. This war-mindedness was to a certain extent the result of historical and geographical conditions, for the Assyrian had to defend his fields and orchards on the left bank of the Tigris from the raids of the rough mountain folk who were his neighbours

17   c

on the north and east, while on the south and west the country had no natural defences. Assyria had first to free itself from the bondage of Babylonia (in the days of Hammurabi and his dynasty, for example), then of Mitanni (in the days of Tel-el-Amarna), and when freedom was assured it continued to harass its neighbours. By 1300 it had conquered the territories belonging to its former rulers, but it lost them again. About 1100, however, Tiglath Pileser I once more took possession of Babylon. On the west he reached the Mediterranean at Arvad, in the north of Phenicia.

These rapid expansions and contractions of subjugated areas are characteristic of Assyrian conquest. The empire of the kings of Asshur could not boast of even the relative solidarity of that of the Pharaohs of the eighteenth and nineteenth dynasties. This was due in part to a difference of method. For the maintenance of their authority, the kings of Egypt relied to a much greater extent on carefully fostered discord among their vassals than on the inadequate forces which they sent to guard the provinces. They observed, moreover, a policy of tolerance and assimilation, most evident in their attitude to native gods, which they worshipped, identifying them with Egyptian divinities or even admitting them to the pantheon of the metropolis.[1] The Assyrians, on the contrary, preferred the alternative of brute force, destroying everything which they could not carry off, cutting down fruit-trees, levying exorbitant taxes, inflicting barbarous punishments upon rebels, whom they impaled or flayed alive, sometimes exhuming the dead in order to deprive them of the honours of burial. Nor did they scruple to humiliate the divinities of conquered nations, taking them captive or even destroying their statues. In this way the seeds of implacable hatred were sown, which bore fruit in refusals to pay tribute, and in revolt whenever the Assyrian troops were recalled to deal with disorder at home or to wage war on other frontiers. The king's death was often a signal for the dissolution of his empire, which his successor had to reconquer.

It is only fair to add that while the Egyptians had ruled only over populations endlessly subdivided and disintegrated, the Assyrians measured their strength against strong and virile

---

[1] *Cf.* **LVII,** 161-2.

Fig. 1.—Assyrian horsemen of the ninth or eighth century, after a mural painting discovered by M. Thureau-Dangin in the palace of Tell Ahmar (*Syria*, xi (1930), fig. 7, p. 126).

nations : Babylonians, Elamites, nomadic or sedentary Aramæans (particularly the Chaldeans), Medes, Khaldi from the country of Urartu (Ararat) in Armenia, Hittites, barbarians from the north—such as the Moschi, the Cimmerians, the Akkhuzi (Scythians), Arabs, Egyptians, and Ethiopians.

It was in the course of the eighth century that, having perfected their methods of conquest, the Assyrians reached the zenith of their power. Instead of allowing conquered states a certain amount of autonomy under native rulers, from the time of Tiglath Pileser III onwards (745–727) they show a preference for transforming these states into provinces administered by Assyrian governors. Tiglath Pileser III also seems to have been the first to make systematic use of deportation on a large scale, a procedure less cruel and much more effective than the traditional terrorism. His plan was to deport in a body the pick of the conquered population, which he replaced by foreign colonists from some other rebellious city. The Syrian prince Panammu says of him in an inscription :—

" He transported to the west the populations of the east, and to the east those of the west."[1]

As a rule, the Assyrians succeeded in finally undermining the entire fabric of national existence in the communities so treated.

By thus shuffling and reshuffling the populations of Asia and by obliterating frontiers, the Assyrians were chiefly responsible for the levelling process which prepared the ground for the great empires of Babylonia, Persia, Greece, and Rome.[2]

Before the end of the eighth century the Israelites had already come in contact more than once with these redoubtable invaders—at the battle of Qarqar (854), at which Ahab joined forces with the King of Damascus against Shalmaneser III,[3] at the battles fought by Joram in 849 and 846[4] against the same ruler, when Jehu paid tribute-money to the same Shalmaneser in 842,[5] and Joash, King of Israel, a subsidy to Adadnirari IV for his campaign against Damascus between 806 and 803.[6] None of these unfortunate

---

[1] L. 14 of Panammu's inscription ; cf. Lagrange, Études, 2nd ed., 495–8.
[2] H. Gunkel, XXVIII, ii, 2², p. x.   [3] LVII, 441–2.
[4] LVII, 443.   [5] LVII, 445.   [6] LVII, 447 ; cf. XLIII, 243–4.

encounters, however, had lasting consequences. The Assyrians renewed warlike operations near the borders of Palestine at the time of the expeditions of Shalmaneser IV against Damascus (773) and Hadrach (772), and of Asshurdan against the last-named city (765 and 755)[1]; but there is no proof that Israel was involved in the struggle.

The situation grew rapidly worse in the reign of Tiglath Pileser III,[2] an energetic ruler and skilful warrior who, after having taken possession of the throne by force, restored on all frontiers that favourable state of affairs which the weakness of the last princes of the overthrown dynasty had compromised : at Babylon (745), on the borders of Media (744), then on the Syrian side, where he drove out the King of Urartu (743). He took three years to reconquer the city of Arpad (the present-day Erfad, to the north of Aleppo). He made an Assyrian province of the territory belonging to it and did the same with that of the princes of Unqi and Yaudi[3] in 739. Warned by this success, the petty kings of Syria, Palestine, and southern Asia Minor, and even an Arabian queen, sent tribute (738). Tiglath Pileser names, among others, Rasunnu (Reṣôn) of Damascus, and Me-ni-khi-im of Sa-me-ri-na-ai, that is to say, Menahem of Samaria.[4]

The kingdom of Israel had indeed fallen from the high estate it had known only a few years before, when Jeroboam II, after his decisive victory over the Aramæans of Damascus,[5] the hereditary enemies of his country, had been in the forefront of the rulers of that region (Am. vi, 1). His son Zechariah, after reigning for six months, was assassinated and supplanted by one Shallum, son of Jabesh, possibly a native of Jabesh in Transjordan. It may be gathered from this that the overthrow of the house of Jeroboam was due to tribal rivalries ; Isaiah mentions strife between Ephraim and Manasseh (ix, 21). A month later

---

[1] **XII**, 278.

[2] Some historians call him Tiglath Pileser IV.

[3] From the names of the towns enumerated, the province of Yadi, to the north-west of Aleppo, is apparently meant (**XCII**, 1 ; **XCV**, 54, 262, 465 ; **LXXIII**, 311 ; **XXVII**, 345). As the prince of this country was called Azriyahu, others identify him with Azariah, who was king of Judah at this time (Schrader, *Keilinschr. und Geschichtforschung*, 395 *ff.* ; Tiele, *Bab.-ass. Gesch.*, 230 *ff.* Luckenbill, **AJSL**, 41, p. 217 *ff.* ; **CLXIII**, 2.

[4] Annals, i, 148–157 ; *cf.* **XLIII**, 244.   [5] **LVII**, 447–8.

Shallum was put to death by Menahem, another claimant
to the throne who ruled over Tirzah, the former capital of
the country. As he was " the son of a Gadite ", it has
been supposed that he also came from Transjordan, but
the translation might equally well read " the son of Gadi ".
In any case, it was owing to these civil wars, marked by
episodes of the utmost barbarity, such as the massacre of the
people of Tappuah by Menahem, that the country lay at the
mercy of the stranger. According to the book of Kings, the
tribute of a thousand talents of silver sent by Menahem to
Tiglath Pileser was paid in the hope of strengthening his
position ; he obtained the money by levying a tax of fifty
shekels on every citizen capable of bearing arms. According to the Hebrew account, the King of Assyria then
invaded the country, but the silence of the cuneiform
records on this point suggests that he merely sent one of
his officers.

During the years 737–735 Tiglath Pileser's whole
attention was absorbed by the campaigns in Media and
Armenia. Reṣôn—or Reṣîn—of Damascus seized the
opportunity to organize a general rebellion of the States of
Syria against the governor who had been imposed on them
in 738. Israel joined the coalition. Pekahiah, son and successor
of Menahem and considered as the puppet of the King of
Assyria, was overthrown and assassinated by one of his
officers, Pekah, son of Remaliah, at the head of fifty men of
Gilead. The new king of Samaria and his ally Reṣôn declared
war against Jotham, king of Judah, probably because the
latter refused to take part in a rising against Assyria. Under
Ahaz, the son of Jotham, the situation became critical.
Israelites and Aramæans marched upon Jerusalem with the
avowed intention of setting up the " son of Tab-el "—possibly
Reṣôn himself—on the throne of David.[1] The Edomites
retook Elath, the port on the Elanitic gulf, which
Azariah, the grandfather of Ahaz, had succeeded in wresting
from them.[2] It was doubtless also at this time that the
Philistines took possession of various towns in the south-
west.[3] In his extremity Ahaz, against the advice of Isaiah,

[1] **XCIII**, 74 ; **XCV**, 55, 135.
[2] 2 Kings xvi, 6 (for Aram read Edom) ; 2 Chron. xxviii, 17.
[3] 2 Chron. xxviii, 18.

enlisted the help of Tiglath Pileser by sending him the entire wealth of the Temple and the royal palace.

In consequence the King of Assyria came to chastise the rebels. According to the eponym list he penetrated as far as Philistia. It was therefore probably in the same year that he invaded and dismembered the kingdom of Israel (2 Kings xv, 29), making of Transjordan (Gilead) and Galilee—whose population had to submit to the usual deportation—an Assyrian province. Pekah was overthrown by the pro-Assyrian party in Samaria ; the murderer, Hoshea, son of Elah, prevailed upon Tiglath Pileser to recognize him as king. During the years 733 and 732 Tiglath Pileser concentrated all his energy on the task of subjugating Damascus. When at length the town yielded, Resôn was executed and the surrounding territory annexed to Assyria. Tiglath Pileser received tribute in the conquered town from Ammon, Moab, Ascalon, Gaza, and Edom, while Ahaz himself brought that of Judah. It was in Damascus that Ahaz saw an altar, obviously Assyrian, and had a copy made in order to curry favour by having it set up in the Temple at Jerusalem. It was perhaps at this time that he made an attempt to exalt himself at Israel's expense (Hos. v, 10), probably without success.

From 732 the two kingdoms of Israel and Judah were in almost desperate straits. There was no longer any bulwark to defend them from the empire of Assyria. The northern kingdom, three-quarters of which had been annexed, now consisted solely of the tribe of Ephraim, which, however, had the insane audacity to engage once more in open combat with the enemy.

Tiglath Pileser died in 727, having assumed the title of King of Babylon, but under the name of Pulu (Pul, 2 Kings xv, 19), so as to give the inhabitants of the famous city the illusion of independence. Thinking to avail himself of the change of ruler in order to regain his liberty, Hoshea sought the help of So, whom the book of Kings describes as King of Egypt, but who is certainly to be identified with Sabe' or Sibi', " Pharaoh's commander-in-chief," mentioned in Assyrian documents. This personage, the Hebraic version of whose name was doubtless Sévé, was perhaps at the same time one of the minor " kings " who shared the Delta among them. Hoshea also probably joined forces with the King of

Tyre, Luli or Elulæus, who at that time recovered the country of the Kittim (in Cyprus), which the Assyrians had taken from him.[1] Hoshea did not go beyond suspending payment of tribute, but Shalmaneser V, son of Tiglath Pileser III, took him prisoner, probably in 725, in the course of the campaign in which he conquered the whole of Phenicia with the exception of the island on which the town of Tyre was built.[2] As Samaria had not surrendered, Shalmaneser returned the following year and laid siege both to it and to Tyre. After a five years' siege the Assyrians failed to capture Tyre,[3] but Samaria capitulated after a heroic resistance lasting three years (724–722).

Shalmaneser died during the siege, and a new sovereign, Sargon II—who had usurped the throne in 722—sealed the fate of the residue of northern Israel. He deported 27,290 inhabitants of Samaria, evidently the pick of the population, settling them partly in Ḥalaḥ (not far from Ḥarran in Upper Mesopotamia), partly on the banks of the Ḥabur, a tributary of the Euphrates, in the province of Gozan [4] further to the south-east, partly in the mountains (or, according to the Septuagint, the towns) of Media. It is quite likely, however, that the mention of Media concerns the previous deportation of Galileans and men of Gilead under Tiglath Pileser in 734, for this ruler had then just organized an Assyrian province on the frontier of Media and would, as a matter of course, colonize the region with foreign immigrants.[5]

In the place of the deported Israelites the conquerors, according to their usual policy, imported groups of settlers drawn from regions which they wished to subdue.[6] Some may have been sent by Sargon after the rising of 720, as was the case with the rebels who came from Syria, namely those of Ḥamath, and perhaps those of Sepharvaim and of Awwa, if by these two names we may understand Sibraim, near Hermon—cf. Ez. xlvii, 16 [7]—and Imm in Northern Syria.[8]

---

[1] Menander, in Josephus, A.J., ix, 14, 2, § 284.
[2] Menander, ibid., § 284–5.
[3] Menander, ibid., § 285–7.
[4] Cf. **XIX**, 490.   [5] **XCV**, 69–70.
[6] 2 Kings xvii, 6 ; xviii, 11.
[7] Or Sipri, in northern Syria (Kandersdorfer, **TQS**, 99, 377).
[8] **CXII**, 5–6.

Sargon also seems to have settled conquered Arabs there at a later date.[1] Others were transplanted still later by Esarhaddon and Asshurbanipal,[2] among them doubtless the Babylonians from Cuthah, Susa, and Elam, after the revolt of 648.[3] The newcomers received not only quarters and land, but also privileges[4] intended to isolate them from the native population and to keep the latter in check. Nevertheless, they lost no time in intermingling, even adopting the worship of Yahweh, the Elohim of the country.[5]

The fate of the Israelite settlers in Mesopotamia and Media is so mysterious that popular tale and learned legend alike have sought their descendants in the four corners of the earth, not excluding America.

It seems certain that in the seventh century a good many still survived in that part of Mesopotamia to which they had been deported. In various Assyrian documents[6] dating from the last years of the Empire (between 692 and 612), and originating chiefly from the countries of Ḥalaḥ and Kannu,[7] Mr. Sinaï Schiffer has pointed out[8] a number of authentic Jahivistic names such as Nadbi-ia-au (Nedabyahu),[9] Il-ia-au (Eliyahu),[10] Niri-yau (Neriyahu),[11] Paltiyahu,[12] or Hebrew names such as Sauli (Saul),[13] Ḥanina,[14] Abidanu,[15]

---

[1] Cf. **CXCII**, ii, 42 ; **XXVII**, i, 349–350.
[2] Ezr. iv, 2, 10.
[3] Cf. **XXX**, 219, 236–7.
[4] Ezr. iv, 14.
[5] This is to be inferred from the tendencious account given in 2 Kings xvii, 24–34 ; cf. **LXVIII**, ii, 146.
[6] Published by Ungnad (*Vorderasiatische Schriftdenkmäler der kgl. Museen zu Berlin*, i, Leipzig, Hinrichs, 1907) and Peiser (**OLZ**, 1905, 130 *ff.*).
[7] Perhaps to be identified with Kanne, which Ezekiel places between Harran and Eden (Bit adini on both banks of the middle Euphrates).
[8] *Keilinschriftliche Spuren der in der zweiten Hälfte des 8 Jahrhunderts von den Assyrern nach Mesopotamien deportierten Samarier* (10 *Stämme*), *Beihefte zur* **OLZ**, i (1907) ; *Oriens*, i, 1, Paris, 1926, p. 29 ; i, 2, pp. 29–30 ; cf. Gry, **MUS**, 1922, pp. 153–185 ; 1923, pp. 1–26 ; Abraham Levy, *The Song of Moses* (Deut. xxxii), Scientific Series of Oriens—The Oriental Review, i, 1930, pp. 12–25.
[9] **K**, 383, rev. 9 (Schiffer, *Keil. Spuren*, p. 37).
[10] **K**, 428, l. 1, 6, 10 (*op. cit.* 38).
[11] *Oriens*, i, 1, p. 29.
[12] Ibid.   [13] **VA Th**, 5391, l. 1 (Schiffer, *K.S.*, 5).
[14] **VA Th**, 5394, l. 4 (*op. cit.* 7).
[15] **K** 3789*a*, rev. 4 ; 3789*b*, rev. 3 (*op. cit.* 34).

Aḥiramu,[1] Pekah,[2] Usi (Hosea),[3] Menahem,[4] Aḥiiaqamu (Aḥiqam),[5] Amram, Naboth.[6] Some of these are the names of slaves, but there are also slave-traders, a secretary-treasurer (Ahiram), the head of a town (Pekah), a steward (Nedabiah), a master-weaver (Naboth)[7]; two others are friends of the Governor of Gozan, who has relations with Samaria.[8]

To judge by some of their names, the Israelites had remained faithful to their national God. Schiffer even believes himself justified in stating that they had obtained—like the Jews of Elephantine in Egypt—permission to erect a temple to Jahweh; in A-U, a god whose temple was situated in one of the towns of the region named Kar A-U (fortress of A-U), he recognizes Jahweh himself, whose name, he thinks, had been shortened to the vowels A-U. This seems less certain, for Assyriologists differ in their reading of the signs representing the name of this god.[9] Moreover, the numerous names into whose composition the divine vocable A-U enters are almost all undoubtedly Assyrian.

However this may be, the deported Israelites must still have formed communities fully conscious of their origin in the days of Jeremiah and Ezekiel, since these two prophets look forward to their return to Palestine.[10]

Some historians think they must have swelled the numbers of the Judæans exiled to Babylonia in 597 and 586.[11] This is not impossible. It is true that according to Ezra ii, those who returned to Judæa in 538 were all the sons of former inhabitants of Judah and Benjamin, which would be very strange if the Jewish settlements of Babylonia had

---

[1] **K** 383, rev. 7 (op. cit. 37).
[2] **K** 383, rev. 8 (op. cit. 37).
[3] **K** 76, l. 3, and Aramæan note (op. cit. 39).
[4] 81-2-4, 152, l. 1 and 6; **K** 411, l. 2, and rev. 3 (op. cit. 39-41).
[5] Oriens, i, 2, p. 29.   [6] 80-7-19, 48 (Schiffer, K.S., 31).
[7] Op. cit., p. 31.   [8] Oriens, i, 1, 29.
[9] Jensen, in Johns, Assyrian Deeds and Documents . . ., iii, 235. H. Zimmern, **XCV**, 468; Ungnad, op. cit.; Sayce, etc.
[10] Jer. iii, 6-25; xxxi, 15-17; Ez. iv, 4-6; xxxvii, 15-28.
[11] Thus **VIII**, 14-16, 32-4. According to Abraham Levy (The Song of Moses, pp. 28-32), it is these exiles of Israelite origin whom Ezekiel apostrophizes with the words " House of Israel ". This interpretation would do violence, however, to the obvious meaning of texts such as xiii, 16; xvii, 12; xxii, 6; for Ezekiel, as for all Judæan writers after 722, " Israel," unless the contrary is expressly implied, was merely a synonym for " Judah ".

experienced any extensive addition of Israelite elements. But it is not certain that the passage in Ezra is undeniably a list of immigrants.[1]

A few Jewish communities of Israelitish origin persisted for some time in the neighbourhood of Nisibis.[2] Nevertheless, the majority probably became amalgamated with the surrounding mass of pagans. If not, how can the circumstance be explained that the deported Jews from the northern kingdom did not solicit and obtain from Cyrus an authorization to return to the land of their fathers like the exiles of Judah or those of Gutium.

[1] See below, pp. 190–3.   [2] **LXXV**, iii², 8.

CHAPTER II

THE END OF THE KINGDOM OF JUDAH

I

ASSYRIAN POWER AT ITS HEIGHT. REIGNS OF HEZEKIAH, MANASSEH, AND AMON (ABOUT 720–638)

AFTER the war of 734, when Ahaz had placed himself under the protection of Tiglath Pileser, Judah was dominated, at first effectively, then nominally, by Assyria until 609. That it escaped the annexation which befell all the neighbouring states, one after the other, and that it out-lived Assyria itself, the little kingdom owed to its acceptance of its subordinate position. Such departures from the attitude of submissiveness as it did make nearly proved fatal.

But though the political rôle of the kingdom of Judah was one of self-effacement and humiliation, it was none the less the champion of the cause of Israel ; it is therefore not surprising that the intense spiritual fervour radiating at this period from Jerusalem should have affected the population of what had once been the northern kingdom, and, in fact, we find that even after the destruction of Jerusalem in 586, pilgrims from Samaria, Shechem, and Shiloh brought offerings to the site of the Temple (Jer. xli, 5) ; how much stronger then must the attraction of Zion have been before the Temple was destroyed.

But let us trace the succession of events. Hezekiah succeeded Ahaz probably about 720.[1] Unlike his father, he

---

[1] According to 2 Kings xviii, 10, he came to the throne as early as 727, since Samaria is said to have been taken in the sixth year of his reign (722). According to another passage in the same book (xviii, 13), the beginning of his reign must be dated much later, in 715 ; for Sennacherib's attack on Jerusalem is supposed to have taken place in the fourteenth year of his reign. It is better to take the destruction of Jerusalem as starting-point and work backwards, reckoning by the length of each reign, as stated in the book of Kings ; this being apparently the most reliable element of Hebrew chronology. In this way the mean date 720 is obtained.

PLATE II

Sennacherib receives the surrender of the city of Lachish (2 Kings xviii. 13-17).
Bas-relief in the British Museum

[face p. 28

made several attempts to shake off the yoke of Assyria, taking advantage of the incessant conflict between the kings of Assyria and their neighbours—especially Urartu (Armenia)—and their rebellious dependencies.

The most redoubtable adversary of Sargon II was Marduk-aplu-iddina, the Merodach-baladan of the Hebrew Bible. He was a Chaldean prince, a descendant, namely, of those nomads, probably Aramæan, who had settled in "the sea-country", on the borders of the Persian Gulf, to the south of Babylonia. By exploiting—in Babylon, that ancient home of science, religion, and commerce—the hatred felt for the Assyrian masters, who in spite of their omnipotence were looked upon as barbarians and parvenus, Marduk-aplu-iddina succeeded in getting himself recognized as King of Babylon (as early as 721). It may have been at this time that he sent to Hezekiah that ambassador whose mission is related, none too clearly, in the book of Kings,[1] its avowed object being to inquire for the health of the king of Judah, its real intention an effort to persuade him to take part in a general revolt secretly instigated in the west by the Chaldean prince. Hence the interest shown by the envoys in the arsenals and treasury of their host.

And, in fact, in 720 a great rebellion broke out in Syria, probably when tidings were brought that the Elamites, the allies of the Chaldeans, had defeated Sargon at Dur-ilu in north Babylonia. The chiefs of the movement in the west were the king of Hamath, Ilubi'di or Yaubi'di,[2] and Hanun of Gaza. The populations of Arpad, Simirra, Damascus, and Samaria had also been involved, although these provinces had already been subjugated by Assyria. The Gaza revolt was supported by Sibe at the head of an Egyptian army.[3]

The King of Hamath was defeated at Qarqar, the King of Gaza and his ally Sibe at Raphia, on the road to Egypt. The possibility that Hezekiah joined the insurrection rests upon

[1] 2 Kings xx, 12–19 ; Isa. xxxix.

[2] This name, which bears witness to the extension of the worship of the god Jahu (Jahweh) beyond the borders of Israel, is further discussed, **LVII**, 371; cf. 150–1, 370–7.

[3] The title of " tartan of Pir'u, king of Musri ", given to Sibe, should be interpreted as " general of the Pharaoh, King of Egypt ", in preference to Winckler's rendering " general of Piru, King (unknown) of the Arab country of Musri " (**XCV**, 67, 146).

a single piece of evidence. In an inscription of 717 Sargon gives himself the title of " conqueror of the distant country of Ya-u-du ". This, however, may refer to the kingdom of Yaudi, in northern Syria,[1] or else Sargon, having received the homage of Hezekiah, may have added Judah to the list of the vanquished, to lengthen the list.

Knowing that the King of Assyria was preoccupied with struggles against Urartu and allied powers (719–711), the west once more seized the opportunity to revolt during the three years 713 to 711. This time the centre of insurrection was the city of Ashdod, in Philistia, from which city a certain Yamani or Yawani (perhaps an " Ionian " adventurer) drove away its prince, the vassal of Asshur. Once more Sibe was looked to for help. Among the rebellious states Sargon names Philistia, Judah, Edom, and Moab. The mention of Judah is confirmed by a strange scene described in the book of Isaiah (ch. xx), which shows that at least the temptation to join forces with the rebels was strongly felt there : the prophet, we are told, appeared for three years in the streets, naked and barefoot, endeavouring to convince his people that the Egyptians and the Ethiopians, whose help they relied on, would also be despoiled and led captive by the Assyrians. The Ethiopians are named in conjunction with the Egyptians because Shabako, a Nubian prince, succeeded at this time [2] in extending his rule over the whole of the Nile valley, and became the founder of the twenty-fifth or Ethiopian dynasty. It was doubtless these internecine disturbances which prevented Sibe from intervening in Palestine. Ashdod was taken without difficulty by the tartan or general acting for Sargon at the head of a detachment of the royal guard (711). The inhabitants of the town were deported and the surrounding territory became an Assyrian province with new settlers. Judah's escape from the same fate was no doubt due to Hezekiah's opportune payment of arrears of tribute.

Sargon II died in 705 in the course of a campaign, and was succeeded by his son Sennacherib. As usual, the vassal states of the empire took advantage of the change of sovereign,

---

[1] **XCV**, 67–8 ; for the opposite view, **CLXIII**, 6.
[2] **XLIX**, ii, 378 ; **CLXIII**, 237 (about 714). Reisner (**CLXV**) gives the date of Shabako's succession as between 734 and 711, probably about 722.

PLATE III

Esarhaddon holding conquered princes by a leash (from RICCIOTTI, *Storia d'Israele*, Società Editrice internationale, I, 463)

Sargon II puts out the eyes of a conquered enemy
(From XLV, 4th ed. p. 599)

attended this time by the confusion of a defeat, to make an attempt at recovering their independence.

A rebellion broke out in Babylon. Marduk-aplu-iddin once more intervened, but after six months he was driven from the city by Sennacherib's army and had to take refuge in Elamite territory. The King of Assyria deemed it prudent to allow the Babylonians the meagre satisfaction of a prince of their own, bearing the ancient title of " King of Sumer and Accad ", namely Bel-ibni (704–700) ; it was not long, however, before Bel-ibni allied himself with the Chaldeans.

During this time, and there can be no doubt that the rebellion was due to concerted planning (some historians think that the sending of the envoy from Baladan to Hezekiah should be placed here), the whole of the south-west part of the empire was seething with revolt. By the most energetic inducements at their disposal the more determined rebels coerced the hesitant or the reluctant to take part in the coalition, until finally even the cities of Phenicia were drawn in, except perhaps Sidon, which Elulæus, King of Tyre, tried to include by force, as well as the towns of Philistia, and Judah, Moab, and Edom. At Jerusalem the anti-Assyrian party gained the upper hand to such an extent that Hezekiah became the chief of the rebellion in Palestine. He entered into active negotiation with Egypt, and from Shabako, the Ethiopian Pharaoh, he obtained, by bribing him with gold,[1] a promise of an army. He then ravaged the land of the Philistines,[2] which term applies probably to such Philistines as wished to remain faithful to Assyria, and was entrusted with the care of Padi, the pro-Assyrian prince of Ekron, who had been deposed by his subjects. Hezekiah recruited Arab mercenaries and set about great preparations for restoring the ramparts of Jerusalem to a state of defence, especially those of the city of David, that is to say of the citadel ; it was perhaps at this time that he made what is now called the pool of Siloam, in the interior of the town, and the subterranean conduit to it, out of sight of the enemy, from the spring of Gihon.[3]

Sennacherib finally appeared in Syria with his army in

---

[1] Ez. xxx, 6.   [2] 2 Kings xviii, 8.
[3] Now the Virgin's Well. 2 Kings xx, 20 ; 2 Chron. xxxii, 30.   Sir. xlviii, 17. *Cf.* **CL.**

701. This campaign, which to all appearances ushered in Judah's last hour, is still to a great extent veiled in obscurity ; not that documents are lacking—on the contrary, this event is more richly documented than any other event of ancient times. But not one of all these texts furnishes a complete and consecutive account, and it is not always possible to piece together the reliable facts which can be extracted from them.[1] Sennacherib's own account of the facts, contained in contemporary inscriptions,[2] must, of course, be taken as our starting-point, remembering, however, that the royal scribes may have omitted events which did not redound to their master's glory, and that we cannot be sure that they followed a strictly chronological order : they seem, for instance, to have grouped together everything which concerned each of the king's enemies respectively.

The passages in the book of Kings which refer to this campaign—reproduced in the book of Isaiah, and, with supplementary details, in the much later book of Chronicles (2 Chron. xxxii)—are apparently the result of the inter-weaving of three distinct versions. One, the most ancient, agrees in almost every point with the cuneiform account (2 Kings xviii, 13b–16), the second (2 Kings xviii, 17–20a, 23–37 ; xix, 1–9a, 36–7) was written at least twenty years after the event, since it records the murder of Sennacherib (681), but not necessarily much later than that, for, in spite of its bias, it is sober and definite, and the more recent details it contains seem to have been inserted subsequently.[3] The third (2 Kings xix, 19b–20, 35) is in the nature of a belated popular legend, but seems to have preserved for us a certain amount of usable material.

About 440, Herodotus noted an Egyptian tradition which, freed from its legendary trappings, confirms in an interesting way one of the Hebrew accounts.

---

[1] On this problem cf. **CLIV, CLVIII** ; Prasek, **MVAG,** 1903 ; **CXCI, CXVII, XCVIII, CXIII** ; Fullerton, **AJSL,** 42 (1925), 1, ff. ; **XLIX,** ii, 430 ff. ; Rudolph, **PJ, XXV,** 59 ff. ; **CLXIII,** 439–460 ; A. Alt, **RGG,** 2nd ed., ii ; **LXVIII,** i, 409–410.

[2] Taylor Prism, a clay prism found at Nineveh in 1830 ; a replica was published in **CLIII** ; cf. Breasted, **AJSL,** 38 (1922), 284–6. This text was reproduced on the bulls at Kuyundjik.

[3] xviii, 21, reminiscent of Ez. xxix, 6, is a doublet of xviii, 24 ; and xviii, 22, which ascribes to Hezekiah the reforms of Josiah, does not ring true in the context owing to the use of the second person plural.

Finally, we may make use of the allusions contained in those prophecies of Isaiah, whose date and authenticity are undeniable, e.g. xxii, 1–14.

The order of events may be reconstructed as follows. In the north of Phenicia, Sennacherib had no difficulty in restoring his authority. Sidon, where the partisans of Assyria had the upper hand, accepted the king whom he set on the throne, Ithobaal ; the princes of the towns, which owed allegiance to Sidon, such as Arvad and Byblos, paid tribute. Tyre on its island was almost impregnable. Sennacherib left it invested, and went south along the coast. The kings of Edom and Moab immediately surrendered. At Ascalon, Sennacherib deposed and banished to Assyria the prince proclaimed by the rebels, and restored to the throne the prince who had remained loyal to him.

He then retraced his steps and laid siege to Ekron, one of the principal centres of the rebellion. The promised Egyptian army advanced to the rescue of the town. Sennacherib states that he defeated it at Altaqu (Elteqeh, half-way between Ekron and Jerusalem) : he did in fact force it to retreat, but his success must have been dearly bought, for he did not pursue the Egyptians. He returned to finish the siege of Ekron.

He now had only one enemy to overcome, Hezekiah. Sennacherib, however, did not march with the bulk of his army against Jerusalem, but laid siege to Lachish (Tell el-Hesy ?),[1] and his troops captured the other small fortified towns in the neighbourhood which belonged to Judah. He boasts of having taken forty-six of them, and of leading captive 200,150 men, women, and children. As to the capital itself, he contented himself for the time being with surrounding it with a detachment of guards, who kept watch, blocked the roads with entrenchments, and captured anyone attempting to leave the town. " I shut him up in Jerusalem, his capital, like a bird in its cage," says Sennacherib of Hezekiah, the usual simile for operations of this kind.[2]

---

[1] Tell Duweir is now accepted generally as the site of Lachish.— *Translator's note.*

[2] *Cf.* Tell el-Amarna, ed. Hugo Winckler (**KB**, v), 55, l. 45–8 ; 60, l. 35–8 ; 62, l. 13–16 ; 64, l. 34–6 ; 84, l. 7–10 ; 87, l. 19–21.

It must have been at this time that an encounter took place which ended in the disgraceful flight of the fine mercenary troops of Hezekiah, along with the princes of Judah.[1]

His last hope gone, the king had no choice but to send officers to Lachish to ask for terms. Sennacherib did not spare him. He was required to set Padi at liberty (it is possible that Hezekiah freed him of his own accord), that the King of Assyria might restore him to the throne of Ekron, and to pay, in addition to the usual tribute, a heavy indemnity : in all 30 talents of gold and 300 talents of silver,[2] roughly 280,000 pounds sterling, not counting numerous articles of value, his daughters, the ladies of his palace, and his musicians, male and female. Furthermore, the cities taken by the Assyrians were divided among the kings of Ekron, Ashdod, and Gaza, who had not rebelled.

The terms laid down for the King of Judah were severe. Nevertheless, he hastened to accept them, astonished no doubt that they were not more rigorous still, and that Sennacherib did not demand, as was the Assyrian custom when inflicting penalties for rebellion, that the town should be given up, the delinquent ruler deposed, and the *élite* of the inhabitants deported.

Sennacherib himself seems soon to have regretted his moderation, for it must have been after Hezekiah had sent the treasure and the captives required of him to the Assyrian camp at Lachish [3] that there appeared beneath the walls of Jerusalem one of the chief officers of the great king, namely his *rabshakeh* or chief cup-bearer, at the head of a strong detachment to demand the surrender of the town, whose inhabitants were to be deported. The speech of the Assyrian envoy was doubtless composed after the event by the Israelite historian, but it gives us a very vivid and certainly correct idea of the methods by which the conquerors brought pressure to bear upon the vanquished. He stands beneath

---

[1] Taylor Prism, iii, 31–3 ; *cf.* Ez. xxii, 2–3.

[2] Eight hundred according to the Assyrian text. The difference may be due to the fact that the Judæans and the Assyrians used similar terms for monies of different value.

[3] Such at least is the conclusion to be drawn from the sequence of the Hebrew text as it now stands (2 Kings xviii, 14–17). According to the Assyrian account, Hezekiah sent them after Sennacherib to Nineveh. And, in fact, the formal payment of the tribute may have been made in the Assyrian capital.

the walls of the town and in a loud voice harangues the envoys of Hezekiah, not in Aramæan, the diplomatic language of the time, but in the Jewish language, namely Hebrew, so that all the common people on the ramparts, whom he even addresses directly, might understand him. He scoffs at the impotence of the states already vanquished by the Assyrian, of their gods, of their Egyptian ally, of Hezekiah himself who, even if he had horses, would no longer have riders to set upon them ; he threatens, he promises ; he even declares that his master has been sent by Jahweh. We are not told Hezekiah's answer to these disloyal exhortations, but whatever it was he did not open the gates.

And, strange to say, the Assyrian officer departed with his forces and did not return. One of the Hebrew versions of the story gives us the explanation of the peculiar behaviour of the Assyrians. Sennacherib had just received news of the approach of an Egyptian army under the leadership of " Tirhaqah, King of Ethiopia ".

This also explains the moderation, so foreign to his vengeful nature, shown by Sennacherib in the terms imposed on Hezekiah. In danger of being attacked in the rear by an enemy of whose mettle he had had experience at Altaqu, he had realized that he could not hope to undertake the siege of a stronghold like Jerusalem and had contented himself with exacting tribute. He had on second thoughts tried by intimidation to make the town give way, but had not resorted to a regular blockade. At the very moment when his expedition left for Jerusalem he was probably on the point of retreating ; and, in fact, while he was still at Lachish when the *rabshakeh* took his departure, he had already reached Libnah, farther north,[1] when his envoy rejoined him.[2]

The taking of Lachish was the last triumph of the campaign ; Sennacherib had it portrayed on a bas-relief in his palace at Nineveh.[3]

There was still another deterrent to inspire him with prudence ; an epidemic seems to have broken out in his army.

---

[1] See Jos. x, 29–32.
[2] 2 Kings xix, 8. This detail proves that the episode of the *rabshakeh* took place after and not before (**XXX**) Hezekiah's surrender, since it was before Lachish that the king of Judah asked for and received Sennacherib's conditions (2 Kings xviii, 14).
[3] British Museum. See pl. ii ; *cf.* **XXVII**, ii, figs. 138 and 141.

One of the Hebrew accounts of the episode records that the angel of Jahweh struck down in a single night 185,000 men of the Assyrian camp. According to Egyptian tradition, of a still more legendary nature, noted by Herodotus, rats gnawed away the bows and buckler-straps of the soldiers of Sanacharibos, King of the Arabs and Assyrians, leaving them unable to defend themselves against the merchants and the artisans composing the army of the Pharaoh Sethon.

The ancients were already well aware of the connection, confirmed and explained by modern science, between rats and the plague : in India the plague was called " rat disease ", and one is perhaps justified in inferring from an old Hebrew story that in Palestine mice were held as the symbol of the terrible scourge (1 Sam. vi, 4).

But the event which more than anything must have compelled Sennacherib to leave the west in the utmost haste and without chastising Hezekiah as thoroughly as he would have wished, was a fresh outbreak of revolt in Babylon.

Judah came out of the conflict with territory reduced, population decimated, countryside laid waste, and treasury empty. Hezekiah was still the vassal of the King of Assyria, and even had to pay increased tribute. Nevertheless, since the inhabitants of Jerusalem had had every reason to fear a much worse fate, they greeted the unexpected departure of the invaders with transports of joy,[1] and legend was not long in celebrating the partial setback experienced by Sennacherib as a shining proof of the protection afforded by Jahweh to his temple and his sacred city.

From 700 to 689 Sennacherib's attention was absorbed by the eastern provinces of his empire, especially Babylonia. Nothing positive is known about the eight last years of his reign, except that he died by assassination, probably at Babylon,[2] at the hands of one [3] or two [4] of his sons, falling

---

[1] Isa. xxii, 1–2, 13.

[2] For it was there that his grandson afterwards offered expiatory sacrifices. (Cf. Schmidtke, **OLZ**, 21, 169 ; Streck, *Assurbanipal*, ii, 38–9.) According to 2 Kings xix, 36–7, the murder was at Nineveh : a view supported by Lehmann-Haupt, **LII**, 124 ; **OLZ**, 21, 273 ; Ungnad, **OLZ**, 20, 359 ; B. Meissner, **SBA**, 1932, p. 250 *ff.* ; Sidney Smith, **CAH**, iii, 79 ; Proksch, **CLXIII**.

[3] Chron. Bab., iii, 34–5.

[4] 2 Kings, xix, 37 ; Esarhaddon's prism has " my brothers ". *Cf.* B. Meissner, *ibid.*

without doubt a victim to the hatred he had inspired by his destruction of the capital of the rebel Babylonians (689).

Winckler,[1] whose opinion has been adopted by other critics,[2] considers that between 689 and 681, in the course of a campaign against the Arabs of the oasis of Dumah, he penetrated as far as the borders of Egypt, and engaged in battle with Tirhaqah, and that he again marched into Palestine and threatened Jerusalem. In his opinion it is to this campaign, and not to that of 701, that both the third Hebrew narrative and the Egyptian legend recounted by Herodotus refer, the Hebrew account in question being the one which describes the destruction of the Assyrian army by the plague, and which, according to him, should contain the verse about the intervention of Tirhaqah, " king of Ethiopia."

This hypothesis is supported by the chronology. Tirhaqah was not king of Ethiopia (and Egypt) in 701, nor until about 689 or 688. On the other hand, are we to believe that the Hebrew narrator was mistaken in the chronology of the kings of Judah ? For between 689 and 681 the throne of Jerusalem had become the heritage of Manasseh, Hezekiah having died about 692. Moreover, it is hard to believe that Sennacherib could have led, right across the great deserts of Central Arabia, an army powerful enough to attack Egypt and lay siege to Jerusalem ; it is equally difficult to suppose that the second and third accounts in the book of Kings, in both of which the same characters appear, using words almost identical, should refer to two entirely distinct events. On the contrary, everything points to their being two versions of the same tradition. As to the sentence about Tirhaqah (2 Kings xix, 2a), it would seem to belong to the second narrative, the rumour of the immediate intervention of this enemy being responsible, in accordance with Isaiah's prophecy (xix, 7), for Sennacherib's decision to retreat.

A hieroglyphic inscription from Tanis proves that Tirhaqah was already a person of considerable importance during the reign of his predecessor, whose nephew he was [3] ;

---

[1] **XCII**, 26 *ff.* ; **XCV**, 273.
[2] e.g. Dhorme, **RB**, 1910, 511–18 ; *The Lands of the Bible and Assyria*, 75 *ff.*, 80 *ff.*, Guthe, **XXX** ; R. W. Rogers, **CLXXI** ; Delaporte, **XII**.
[3] *Cf.* **LII**, 114.

it would therefore not be surprising if a somewhat later historian, relating an event which took place in 701, had anticipated Tirhaqah's title of "king of Ethiopia" at a time when he
was still only crown prince and his uncle's general. It is also
possible that this historian named Tirhaqah by mistake for
Shabako, the former being the best known sovereign of the
Ethiopian dynasty, and above all renowned for his subsequent
affrays with Assyria.

Manasseh, who succeeded Hezekiah about 692, unlike his
father, does not seem to have departed from the attitude of
subservience which it behoved a faithful vassal of the King
of Asshur to cultivate. He introduced the worship of his
sovereign's gods into the temple at Jerusalem, and he is
mentioned among the contributors towards the building of a
new arsenal at Nineveh,[1] paying his dues to Esarhaddon (681–
668) as one of twenty-two western vassals. The example of
Sidon which, after a rebellion (679–676), was razed to the
ground while another town was built in its stead upon another
site, and given the name of citadel of Esarhaddon, doubtless
helped to inspire Manasseh with caution. The book of
Chronicles relates, it is true, that the chiefs of the Assyrian
army marched against him and took him to Babylon in
chains,[2] but adds that having called upon Jahweh he was
delivered, and that he then restored the worship of the true
God in Israel.[3] But this edifying tale, about which the book
of Kings is silent, contains at best a few historical allusions
dressed in a garb which is anything but historical. It is not
impossible that Manasseh's loyalty may have been suspected
at some time during his long reign, perhaps when there was
trouble in Samaria, as there must have been, for Esarhaddon
and Asshurbanipal brought in new colonists [4]; it is also
conceivable that he was led captive to Babylon, where each
of those sovereigns lived fairly frequently, and that, having

---

[1] Prism B, l. 13 (**KB**, ii, 140–1).

[2] Esarhaddon had himself portrayed on steles found at Sendjirli
and Tell Ahmar, holding conquered kings in leash (probably Abdi-
Milkutti, King of Sidon, and the son of Tirhaqah) by means of rings
passed through their lips ; *cf.* Dussaud, **SY**, viii (1927), pp. 366–7 ;
Fr. Thureau-Dangin, **SY**, x (1929), pp. 189–196. See pl. iii, 1.

[3] 2 Chron. xxxiii, 11–13, 15–17, 19.

[4] Ezr. iv, 2, 9–10. From the gloss in Isa. vii, 8, it is perhaps allowable
to infer that the colonization under Esarhaddon took place sixty-five
years after 734, therefore about 670.

succeeded in proving the blamelessness of his conduct, he was restored to favour, as was the case at that time with another vassal of Assyria, the Egyptian Necho. However that may be, Manasseh made no change in his religious policy towards the end of his life.[1]

The moment was not propitious for taking liberties with the Assyrian rulers. Never had they been more powerful than they were under Esarhaddon and his son Assurbanipal (668–626). The conquest of Egypt laid the whole of the civilized world at their feet. A first attempt having failed (676), Esarhaddon succeeded in subduing the country as far as Thebes, and in driving out Tirhaqah (671), whom he defeated in three encounters. Under Asshurbanipal a third expedition, in which twenty-two vassal kings took part (Manasseh was certainly one of them), ended in the taking of Thebes (667), an event so striking that the deep impression it made had not been obliterated half a century later.[2] Tyre itself, the impregnable city, made its submission to the great king.

No less crushing was the defeat which Asshurbanipal inflicted in 648, after a long and severe struggle, on Babylon, once more rebellious, and on Babylon's faithful ally, the kingdom of Elam, whose capital, Susa, he destroyed. Taking advantage of these disorders, the Arabs had begun raiding and looting. They were beaten in several battles on the borders of Palestine, and in the same campaign the King took possession of the towns of Usu (the continental Tyre) and Akko, and deported the inhabitants. Even in Judæa there seem to have been Assyrian settlers at Gaza.[3]

The " Assyrian peace " seemed so firmly established that Asshurbanipal was able to contemplate a future in which his people should excel in art and literature as they had hitherto excelled in war. The temples, both in Assyria and Babylon, were rebuilt and splendidly adorned by artists of renown, while at Nineveh the king made a library containing copies of all the literary and scientific works of Assyria, and more especially of Babylon, a move of far-reaching importance to which, as is well-known, we owe the greater part of our acquaintance with Sumero-Accadian civilization.

---

[1] Jer. xv, 4; 2 Kings xxi, 10–15; evidence rejected by Lehmann-Haupt (**LII,** 136–7).
[2] Nah. iii, 8.   [3] See pp. 4–5.

Manasseh's son, Amon, continued his father's policy of obedience to Assyria. He fell a victim to a palace intrigue (about 638). But the populace no doubt approved of the line of conduct followed by the prince, for the " people of the land " struck down the murderers and, still faithful to the ancient house of David, set upon the throne Josiah, the young son of the assassinated sovereign.

II

The Decline of Assyria

Judah's Last Period of Greatness : Josiah (about 637–609)

It had taken centuries to build up the might of Assyria. Less than forty years sufficed for its decline and fall, from the moment, during the lifetime of Asshurbanipal,[1] when it first began to totter, to that of its complete annihilation.

The Assyrians had emerged victorious but exhausted from their struggle with Babylon and Elam.

About the same time Asshurbanipal lost Egypt. Psammetichus I (664–610), son of Necho I, at first Prince of Sais in the Delta, and under Assyrian rule, seized the entire country, and about 645 [2] made himself completely independent. The short period of Assyrian domination had only served to rid Egypt of its Ethiopian sovereigns and inaugurate a national dynasty, the twenty-sixth. Like the Pharaohs of the middle and later empires, Egypt once more began to have designs on Syria. Psammetichus took possession of Ashdod after a siege which, according to the improbable account of Herodotus, lasted twenty-nine years.

The power of the Medes in the east was developing simultaneously. These Medes were merely the forerunners of a host of barbarians, largely of Indo-European origin like themselves, who came from the south of Russia and who, since the beginning of the seventh century, had poured into Asia Minor over the Caucasus or through the Straits : Cimmerians,

[1] See his lament, **XLI**, 107 ; **CAH**, iii, 127 ; **LXVIII**, ii, 8.
[2] In 652 according to **LXVIII**, ii, 410, 412.

Treres, Bithynians, and, most terrible of all, the Akhkhuza,[1] whose name has been preserved in the Old Testament in the corrupted form Ashkenaz, and in Greek transcribed as Σκύθαι, the Scythians.

The Assyrians, as in later days the Romans, tried at first to utilize these barbarians to defend the empire. It was with the aid of the Scythians that the Cimmerian invasion was diverted westwards to Asia Minor, and it was thanks to a Scythian chief that Nineveh itself was saved when, a short time after the death of Asshurbanipal, Cyaxares, King of the Medes, first laid siege (about 625) to the capital.[2]

But when Asshur-etil-ilani and Sinšariškun, the inadequate successors of the great king, came to the throne (in 625 and 620 respectively), the Assyrians, like the Romans when Rome was declining, were incapable of restraining the inroads of these redoubtable allies. A Scythian invasion, according to Herodotus,[3] after traversing the whole length of the empire, spread terror as far as the frontiers of Egypt ; Psammetichus bribed them to retreat but on their way they pillaged the temple of Ascalon. For twenty-eight years, according to the same historian, the Scythians were masters of Asia ; the Greek writer may have been thinking more especially of Asia Minor, but the fact is none the less significant.

And, finally, in the south the Assyrians were unable to prevent the Chaldean prince Nabopolassar from making himself independent at Babylon (625).

These upheavals naturally had their counterpart in the land of Judah. A precept recorded in Deuteronomy laid down that the king should not " cause the people to return to Egypt to the end that he should multiply horses ",[4] which shows indirectly that among some of the rulers of Judah the practice existed of bartering their subjects, to act as mercenaries for the Pharaohs, in exchange for consignments of war-horses. The allusion must be to the Pharaohs of the Sais dynasty, who in order to carry on their military operations drew extensively on foreigners, Greeks, Carians, Phenicians. On the colossi of Ipsambul the names of many of

---

[1] A new transcription figures on Esarhaddon's stele found at Tell Ahmar near Aleppo (**SY**, viii (1927), 367).

[2] According to Herodotus at least.

[3] **I,** 103–6.   [4] Deut. xvii, 10.

these legionaries can still be read, roughly inscribed by their own hand as they passed by, marching against the Ethiopians.[1] If the rulers of Judah at whom the stricture was aimed were, as is probable, Manasseh, Amon, or the guardians of the young Josiah, we may infer that, after the middle of the seventh century, the Jewish authorities no longer were afraid to take steps which in earlier times would have caused suspicion and brought down the wrath of the Assyrian overlord, since they were not only assisting a rebellious vassal but also reinforcing their own army. It was doubtless one of these groups of Palestinian soldiery which, ceded to a Pharaoh, formed the nucleus of the military colony at Elephantine which reappears in the fifth century, observing the worship of Yahu (Jahweh), as it had been observed in Judæa and Samaria before the reforms of Josiah ; these Jews of Upper Egypt knew that their sanctuary of Yahu had been in existence since the days of the dynasty of Sais (645–525) ; Herodotus, on the other hand, relates that Psammetichus I had put a garrison in Elephantine, and the letter of Aristeas (§ 13) states that Jews had been sent as reinforcements to Psammetichus [2] in his campaign against the Ethiopians.

Assyrian authority in Judæa waned rapidly ; by 622 it was almost non-existent. Besides its religious aspect, to which we will return later, the reform which Josiah carried out at this date was, from the political point of view, virtually a proclamation of independence. He removed from the Temple and destroyed all the emblems of the worship of the " heavenly hosts ", that is to say of the star-cults of Assyria, which Manasseh as a faithful vassal had introduced. To restore to his exclusive rights the God of Israel was tantamount to a restoration of nationality, such as was being carried out in Egypt and Babylonia in similar political conditions.

Josiah enforced his measures of reform not only in Judæa but also at Bethel, at a date of which we cannot be sure, a proof that he had been able to extend his political authority to territory which had been an Assyrian province ever since the fall of Samaria (722). This is further borne out by the fact that when the independence of his people was at stake

---

[1] **CIS**, i, 112 c ; *cf.* Mark Lidzbarski, **LIV**, ii, 5 ; *Altsem, Texte*, i, Giessen, Töpelmann, 1907, p. 37.
[2] Psammetichus II is meant (594–588).

he defended it, as we shall see, from Megiddo, that is to say from the centre of the former kingdom of Israel.

The period of expansion and liberty which Judah experienced in the reign of Josiah, especially in the second half, was of short duration. By 609 the series of disasters had begun again, to culminate only in the complete destruction of the last of the Israelite states.

III

THE EGYPTIAN CONQUEST. THE NEW BABYLONIAN EMPIRE. THE LAST YEARS OF THE KINGDOM OF JUDAH (609–586)

A fragment of Babylonian chronicle published in 1923 by Gadd,[1] recounting the exploits of Nabopolassar during the years 616–609, sheds new light on and discloses some curious details about the final stages of Assyrian decay. When the chronicle opens, Nabopolassar, Chaldean prince of Babylon, is already in open revolt against his Ninevite overlord. The latter is simultaneously attacked by him and by Cyaxares, King of the Medes, the date of the alliance being 614. From at least 612, the people of the Umman Manda, whose identity we shall discuss later, also figured among the enemies of Assyria. In this death struggle, however, the king of Assyria had a somewhat unexpected ally, the Pharaoh : as early as 616, an Egyptian army had been fighting on the Euphrates side by side with the troops of Asshur. Psammetichus I (645–610), having driven the Assyrians out of his own country, had apparently understood that a military state like Assyria was a most effective bulwark, between himself and the hordes of barbarians from the north who, a few years before, had reached the very borders of Egypt. Psammetichus had, moreover, in all probability demanded, as the price of his assistance, the rights hitherto enjoyed by Asshur over all or part of Syria.

In spite of his help, Nineveh was taken by storm (612) ; the king Sinšariškun perished and the town was reduced to a heap of ruins.[2]

---

[1] **CXV** ; **CLII**, ii, 413–423.
[2] *Cf.* Xenophon, *Anabasis*, iii, 4.

Nevertheless, under a prince named Aššuruballit, who took as his capital Harran, in the north-east of Mesopotamia, Assyria was able to hold some years longer. Harran succumbed in its turn in 610, under the combined onslaught of the Umman Manda [1] and the Babylonians.

Aššuruballit had to take refuge on the western bank of the Euphrates, apparently in the region of Carchemish.

In 609, as we are further informed by the chronicle, a great Egyptian army came to his assistance, but that did not prevent his attempt to recapture Harran from being a failure.

It is extremely probable that it was at the beginning of this campaign of 609, on his way to the Euphrates, that the Pharaoh Necho II, son of Psammetichus I (610–594), slew Josiah at Megiddo and subjected Judah to Egyptian domination.[2]

The details of this disaster have not yet been fully explained. Welch has recently made the suggestion that Necho, as he passed through Palestine, summoned Josiah to appear before him at Megiddo, and that, finding his loyalty open to suspicion, he had him executed.[3] The words of the story as it appears in the book of Kings are certainly capable of this interpretation :

[1] The term, which perhaps signifies nomads in general (ed. Dhorme, **SY**, xiii (1932), p. 34), here means, according to some critics, the Medes (Schnabel, **ZA**, N.F., xxxvi (1924–5), 316–18, *cf*. **CXLIV**, 3 ; **LXVIII**, ii, 8), according to others a Scythian people. A letter from Nebuchadnezzar mentioning the Medes as allies of his father in his campaign against Harran (Thureau Dangin, **RA**, xxi, 198 ; xxii, 27 *ff*. ; *cf*. Dhorme, **RB**, 1927, p. 152 ; **SY**, 1932, pp. 30, 33, 34) would seem to favour the first hypothesis. However that may be, the fact and the date are also attested by an inscription by Nabonidus, who attributes to the destruction of the great temple at Harran by the Umman Manda a date fifty-four years earlier than the rebuilding of the temple by this prince at the beginning of his reign (555) : V. Scheil, **RTEA**, xviii (1896), 15–29, 77–8, 217 ; **CXV**, 22.

[2] The book of Kings states (2 Kings xxiii, 29), it is true, that Necho was then setting out "against the King of Asshur". But these words, lacking in the Syriac version and also in the parallel passage in Chronicles (2 Chron. xxxv, 20), might perhaps be a gloss (**RHP**, iv (1924), 382–3 ; **CIX**, 117). In any case, Josephus also says that the King of Egypt was marching " To wage war on the Medes and the Babylonians who were destroying the power of the Assyrians " (A.J., x, 5, i, § 74).

[3] **ET**, Jan., 1924, 171 ; **ZATW**, xliii (N.F. ii), 1925, pp. 225–260 ; **LXVIII**, 424. On this question see Condamin, **RSR**, xiv (1924), 67–8 ; W. W. Cannon, **ZATW**, xliv (1926), 63–4 ; Ad. Lods, **RHP**, iv (1924), 383.

" And King Josiah went against him ; and he slew him at Megiddo when he had seen him." [1]

It is, however, more probable that, as the author of the book of Chronicles expressly states,[2] no doubt basing his assertion on tradition,[3] Josiah fell in battle at Megiddo.[4] It is very natural that the King of Judah should have tried to defend the independence which was his in all but name, and should have opposed by force the passage of the Egyptians through the territory of the former kingdom of Israel which he had annexed. No doubt he relied on the power of Jahweh, whose worship he had restored, free of all impurities. Herodotus also reports that Necho, in this campaign, had to engage in battle with the " Syrians " [5] : his only mistake is as to the scene of the encounter, for instead of Megiddo, a name which perhaps he did not know, he writes " Migdol in Egypt ", meaning a frontier city near Pelusium.[6] He also tells us that others besides Josiah attempted open resistance. And in fact Necho had to conquer " Kadytis, a great town in Syria ", by which most certainly Qadesh on the Orontes is meant.[7] The reason why, as far as we know, the Egyptian troops did not come to blows with the army of Judah in 616, when the Pharaoh had previously intervened in Mesopotamian affairs, may have been that they had been transported by sea to northern Phenicia, or else that Josiah had not yet annexed the plain of Jezreel.

When the news of the death of the king who had initiated so many reforms reached Jerusalem, the " people of the land " elected as his successor his second son Jehoahaz, doubtless because he shared the political ideas of his father. But he was summoned to Riblah to the Pharaoh, who deposed him after he had reigned scarcely three months, and sent him to end his

[1] 2 Kings xxiii, 29.   [2] 2 Chron. xxxv, 20–25.
[3] See the mention of Carchemish (v. 20), that of the second chariot (v. 24), and of the lamentations (v. 25).
[4] " As soon as he saw him " may mean " at the beginning of the battle ". The expression " let us look one another in the face " meant " let us measure each other's strength " (2 Kings xiv, 8, 11).
[5] II, 159.
[6] According to Winckler, the reference is to Migdal-Ashtoreth, the old name of Cæsarea (Strato's tower), XCV, 98, 105 ; according to W. W. Cannon (ZATW, 1926, p. 64) Migdal-El (Magdala), near Tiberias, may be meant (Jos. xix, 38).
[7] And not Gaza (Hitzig, Stark) ; cf. CAH, iii, 297 ; Cannon, loc. cit. ; XLIX, ii⁶, 417.

days in Egypt. In his stead Necho set on the throne the elder
son of Josiah, Eliakim, henceforth called Jehoiakim, a new
name given him by the Pharaoh to impress upon him the fact
that he owed his position to him and must behave with due
humility. Jehoiakim had to pay an indemnity of 100 talents
of silver and one talent of gold (about 11,000 pounds sterling);
he obtained them by levying taxes on his subjects. He
nevertheless began a series of building operations whose
costliness disgusted the unfortunate Judæans, who were
obliged to find the money.[1]

All this time, the struggle on the banks of the Euphrates
was going on between the Assyrians and Egyptians on the
one hand, and the Babylonians and Medes on the other, a
struggle in which the Babylonians took a particularly active
part, for they hoped that when the moribund Assyrian empire
should be parcelled out, they would obtain the southern and
western districts, while the Medes made sure of the eastern
and northern provinces.

We do not know the exact date at which the last vestiges
of the might of Asshur disappeared, but by 605 it was at an
end. For in that year the Egyptians were completely routed,
probably at Carchemish (the modern Djerabis), on the west
bank of the Euphrates, by the son of Nabopolassar, the
crown prince Nabu-kudur-usur, who was called in Hebrew
Nebuchadrezzar or Nebuchadnezzar, and whose name was
transcribed by the Greeks in the much more exact form
Nabuchodonosor.

Thus was founded the neo-Babylonian or Chaldean
empire.

Nebuchadnezzar was hindered from reaping immediately
the full harvest of his victories by the news that his father
had died, which necessitated his return to Babylon to assume
the reins of government.[2]

Convinced of the inviolability of the Temple, the people
of Judah flattered themselves that Jerusalem would elude
the clutches of the new conqueror, as it had eluded Sennacherib. Jeremiah's protest against this illusion almost
cost him his life.[3] Nebuchadnezzar in fact entered the

---

[1] Jer. xxii, 13, 14.
[2] Berossus in *Josephus, C. Ap.* i, 19.
[3] Jer. vii, 1–15; xxvi.

country some time between 604 and 600, perhaps in 602, if it is to his reign that an inscription belongs, which tells of a revolt in Syria put down by an unnamed king in the third year of his rule.[1] After three years, Jehoiakim refused tribute. The King of Babylon first launched against him the standing army of Chaldean troops, then those of the neighbouring loyal states, Aramæans, Moabites, Ammonites. Jehoiakim perished, it would seem, in one of these encounters, his body being denied the rights of sepulture. " He shall be buried with the burial of an ass," Jeremiah had prophesied, and his prophecy, not having been recorded until a later date, had probably been realized.[2] Be that as it may, when Nebuchadnezzar arrived in person before Jerusalem, he no longer found Jehoiakim on the throne, but his young son Jehoiakin or Jeconiah (597), who surrendered at once, having reigned scarcely three months. He was exiled into Babylonia with his mother, his court, the chief men of the government and the army and the craftsmen—the pick of the nation. This was the first deportation from Judah, and was shared by the prophet-priest Ezekiel. A curious estimate gives the strength of this first convoy as only 3,023 men.[3] Another document mentions the figure 10,000.[4]

Thinking that this lesson was a sufficient warning, the King of Babylon allowed the country its autonomy under a prince of the house of David, Mattaniah, a third son of Josiah,[5] whose name he changed to Zedekiah and from whom he contented himself with exacting the oath of fidelity.

But at the news of a revolt of Elam against Babylon, the

---

[1] Cf. **XCV**, 108-9 ; **XLIX**, ii [6], 421.

[2] Jer. xxii, 19 ; cf. xxxvi, 30. The evidence of the Greek translator of Chronicles (2 Chron. xxxvi, 8) is less certain : he may have thought that the parallel passage in Kings (" he slept with his fathers ", 2 Kings xxiv, 6) referred to the king's burial, whereas it only meant that he was dead.

[3] Jer. lii, 28.   [4] 2 Kings xxiv, 14.

[5] Julius Lewy, giving preference to the Hebrew text of 2 Chron. xxxvi, 10, and 1 Chron. iii, 16, over 2 Kings xxiii, 31 ; xxiv, 18, and the Greek text of 2 Chron. xxxvi, 10, is of the opinion that Zedekiah was the elder brother, not the uncle, of Jeconiah (**CXLV**, 42-6). But the evidence of the compiler of the book of Kings cannot be lightly disregarded, and he, naming as he always does with the kings of Judah, the king's mother, says that Hamutal, mother of Zedekiah, had also given birth to Jehoahaz, son of Josiah and his successor (2 Kings xxiii, 31 ; xxiv, 18).

country once more began to seethe with patriotic fervour, possibly at the very beginning of the reign of Zedekiah.[1] Far from being cast down by the recent deportation, most of the population of Jerusalem saw in it a proof that Jahweh would one day restore to those who had remained in the Holy Land the possession of their country, while chastising those who had been exiled. A number of prophets, both in Palestine and among the exiles, foretold that the yoke of Babylon would be broken. As early as 594, negotiations were being made in Jerusalem with Edom, Moab, Ammon, Tyre, and Sidon, with a view to a general revolt.[2]

The insurrection did not break out, however, perhaps because it was impossible to persuade Necho II, who had been defeated at Carchemish, to leave Egypt again in support of the coalition.[3] The Chaldean police, moreover, were energetic in quelling discontent, at least among those who had been deported.[4] Zedekiah sent a special mission to Babylon to assure Nebuchadnezzar of his fidelity.[5]

Under Necho's successor, Psammetichus II (594–588), the attitude of the Egyptian court changed, and this prince undertook a campaign in Palestine in 590.[6] His son Hophra (the Apries of the Greeks) stimulated to still greater activity the struggle against Babylon. Herodotus tells us that he made war on the Sidonians, and fought a naval battle against the Tyrians,[7] doubtless with the intention of forcing them to join the coalition. Tyre probably did join it, and also Ammon.[8]

---

[1] Jer. xlix, 34–8. *Cf.* **LXVIII**, ii, 31.

[2] Jer. xxvii–xxix   [3] 2 Kings xxiv, 7.

[4] Jer. xxix, 21–3. According to Erich Klamroth (*Die wirtschaftliche Lage und das geistliche Leben der jüdischen Exulanten in Babylon*, Inaug. Diss ; Koenigsberg, Kümmel, 1912, pp. 22–9) the Babylonians also used severe measures in Palestine ; in 595–594 a second deportation is supposed to have taken place which included prophets and priests ; Ezekiel is said to have been one of them. Jer. xxix, 1–2, certainly seems to place a deportation of this kind " after " that of Jeconiah —but at a date not determined. But it is generally recognized that v. 2 is an unintelligent gloss taken from 2 Kings xxiv, 15–16. The new chronology proposed by Klamroth for the prophecies of Ezekiel would offer certain advantages but would also be open to many objections.

[5] Jer. xxix, 3, and li, 59 (Septuagint version). According to the Massoretic text of the latter passage, he even went there in person.

[6] Papyrus found at Hibeh, published by F. L. Griffith, **CXX**; *cf.* **CXVIII** ; Alt, **ZATW**, 1910, pp. 288 *ff.*

[7] ii, 161 ; *cf.* Diod., i, 69.   [8] Ez. xxi, 23–37.

Fortified by their support, and in spite of the abstention of the Edomites and the Philistines, who allied themselves with the Babylonians,[1] the militarists, who had the upper hand in Judah, overruled the objections of Zedekiah, who weakly gave way, and revolt was openly declared.

On the tenth day of the tenth month of the tenth year of this prince's reign (January, 587), the Chaldeans began to besiege Jerusalem, which soon was suffering the ravages of a terrible famine. For a brief moment, the besieged thought that they were saved, for the Babylonian troops had to withdraw in order to cope with an army which the Pharaoh sent to the assistance of the town. But whether as a result of defeat[2] or of bribery, the Egyptians fell back, and the Chaldeans resumed the siege. On the ninth day of the fourth month of the eleventh year (July, 586), a breach was made in the north wall of the town. During the night, Zedekiah and the garrison fled in the opposite direction, through the " gate between the two walls ", and went towards the Dead Sea, hoping perhaps to reach the land of Ammon in Transjordan. But they were overtaken near Jericho. Zedekiah was taken to Riblah, where he was tried for perjury. His sons were killed before his eyes ; then his eyes were put out[3] and he was taken to Babylon laden with fetters.

In the month of August of the same year, Nebuzaradan, chief of the guards of the King of Babylon, set fire to the Temple, the palace, and all the houses of importance in Jerusalem, having first pillaged any valuables they might contain. The walls were levelled to the ground. Eighty of the principal men, among them the chief priests, were executed. The rest of the inhabitants, found either in the ruins of the town or in the Chaldean camp where many had taken refuge during the siege, were sent to Babylonia, to join those who had been deported in 597. One estimate, surprisingly low, gives the strength of this convoy as only 832.[4]

The country dwellers and the poor were left in the land under a Jewish governor Gedaliah, who took up his residence at Mizpah. But this brave and intelligent man was assassinated in October of the same year, by one Ishmael, a

[1] Ez. xxv, 12–14, 15–17.
[2] Ez. xxx, 20–26.
[3] Cf. Pl. iii, 2.
[4] Jer. lii, 29.

E

fanatically patriotic member of the royal family, urged on by Baalis, King of the Ammonites, who with Tyre was still able to hold out against Nebuchadnezzar. The little group of Jews which had begun to gather round Gedaliah dispersed. Many took refuge in Egypt, where they swelled the ranks of the Judæan settlers already established in the Delta, even going as far as Pathros, that is to say to Upper Egypt, the " land of the south " (*pa-tu-risi*).[1]

There were doubtless fresh disturbances in Palestine five years later (581), for Nebuzaradan, at that date, again deported 745 Jews.[2] They were, however, only the despairing efforts of the last Israelite monarchy before its final extinction.

[1] *Cf*. Adolf Erman, **ZATW**, x (1890), pp. 118–19.
[2] Jer. lii, 30. Erich Klamroth (*op. cit.*, p. 34) and Theodore H. Robinson (**LXVIII**, i, 442–3) consider that this measure was intended as revenge for the murder of Gedaliah, which in that case would have taken place only three or four years after the destruction of Jerusalem. But the obvious meaning of the text would rather seem to be that Ishmael's plot was carried out a short time after the grape-harvest of the year 586.

BOOK II

THE RELIGIOUS CONFLICT. THE PROPHETS IN CONFLICT WITH THE NATIONAL RELIGION

CHAPTER I

GENERAL CHARACTERISTICS OF THE PROPHETIC MOVEMENT

DURING the dramatic changes which marked the political life of Judah and Israel from the middle of the eighth century until the fall of Jerusalem, a religious movement, periodic in its intensity, stirred the minds of men in both kingdoms. It was kept alive mainly by the burning words of a group of prophets who interpreted events in a sense diametrically opposed to that of the other prophets— the spokesmen of the traditional national religion.

These new prophets are called, for lack of a better name, the great prophets, or the writing prophets, because certain writings, directly or indirectly coming from them have been preserved for us in the Old Testament.

I

THE PHENOMENA OF INSPIRATION AMONG THE GREAT PROPHETS

One day when Amos, the earliest of the new prophets known to us, had been called a " seer ", and had been requested to go elsewhere to earn his bread and prophesy, he replied, " I am no prophet (*nâbî'*), neither am I a prophet's son " (vii, 14).

There can be little doubt that by these words he meant to declare that he was not one of those professional ecstatics, of whom there were plenty at the time, who made a living by

prophecy,[1] but that he was a layman, who had been torn
from his daily work by the irresistible command of his God
—which indeed was true, at least in theory, of all the genuine
ecstatics, of Moses and Samuel as well as of Amos. Nevertheless, the brief statement of the shepherd of Tekoah has
a distinctive note.[2]

He felt that he was the mouthpiece of a new power, essentially different from that which had been hitherto represented
and which was still being represented by the prophets and
seers and " sons of prophets ", as the members of bands of
ecstatics who gathered round Elisha in the preceding century
were called.

But it is important to realize that this difference, fundamental as it was, concerned the matter much more than the
manner of the message which Amos and his successors felt
called upon to deliver. An attempt has often been made
to modernize the great prophets, and to relegate to the background the elements common to them, and to the vision-
aries of Saul's day, the " sons of the prophets " of the period
of Elisha, and, through them, to the soothsayers, the ecstatics
of every kind, even to the necromancers and magicians of
primitive Semitism.[3] This is a mistake. The form—and
the term includes not only the outward manifestations of
prophecy, but also the psychic phenomena which characterized
it—remained essentially the same for the new prophets as
for their predecessors ; it was the spiritual content of the
ancient form that was the new thing.

By the names they give themselves, by the functions
they assume, by their conception of the origin of their revelations, by the psychological processes traceable in the method
of these revelations and in their manner of communicating
them, they belong to the category of the ecstatics of an
older day.

Amos himself, although he declared that he was neither
a " prophet " nor " a prophet's son ", cannot define his
activity otherwise than by saying he " prophesies " (iii, 8).
Isaiah calls his wife " the prophetess " (viii, 3), and the term
nâbî was commonly applied to Hosea and Jeremiah by their
contemporaries.

---

[1] *Cf.* **LVII**, p. 518.   [2] *Cf.* Micah iii, 5–8.
[3] *Cf.* **LVII**, 345–351, 513–520.

The utterances of the great prophets, like those of other inspired men of ancient times—whether among the Hebrews, the pagan Arabs,[1] the Greeks or the Romans—were couched in the rhythmic form of poetry. Hence they always strike the note of intensity, abruptness, and violence, characteristic of the tranced ecstatic. When describing the future, the prophets preferred to veil it in that half-light favoured by the older oracles. Amos does not name the Assyrians, although he indicates them transparently enough as the future instruments of divine wrath (vi, 14).

The great prophets do not depart from the conception of inspiration common to the whole of Semitic antiquity : for them it is the invasion of a human personality by a power foreign to it, which they usually call the spirit or the word of Jahweh.

They think of themselves as grasped by the hand of Jahweh (Is. viii, 11), on terms of the closest intimacy with him (Amos iii, 7, 8 ; Jer. xxiii, 18, 22), filled with his spirit (Is. xxxvii, 1 ; xlii, 1, etc.). " Thou hast deceived me," says Jeremiah to his God ; " thou art stronger than I and hast prevailed " (xx, 7).

The words which they speak are not their own : they accompany them with the formula " Thus saith Jahweh " or " the word of Jahweh ". When they speak in the first person, it is a matter of indifference to them whether they use their own name or that of Jahweh. In reporting a conversation between the prophet Isaiah and King Ahaz, the narrator says :—

" And the Lord spake again unto Ahaz, saying : Ask thee a sign of the Lord thy God," etc. (Is. vii, 10–11).

Among the new prophets, as among their predecessors, this divine presence manifests itself not only in words but also in deeds, sometimes very strange deeds, which they feel constrained to perform. These have been, and still frequently are, interpreted as " symbolic " gestures, as a kind of parable in action, invented and mimed by the prophets in order to heighten the impression they desired to make upon their audiences.[2] But this explanation fits only

[1] **XXXVI,** 87–8, 93–100, 121.
[2] **LXXI,** ii, 485 ; **VII** ; A. Causse, **RHP,** 1922, 354 ; **CIX,** xv, 126, 145.

a few of these scenes (e.g. Jer. xxxv) ; it could not apply to those
which were not witnessed by any audience, and does not
account for the considerable importance attached to these
gestures by prophets and spectators alike. In certain cases
it is clear that they were thought to have a definite influence
on the future. This was already the case as far as the *words*
of the prophet were concerned : Jeremiah destroys or builds,
uproots or plants kingdoms by merely foretelling their
destruction or their restoration (i, 10). All the more surely
do the *actions* of the man of God give glimpses of the reality
of the future events which they symbolize. Jeremiah commands a prophecy to be read at Babylon—apparently with
no one to hear it—condemning that city, which prophecy
is then to be tied to a stone and thrown into the Euphrates,
in order to ensure that his curse shall penetrate literally
and materially into the heart of the country and cause the
destruction of the city.[1] The pitcher broken by the same
prophet at the gate of Jerusalem was doubtless in the same
way intended to bring about, and not only to foretell, the
overthrow of the town [2] ; it is for this reason that Pashhur,
the priest, has Jeremiah arrested after this scene and put
in the stocks.[3] It was thought then that the prophet could
influence events by word and by action, as did the ecstatics
of a bygone age,[4] and as the " men of God " did before them,
using the same methods of imitative magic,[5] but with this
difference that the prophet exercised his formidable powers
only by God's command and according to his will.

In other cases one wonders whether the prophet's act
was supposed to influence the future or whether the future was
reflected in the action of " the man of the spirit ". Doubtless
a clear line of distinction was not always drawn between the
action and reaction of visible upon invisible, and *vice versa*,
but the fact remains that the act accompanying the
prophecy was a part, and a part which had already " come
true ", of the event foretold, and therefore a guarantee
that the whole would shortly be accomplished. This was
the case when Hosea and Isaiah gave their children names
predicting in so many words the fate of Israel or of some other

---

[1] Jer. li, 59–64a.   [2] Jer. xix.
[3] Jer. xx.   [4] *Cf.* **LVII**, 242–4.
[5] See below, pp. 163–4.

nation,[1] when Isaiah, by walking in the streets naked and barefoot, prefigured the captivity of the Egyptians and the Ethiopians,[2] or when Jeremiah by going about with a yoke upon his neck foretold that the Chaldeans would lord it over all the nations of Western Asia,[3] or again when the same prophet, in front of the palace of the Pharaoh at Taḥpanḥés in Egypt, secretly laid the foundations of the throne which Nebuchadnezzar after his victory was soon to set up there.[4]

The acts most commonly reputed to exercise an influence on the future, or a bearing on the prophecy, were probably those done by the prophet when in trance, because of the tendency to transform symbolism into action,[5] for example when Ezekiel claps his hands, utters inarticulate cries, shakes a sword to and fro.[6] But the actions supposed to be prophetic were not all of this ecstatic nature.

The prophet was thought to be in such constant touch with the unseen that the future was reflected, often without his knowledge, in the everyday events of his life and of those of his family, as for instance the unhappy marriage of Hosea or the celibacy of Jeremiah. " Behold," says Isaiah, " I and the children whom the Lord hath given me are for signs and for wonders in Israel from the Lord of hosts." [7]

This illustration shows how much the rôle of *nâbî*, as understood by the great prophets and their contemporaries, resembled that of the primitive possessor of potent *mana* whose slightest action might shake heaven and earth.

Many modern historians of the religion of Israel, without denying the facts we have just noted, but deeming them at too great odds with the vigour and the loftiness of thought found elsewhere in the preaching of the great prophets, hold that the excited, ecstatic tone of their discourse, their strange acts, the supernatural powers they claim for themselves, are nothing but survivals from a past already obsolete ; the prophets seem to them to be profound thinkers systematically teaching coherent and connected doctrines ; ecstatic frenzy, a sign of psychological disintegration, can

---

[1] Hos. i, 4, 6, 9 ; Is. vii, 3 ; viii, 3.
[2] Is. xx, 2 ; see above, p. 30.
[3] Jer. xxvii–xxviii.　　　　[4] Jer. xliii, 8–13.
[5] **XXXVI**, 304.　　　　[6] Ez. xxi, 17, 19, 21–2.
[7] Is. viii, 18 ; *cf.* Hos. i–iii ; Jer. xvi, 2.

in their opinion have been nothing more than an accidental phenomenon.[1] Abraham Kuenen considered that many of the descriptions of visions to be met with in the prophetic books, particularly in Ezekiel, were merely literary forms necessitated by tradition.[2] So did Eduard Reuss. Bernhard Duhm held that most of the prophetic acts described in the book of Jeremiah had never been carried out. Renan believed in the reality of these little " symbolic dramas ", but classed them among the " poses ", the " manœuvres ", the " tricks ", which the manner of life of the prophets entailed[3]; he imagined Isaiah as a kind of " Carrel or Girardin, with a good topical knowledge of events and the ability to clothe his ideas in lively and spirited language ".[4] Hugo Winckler went so far as to look upon the prophets as political agitators, as secret agents carrying out in Palestine schemes dictated by the court at Nineveh or Babylon.

Important works dealing with the psychology of the great prophets have lately been published.[5] These would seem to have established the fact that ecstatic phenomena occupied a much more important place among them than critics had seen fit to admit. Thanks to these researches the various mental states which modern psychiatrists distinguish among the individuals whom they analyse can be clearly distinguished : active and passive trance, insensibility to pain, glossolaly, hallucinations of sight, hearing, taste and touch, sense illusions, sometimes even hypnosis and auto-suggestion. The body of evidence is too extensive to allow of the explanation that these were mere literary fictions : the prophets did in fact go through the psychological experiences which they said they had gone through. This must be our starting-point if we wish to understand either themselves or the writings which bear their names. These books are not

---

[1] Ant. Causse, **RHP**, ii, 354.   [2] **CXLIII.**
[3] **LXXI**, ii, 485.   [4] *Op. cit.*, p. 483.
[5] The ecstatic nature of their mentality has been emphasized by Hoelscher (**XXXVI**), Gunkel (**XXVIII**, ii, 2², pp. xviii–xxvi), Jacobi (**CXXXVI**), Lindblom (**CXLVI ; CXLVII ; CXLVIII**), Herzberg (**CXXII ;** L. P. Horst (**RHP**, 1922, 337-048), Theodore H. Robinson (**CLXVII**), **CLXVIII ; CLXIX ; TR**, N.F. iii (1931), 75–103), Ad. Lods (**RHP**, ix (1929), 170–5 ; **RHR**, civ (1931), 279–297). These views have been disputed by, among others, Aalders (**XCVI**) and Junker (**CXXXVIII**) ; and to some extent accepted by Skinner (**CLXXVII**), Wheeler Robinson (**CLXX ; ZATW**, 41, pp. 1 *ff.*), A. Causse (**RHP**, 1922, pp. 349–356).

essentially collections of discourses addressed *by the prophet to the people*, but primarily and principally they are collections of words addressed *by Jahweh to the prophet*, that is to say, like similar collections of the utterances of the Montanist prophets, or of the medieval mystics, or of the ecstatics of the Cevennes,—they are the records made by the inspired man himself or by a third party, of the divine words heard by him when in trance [1] ; this explains why the book of Jeremiah contains revelations which have nothing to do with his people, but concern himself or his friends, and also why, when the revelation is to be made public, the account of the execution of the order is so often omitted.[2]

It would be necessary to disregard the evidence of history, and to forget the instances of Paul, Mahommed, Luther, Pascal in order to maintain that a tendency to ecstasy is incompatible with a sane and vigorous mind. According to modern psychology, hallucination is nothing but the awakening of a *memory* with particular intensity : what the ecstatic sees and hears in trance is the expression of his personality : it is the fruit, perhaps ripened in unconsciousness, of his reflections, of his previous religious experiences, of the deep tendencies of his whole being, rising to the threshold of consciousness like something which appears to him to come from outside himself.

Let us add that pneumatic phenomena are found to have spread almost like an epidemic at certain periods, when these phenomena were appreciated, and consequently desired, by all, as the supreme manifestation of religious life ; the great prophets lived at one of these periods of ardent belief in the spirit ; they could hardly have escaped their share in the aspirations of their time.

And in fact, while, in Samuel's day, we are told that " there was no open vision " [3] and that in the Jewish period the few seers who arose were looked upon with suspicion,[4] in the second half of the eighth century,[5] and at the beginning of the sixth,[6] the two periods when most of the major

---

[1] *Cf.* Lindblom, *op. cit.*, and **RHR,** civ (1931), pp. 295–7.
[2] *Cf.* **CI,** 148.　　　　　　　　[3] 1 Sam. iii, 1.
[4] Zech. xiii, 3, 6 ; *cf.* Ps. lxxiv, 9 ; 1 Macc. iv, 46.
[5] Micah iii, 5–8, 11.
[6] Jer. xxvi, 7–8, 11, 16, 20–3 ; xxviii ; xxix, 24–7 ; *cf.* xx, 1–6 ; Ez. xiii.

prophets were living, there was an abundance of prophets in general, as there had been in Saul's day—the eleventh century,[1] or in the time of Ahab or Elisha—the ninth century [2] ; there can be no doubt that these were the periods when the ecstatic fever in Israel reached its highest point.[3]

The ecstatic fervour of the prophets of the eighth and sixth centuries is doubtless no longer exactly what it was in ancient Israel. The loftiness of the moral and spiritual ideal animating those who came later, led them to avoid or to reprove certain practices and even certain manifestations of the spirit which had previously been considered legitimate. They condemned those of their kind who accepted payment for their prophecies [4] ; dreams are discredited [5] ; the great prophets will no longer provoke inspiration by physical means,[6] such as collective excitement, music, dances, a night spent in a temple, the use of intoxicating drinks ; they expressly condemn those of the *nebî'îm* of their day who still have recourse to the last-named means.[7] Those who come to a prophet to ask for divine counsel, must wait for him to receive Jahweh's answer, with no means of solicitation except prayer ; on an occasion of this sort Jeremiah was unable for ten days to give the desired message.[8] It is also quite likely that the great prophets thought they heard within themselves the " word of Jahweh ", not only when they were really in ecstatic trance, but also when they were in a state of excitement analogous to what we call poetic or artistic inspiration, when words and images seem to crowd of their own accord into the mind and are apparently dictated to it : this was the case with the medieval mystics [9] ; it must have been the same with the Hebrews, who explained the most diverse psychic phenomena, if only they were sufficiently

[1] 1 Sam. x, 5–6, 10–13 ; xix, 18–24.

[2] 1 Kings xviii, 4, 19–40 ; xix, 1, 10, 14 ; xxii, 6 ; 2 Kings ii, 3, 5, 7, 15–18 ; iv, 38–44 ; vi, 1–7 ; ix, 1–12.

[3] *Cf.* Ad. Lods, **RHR**, civ (1931), 290–3.

[4] Micah iii, 5, 11 ; Ez. xiii, 19 ; *cf.* Am. vii, 12 ; 2 Kings v. See, on the other hand, 1 Sam. ix, 7–10 ; 1 Kings xiv, 1–3 ; etc. *Cf.* **LVII**, 518, n. 4.

[5] Jer. xxiii, 25 ; *cf.* Deut. xiii, 2, 4, 6. See, on the other hand, Gen. xxxvii, 19 ; 1 Sam. xxviii, 6 ; etc.

[6] **LVII**, 343–4, 347.

[7] Micah ii, 11 ; Is. xxviii, 7, 8 ; xxix, 9 (?) ; *cf.* 4 Esdras. xiv, 40.

[8] xlii, 7 ; *cf.* xxviii, 12–16.   [9] *Cf.* **CXLVII**, 27–9.

violent and seemed abnormal, by attributing them to possession by a spirit.

But the new prophets, if they noticed any differences at
all between themselves and their predecessors or contemporaries, looked upon them as very slight. The great prophets
*knew of no exterior sign by which the genuinely inspired of
Jahweh could be distinguished* : he was recognized only by
the fulfilment of his predictions [1] or by the moral content of
his message.[2] Jeremiah, meeting one day another prophet,
Hananiah, who, on behalf of Jahweh foretold immediate
deliverance and broke the yoke which Jeremiah wore about
his neck, exclaimed : " Amen : the Lord perform thy words
which thou hast prophesied." It was only later, as the result
of a special revelation, that he realized him to be a false
prophet.[3] Sometimes the great prophets even admit that their
opponents are genuinely inspired by Jahweh, but infer that
he has intentionally misled them,[4] or that they themselves
from interested motives altered the revelations they received.[5]
The behaviour and appearance of an Isaiah and a Jeremiah
were apparently not enough to mark them out from the
multitudes of those victims of the divine afflatus who thronged
the Temple courtyard, and whose supervision was the social
care of a particular priest [6] : Hosea and Jeremiah were called
madmen,[7] as had been the " sons of the prophets " in the
time of Elisha.[8]

II

THE SPIRITUAL CONTENT OF THE MESSAGE OF THE GREAT
PROPHETS

Though the form in which the message of the great
prophets was conveyed to them, and the way in which they
handed it on, were more or less those which the people had
long been accustomed to expect from its seers, the message

[1] Jer. xxviii, 9 ; Deut. xviii, 21–2.
[2] Micah iii, 8 ; *cf.* Deut. xiii, 2–6.
[3] Jer. xxviii, 6, 12–16.
[4] Ez. xiv, 9 ; *cf.* Jer. xx, 7 ; 1 Kings xxii, 20–3.
[5] Micah iii, 5–7.   [6] Jer. xx, 1–3 ; xxix, 24–9.
[7] Hos. ix, 7 ; Jer. xxix, 26.   [8] 2 Kings ix, 11.

of the new envoys of Jahweh was radically different, as far as its contents were concerned, from all that had hitherto been transmitted.

We will confine ourselves here to indicating two particularly striking points of contrast.

At the time when the first of the new prophets arose, the Assyrian menace was becoming more definite. His successors were to witness the life and death struggle of the two kingdoms of Israel, first with the redoubtable armies of Asshur, then with Babylon. Now the great prophets foretold that both Israel and Judah would be overthrown by the invaders, that the nation would perish, and that by the will of God. It is hard for us to realize to-day that such a declaration must have been not only repellent to the patriotic feeling of their hearers, but an offence to their faith, and intolerable to their reason : if a national God can destroy his own nation, what will become of the honour of his name, which is closely bound up with the greatness of his people ? One might as well say that he desires his own humiliation, his absolute discrediting.

This declaration that the God of Israel would himself destroy Israel entailed a complete reversal of the idea of Jahweh which had hitherto been held, it seriously implied that Jahweh was something different from and infinitely more than the particular God of a peculiar people, a conception implicit no doubt in the old traditions of the compact made in the time of Moses, but until then a dead letter ; the new prophets hail him as the supreme ruler of humanity and the universe, the judge of all nations. Some of them even proclaim him at times—intuitively, be it said, rather than doctrinally—as the only God of the whole universe, asserting that his worship must and shall one day become the worship of all the nations of the earth. Monotheism, universalism, the idea of Israel's mission to humanity will not be preached or clearly defined until the last of the great prophets arises, the second Isaiah,[1] but the ideas themselves, shattering the narrow moulds of the national religion which up till then had been the whole of Jahwism, are already outlined in the preaching of Amos.[2]

The second distinctive feature of the message of the new

[1] xlv, 22, 23 ; li, 5 ; xlii, 4, etc.   [2] i–ii ; ix, 7.

prophets is the unexampled severity and, more important
still, the lofty morality and spirituality, hitherto unknown,
of the judgment passed by them on the social, political,
and religious condition of their people, a judgment which
in their eyes is sufficient justification for the sentence of
death which they pronounce against Israel. In bygone
centuries the prophets of Jahweh had sometimes censured
a particular crime of a particular king, or had blamed some
defect in the people's worship or in one individual, or had
called to account the religious infidelities of a dynasty. But
in the eyes of the new prophets, the life of the nation is rotten
at the core.

> " Can the Ethiopian change his skin ? " says Jeremiah,[1] " or
> the leopard his spots ? Then may ye also do good, that are
> accustomed to do evil."

If the nation is to be saved, the very orientation of national
life must be changed. Each of the great prophets, in his own
highly individual way, has a sharply defined view of the
nation's shortcomings. Amos and Micah find fault chiefly
with social sins, Hosea with lack of love, Isaiah with pride,
Jeremiah with stubbornness. But their censure has this
in common : it sets a higher value than had been set by any
other people in antiquity on morality and inward piety.
A century before Confucius and Buddha, two centuries before
Æschylus, and much more categorically than any of these
religious thinkers and reformers, they declare that God
demands purity of life rather than burnt-offerings. Jahweh
hates sacrifices, despises feast-days and psalm-singing when
justice and love are lacking.[2] He demands nothing of man
but that he shall do justly, and love mercy, and walk humbly
with his God.[3] Some of the prophets declare that outward
forms of worship are useless and even reprehensible.[4]

When reviewing the different representatives of the
prophetic movement, we shall have occasion to observe the
variety of ways in which these fundamental ideas and
tendencies occurred to them, the diversity of conclusions they
drew from them, each according to his temperament or the
circumstances of the time, and the extent to which they

[1] xiii, 23.
[2] Amos v, 21–5 ; Hos. vi, 6 ; Is. i, 10–17.
[3] Micah vi, 8.
[4] Amos iv, 4 ; v, 25.

enriched every aspect of religious thought : the idea of God, of morality, of worship, and of the relations of the individual to society.

From now it may be taken for granted that the great prophets were responsible for a new conception of religion, and that, although like most reformers they claimed merely to restore the past, they demanded nothing less than the radical transformation of Jahwism.

III

ORIGIN OF THE VARIOUS ELEMENTS OF THE PROPHETIC MESSAGE

There is one question which a historian cannot avoid. How, by what psychological process, under what influences, whether Israelite or foreign, did these men come by the convictions which inspired them ?

1. *Certainty of the Imminent Downfall of the Nation.*— It is evident that the tragic political circumstances in which their people were placed, menaced as they were by the advance of the Assyrians, then of the Babylonians, were largely responsible for their positive belief that Israel's doom was imminent. The question then arises, and it is one which has been much disputed—did the prophets see in the Mesopotamian menace the *fulfilment* of the sentence *previously* pronounced by them against their people in the name of their moral and religious ideals, or did they find them guilty because they knew they were condemned to death ? Foreseeing, whether by some mysterious presentiment, or merely because they had formed a saner estimate of the irresistible power of Asshur and Babylon, the annihilation of their little country, they might have argued thus : Israel is about to perish, there-fore Israel has committed unforgivable crimes. A process of reasoning quite in keeping with " primitive mentality ", which regards every victim of misfortune as the object of the animosity of invisible powers : it is this principle which prompts the non-civilized to throw a shipwrecked man back into the sea, to abandon one who is ill, or to rob the victims of a fire.[1]

---

[1] **LIII.**

Granted that the gravity of the punishment foreseen must have led the prophets to take a more serious view of the faults which, in their eyes, had provoked it—thus far we are in agreement with those who favour the second hypothesis— it, nevertheless, seems evident that those who were animated by a faith as invincible as that of Isaiah, would never have admitted the remotest possibility of defeat overtaking the people of Jahweh merely because the enemy had the bigger battalions. Did not Isaiah promise victory to Ahaz and Hezekiah with neither warhorses nor foreign allies provided they put their trust in God alone ? Jeremiah, moreover, persistently foretold the overthrow of Judah when the Assyrians and the Scythians had disappeared from the horizon and the Chaldean had not yet made their presence felt.

The prophets' unshakable belief that their nation was to be destroyed must then have been due chiefly to the acknow-ledgment by their conscience, so long outraged by the ingrati-tude, worldliness, and corruption of Israel, of which they had a direct personal experience, that such faults deserved the most ruthless sentence. As Loisy says [1] :—

" It seems clear that it was not their clear-sightedness " (politically) " which made pessimists of them " (in their estimate of the moral condition of their people), " but their pessimism which made them clear-sighted."

2. *The Prophets and Civilization.*—The national existence of Israel and Judah was threatened not only by the political state of Asia, but also by internal social conditions, which, becoming more and more intolerable in both kingdoms, were certainly largely responsible for the origin of the prophetic movement. When the Hebrews had settled in Palestine, the group systems, tribal, family or patriarchal, which they had brought with them from the desert, had gradually disappeared ; for a long time they had tried to retain them in their new surroundings, but in vain. Private property was substituted for the collective possession of the soil ; the solidarity of the clan, so strictly observed by nomads, had relaxed, and the spirit of fraternity which had previously obtained among them had given way to private interest ; the autonomy of the little groups (tribes or clans),

[1] **LIX**, 160.

innumerably subdivided, had been broken by the establishment of a national unity, embodied in the king ; power
gradually passed from the " elders of the people " and
became vested in the officials of the central power. Plunged
into civilized surroundings, the Israelites lost their hold on
that simplicity of life which, among nomads, results in an
almost complete equality between rich and poor ; new wants
were discovered, luxurious tastes which only fortune's
favourites could satisfy. Hence the growing cleavage of
the nation into more and more sharply defined social classes.
Hence also an ever-increasing shameless exploitation of the
poor by the rich, who were at once the judges, the " elders ",
that is to say, responsible for administration, the controllers
of commerce and the money-lenders.[1]

At least as early as the ninth century this state of affairs
had given rise to a vigorous reaction in circles particularly
attached to ancestral customs. The small collection of civil
laws preserved for us in the " Book of the Covenant " and
probably compiled at this time by the priests of some sanctuary, aims at. re-establishing the ancient fraternity by
moderating the severity of the regulations about debt.

The prophet Elijah, at about this time, defends the sacred
rights of the Israelitish family against the arbitrary power
of the king himself : he appears before Ahab and foretells
that Jahweh will slay him and all his family because he
has caused the death of humble vinedressers, Naboth and
his sons, in order to take possession of the land of their
fathers.[2]

More drastic still is the action of one Jonadab, son of
Rechab, who obliges the members of the brotherhood whom
he groups about him to live in tents, to own neither field
nor vineyard, to drink no wine, in a word to adhere rigorously,
or rather to return to, the conditions of nomad life as known
to their fathers, the only life which, according to him, can be
pleasing to the God of the desert ; in other words, he
repudiates civilization, finding it doubtless to blame for all
the evils of his day.[3]

---

[1] Cf. **LVII**, pp. 449–461 ; Antonin Causse, *La crise de la solidarité
de famille et de clan dans l'ancien Israël*, **RHP**, x (1930), 24–60.
[2] 1 Kings xxi ; 2 Kings ix, 25–6 ; *cf.* **LVII**, 490.
[3] **LVII**, 463–4.

These aspirations must have been fairly widespread, for they are reflected in several of the popular traditions collected by the Jahwist and Elohist narrators : the tale of the city and the tower of Babel condemns, as the fruit of impious pride, the civilization of the monstrous cities of Mesopotamia (Gen. ii, 1–9) ; the stories of the patriarchs give an idyllic picture of the wandering life of the fathers.

The new prophets of the eighth century are clearly related to those circles which saw their only salvation in a return to the past. From the social point of view, they, too, are reactionaries. " Ask for the old paths, (see) where is the good way and walk therein." [1] They even frequently speak as if they shared the " nomadic ideal " of a Jonadab. For Amos, for Hosea, for Jeremiah, the time of the sojourn in the desert was the ideal time, as far as the relations between Israel and Jahweh were concerned.[2] The entry into the fertile land of Canaan, with the consequent increase in wealth, was the signal for the corruption of the people.[3] To bring the nation back to himself, Jahweh will make it return to the desert—there to speak to its heart.[4] In one passage Isaiah describes the golden age of the future as a time when vines will no longer be cultivated, and the sole means of livelihood will be the breeding of cattle.[5]

Does this mean that this tendency to react against Canaanite civiliation is sufficient to explain the attitude of uncompromising disapproval adopted by the great prophets with regard to every political and social aspect of the life of their people ? Some historians of Israel incline to this point of view.[6] It seems to us that though the prophets shared to a great extent the sympathies and antipathies of Jonadab, they saw much farther than he did ; they could not overlook the superficiality and inadequacy under-lying the facile solution of a return to a nomadic existence. Hosea himself, whom Paul Humbert calls the Bedouin prophet, and who seems to him to have applied the nomadic idea with " inexorable logic ", looks upon the future sojourn in the desert as only a transitory trial.[7] God will

---

[1] Jer. vi, 16.
[2] Amos v, 25 ; Hos. ix, 10 ; x, 1 ; xi, 1 ; Jer. ii, 1–3.
[3] Hos. x, 1 ; xi, 1–2.   [4] Hos. ii, 16.   [5] Is. vii, 21–5.
[6] **CVI ; CXXXI ; CXXXII ; VIII.**   [7] iii, 3–4.

F

bring back the nation to its own land, where he will once more enrich it with the blessings of a settled civilization. Corn, wine, and oil are indeed gifts from Jahweh.[1] For Hosea, as for Jeremiah, fertile Palestine is—as no other land — the land of Jahweh.[2] For Isaiah, agriculture is a divine science, whose smallest details have been revealed by Jahweh.[3] He hopes for the reform, not the destruction, of cities like Jerusalem (i, 26). There can be no doubt that the prophets long for a return to the past ; but what they foretell is often the reinstatement of the Israelite peasant in the patriarchal existence of the time of the Judges, or even the restoration of royalty to its original purity, as in the days of David, that is to say, a time when Israel had already assimilated the urban civilization of the Canaanites.[4]

This shows that the prophets were not, on principle, disposed to look upon the adoption of any particular habitat or mode of life as a sovereign remedy. They never said, as Jonadab would doubtless have said, that the way to ensure the salvation of the nation was to pluck up the vines and give up drinking wine, to transform cornfields into pasture and destroy the towns. Jeremiah, when he meets disciples of Jonadab holds up their fidelity to their master's rule as an example, but not his rule itself.[5] To change nothing but institutions would be, as the same prophet says later, with regard to the reform of Josiah, " to sow among thorns." What is necessary is a thorough cleansing of the soil, a circumcision *of the heart* to Jahweh.[6] The new prophets demand, not merely certain social reforms, but moral reformation.

As has been well said by M. Causse,[7] they also, without knowing it, helped to bring about the final disintegration of the ancient system of tribal and family life, by combating petty domestic exclusiveness and the worship of ancestors, by condemning the use of local high-places where the unity of the family was strengthened, and by sapping the very foundations of ritual institutions, " the mystical basis of primitive society."

3. *The Prophets and the Cult.*—The attitude of hostility

---

[1] Hos. ii, 10–11.
[2] Hos. ix, 3–6 ; Jer. xii, 14.
[3] xxviii, 23–9.
[4] *Cf.* **XXXVI**, 247.
[5] Jer. xxxv.
[6] Jer. iv, 3–4.
[7] **RHP**, xii (1932), 124–133.

adopted by the prophets towards the traditional religion of their people had also had its antecedents in previous centuries. But here again, above all, it is clear that the new prophets went farther and deeper than their predecessors.

The establishment of the Israelites in the land of Baal had resulted in so extensive an influx of Canaanitish ideas and practices into their traditional cult that the religion of the newcomers may be said to have fused with that of the natives. This had sometimes threatened the very roots of Israelite faith, the principle that Jahweh is and will be the only Elohim of his people.[1]

This " Canaanization " of the religion of their fathers, gradual though the process usually was, had now and then aroused protest : the Rechabites would seem to be a case in point, equally attached as they were to both the manner of worship and the way of life of their fathers, and the Levites, trustees of the tradition of Moses, their father.[2] However that may be, certain of the prophets, Elijah, Micaiah, son of Imlah, Elisha, entered upon a life and death struggle with the dynasty of Omri, when the latter for political reasons violated the principle of monolatry by sacrificing to the Tyrian Baal in the very capital of the kingdom of Israel.[3] Several of the kings prohibited obviously Canaanitish rites, as, for instance, temple prostitution.[4] And the ritual decalogues compiled about the ninth century, while sanctioning the transformation of Jahwism into an agrarian religion, at least endeavoured to perpetuate the ancient simplicity of the nomad days by forbidding, for example, " molten gods " and condemning altars built of hewn stone or raised upon steps, in favour of those made in the Bedouin style, of rough stones or of clay.[5]

Among the great prophets we also find this watchword of rebellion against the Canaanization of the religion of Jahweh. Hosea, Isaiah, Jeremiah, Ezekiel, all inveighed against certain practices borrowed from the native population or considered by them to be of Canaanitish origin, the worship of idols, of pillars and sacred poles, ritual prostitution, and the

[1] LVII, 465–485, 489. [2] LVII, 476–7.
[3] LVII, 487–491. [4] 1 Kings xv, 12 ; xxii, 47.
[5] Ex. xxxiv, 17 ; xx, 23–6.

sacrifice of children. But to consider, as some historians do,[1] that the prophets were only denouncing a cult because it had been contaminated by certain foreign importations such as *local* worship, as celebrated in the temples of the northern kingdoms and the high places of Judah, is to put too narrow an interpretation on the facts. Many of the great prophets [2] abstain entirely from any polemic against *individual* so-called Canaanitish practices in worship, and only their successors or disciples give it the first place.[3] The dominant motive of the real leaders of the prophetic movement, Amos, Hosea, Isaiah, Micah, and Jeremiah, is much profounder : they challenge the efficacy of the rites, in particular the rite of sacrifice, which all ancient religions had held to be infallible. In their view, whatever these rites may be, and in whatever place they are observed, in the sight of God they are but meaningless gestures, and exercise no influence upon him : he is indifferent to them.[4]

> " I desire mercy and not sacrifice and the knowledge of God more than burnt offerings." [5]

Nor do sacrifices have any effect on those who offer them :

> " Shall prayers and the holy flesh of burnt-offerings take away thy sin ? "

asks Jahweh of Jerusalem.[6]

Having in view not the worship of the high places, but that of the temple at Jerusalem after Josiah's reforms had purified it, Jeremiah still declares that it is vain for the followers of Jahweh to put their trust in the possession of this temple.[7] He states clearly that God asks for no sacrifices.

> " Thus saith the Lord of hosts, I spake not unto your fathers, nor commanded them in the day that I brought them out of the land of Egypt, concerning burnt offerings or sacrifices : but this thing I commanded them, saying Hearken unto my voice, and I will be your God, and ye shall be my people . . ." [8]

This does not necessarily imply that the great prophets demanded the abolition of sacrifices and the creation of a new and purely spiritual worship. They understood quite well—

---

[1] **XVIII,** 16–19 (on the other hand, see pp. 20–1) ; **XXXVI,** 203–4.

[2] Amos, Micah.

[3] See Ezekiel, Is. lvii, 5–10 ; lxv, 3–5, 11.

[4] *Cf.* **XXVI,** 43–4.   [5] Hos. vi, 6.

[6] Jer. xi, 15 (**LXX**).   [7] Jer. vii, 1–15.

[8] Jer. vii, 22–3.

no doubt because they would share it themselves, like any other devout-minded man in ancient times—the appalling distress which the exiles would feel if these venerated rites were forcibly suspended :—

> " What will ye do in the day of solemn assembly and in the day of the feast of the Lord ? " [1]

Nevertheless, some of the boldest among them do not recoil from the consequences implicit in their principles. Amos declares that Israel, in the golden age of its relations with its God, brought him no burnt offerings.

> " Did ye bring unto me sacrifices and offerings in the wilderness forty years, O house of Israel ? " [2]

For Hosea, the nation will 'only cease to be a " harlot ", that is to say, unfaithful to Jahweh, when its sacrifices have come to an end.[3]

Though they do not all go so far as this, the great prophets of the days before the exile have broken with the conception of ritual as something half mystical, half magical ; an advance, in fact, of much greater import than the condemnation of this or that practice more or less incompatible with reason or morality.

4. *The Prophets' Vision of the Future.*—In their conception of the future the new prophets naturally took as their starting-point the beliefs current in their time in Israel, or even in the East in general. Had there been a traditional eschatology before ? And if so, to what extent did the prophets accept it ? How far did they transform it ? The question is a delicate one, and one which is much discussed at the moment.[4]

It seems certain that the Egyptians had, long before the first of the Hebrew prophets appeared, looked for a Messiah, and that this hope enabled them to bear present ills, and was closely connected with their belief in the divine nature of the king, son of Ra. It is true that most of the texts in which it

---

[1] Hos. ix, 3–5.   [2] Amos v, 25 (emend.).
[3] Hos. iii, 3–4.
[4] Since the publications of H. O. Lange (**SBA,** 1903, pp. 601 *ff.*), Hugo Gressmann (*Der Ursprung der israelit.-jüd. Eschatologie,* Gottingen, 1905 ; **XXVIII,** ii, 2, 1st ed. (1909), pp. 327–9), Edward Meyer (*Die Israeliten und ihre Nachbarstämme,* Halle, 1906, pp. 451 *ff.* ; *Gesch. des Alt.,* i, 2 [2], Stuttgart, 1909, pp. 274 *ff.*), J. M. P. Smith (**AJSL,** xxxv (1918), 1–19 ; *The Prophet and his Problems,* Chicago, 1914, pp. 16–35).

was thought that this hope was expressed are very obscure, and that one of the most important, and the most ancient— that containing the " predictions of Ipuwer " [1]—is perhaps, as Alan Gardiner on the one hand,[2] and Erman on the other,[3] confidently affirm, a collection of political sayings and not a prediction. It is none the less true that the " vision of Neferrehu ", dating from the Middle Kingdom (about 2000), already offers characteristics which reappear later as typical of Jewish apocalypses.[4] It is related that Neferrehu predicted to the pharaoh Snefru (who reigned about 2950) that calamities of all kinds would descend upon Egypt, but also foretold the advent of a king Ameny, who would bring deliverance, build the " Prince's wall ", and put an end to the incursions of the Asiatics : meaning Amen-em-het I (twelfth dynasty). Of course, the real author of this work was a contemporary of the latter sovereign and looked for the salvation of the country through him ; the evils represented as taking place in the future belonged in reality to the past, or to the time of the author.

The Israelites, for their part, had cherished similar hopes even before the coming of the great prophets. They looked for " the day of Jahweh ", thinking it of as a day of light, that is to say one which should bring joy to the nation (Amos v, 18–20). The feast of the new year, which doubtless from this time onward included a ceremony of dedication to Jahweh, was intended as a reminder that the God of the nation would shortly come to reign for ever. He was acclaimed with cries of " Jahweh reigns ", that is to say " becomes king ".[5] There is every reason to think that in Israel, as in Egypt, and doubtless under the more or less direct influence of the subjects of the son of Ra, these proceedings crystallized even before the eighth century into the idea of a triumphant prince bringing victory and peace in his train : the Israelites did, in fact, adopt, along with the system of monarchy, the ideas and the customs which for centuries had been part and

---

[1] Translated in Adolf Erman, *Die Literatur der Aegypter*, 1923, pp. 132 *ff.* ; also partially in **XLIV**, ii, 149–151 ; **XXVII**, i, 52–5.
[2] **CXVI** ; **JEA**, x, 11, 13–14, 18.   [3] **SBA**, 1919, pp. 804 *ff.*
[4] Translation in Erman, *Lit.*, pp. 151 *ff.* ; partial in **XLIV**, ii, 145–8 ; **XXVII**, i, 47–8.
[5] **LVII**, 506–7, 548–9.

parcel of the institution of royalty, and in particular the belief in the supernatural powers and almost divine character of the king, " son of God." [1]

According to an hypothesis of Hugo Gressmann,[2] this popular eschatology, both Egyptian and Israelite, was itself the by-product of more learned speculations as to the destruction and renewal of the world, the return to primitive chaos being foreshadowed by calamities announced before-hand, and the restoration to the joys of Paradise symbolized by the coming of the Messianic era. If Gressmann is right, the ancient Israelites made this conception of the future their own, with this difference, that their patriotism prompted them to think of themselves as the only nation to escape the general cataclysm. He holds that in this respect the great prophets accepted the traditional outlook, but foretold that, contrary to the hopes of their compatriots, and as punish-ment for sin, Israel also would be involved in disaster, and that only after this had happened could the return to the Golden Age begin.

The idea that popular eschatology was of cosmic origin is not, however, borne out by the texts. It does not seem as if the masses of the people of Israel believed, as the Jews round about the time of the Christian era believed, that the calamities of the present were necessarily the forerunners of the felicity they hoped for, so that the unhappier they were, the surer they could be of imminent deliverance. It is still less likely that the great prophets admitted that an " eschatology of misfortune " must inevitably be followed by an " eschatology of happiness ", as winter is followed by summer. This is the view held by Hugo Gressmann and by MacCown,[3] who come to the conclusion that therefore the prophecies of happiness, which are very rare, to be found in the books of the older prophets, must be considered as authentic,[4] unless absolute proof to the contrary is forth-coming, and that each of their threats must be understood to imply similar foreshadowings of joy. The unprejudiced reader, perusing their sombre predictions, does not gather the

---

[1] 2 Sam. vii, 14. *Cf.* **CXLIX**, 267–272. [2] *Op. cit.*
[3] *Hebrew and Egyptian Apocalyptic Literature*, **HTR**, xviii (1925), 357–411.
[4] *Cf.* T. H. Robinson, **ZATW**, 45 (N.F. 1), 1927, pp. 3–9.

impression that the misfortunes they foretell are intended merely as the traditional, necessary precursor of future happiness. Chastisement is still avoidable, calamities are *undreamt of*, the hearers shudder at their very prospect, and lastly, punishment as a rule is *final*, " the end of Israel ". With regard to such hopes of happiness as were entertained by his people, the first at least of the great prophets adopted a resolutely negative attitude.

> " Woe unto you that desire the day of the Lord ! It is darkness and not light." (v, 18–20.)

Amos does not say : " It will only come after a period of darkness," but " it shall itself be darkness."

The successors of the shepherd of Tekoa, less logical than he, made concessions to the old national optimism : Hosea dreamt—it may have been only for a time, it is true [1]— of a return of the nation to Jahweh after the chastisement ; Isaiah foretold the conversion and salvation of a " remnant ", and probably the coming of a king, son of David, " whose delight should be in the fear of the Lord," and who " should judge the poor with righteousness ".[2] Even the prophets of the time before the exile made the realization of these hopes depend on moral conditions of great stringency. Hence the great prophets rebelled first of all against the popular eschatology of their time, which they opposed ; they next appropriated certain elements of it, but transformed them more or less fundamentally. Finally, after the exile, urged on by the trend of events, their denunciations are converted into a cry of hope ; but however nearly their eschatology may then have approached that of ancient Israel, it differs from it in the emphasis laid upon morality, and in the profoundly religious nature of the exhortations based thereon.

5. *Ethical monotheism.*—Ethical monotheism, to us the most specific and original feature of the prophets' mode of thought, was not entirely new.

Egyptian and Babylonian texts show that certain priests had arrived at the conception that the various gods were simply one divine Being with many names, each name descriptive of the diverse activities by which that Being was

---

[1] **CXLVI.** See below, pp. 97–8.
[2] Is. xi, 1–8 ; *cf.* ix, 5–6.

manifested. But it is generally recognized that there cannot
be any historical connection between these pantheistic
speculations, fusing all gods into one, and the prophetic
attitude, which belittles, and finally eliminates, the multitude
of divine beings, in favour of the supreme personality of one of
them : the nearest approach to an echo of this doctrine of
universal theocracy is perhaps to be found in a very late
prophetic book,[1] in a passage in which Jahweh declares :—

> " From the rising of the sun even unto the going down of the
> same my name is great among the Gentiles ; and in every place
> unto my name a pure offering is burned." [2]

The prophets' conception bears a closer resemblance
to that of Amenophis IV, the fourteenth-century Pharaoh
responsible for many reforms, who tried to substitute the
worship of Atôn for that of Amon-Ra, and who wrote a
hymn known to and adapted by a Hebrew psalmist,[3] or to
the thought which prompted Adadnirari III, King of Assyria
(812–783), to write upon a statue of Nebo : " Put thy trust in
no other god ! " But in this latter case nothing more may
perhaps be involved than pious hyperbole, or even a witticism
with a political point, directed against Marduk [4] ; as to
Amenophis, he does not seem to have denied the existence
of all gods save his patron.

Between the thought of the prophets and certain features
or tendencies characteristic of the national religion of their
people, no doubt from the very beginning, the links are more
obvious : the ancient Israelite had a very lofty idea of the
might of his God, who is able to protect him even on foreign
soil, who once overthrew the Elohim of Egypt, who in the
beginning created the heavens and the earth ; he extolled
the sublimity of Jahweh's moral claims, Jahweh who
" rewards the wicked doer according to his wickedness "
and " renders to every man his righteousness and his faithfulness ".[5] In this, and also in the traditions as to the alliance
with Israel, there are the germs of moral monotheism, even
of universalism,[6] although the religion of Israel remained

---

[1] Malachi i, 11. On this passage see pp. 275–7.
[2] Omit *muggás* and *u* before *minhah*.
[3] The author of Ps. civ.   [4] **XLV**, 1st ed., 45.
[5] 1 Sam. xxvi, 23 ; 2 Sam. iii, 39.
[6] *Cf.* **LVII**, 361–5, 528–9, 554–5, 564.

essentially a *national* religion and closely resembles the other national religions of antiquity.

Another factor may have helped to create, in the time of the great prophets, an atmosphere favourable to the emergence of moral monotheism, namely the influence of writings of the moralists. It is true that we have no gnomic Hebrew work to which we can with certainty attribute a date prior to the eighth century. But we know now that Wisdom literature in the East had an international character ; it was the work of scribes who, as we can see from the letters of Tell el-Amarna or the bilingual vocabularies found at Ras Shamra,[1] mastered foreign languages with a view to their diplomatic functions ; the Jewish moralists in particular set great store by the wisdom of their Egyptian, " Eastern " and Edomite fellow-writers [2] ; in the book of Proverbs they preserved two collections of maxims attributed to Arabian princes of Massa, Agur and Lemuel, [3] and a series of aphorisms [4] of which the Egyptian model has lately been discovered, namely the *Wisdom of Amen-em-ope*.[5]   Now certain gnomic writers of Egypt, as for instance the author of the *Instructions to Merikere*,[6] like various Babylonian " sages ", use expressions which have an undeniably monotheistic air about them : they speak of " God " or " the god " rather than of this or that divinity ; thus :—

> Man is clay and straw,
>   and it is the god who fashions it.[7]

They hold lofty ideas about divine justice : one of their basic doctrines is that God punishes the wicked and rewards the righteous :—

> He who nourishes the weak,
>   God will reward him.[8]

The significance of these observations must not, however, be exaggerated, nor must it be inferred that the prophets of

---

[1] François Thureau-Dangin, **SY**, xii (1931), 225–266 ; xiii (1932), 233–241.
[2] 1 Kings v, 10 ; Jer. xlix, 7 ; Obad. 8–9 ; Bar. iii, 22–3.
[3] xxx and xxxi, 1–9.
[4] The " words of the wise " (Prov. xxii, 17–23, 11).
[5] *Cf.* p. 13, n. 1.
[6] The manuscript belongs to the xxth century (**XXXIX**), 32.
[7] Amen-em-ope, xxiv, 13–14 ; *cf.* **XXXIX**, 58.
[8] Insinger Papyrus, 16, 13.

Israel ultimately derived their purer ideas about God and his righteousness from ancient Eastern morality in general.[1]

Although Amen-em-ope often speaks of " God " or " the God ", he also occasionally mentions Khnum, Ra, Thoth, Shaï, and Renent ; he calls himself the scribe who " assesses the dues of all the gods ".[2] The expression " God " or " the god ", as used by the moralists of the ancient East, probably means, therefore, " divinity " in general, which is practically the same as the gods.[3] To convey the same meaning the Greek polytheists used θεός as well as θεοί, and the ancient Israelites, to describe piety, used the term " fear of Elohim ", even when speaking of foreigners, which did not mean that the latter feared the one God, but that, if they were pious, each feared his own god or gods.

On the other hand, when they affirm that " the divinity " favours the righteous and severely punishes the wicked, they are only proclaiming a principle contained in all the religions of antiquity, the Egyptian, the Assyro-Babylonian, or the Greek as well as that of ancient Israel. But, in accordance with current beliefs, the principle admitted of numerous exceptions which considerably lessened its scope : it was thought that the gods were subject to ignorance or forgetfulness, that they were mindful of the sacrifices made to them, and of the ties which bound them to a nation or a family, that they had inexplicable dislikes or predilections, that they often smote an innocent man for a fault committed by one of his relations, etc.[4]

The originality of the great prophets in this connection consists in their declaring that divine justice is absolute, strictly impartial, unequivocal, and without reservation ; Jahweh is above caprice as he is above self-interest ; neither offerings nor a ritual more or less magical can influence him.

It seems that the early moralists of the East as a rule contented themselves with stating the general principle of divine justice, as to which all were agreed, without com-

---

[1] As H. Gressmann did, at least with regard to their conception of retribution (**ZATW**, 1924, p. 288).

[2] ii, 3.

[3] Cf. Ad. Lods, *Le monothéisme israélite a-t-il eu des précurseurs parmi les " sages " de l'ancien Orient ?* **RHP**, xiv (1934), 197–205.

[4] Cf. **LVII**, 540–5.

bating the beliefs which too often nullified it in practice, particularly the belief in the efficacy of ritual to gain or recover divine favour ; we read in a Babylonian collection, for instance, this maxim, the tenor of which is certainly lofty enough :—

> The fear of God obtains favour,
>   an offering enriches life,
> And prayer secures the forgiveness of sins.[1]

In the instructions to Merikere this precept is to be found :—

> *Let the table be laden with offerings. Bring much bread. Increase the daily sacrifices, for he who does so shall profit thereby.*[2]

The works of these ancient moralists are interesting in that they reveal to us the existence of the desire for a higher and morally purer conception of religion among the most cultivated class of ancient Eastern society. But these rather timid and vague aspirations would hardly suffice to explain the truly heroic passion for righteousness of an Amos or a Jeremiah, which can approve, which can even demand the condemnation of their own people in the name of God, or the profound religious conviction with which the second Isaiah calls upon Israel, " the servant of Jahweh," to accept all suffering in order to fulfil his mission in the world, and to bring all nations to the worship of the only true God.

IV

The Main Lines of Development of the Prophetic Movement

As we have pointed out,[3] the appearance in Israel, in the course of two and a half centuries, of a series of personalities who, in forcefulness and originality, are without parallel in history, brought about an increasing enrichment of the new type of religious life for which these men stood and which they sought to propagate. The last great representatives of the movement, Jeremiah, Ezekiel, and the

---

[1] Ll. 76–8 ; *cf.* **XXVII**, i, 293.
[2] Ll. 65–6 ; *cf.* **XXVII**, i, 35.   [3] Pp. 61–2.

second Isaiah, not only provide their own personal and original contribution, but also a synthesis of the particular views of their various predecessors. They are conscious of their continuity with them,[1] and what they are anxious to formulate is the revelation common to the true prophets of Jahweh, which Jeremiah interprets spiritually, which Ezekiel translates into institutions, and the second Isaiah enunciates in clear and simple teachings, such as may be easily disseminated throughout all nations.

This general statement must not, however, be taken to indicate that the evolution of the prophetic movement always followed a straight line, or that, by a process of simple addition, a primitive nucleus was enlarged by homogeneous accretions. As time passed, important internal changes took place. The chief point to notice is, that in spite of temporary individual reactions, as in the case of Jeremiah, there was a general increase of agreement between the views of the prophets and those of their political and religious adversaries. The first of the new prophets stand alone, in uncompromising opposition to all the beliefs and hopes of their people. The last of the new prophets, Haggai, Zechariah, Malachi, are in full agreement with the representatives of the official religion of their time : Haggai and Zechariah have the ear of the masses, of whose hopes they are the mouthpiece.

This reconciliation was due no doubt partly to the leavening, first of an *élite*, i.e. some of the rulers, then of the general run of the people, by those ideals which the prophets had preached : it was owing to their influence that Hezekiah, Josiah, and Ezra officially introduced certain reforms into traditional religion. But a factor which must not be lost sight of is the increasing tendency, noticeable in some of the prophets, to return to the older beliefs : Isaiah was already nearer to them than Amos or Hosea ; Ezekiel, priest as well as prophet, was saturated with the ideas of Semitic antiquity with regard to ritual and its efficacy ; Haggai and Zechariah devoted their best energies to the cause of the rebuilding of the Temple. Like Ezekiel, they combined with monotheistic ideas a spirit of narrow nationalism.

---

[1] *Cf.* Jer. xxviii, 8 ; vii, 25 ; xxv, 4 ; xxix, 19 ; Ezek. xxxviii, 17 ; xxxix, 8 ; Micah vii, 4 ; Is. xli, 21–2, 26–9, etc.

This evolution of the teaching of the prophets simultaneously with Jahwism of the old type, and their gradual convergence, was to some extent the product of circumstances : when Manasseh introduced the Assyrian pantheon, the outcry which was raised by the prophets made them appear to the masses of the people as the champions of the religion of their fathers, and doubtless had a great deal to do with their popularity. The catastrophes of the period of the exile obliged them to become the comforters and spiritual directors of their people, the rebuilders of the city : confronted by stern reality and all the strength of the past, they ceased to dwell in the peaceful realm of ideals.

Thus, both in the midst of the prophetic group itself and among the masses who clung to traditional beliefs, the ground was being prepared for that synthesis which was the characteristic of Judaism.

CHAPTER II

THE PROPHETS OF ISRAEL IN THE EIGHTH CENTURY

I

AMOS

AMOS, the earliest of the new prophets known to us, belongs to the type of the solitary ecstatic, attacking all interests and every tradition, in the complete conviction that he expresses the mind of God, carrying his principles to their ultimate consequences however, desperate.

1. *The Life of the Prophet.*—We only know one scene of his life. It was in the time of Jeroboam II, King of Israel (about 783–743),[1] just when this ruler had brought to a victorious conclusion the hundred years' war against the Aramæans of Damascus. Moab also was subdued, for the kingdom of Israel extended once more from the outskirts of Hamath [2] to the brook of the Arabah, that is to say to the south of the Dead Sea (Amos vi, 14). Israel was full of rejoicing and looked to the future with confidence, trusting in its own strength, which had enabled it to retake Lodebar and Karnaim in Transjordan (vi, 13), and relying on help from Jahweh, who had just shown that he was with his people (v, 14). And so pilgrims flocked to the venerated shrines of the national God, at Bethel, Gilgal, and Beersheba, where they multiplied offerings and sacrifices in his honour (iv, 5 ; v, 5, 21–3). They looked forward to the " day of Jahweh ", when the nation would be assured of still more brilliant triumphs (v, 18–20).

But in the midst of the general rejoicing a dissenting voice is heard. It is the voice of Amos, predicting the woes which are to come upon the kingdom, the royal house, and the nobles.

---

[1] From 790/89 to 749/48, according to **CLVI**, 234, 271.
[2] **LVII**, 20–1.

It is probable that he went through the length and breadth
of the land, and that it was in Samaria itself that he addressed
the great ladies of the capital as " kine of Bashan " (iv, 1–3 ;
cf. iii, 9–11, 12), and at Gilgal that he declared " Enter not
into Gilgal " (v, 5). Finally he went to Bethel, the principal
sanctuary of the country. Everywhere he foretold in the name
of Jahweh that Israel would be destroyed (viii, 2). Over the
" virgin of Israel " he sang the lament whose characteristic
melody was heard at burials (v, 1–3), or like the old warlike
nabis he broke out into fulminations against the neighbouring
nations, which were all more or less at enmity with his own,
hurling threats against them which could not fail to flatter
the patriotism of his hearers, but ending by a still more
terrible prophecy against Israel itself (ch. i–ii).

The nature of the calamity which was to bring about the
final overthrow of the nation was only darkly hinted at : in
the sinister visions of Amos there is diversity of horror ;
earthquake (ii, 11), plague (vi, 9–10), eclipses (viii, 9),
universal mourning (v, 16–17 ; viii, 3–10), a " famine of the
word of the Lord " (viii, 11–16), drought (viii, 13–14).
But as a rule he saw the country invaded by an enemy nation
which would destroy ramparts and despoil palaces (iii, 11),
subjugate the land from the north to the south (vi, 14), and
deport the population beyond Damascus (v, 27 ; *cf.* v, 5, 11 ;
vi, 7 ; vii, 11, 17). This pointed clearly enough to the
Assyrians as the instrument of Jahweh's wrath. It may
perhaps be concluded that Assyria was then beginning to
recover from the long period of impotence which for nearly
a century had rendered successful interference in Western
affairs impossible, and that the energetic Tiglath Pileser III,
the organizer of systematic deportations, had just begun his
career (745).

Amos explicitly foretells that in his anger Jahweh will
spare neither the holy places nor the reigning dynasty.

> " The sanctuaries of Israel shall be laid waste ; and I will rise
> against the house of Jeroboam with the sword " (vii, 9).

Amaziah, the priest of Bethel, informed the king of the
blasphemous and seditious words : what if Amos were
preparing the way for some leader of rebellion, as Ahijah
had done for Jeroboam I, or Elisha for Jehu, the ancestor

of Jeroboam II ? However, Amaziah contented himself with disdainfully intimating to Amos that he must leave the country, his moderation being dictated perhaps less by the contempt which the priest professed to feel, than by the fear which even the most sceptical entertained with regard to the supernatural powers of a " man of the spirit ".

> " O thou seer, go,"

he says to him,

> " flee thee away into the land of Judah, and there eat bread and prophesy there."

Amaziah insinuated that Amos was one of those men who lived by the trade of a *nabi*, foretelling peace when they were given enough to eat, and war when food was refused them [1] : if he threatens it is merely to induce the court to buy his silence.

Amos replied proudly, " I am no prophet, neither am I a prophet's son," meaning that he was neither a professional prophet nor a member of a guild. " I am a shepherd,[2] and a dresser of sycamore trees." Two trades, therefore, ensure me a living. " But the Lord took me from following the flock, and the Lord said unto me, Go, prophesy unto my people Israel." He then reiterates his threats, adding that the calamity foretold shall overtake even the city of Bethel, the priest Amaziah, his wife, who shall be delivered over to the enemy soldiery, his children, and his goods (vii, 10–17).

This scene, in which official religion and personal religious experience are confronted, is the only one which remains to us of the life of Amos. But from some of its details, as well as from various other passages in the book, we are able to draw some conclusions about the prophet's past. The land of Judah, to which he is ordered to flee, was doubtless his own native land : there is no real reason for main-

---

[1] Micah iii, 5.

[2] The correct reading is *noqed*, found in both the Septuagint and the Targum, as in i, 1, and not *boqer* " herdsman ", as the Massoretic text has it. In v. 15 we read that the Lord took Amos " from following the flock " : grazing sheep and goats was his usual occupation. Consequently it seems impossible to admit, with Hans Schmidt (**CLXXIV**) and Otto Eissfeldt (**XX**, 440), that the future prophet was a breeder of *both* large and small beasts.

taining, as has been supposed, that he was an Israelite,[1] and that Tekoa, a village situated about 6 miles to the south of Bethlehem, was not his place of origin, but the retreat in which he took refuge.[2]   It is not surprising that an inhabitant of the southern kingdom should have taken so deep an interest in what was happening in Israel : in spite of political divisions, the two countries were conscious that they were both the people of Jahweh.[3] Amos therefore was one of the southern Hebrews, who clung more faithfully to the customs and beliefs of the past than those of the great northern towns.   In his wild setting of the Judæan desert, he himself lived the life of his fathers, the rough, austere life of a breeder of sheep and goats, merely adding to his shepherd's trade the temporary pursuit of a stay-at-home peasant : skilled in splitting the sycamore seeds, so as to make them less bitter, when the time for gathering them drew near he doubtless went down to the hilly region called the Shephelah, where these trees abounded.[4]

But in the East, simplicity of life, particularly the life of a desert shepherd, does not preclude mental culture, nor even a literary vocation.[5] With grief and indignation, Amos, the lonely ascetic, heard the rumours of scandal after scandal in the cities of Israel, in spite of public calamities such as famine, drought, blighted harvests, the scourge of locusts, defeats, epidemics, which from time to time befell the land, and which Amos interpreted as so many warnings from Jahweh (iv, 6–11). He himself relates that in two visions [6] Jahweh revealed to him that he would send locusts to lay waste the country, and that by a divine fire he would devour the " great deep ", the reservoir of the springs. Amos implored forgiveness for Jacob : " He is so small ! " And twice did Jahweh repent him of the evil (vii, 1–6). But in two other visions, of which the first is obscure in meaning, and the second represented a basket of fruit whose name

---

[1] Oort, **TT**, 1880, pp. 122–9 ; 1891, pp. 121 *ff.* ; Zeydner, *Stemmen voor Waarh. en Vrede*, 1886, pp. 548 *ff.* ; Hans Schmidt (**CLXXIV**). See the criticisms of Karl Budde, **JBL**, 1925, p. 81.

[2] Oort (1891).   [3] *Cf.* **LVII**, 482–6.

[4] 1 Kings x, 27 ; 1 Chron. xxvii, 28 ; 2 Chron. i, 15 ; ix, 27.

[5] *Cf.* traditions about David, shepherd and poet.

[6] He must have had these before he received his call. *Cf.* Karl Budde, **JBL**, 1925, p. 65.

in Hebrew (*qayiṣ*) was a portent of the end (*qeṣ*) of the nation—
Jahweh announced to him : " I will pardon Israel no more "
(vii, 7–8). Amos then left everything to proclaim the gloomy
tidings :—

> " The lion hath roared, who will not fear ? The Lord God hath
> spoken, who can but prophesy ? " (iii, 8.)

The prophetic activity of Amos must have been very
brief : according to the prefatory title of the book the
revelations were all made to him at a definite date, " two
years before the earthquake " (i, 1). Having borne his
testimony, he probably returned to Tekoah and resumed
his life as a shepherd.

2. *The Mission of Amos.*—The mission which Amos had
felt called to deliver was obviously embodied in the very
visions which had made him a prophet : he must warn the
condemned nation of the fate which threatened it, evidently
in the hope that the guilty would finally return to the paths
of righteousness, and perhaps win their reprieve :

> " Hate the evil and love the good, and establish judgment in
> the gate : it may be that the Lord, the God of hosts, will be gracious
> to the remnant of Joseph " (v, 15).

Nevertheless, this gleam of hope appears only in a single
passage in the book (v, 4–6, 14–15). Everywhere else Amos
represents the end of Israel as a certainty, the death-sentence
as irrevocable (ii, 6). The impression that Amos is
unshakably convinced of Israel's approaching doom may
in part be due to the fact that his prophecies were only
recorded in writing after his mission had been interrupted,
when he already knew by experience that the Israelites said
to the messengers of Jahweh : " Prophesy not " (ii, 12 ;
vii, 16). But the chief reason is that the crimes of the nation
are, in his eyes, beyond redemption.

The grievances of Jahweh against this people are many,
he declared : he reproaches it with ingratitude (ii, 9–10),
with failing to understand the intentions of God, clearly
manifested by contemporary events (iv, 6–11 ; vi, 1–6),
pride (vi, 8), and once he apparently makes an allusion to
temple prostitution (ii, 7) ; also, in two passages of which both
the interpretation and the text itself are uncertain, to the

worship of other gods, Ashima of Samaria,[1] Sakkuth and Kēvān.[2] But what he considers the most heinous offence of the Israelite community, its unforgivable sin, the crime to which he constantly and indignantly reverts, is the exploitation of the small by the great, creditors that know no pity, judges without a conscience, who will deliver up the innocent to their enemies for the price of a pair of sandals (ii, 6), hypocritical and unscrupulous traders (viii, 4–7). He taunts them with their fine houses of hewn stone, their luxurious feasts, at which they recline like the Assyrians, instead of sitting on the ground like their fathers, their love of music, inveighing against luxury which is paid for by corn-levies wrung from the poor (vi, 4–7 ; v, 11–12 ; iv, 1–2). These abuses were, as we have seen, the result of the transition of the Israelites from the habits of equality and fraternity which prevailed in nomadic times, to the civilization of the towns.[3] For Amos, a society which tolerates such iniquities *cannot* survive, any more than horses can be made to run over slippery rocks, or oxen to plough the sea.[4]

Jahweh himself will put an end to the kingdom of Israel. This unheard of declaration must immediately have called forth two objections, whose echo we find in the answers the prophet made to them. Jahweh then takes no account of the worship we offer him with so much zeal—a worship which, according to ancient ideas, not only places the god who accepts it under an obligation, but establishes a mysterious bond, a kind of union between him and his worshippers ? Here, according to Amos, is Jahweh's reply :—

" I hate, I despise, your feasts, and I will take no delight in (the smell of) your solemn sacrifices. I will not accept your burnt-offerings, I regard not the sacrifice of your fat beasts. Take thou

---

[1] viii, 14. *Cf.* **LVII**, 469, 586 ; Ed. König, **ZATW**, 1914, pp. 16–30 ; Epstein, **ZATW**, 1912, pp. 139 *ff.* ; **XCIX** ; K. Budde, **JBL**, xliv (1925), 96.

[2] v, 26. According to the theory maintained by us (**V**, *ad loc.*), v. 26, and also v. 27, really contained a threat : the Israelites, when deported beyond Damascus, will have to serve the gods of the country, as one must when one lives in a foreign country (1 Sam. xxvi, 19 ; Jer. xvi, 13). Having corrected v, 26, in accordance with the Greek, we have only to invert the order of 27a and 26, or better still to read *behaglothi* in v. 27.

[3] Pp. 64.

[4] vi, 12 (em.).

away from me the noise of thy songs, for I will not hear the melody
of thy viols. But let judgment roll down as waters, and righteousness like a mighty stream that never runs dry ! Did ye bring unto
me sacrifices and offerings in the wilderness forty years, O house
of Israel ? " [1]

Thus not only is worship an abomination when not
accompanied by righteousness, but it is never indispensable.
Amos actually says that it may be sin, not indeed because
of the more or less immoral rites which the northern Israelites
included in it, but because of the illusory efficacy attributed
to these practices (v, 4–6, 14–15). For Amos the demands
of Jahweh are of an *exclusively moral and spiritual order.*

The second objection was equally inevitable : Jahweh
has but one people, the nation which he brought out of
Egypt : if he destroys the only nation which worships him,
what shall he do then for the honour of his name ? With
scathing irony Jahweh replies :—

" You only have I known of all the families of the earth : therefore I will visit upon you all your iniquities " (iii, 1–2).

The worshippers of a just God must be the first to feel
the effects of his justice. Moreover, Jahweh rigorously applies
to other nations the same laws as to Israel (i, 3–ii, 16) : he
requires equity and loving kindness from all alike. He punishes
foreign nations not only for the wrongs done by them to his
people, but for their cruelty one to the other (ii, 1). Both
alike are the objects of his righteousness and of his
providence :—

" Have not I brought up Israel out of the land of Egypt, and
the Philistines from Caphtor,[2] and the Syrians from Kir ? " (ix, 7)

Amos simply denies that the sons of Israel are privileged
beings : in the sight of Jahweh they rank no higher than the
negroes of Cush (ix, 7 ; *cf.* Jer. xiii, 23). The God of Amos
is no longer the particular god of one nation : he is the
supremely just judge and the protector of all nations.

These assertions, which opened up vistas of thought so
new, but so disturbing to the minds of antiquity, are
immediately followed, in the book as it now stands, by an
appendix so full of consolation, that if it were authentic it
would reduce the daring denunciations of Amos to the

[1] v, 21–5 (emended, *cf.* **V**).
[2] Doubtless from Crete (Deut. ii, 23 ; Jer. xlvii, 4).

proportions of a village squabble : it is explained that
Jahweh's threats concerned " the sinful kingdom ", that is to
say, according to the most natural interpretation, the kingdom
of Israel, as opposed to that of Judah, which was therefore
a righteous kingdom [1] ; they were even directed solely
against the guilty members of the people of Israel. Judah,
on the contrary, which the author calls " the tabernacle of
David that is fallen "—although in the time of Amos the house
of David was more powerful than it had ever been since
Solomon—will once more subjugate Edom and all the nations
formerly conquered by Jahweh (that is to say by Israel).
The whole passage contradicts the thought of Amos. An
imperialist and militarist conception of national greatness
is certainly foreign to the thought of the man who indignantly
upbraids the nations which do wrong in order that " their
borders may be enlarged " (i, 13). The expression " the
remnant of Edom " implies that the territory of the
Edomites had already been conquered by the Nabatæan
invasions of the sixth and fifth centuries. It is also very
improbable that Amos would have foretold the restoration of
the kingdom of David without attaching any moral condition
to the promise. We may be sure that even if ii, 4–5, is not
authentic, Amos judged the spiritual and moral condition
of Judah by a standard at least as severe as the prophets who
were his contemporaries, Hosea, Isaiah, and Micah, and that
he considered the nation doomed, as they did, unless it was
saved by complete regeneration.

It seems clear to us that this appendix was added as an
afterthought, by one who deemed the predictions of the
shepherd of Tekoah to be too sombre, and wished to modify
them.[2]

[1] Like Calvin, Mercerius, and Pusey, Budde understands thereby
" every sinful kingdom " (**JBL**, 1925, pp. 110–11). But the expression
would be a clumsy one ; for the nations of which Amos has just spoken
(v. 7), and to which he here makes allusion, Israel (in the wider sense),
the Philistines, and Aram, did not, strictly speaking, constitute so
many " kingdoms ", but each of them were made up of *several* States,
which, at that time, were not even perhaps all kingdoms. Besides,
Amos would be making an abrupt return from his idea of God's care
being the same for all, to the idea of impartial justice (v. 8). Finally,
in v. 9, " that is why " would be necessary instead of " for ".

[2] The authenticity, at least in part, of this conclusion has recently
been defended by von Orelli, Oettli, König, Hans Schmidt, Ludwig

In reality Amos took quite literally the divine prediction of the end of Israel. But he is hardly likely to have thought that with this catastrophe history would also come to an end : the religious mind is unable to stop short at the idea of final annihilation. He hints in the last certainly authentic words of the book (ix, 7) that, though the nation fall, Jahweh will still remain, and that, to realize his plans for humanity, he may make use of another people, the Philistines, the Syrians, even the negroes of Ethiopia.[1]

II

Hosea

Hosea, the son of Beeri, came from the northern kingdom (i, 2 ; vii, 8), perhaps from the land of Benjamin, which he seems to know particularly well,[2] but not from that part which belonged to Judah.[3] The divine mission with which he felt himself entrusted was essentially the same as that of Amos : to warn Israel that, as a punishment for its sins, Jahweh would blot it out. As early as the reign of Jeroboam II, the contemporary of Amos, Hosea, at Jahweh's command, had given his eldest son the name of Jezreel [4] :—

"For yet a little while and I will avenge the blood of Jezreel upon the house of Jehu (the blood of the Omrides shed at Jezreel),[5] and will cause the kingdom of the house of Israel to cease " (i, 4).

Soon afterwards he called the two other children borne him by his wife, Lo-ru-hamah (Not beloved)—for Jahweh would no longer have mercy on the house of Israel—and Lo-ammi (Not my people), for Israel was no longer the people of Jahweh (i, 6, 9). For Hosea, too, it is the Assyrians who will execute divine judgment (viii, 10 ; ix, 3 ; x, 6 ; xi, 5, etc.). And the prophet witnessed with his own eyes the first signs

Köhler (**TR**, iv (1932), 195–213), Sellin, Budde (1900, 1906, 1925), Walter Baumgartner (1913), Baudissin, MacCown ; on the other hand, Hugo Gressmann, having supported the same view (**XXVIII**, ii, 2, 356), abandoned it in the 2nd edition (p. 358). It does not seem to us that, even setting aside as glosses vv. 8*b*, 12, and 13 (Budde, 1925), a sequence can be obtained which will fit in perfectly with the parts of the book which are certainly authentic.

[1] *Cf.* **CXXXIV**, 12–13.   [2] v, 8 ; vi, 7 ; ix, 9 ; x, 9 ; xi, 8.
[3] **XXXVI**, 205–6.   [4] *Cf.* pp. 54–5, on such predictions.
[5] 2 Kings ix–x ; *cf.* **LVII**, 444–5, 491.

that the sentence was being carried out : he saw the bloodshed at those palace revolts which followed the assassination of Zechariah, son of Jeroboam II, and knew of the appeal which the short-lived usurpers made to the King of Assyria and of the support paid for with huge sums of tribute money (v, 13) ; perhaps he may have witnessed the conflict with Judah which, in 734, gave Tiglath-pileser an opportunity to dismember the Northern kingdom : Hosea already uses the name Ephraim instead of Israel.[1] It is even possible that the prophet was a spectator of his namesake's efforts, when the last King of Samaria attempted to resist Assyria with the help of Egypt.[2]

But though Hosea's prophecy of a catastrophe which was becoming increasingly easy to foresee, agrees with that of Amos, the motive he gives for the punishment to be meted out by God is very different. It was social injustice which chiefly called forth censure from Amos ; Hosea's chief quarrel is with what he calls the nation's harlotry, that is to say its infidelity to its God.

Amos imagines Jahweh as the supreme judge of all the nations of the world, applying to all impartially the universal law of righteousness ; he relaxed, as it were, the bonds between Israel and the God of the Universe. For Hosea, the relations between Jahweh and his people are of the closest conceivable kind. He loves to compare them to those of a father with his children,[3] or, better still, to those of a husband with his wife. In this respect Hosea at first seems to share the popular religious views of his time to a far greater extent than Amos did ; universal monotheism means nothing to him : Jahweh appears to him only as the God of Israel. The figures of speech which he uses are precisely those which the ancient Israelites, and the Semites in general, used to describe their relations with their national gods : they called them their father, their mother, their kinsmen.[4] As to the idea of a conjugal relation between the god and his worshippers, the prevalence of temple prostitution is a sufficient indication of the frequency with which it occurred in the agricultural religions of the Semites.

But while the Gentile nations and also the Israelites who

---

[1] Cf. **XXXVI**, 213.

[2] vii, 11, 16 ; xii, 2.

[3] i ; ii, 4, 6 ; xi, 1, 3–4.

[4] **LVII**, 278–280.

were contemporaries of Hosea, gave to these relations of father and son, or of husband and wife, a material interpretation of varying degrees of literalness, the prophet looks upon them as the symbol of those bonds of holy love which should unite God and his people. When he calls Israel the son of Jahweh it is because Jahweh loves Israel as a father loves his child (xi, 1, 3–4). When Jahweh speaks of the land of Israel as his wife (ii, 3), it is because he feels for the nation which dwells therein the same deep, tender, and pure affection as the bride-groom feels for the bride (ii, 21–2 ; xiv, 5). And he expects from her the obedience, the complete trustfulness of a faithful wife, and also—these expressions are new to the religious language of the Semites—the gift of the heart, love (vii, 14). According to Amos, it is righteousness that Jahweh above all requires instead of sacrifice (v, 21–4). Hosea expresses a similar thought, but with a characteristic alteration :—

" I desire *hèsèd*, and not sacrifice, and the knowledge of God more than burnt-offerings " (vi, 6).

According to Hosea, Jahweh's demands are summed up in the word *hèsèd*, a very comprehensive word, which, for want of an adequate equivalent, we are obliged to translate, now by piety, now by mercy, love, or grace : it corresponded fairly closely to the Latin *pietas*, meaning not only the feeling of a faithful believer towards God, or of a son towards his father (filial piety), but also the feeling of God or of a leader towards his subordinates, and, in a general way, the natural feeling which prompts a man, apart from the constraint of law, to be kind and indulgent towards the members of his family or tribe.[1] According to Hosea, the " knowledge of God ", by which he means the knowledge of God's will, can never be attained without this *hèsèd*. Amos had *widened* the national religion of his people until, in principle, it embraced all peoples. Hosea *deepened* it, by making it consist solely of an interchange of love between the nation and its God. With a greater aptitude than Amos had for probing to the heart of things, he is not contented with external rules of conduct, he must search out the secret feelings by which actions are prompted.[2]

If Hosea shows himself less sensitive to social injustice

[1] *Cf. hsiâo* in the doctrine of Confucius, see **LXXXV**, 44, 46.
[2] *Cf.* **LXVII**, 207.

than Amos, it may be because he was not a member of the
poorer classes as Amos was : it has been thought, but without
any very convincing proof, that he was a priest,[1] or a well-
to-do peasant.[2] But the difference in the attitude of the two
men was doubtless chiefly due to diversity of temperament.
Amos is above all the voice of conscience : unflinchingly
he draws the last consequences of the demands of righteousness. Hosea's nature is sensitive, ardent, passionate : he
naturally approaches religion by the avenues of emotion and
of mysticism.

Another of the factors which contributed to the originality
of his thought may perhaps be sought in those unhappy
episodes of his private life which are related at the beginning
of the book, and whose meaning is unfortunately somewhat
enigmatic (ch. i and iii). The gist would seem to be as follows :
At the beginning of his career Hosea felt irresistibly drawn to
a woman of easy virtue, a " wife of whoredom ", as the first
chapter bluntly states, a " woman beloved of her friend ",
as chapter iii explains. He married her. Perhaps it was
only after the event that his passion, by reason of its very
ardour, seemed to him to have been inspired by Jahweh ;
as is well known, the ancients attributed all violent
sentiments, especially when they plunged a man into misfortune, to the intervention of some *Elohim*.[3] It seems, however, more probable from the text that he conscientiously,
and from the very beginning, looked upon his marriage with
this woman of depraved instincts as part of his vocation
as a prophet, who should show forth by his actions and by
the events of his life, what it is that the God by whom he is
inspired desires and feels. He heard the voice of Jahweh
saying to him :

> " Go, take unto thee a wife of whoredom and children of
> whoredom ; for the land doth commit great whoredom, departing
> from the Lord " (i, 2).
> " Go, love a woman beloved of her friend . . . even as the Lord
> loveth the children of Israel, though they turn unto other
> gods " (iii, 1).

Gomer (such was the name of the bride in chapter i)
bore three children. But as early as the birth of the second,

---

[1] Duhm, according to ix, 8.
[2] **CXLVI**, 125 ; *cf.* **XXXVI**, 207–8.
[3] **LVII**, 534, 544, 551.

Hosea seems to have realized that his wife was unfaithful
to him, and that these children were not his : he called them
" Not-beloved " and " Not my people ", for Jahweh also
had ceased to love the house of Israel and to recognize it as
his people. Thus in his bitter personal experiences the
prophet saw a sign from heaven : Jahweh was seeking to
reveal to him through such experiences what he himself
felt when his holy love was despised and made light of by an
unfaithful nation.

This domestic tragedy of which Hosea's home was the
scene has been interpreted by some as a mere allegory
invented by the prophet.[1] But the tale includes circumstantial details which it has not been found possible to explain
figuratively, as, for instance, the name of the wife and that
of her father, and the price paid for her by the prophet.
Moreover, it is hard to see what impression such a tale, if
it had been imaginary, could have made on those who first
heard Hosea, and were well acquainted with the facts :—

" He would have made himself ridiculous if he had spoken of
himself as the hero of a story of adultery, when in reality his home
was a happy one." [2]

According to other explanations Hosea did, indeed,
believe himself to have taken part in the scenes he recounts,
but he did so only in a vision,[3] or else in a state bordering
upon ecstasy.[4] There is nothing in the text to support
these conjectures.

It seems to us much more likely that the strange events
related at the beginning of the book did in reality take place.
The methods of psychoanalysis, too often abused, but which
it seems natural enough to apply in Hosea's case, may help
us to arrive at a better explanation, both of this particular
incident and of the prophet's general attitude of mind.
These are the methods recently used by Allwohn.[5] This
scholar is of the opinion that the future prophet was
temperamentally sex-obsessed, but that, for this very reason,

[1] e.g. Calvin, Hitzig, Edouard Reuss, Van Hoonacker (*Les Douze
Petits Prophètes*, Paris, Gabalda, 1908, p. 40), Gressmann (**XXVIII**,
ii, 1), Day (**AJSL**, 26, pp. 105–6), C. H. Toy (**JBL**, 32, 1913).
[2] Paul Humbert, **RHR,** lxxvii (1918), 158.
[3] Jerome, Hengstenberg, Keil.   [4] König.
[5] **XCVII.** See also W. O. E. Oesterley and Theodore H. Robinson,
An Introduction to the Books of the O.T., S.P.C.K., 1934, pp. 351–2.

he was more impressed than others were by the austerity demanded by Jahweh, the God of the nomads. Hence a lack of mental balance which may have predisposed him to states of ecstasy. But these unconscious tendencies when sternly repressed, erupted all the more violently ; hence the crisis related at the beginning of the book ; the particular form which it took was due to Hosea's consciousness that he was a prophet, and therefore united to Jahweh in the closest possible way, reflecting in his life the thoughts of his God. In this way it would be possible to explain psychologically his mental preoccupation with the concepts of marriage and prostitution, although, imbued as he was with the high moral ideals which had inspired Amos, he himself sees in these concepts nothing but the *figures of speech* illustrating an essentially *spiritual* tale.

Be that as it may, Israel, according to Hosea, ought to bring to Jahweh, in return for his divine love, the offering of an undivided love, of absolute obedience and trust. Now this ideal had only been realized to some extent during the short period of the nation's youth, when it came out from Egypt.[1] In any case, since the day when it set foot in the land of Baal there had been nothing but ingratitude, infidelity, prostitution (ix, 10 ; xi, 1–2 ; xiii, 1).

When he reviews the past and present conduct of his people he finds three capital crimes, three misdeeds which more than any others move him to wrath. First, there is the resort to arms and to alliances. Israel goes begging for help from Egypt and Assyria, and forgets to turn to Jahweh, who longs to save his people (vii, 8–13 ; viii, 8–9). War-horses, fortified towns, all the military equipment on which the nation relies, are so many insults to the God who is capable of delivering them without any of these aids (viii, 14 ; x, 13 ; xiv, 4 ; *cf.* ii, 20). By thus setting up an antinomy between the employment of human means and the resort to divine help, Hosea broke away from the old conception, according to which Jahweh manifested his co-operation chiefly in the strength, the number, and the courage of the heroes of Israel, and in the efficacy of their sword-thrusts [2] ; by his condemnation of material weapons in the name of spiritual weapons,

---

[1] ii, 17. The authenticity is contested.
[2] Judges v, 2, 14, 15, 18 ; xiv, 19 ; xv, 14, 18 ; etc.

omnipotent and irresistible, he laid down a new principle, one whose intrepid idealism seems to most people, even to-day, to go beyond the limits of what is practicable if the existence of the state is not to be jeopardized.

The institution of the kingship furnishes Hosea with another proof of the spirit of infidelity which is leading his people astray. It has been asserted, and the assertion is founded partly on the passages in which the return of Israel to David is foretold, that Hosea was simply condemning the illegitimate dynasties of the northern kingdom. Some of his attacks might be directed solely against individual rulers of his time, it is true (vii, 3–7). But passages such as iii, 3–5, and xiii, 9–11, seem to us to be clearly aimed at the institution of monarchy itself : in the first we read that the nation will only cease from " playing the harlot " when it is without a king as well as without an ephod and without teraphim. In the second, the choice is between a king and Jahweh ; and there is no question here of an unlawful king, but of one appointed by Jahweh : Hosea is thinking of Saul. The passages ix, 15 ; x, 3, 9, and perhaps viii, 4,[1] are probably also to be read as implying a protest against the principle of monarchy. Here, again, Hosea is in complete opposition to the ancient Israelite conception, which, since the foundation of the national monarchy, had acclaimed the institution as one of Jahweh's most beneficent acts.[2] It was not because Hosea was in any sense a logical believer in the return to nomadic life [3] that he adopted this uncompromising attitude towards the Anointed of the Lord, but doubtless chiefly because he saw in the monarchy one of those human means of salvation which seemed to him to exclude the possibility of trust in God : the king, invested by the Israelites, like all Orientals, with a halo of divinity,[4] must have seemed to him a rival to Jahweh.

And besides, since its very beginnings, royalty was the embodiment of the political and military greatness of the state, it had not striven to forge bonds of love between the nation and its God. This being the case, it is more than

---

[1] **LXXXII**, i, 223.
[2] *Cf.* **LVII**, 410, 413, 477.
[3] See pp. 64–5.
[4] **LVII**, 456–9 ; *cf.* pp. 135–7, 351–2 ; **CXLIX**.

probable that those passages which foretell Israel's return
to the rule of David were interpolated later, as many of the
passages relative to Judah obviously were.

But in Hosea's eyes it is above all with regard to worship
that Israel is inclined to go a-whoring after strange gods.
He accuses the nation of having forsaken Jahweh to worship
the Baals (ch. ii), and of having turned to other gods. Hosea's
chief quarrel is with the worship offered by Israel *to Jahweh* ;
his anger is directed against the high-places of Gilgal and
Bethel, where they swear " As the Lord liveth " (iv, 15) ;
and one of the most melancholy results of the deportation
into Assyria will be that the Israelites will no longer be able
to bring burnt-offerings and oblations *to Jahweh*, nor offer
their bread in the house *of Jahweh*, nor celebrate the feasts
of Jahweh.[1]

But to the prophet this worship is meaningless. The
bull-image which represents Jahweh at Bethel and in
Samaria, and which he disdainfully calls a calf, is merely
the work of a goldsmith, a piece of craftsmanship which
will be broken up : it is not God. If it is anything it is
a false god (xiii, 1–2) ; as far as we know, Hosea was the first
of the Israelites to condemn images of Jahweh as a matter
of principle. The sacred trees are nothing but a pleasant
shade (iv, 12–13) ; the meals which accompanied the sacrifices
are only so many opportunities for eating meat (viii, 13) ;
the sabbaths and the new moons are feasts of Baal (ii, 13).

Concise as he always is, Hosea never gives the precise
reasons for the attacks which he launches against the principal
religious observances of his time. It is very likely that he
repudiates some of them, such as temple prostitution
(iv, 13–14), ritual tattooing,[2] the orgiastic nature of the
ceremonial, perhaps also the worship of images, because he
knew them to be borrowed from Canaanitish cults : he saw
that the worship offered up to Jahweh by the Israelites in the
high places of Palestine was in reality merely the continuation
of that which the former inhabitants of the land had offered up
to false gods in the same sanctuaries ; and the historian
can but admire the perspicacity of his judgment in spite

---

[1] ix, 3–5 ; *cf.* viii, 13 ; v, 6.
[2] vii, 14, where the correct reading, as in several MSS., is *yithgôdâdu*.

of the exaggerated terms [1] in which it is expressed. Hosea certainly also reproached his contemporaries with the lovelessness of their worship, which was therefore worship devoid of the real " knowledge of God ", since the one object of the priests was to exploit the worshipper, and the latter only desired to obtain corn and wine (iv, 6–8 ; vii, 14). But there would seem to be still more than this in Hosea's censure : like Amos, he apparently took exception to the fundamental institution of all the ancient cults, the institution of sacrifice (iii, 3–4). It is a crime in Jahweh's eyes that Israel has *multiplied its altars* and made goodly pillars (x, 1) ; to seek the Lord with sheep and bulls is the way not to find him (v, 6). Jahweh's declaration " I desire *ḥesed* and not sacrifice " must therefore, it seems, be taken literally (vi, 6). In Hosea's mind there was apparently a fundamental incompatibility between the time-honoured ritual, all more or less tainted with self-interest or magic, and the heartfelt love which he considers the essence of religion.

What is to happen in the future, according to Hosea, to the relation between Israel and Jahweh ? The answer to this question varies according to the way in which chapter iii is interpreted. Here is what he says :—

> And the Lord said unto me, Go yet, love a woman beloved of her friend and an adulteress, even as the Lord loveth the children of Israel, though they turn unto other gods. . . . So I bought her to me for fifteen pieces of silver, and an homer of barley, and an half-homer of barley : and I said unto her : Thou shalt abide for me many days : thou shalt not play the harlot . . . For the children of Israel shall abide many days without king, and without prince, and without sacrifice, etc.

According to the explanation now most generally accepted,[2] the woman mentioned here is the same as the wretched heroine of chapter i, and the events related in chapter iii took place after those related in chapter i. After her excesses Gomer left Hosea's house ; having married again, or, as some think, having become a victim of slavery, she was

---

[1] *Cf.* **LVII,** 465–477.
[2] See, for example, Karl Budde, *Der Abschnitt Hosea,* 1-3 (**TSK,** 1925), Hermann Gunkel (**XXVIII,** ii, 2, *Einl.,* xxi), Wheeler Robinson, *The Marriage of Hosea* (Baptist Quarterly, N.S., v, 304–313), A. Allwohn (**XCVII**).

bought back by the prophet, who took her into his home once more, but not until she had been subjected to a severe test. And Hosea found in this new episode of his private life an omen of the future which awaited the guilty nation : Jahweh, whose love has been outraged, will in the end send the nation away. But—such is the depth and richness of his conception of divine love—he knows, as surely as he knows that he loves his own wife in spite of her treachery, that God will receive the faithless spouse back again into favour. And Jahweh will be able to restore the fallen nation without violence to the claims of his righteousness, for when driven into the desert his people's conduct will be radically changed, and their errors forsaken (ii, 16–25 ; v, 15–vi, 3).

The above interpretation is very tempting, for it falls admirably into line with the prophet's thought as a whole ; nevertheless, it is open to serious objections. If the woman whom, according to chapter iii, Hosea is to marry, is none other than Gomer, why does she present herself to his mind as an unknown woman : " Love a woman." Why does the text run " I bought her ", not " I bought her back ", as if Hosea was negotiating his marriage to her for the first time ? And why should the prophet have to pay to get her back ? A husband who took his wife back did not have to pay *mohar* a second time (Judges xix, 2–4 ; 2 Sam. iii, 14). If, as has been supposed, Gomer had in the meantime been repudiated by Hosea, and had then found another husband or had been sold as a slave by her parents, the tale would have been worth the telling, if only for the sake of clearness, and all the more so that remarriage between divorced persons was forbidden, at least by Jewish law in the seventh century (Deut. xxiv, 1–4 ; Jer. iii, 1), as well as by Babylonian civil law.[1]

According to another hypothesis,[2] only the narrative in the first chapter is historical ; that in chapter iii is an allegory. Some adherents of this view [3] deny the authenticity of the second passage on the ground of the discrepancies between the two accounts. These conclusions hardly seem probable ; the version given in chapter iii, which is autobiographical,

---

[1] S. A. Cook, *The Law of Moses and the Code of Hammurabi*, London, Black, 1903, p. 124.

[2] Staerk, Hölscher, Paul Humbert, Guthe, Volz, Marti.

[3] Volz, Marti, Hölscher (**XXXVI**, 426–9).

is more likely to be authentic and historical than that given in chapter i, in which the prophet is spoken of in the third person.

According to many ancient,[1] and some modern,[2] scholars, two different women are referred to, both of whom Hosea married successively and both of whom were equally disreputable. This theory would scarcely fit in with the symbolic meaning attributed to events by the prophet, for in each case the relations of Jahweh with one and the same spouse, the nation of Israel, are symbolized.

But another interpretation is possible [3] : chapters i and iii may be two parallel and independent accounts of a single event, namely, the marriage of Hosea with Gomer. But they are by two different hands, the second alone being the prophet's version. This would explain why the woman in chapter iii is nameless : Hosea saw no purpose in mentioning her name. It would, then, become clear why he said " I bought her ", not " I bought her back ". It is true that the tale as told in chapter iii might be taken as alluding to a former marriage of Hosea, since we read : " And the Lord said unto me, Go *yet*, love a women beloved of her friend and *an adulteress*." But it is quite conceivable that the word *yet* and even the description *adulteress* may have been added by the compiler after collating the two versions. According to Lindblom, one of the most recent critics to favour this interpretation, chapter iii only recounts the beginnings of Hosea's relations with Gomer ; chapter i relates them in a few words (i, 2, 3a), but only emphasizes the subsequent incidents of this unhappy union. The test to which reference is made would then have been imposed by Hosea before his marriage with Gomer, in the hope that such a time of retirement would lead her to amend her ways once for all, a hope that was to be cruelly disappointed.[4] Having reconstructed in this way the sequence of events,

---

[1] Jerome, Dom Calmet.

[2] Vigouroux, Crampon, Fr. Buzy, Duhm, Heermann, Seesemann.

[3] Supported, in somewhat varying forms, by Steuernagel, Caspari, Theodore H. Robinson, Rud. Kittel, Lucien Gautier (**XXIII**), Joh. Lindblom (**CXLVI**).

[4] Theodore H. Robinson, in an unpublished paper written for the *Society for O.T. Study* (1930), and afterwards in a memoir presented to the German Orientalist Congress at Bonn, in Aug.–Sept., 1934 (O.

Lindblom concludes that the parts of the book in which the prophet foretells the restoration of the nation's prosperity after a time of trial in the desert (ii, 16 *ff*. ; v, 15–vi, 3 ; xi, 8–9) must belong to the period during which he still had hopes of curing Gomer of her depraved propensities, while those which testify to his conviction that Israel was incorrigibly corrupt date from the time when he discovered his wife's infidelity. Hosea's optimism would then have been of short duration, and he would afterwards have plumbed the depths of a despair as absolute as that of Amos.

This hypothesis is also not without its difficulties.[1] The symbolic interpretation of events given by Hosea would be somewhat lame and incoherent, since he would first have seen in his marriage an omen of a *future* restoration of Israel after the exile (ch. iii), and then a parable of the state of the nation *at that time*, and of the imminent chastisement awaiting it (ch. i). It is true that these various interpretations are none of them improbable, and that they simply tend to show that the facts on which the prophet was meditating were real.

Whatever the truth of the matter may be, and even if Hosea's hopes for the betterment of Israel were only short-lived, he was the first to make a definite place for hope in the pattern of prophetic ideas, by giving it a moral basis, the love of Jahweh and the repentance of the nation. The fact that the more consoling of his utterances were included in the final collection of his prophecies perhaps suggests that they express his last thoughts, and that if in the darkest moments of his life he abandoned them, he came back to them in the end.

Eissfeldt, **TB**, 13 (1934), 10, col. 282), and also in his *Introd. to the Books of the O.T.*, p. 350, has put forward the theory that this time of retreat was demanded by custom, Gomer having been a *sacred* prostitute, a *qedēśah* : it was necessary to deconsecrate her before it was safe to marry her. It is a plausible conjecture ; nevertheless, no such intention appears in Hosea's words.

[1] See K. Budde's criticism, **TB**, 13 (1924), 12, col. 337–342.

CHAPTER III

THE PROPHETIC MOVEMENT IN THE KINGDOM OF JUDAH IN THE EIGHTH CENTURY

I

ISAIAH

1. *The Career of the Prophet.*—In the year that King Uzziah, also named Azariah, died,[1] and therefore not long after Amos had arisen in Israel and Hosea's career had begun, a man called Ješajahu [2] was in the temple at Jerusalem one day when he had a vision : he saw Jahweh, seated upon an immense throne, while the skirts of his robe filled the sanctuary. He heard the seraphim [3] crying :—

" Holy, holy, holy is the Lord of hosts, the whole earth is full of his glory."

Their voices were so mighty that the very foundations of the thresholds, where doubtless the seer was standing, were shaken. Believing, as all the ancients believed, that no mortal can see an Elohim and live, he cried :

" Woe is me, for I am undone ; because I am a man of unclean lips, and I dwell in the midst of a people of unclean lips : for mine eyes have seen the King, the Lord of Hosts."

But one of the seraphim took a live coal, with the tongs, from the altar and touched his lips with it. He then heard the Lord take counsel with the heavenly host :—

" Whom shall I send, and who will go for us ? "

Without hesitating, Isaiah offered himself as messenger :

" Here am I, send me."

Then Jahweh entrusted him with his mission :

" Go and tell this people, Hear ye indeed, but understand not ; and see ye indeed, but perceive not. Make the heart of this

---

[1] 740, according to some ; 735–734 according to **CLVI.**
[2] Transcribed in the Greek version '*Hσαία*, and in the Vulgate Isaias.
[3] See **LVII,** 275, 277, 284, 533.

people fat . . . lest they see with their eyes, and hear with their ears, and understand with their hearts, and turn again and be healed."

Isaiah, hoping that this was only a temporary sentence cried : " Lord, how long ? " This was his answer :—

" Until the land become utterly waste ; and, if there be yet a tenth of the inhabitants left in it, it shall again be given up to pasture." [1]

In this first vision there were presented to Isaiah's mind, in an objective and concrete form, some of the thoughts and tendencies which must have been taking shape slowly in the subconscious depths of his being. Whether that was the case or not, they were to inspire the whole of his activity as a prophet.

It is as a king that Jahweh appears to him ; and his sovereign majesty is, in fact, the divine attribute which chiefly appeals to Isaiah, and which he most eloquently extols. " The whole earth is full of his glory," cry the seraphim ; the God of Isaiah, like the God of Amos, is, indeed, a universal God, whose rule extends to the uttermost parts of the earth.

On the other hand, the fact that Isaiah had this vision *in the Temple* indicates that he will not attack the cult, root and branch, as did Amos and Hosea. Certainly a native of Judah—for he looks upon the separation of the two kingdoms as the result of *Ephraim's desertion* (vii, 17)— and probably of Jerusalem—for he is fond of metaphors derived from city life [2]—he is convinced that Jahweh dwells in Zion.[3]

The objects and the beings which play a part in his vision are, although more or less transfigured, those which he had seen in the Temple, such as the altar and the tongs. There was in Jerusalem, probably in the Temple, a bronze image which, according to tradition, Moses had set up, and to which burnt-offerings were made (2 Kings xviii, 4) : it represented one of those winged serpents, *seraphim*, which the Israelites had met with of old in the desert : these were the supernatural prototypes of the figure which Isaiah saw

[1] Ch. vi. [2] *Cf.* **XXXVI**, 224–5.
[3] *Cf.* xxxi, 9.

and heard in his vision : they are half-human, for they have
hands, but they have not lost all signs of their animal origin :
they are naked, since they cover " their feet ", as the prophet
euphemistically says, with two of their wings. The ceremony
of expiration of which the seer finds himself the subject was
doubtless inspired by a rite actually practised in the Temple,
perhaps when it was desired to withhold from the fire [1]
any metal objects of special value : all that was done was to
touch them with a live coal taken from the altar.[2] All of which
shows that Isaiah had not the same aversion to ritual practices as Hosea seems to have felt.

On the other hand, it does seem as if these touches of ritual
were for him the symbols of moral realities. The uncleanness
of which the seer feels himself guilty, and of which he accuses
the nation, is an uncleanness *of the lips*, that is to say of
speech, and consequently of the thoughts and feelings which
speech can express. And this is an indication of the important
place which morality is to occupy in his thoughts.

The firm and decisive way in which Isaiah himself offers
his services, in strong contrast with the fears and hesitations
of Jeremiah, Moses, and Gideon, and the passivity of Ezekiel,
has been cited as characteristic of the man of rank, who is not
unduly alarmed by the tasks entrusted to him by his king,
however momentous and dangerous they may be. It is,
indeed, quite likely that Isaiah was, as Richard Simon says,[3]
a " man of quality ", as is to be inferred, not so much from
the nobility of his style,[4] or from the ease of his relations with
the great, as from his aristocratic horror of any upheaval in
the existing order of society : that the " base " should attack
the " honourable " constitutes for him one of the great
calamities which are to overtake the nation (iii, 5).

But the most striking feature of the vision is the tragic
severity of the message with which the prophet is entrusted.
He is to call upon the nation to return to the Lord, who alone
is able to save it, but all the time he knows that the nation
will not be converted—even that Jahweh does not want it to
be converted, as the ancient mentality, unable to distinguish

[1] According to the law codified in Numbers xxxi, 21–3.
[2] *Cf.* Hans Schmidt, **XXVIII**, ii, 2³, p. 30.
[3] *Histoire Critique du Vieux Testament,* ed. 1685, p. 21.
[4] Jerome, Richard Simon.

between what God wills and what he permits, would
inevitably conclude. Isaiah, therefore, feels himself called
to proclaim the imminent ruin of all Jahweh's people,
including Judah, just as Amos and Hosea, at about this
time, were foretelling more especially the overthrow
of Israel. And it is this certainty which impels him to
prophesy.

Did Isaiah think from the beginning that his people was
not to be entirely wiped out, and that of the tenth which was
left a minority would return to the paths of righteousness ?
This is what one might think from the final sentence of this
inaugural vision in the Massoretic text ; but it is very obscure,
has certainly been altered, and is absent from the Greek
version, so that it is open to the suspicion of having been
added later.

Whether or no this conviction was his from the start, it
was brought home to him very early in his career ; for,
evidently acting on a revelation from God, he gave a son who
was born to him the name Shear-jashub, " a remnant shall
return (to God) " (vii, 3).

The chief originality of Isaiah must be sought, not in the
domain of thought, or of the inner life, but in the realm
of practical actualities. While Amos and Hosea could foresee
no possibility other than the wholesale condemnation of the
nation, or—when some slight improvement made itself felt—
its wholesale conversion, Isaiah endeavoured to group around
him a band of disciples [1]—an attempt in which as early as
734 he had been successful—thus creating the nucleus of
that " converted remnant ", which, according to him, was
to survive the approaching cataclysm. In so doing he initiated
the religious emancipation of the individual, whose destiny
no longer coincided entirely with that of the group,[2] and
prepared the way for the replacement of the nation by a
church, as the chief concern of religion.

On the other hand, while Amos declared that in wrath
Jahweh would henceforth refuse to counsel his apostate
people (viii, 11–12), Isaiah, like the *nebî'îm* of old, frequently
intervened in public affairs in order to deliver most precise
commands from his God, and sometimes he succeeded in

---

[1] viii, 2–3 and perhaps 16.
[2] *Cf.* **XXXVI**, 252.

bringing about the adoption of the practical measures he recommended.

The first occasion was when Pekah, King of Israel, and Rezin, King of Damascus, declared war on Israel.[1] Ahaz, the young ruler of the land, and his advisers were about to appeal for help to Tiglath Pileser, King of Assyria, as their only means of salvation. One day, when Ahaz was at the end of the conduit leading to the upper pool,[2] supervising the supply of water to the town in view of the imminent siege, Isaiah appeared before him with his son Shear-jashub, and said to him :—

> " Take heed and be quiet ; fear not, neither let thine heart be faint because of these two tails of smoking firebrands " (by which he meant Rezin and Pekah). " If ye will not believe, surely ye shall not be established " (that is to say, if you do not put your trust in Jahweh alone).

To convince Ahaz the prophet urges him to demand a sign, to confirm the threats and the promises which he has just uttered. The king refuses, with the words : " I will not tempt the Lord." Isaiah, who sees in this pious language nothing but a proof of the king's incredulity, then declares : " The Lord himself shall give you a sign." Before the birth of a child, conceived at the moment at which the prophet is speaking, that is to say within nine months, Judah will be delivered from the dreaded aggressors ; and the child when it is born may be given the joyful name Immanuel, " God with us." [3] But before this same child shall have learnt to refuse the evil and choose the good, that is to say to make use of its reasoning powers, in two or three years in fact, the kingdom of Judah, invaded by these same Assyrians whom in his folly the king summons to his help, and by their enemies the Egyptians, shall become a wilderness covered with brambles and thorns, whose few inhabitants, obliged to revert to their pastoral life, shall live on curds and wild honey. Such, according to the explanation given by Isaiah himself (vii, 16),

---

[1] See p. 21-2.
[2] That is to say, the end of the conduit down the side of the hill which went from the Virgin's spring to Birket el Hamra ; see CL.
[3] According to an ingenious theory of Mowinckel (LXVI, ii, 306) this prediction was a threat and not a promise : by changing the ritualistic cry of triumph to one of distress the prophet meant the name to be interpreted " *May* God be with us ! " If that were the case, however, he would doubtless have indicated it explicitly.

and confirmed by the other prophecies uttered by him at the same period,[1] is the meaning of the celebrated passage, designedly enigmatic (vii, 14), in which the Jews of the last centuries before our era, and after them the Christians, thought they saw a prophecy of the virgin birth of the Messiah. In it there is no question of a virgin, and most probably not of a Messiah.[2] " Behold," it says, " a young woman is pregnant." The word used, *almah*, means a nubile woman, whether married or not : if the sign had consisted in the virginity of the mother, it would have been necessary, to have been rightly understood, to use the correct word, *bethulah* " virgin ".

> " Behold, the young woman is pregnant ; she bears a son ; and she will call him Immanuel. Curds and honey shall he eat, when he knoweth to refuse the evil and choose the good. For before the child shall know to refuse the evil and choose the good, the land [3] shall be forsaken," etc.

In a series of revelations at this period Isaiah repeats his message. He gave to a son born to him the name Maher-shalal-hash-baz, " speed to the spoil, haste to the prey."

> " For before the child shall have knowledge to cry, My father, and My mother, the riches of Damascus and the spoil of Samaria shall be carried away before the King of Assyria " (viii, 3–4).

He inscribed the four fateful words of this prophecy on a tablet, having the date recorded by two faithful witnesses, one of which was the chief priest of the Temple (viii, 1, 2). He foretold that, since the Judæans despised the waters of Shiloah that went softly—the conduit near which he had met the king, and which he took as a symbol of Jahweh's help— the Lord would command the great waters of the Euphrates to flood and lay waste the land, the great waters being the King of Assyria on whom they were counting to save them (viii, 5–10).

---

[1] xvii, 1–11 ; viii, 1–15.

[2] The Messianic interpretation is upheld, for instance, by H. Gressmann, *Urspr. der isr.-jüd. Eschatol.*, 267 ; but see **XXXVI**, 229.

[3] The text has " *the land whose two kings thou abhorrest* ". But in that case the plural would have been necessary, " the lands " (Israel and Aram). Chaps. vii and viii are full of explanatory glosses, generally accurate (vii, 1, 17b, 20 ; viii, 7aβ) ; this one is not. The cultivated lands *of Judah* are meant, which will lie fallow for want of inhabitants (vi, 12). *Cf.* K. Budde (**JBL**, lii, 1 (1933), 29) ; **LXVI**, ii, 306 ; **CLXIII**, *ad loc.*

Ahaz did not listen to the warnings of the prophet, doubtless congratulating himself on his wisdom in refusing to do so. And, in fact, the events which Isaiah foretold did not come to pass in every detail, in particular as regards the intervals of time which elapsed between them—this is, at least, a guarantee that they were accurately reported. Nevertheless, regarded as a whole, his prophecies were fulfilled to a remarkable extent : Damascus fell two years later (732) and ten years afterwards Samaria (722) ; the armies of Assyria and of Egypt came into conflict in Palestine in 720 and 701 ; Judah was laid waste by the Assyrians in 701, and its ruin was completed by their successors, the Babylonians, in 586.

As a result of the step taken by Ahaz, the King of Jerusalem, like the King of Samaria, became a vassal of the King of Asshur from 734. Henceforth Isaiah devoted all his efforts towards restraining the two kingdoms from revolting against their overlord, because the politicians of Judah and Israel were relying on their own strength or on the support of foreign allies for their deliverance, and not on Jahweh alone.

And so he foretold, probably at the time of the rebellion of Hoshea, the last king of Israel, that the enemy would swallow up the country (xviii, 1–6). About 720, or perhaps in 705,[1] he set Hezekiah, the son of Ahaz, who succeeded him, on his guard against Marduk Paliddin, the Chaldean prince of Babylon.[2] When the King of Ethiopia, who had lately become the ruler of Egypt, sent envoys to Jerusalem in the hope of involving Hezekiah in a general revolt of Western Asia against Sargon (713–711), Isaiah, this time by action and gesture instead of by word of mouth, prefigured the miserable fate in store for the populations of Egypt and Ethiopia [3] : by showing himself naked in the streets he symbolized the state to which the Ethiopian soldiers would be reduced when taken captive by the Assyrians. He may have succeeded in persuading the young King of Judah, but on the death of Sargon (705) there was no holding back the movement of revolt any longer. In vain Isaiah declared that the new ruler of Asshur would be more terrible than the last, and that the envoys of the

---

[1] See pp. 29–32.　　　[2] Is. xxxix ; 2 Kings xx, 12–19.
[3] Is. xx ; xviii, 1–6.

Philistines must be told that Judah will rely upon Jahweh alone (xiv, 28–32). Hezekiah put himself at the head of the coalition, and negotiated for help from Egypt. His policy met alternately with indignation and derision from the prophet, who could see in it nothing but madness and contempt for his God.[1] With unwearying insistence Isaiah foretold its fatal consequences : defeat, invasion, the capital wasted by siege to a mere shadow of its former self.[2] One day when the treasurer Shebna, a foreign upstart who was probably one of the leaders of the pro-Egyptian party, was supervising the building of a splendid sepulchre which was being made for him near Jerusalem, Isaiah appeared before him and warned him that his preparations were in vain, for he would die in exile (xxii, 15–18).

It was of no avail, for Hezekiah rebelled. The appalling disaster which he brought upon his country by so doing is well known : the capital escaped annihilation almost by a miracle.

What was the prophet's attitude during the struggle ? According to two of the texts used in the book of Kings, borne out by a good many passages in the book of Isaiah as it now stands, he supported Hezekiah's resistance during the siege.[3] Having predicted the discomfiture of those who were in favour of revolt against Assyria, Isaiah would seem, once the rebellion was an accomplished fact, to have promised that they should escape the consequences of their action. It is generally supposed that this change in his demeanour was caused by the signs of humiliation and repentance shown by the king and his subjects when misfortune overtook them [4] —and that he regarded the Jerusalem of his day as the truly converted " remnant " who alone, according to him, were to be saved.

Such an explanation, if correct, would, it must be admitted, imply a serious lapse in Isaiah's moral standards. If we study the prophet's attitude before, and more particularly after, the crisis, we cannot but conclude that it was

---

[1] xxx, 1–7a ; xxxi, 1–5 ; xxviii, 7–22.

[2] xxviii, 14–22 ; xxix, 1–6 ; xxx, 15–17.

[3] 2 Kings xix, 21–34 ; Is. xxxi, 8–9, etc.

[4] In the time of Jeremiah it was already admitted that Hezekiah and his people had offered supplication to Jahweh, and that he had repented him of the evil with which he had threatened them (Jer. xxvi, 19).

supremely unlikely that he should, under the stress of war, have allowed himself to be so completely deluded as to the real state of his people.

It has also been thought that the promises of victory over the Assyrians which he is said to have uttered, were in reality later additions, inspired by popular legend, which quickly transformed the events of 701, and that during the conflict he did not cease to threaten and admonish. This, too, is difficult to believe, for some of the threats against Assyria attributed to Isaiah bear his unmistakable impress, both in their style and in the ideas which they convey.

The best solution seems to be that during the blockade of the town, while he continued to interpret present calamity as the just punishment of the crimes of Judah, Isaiah nevertheless declared that the final overthrow was not yet, and that Assyria would be checked for a time, not because of the repentance of the citizens of Jerusalem—of that there is no mention in the texts—but solely that the pride of the conqueror might be brought low, because of broken faith and outrages against Jahweh, who will not surrender to the enemy the town in which he dwells. Ideas such as these would be in keeping with those which the prophet had more than once expressed.[1]

Whatever the truth of the matter may be, a scene related in the twenty-second chapter of Isaiah, verses 1–14, gives us an insight into the feelings of the prophet immediately after the retreat of the Assyrian army. They are not feelings of triumph, or of joy at the renewed prosperity of the nation. Jerusalem was giving itself up to delight: everyone was out of doors, everyone was feasting. But Isaiah only asked to be allowed to weep over the disasters of his people; for in his mind's eye he could already see a fresh and more grievous affliction, about to descend upon the guilty city. And the gladness all around him seemed to him as grimly ironic as the gaiety of those condemned to death, who say :—

" Let us eat and drink, for to-morrow we shall die ! " " And the Lord of hosts revealed himself in mine ears, Surely this iniquity shall not be purged from you till ye die " (xxii, 1–14).

The magnificent discourse with which, in its present

---

[1] *Cf.* **XLIX**, ii², 383–7.

state, the book of Isaiah begins, dates from the same period :
the prophet there states his belief that the people of Judah,
in spite of the chastisement of Jahweh, is incorrigibly corrupt,
a people of Gomorrah governed by rulers of Sodom (i, 2–17).

Thus, at the end of his career Isaiah finds that his efforts,
as he had foreseen in his first vision, have not roused his
people from their indifference and hardness of heart. It is
hard to believe that he could ever have identified these men
whose hands are " full of blood " with the " remnant that
shall be saved ", which, according to him, was to be the
nucleus of a new nation. This " remnant " was the group of
disciples whom he left behind him and from which the
prophetic party afterwards arose.

2. *The Personality of Isaiah.*—The outline we have just
given of the prophet's life will have shed light upon some
aspects of this great personality, especially his instinct for
immediate action and the astonishing accuracy of his political
judgment. It is only necessary to add a few touches to the
portrait.

In his language we find a vigour, even a starkness of
expression, a grandeur and vividness of imagery, combined
with a loftiness, an almost classical purity. By turns eloquent
and concise, his oracles, with their sharp outlines, come
nearer perhaps than anything else in ancient Hebrew literature to the idea of symmetry and logical sequence which
we have inherited from the Greeks.

We must, however, be on our guard against modernizing
him too much, against thinking of him merely as the eloquent
orator and far-seeing statesman. First and foremost he is
an ecstatic, retaining many of the features which distinguished so clearly the ancient Israelite *nabi* : he is subject
to ecstasy when the hand of the Lord is laid upon him
(viii, 11) ; he then has visions (ch. vi), hears " with his
ears " the voice of his God (xxviii, 19 ; v, 9 ; xxii, 14 ;
xxviii, 12), and utters words indistinctly.[1] When under
the spirit's influence he sometimes acts eccentrically,[2] he
sings or laments in public (v, 1–6) ; he gives his children
strange and ominous names (vii, 3, 14 ; viii, 3–4, 18). He

---

[1] His enemies deride him by imitating his stammerings in his fits
of glossolaly : *ṣaw laṣaw ṣaw laṣaw qaw laqaw qaw laqaw* (xxviii, 10).
[2] xx, 1–2.

is convinced that he is possessed of superhuman powers ;
for he offers Ahaz the choice of a sign from Sheol or from
heaven.[1] He sometimes fixes definite dates for the fulfilment
of his prophecies (vii, 16 ; viii, 4 ; xxix, 1). His forecasts,
so often correct, of the march of events, are inspired not
by his political acumen but by the demands of morality
and religion.

The ideas which Isaiah defends are to a great extent those
which Amos and Hosea had formulated before him. Like the
latter he condemns idolatry, and protests against foreign
alliances and the use of armed force, which seem to him a
proof of lack of faith in the power of God to help and succour ;
he inveighs against the ingratitude of the Israelites, whom
God has treated with a father's care.[2] More often still he
stands on common ground with Amos : for him, too, Jahweh
is the God whose will is identical with righteousness, who will
judge all nations by the same law, including both Judah and
Assyria, whose anger is directed particularly against social
injustice, and who condemns the practices of worship
when they are associated with crime (i, 10–17). His picture
of " the day of the Lord " is painted with the brush of Amos
(ii, 12–19). He also sees in present calamity a warning from
God.[3]

Nevertheless, Isaiah strikes a personal note of his own.
While Amos looked on the approaching overthrow of Israel
as the consequence of God's *righteousness*, and Hosea recognized in it God's righteous vengeance for despised *love*, Isaiah
regards it as above all the glorious manifestation of the
sovereign *greatness* of God : " Jahweh shall be exalted in
judgment." It is as if the prophet took delight in humiliating
and abasing human pride before the power of God.   His
favourite adjective when speaking of his God is *holy* : holiness,
in the Semitic languages, was synonymous with glory (vi, 3),
with awe-inspiring majesty ; in itself this term implied no idea
of morality : all that was divine, inaccessible, beyond man's
reach was holy.[4] The future evolution of the ideas attaching
to the term holiness was at most foreshadowed in Isaiah's
conception of righteousness [5] as constituting the supreme

---

[1] vii, 11 (read *še'olah*).   [2] i, 2–4 ; *cf.* v, 1–7.
[3] ix, 7–10, 4 ; v, 25b–29.   [4] *Cf.* **LVII,** 539–540.
[5] v, 16 ; *cf.* vi, 3, 5–7.

greatness of God, and that which more than anything else separates God from man.

Since in Isaiah's eyes Jahweh was a king (vi, 5), it is in the form of a rebellion that his mind most readily conceives the nation's sin. Israel is a rebellious people,[1] to whose pride is added ingratitude towards their lawful master (i, 2–4).

Isaiah sometimes defines the normal attitude which Jahweh is entitled to expect from the nation by a word which Christianity was to make extremely popular, namely, faith.

> " If ye will not believe, surely ye shall not be established " (vii, 9). " In quietness and in confidence shall be your strength." [2]

Trust in the Lord was also one of the characteristics of piety among the ancient Israelites.[3] If we want to understand how Isaiah's idea of faith differed from that, and if we would appreciate the depth of significance which the word held for him, we must not separate it from the synonyms which he sometimes either substituted for it or used in conjunction with it—" to hear " (that is, to obey) and " to be willing ".[4] Belief consists first in accepting and welcoming the divine decrees, and then, having loyally obeyed the all-powerful king, in trusting him implicitly, without recourse to force or to human skill : to do this is to testify to faith in a righteous will ruling over the world.

There is a final point to notice. Isaiah's views as to what lies beyond the approaching overthrow of the nation are less despairing than those of Amos, more definite and less visionary than those of Hosea : " A remnant shall return " (to Jahweh) and survive the disaster. It would seem from some passages that those who escape are expected to return to a pastoral manner of life, which was the ideal of the old reactionaries like Jonadab the son of Rechab (vii, 21–5). But in general, Isaiah looks to a reconstruction of the framework of the State and the survival of the capital, provided always that there is a complete change of heart in everyone :—

---

[1] xxviii, 12 ; xxx, 9, 16.
[2] xxx, 15 ; cf. i, 19 ; xxviii, 16.
[3] Cf. **LVII**, 534–9, 548.
[4] i, 19–20 ; xxx, 15.

" I will restore thy judges [1] as at the first, and thy counsellors as at the beginning : afterward thou shalt be called the city of righteousness, the faithful city." [2]

Isaiah even thought that Jahweh, whose home was in Zion, would protect his dwelling-place from the attacks of his presumptuous adversaries, thus emphasizing the dogma of the inviolability of the holy city, a dogma which was to have such dire consequences in the following century.

Perhaps Isaiah may have attributed special importance to the person of the king who was to usher in better times, and perhaps in his visions of the future he gave a place to the popular expectation of a Messiah,[3] a sovereign more or less divine (ix, 5), ruler of a powerful empire and harbinger of everlasting peace—always insisting on the essential justice and piety of such a ruler. Nevertheless, the authenticity of the two passages in which these brilliant prospects are foreshadowed are open to grave objections.[4]

To sum up, Isaiah, however close may be the underlying bond between him and Amos and Hosea, maintained a firmer contact with the traditional modes of thought and feeling than did either of his predecessors [5] : like the nebî'îm of old he took part in current politics, believed in the legitimacy of the house of David (vii, 17), the holiness of Jerusalem, the Temple, and the worship thereof. He counted on the continuance or the restoration of an organized State under a monarchy. By his insistent reminders of the awe-inspiring majesty of Jahweh, he ran counter to popular belief much less violently than Amos did in proclaiming that Jahweh's unbending justice would allow Israel no privileges. With Isaiah the great prophets are moving in the direction of a compromise with traditional religion, towards a traditional religion which shall be both more spiritual and more moral.

II

MICAH

In another prophet of Judah, however, in Micaiah (Micah), the uncompromising spirit of Amos is revived.

He was exactly contemporary with Isaiah. According to

---

[1] i.e. no doubt, " thy kings."   [2] i, 26 ; cf. 27.
[3] See p. 71.   [4] ix, 1–6, and ch. xi.   [5] Cf. XXXVI, 250–2.

the title of his book—added later, it is true—he prophesied
under the same kings. His prophecy against the Temple,
reported in ch. iii, 9–12, was uttered, according to the very
interesting testimony of the biographer of Jeremiah, in the
reign of Hezekiah, since he is said to have led this king to
fear the Lord, to pray to him, and to turn away his anger
(Jer. xxvi, 18–19). As Micah denounces Samaria, it is
generally supposed that the group of prophecies which make
up the first chapter in the book were pronounced before the
taking of the city by the Assyrians in 722.

Against this it must be remembered that the prophet
foretells that the blow which is to fall on Samaria will not
spare Jerusalem (i, 9 and 10–16). Now in 722, Judah, not
being allied to Israel, was not threatened by Assyria. It is
doubtless possible that Micah, like Isaiah in 734,[1] was thinking
that in the future, perhaps far distant, the fall of the northern
kingdom would have a disastrous effect on the fate of the
southern ; which would bear witness to the far-sightedness
of his political instinct. Nevertheless, such a threat against
the two capitals would be more easily visualized at a time
when Samaria and Jerusalem were united against Asshur,
that is to say, either in 705 or, more likely still, during the
insurrection in 720, in which, as we know, Samaria took
part [2] ; in 722 the town had in fact been taken by Sargon,
but had not been destroyed.

Whatever the facts may be, Micah paints the moral,
political, and religious condition of his country in the same
colours that Isaiah used : he speaks of the corruption of the
leaders of the people, the law-givers, the priests, and the
prophets, the greed and the harshness of the rich, coupled
with an irrational trust in Jahweh (iii, 10–11). With regard
to the inspired circle of prophets, Micah also furnishes an
interesting complement to the witness of his contemporaries
Isaiah, Amos, and Hosea. Traditional religion also had its
prophets, a numerous band, supported by custom and popular
esteem (ii, 11), while the prophets of misfortune, such as
Isaiah and Micah himself, aroused horrified protest :
" Prophesy ye not ! " " Reproaches shall not depart " (ii, 6).
Solitary they were, but endowed with the authority which is
conferred by absolute certainty of expressing the divine

---

[1] Is. vii–viii.   [2] See p. 29.

will, and by complete disinterestedness. Many of their opponents, on the contrary, uttered prophecies that were favourable or unfavourable according to whether they had been well or badly paid (iii, 5-8). Nevertheless, it is a remarkable fact that Micah, unlike the prophets of the seventh century, refrains from accusing his opponents of not having been sent by Jahweh. He recognizes them as really inspired, since the punishment which is to descend on them will consist in their *no longer* receiving revelations (iii, 6-7). His only contention is that they corrupt the divine communications to suit their personal interest.

On the other hand, Micah differs from Isaiah and is more akin to Amos, in that his grievances against the nation are not political nor concerned with ritual, but almost exclusively social in character. Micah is the most genuine representative of what might be called democratic tendencies among the prophets. According to him, the great spend their nights devising oppression, which they will put into effect next morning if they can (ii, 1-2). The leaders of the house of Israel devour the flesh of the people, flay the skin from the the humble, and break their bones (iii, 1-3). It is possible to be still more precise. Micah is above all the mouth-piece of the small folk of the countryside. He was from Moresheth : whether the name was a variant of Mareshah— now Khirbet Marash, to the south-west of Beit Djibrin-Eleutheropolis [1]—or, as is more probable, in spite of the uncertainty of the text, whether it was the name of a separate, unidentified hamlet near Gath,[2] the prophet was a native of the extreme south-west of the land of Judah, that is to say, of the coastal plain whose inhabitants were more sorely tried than any others by the Assyrians, who made war there in 734, 720, 711, and 701. This no doubt partly explains his anger against the politicians in Jerusalem, whose heedlessness and foolish intrigues were responsible for these calamities. In any case, he betrays his provincial origin by his way of regarding Jerusalem as the centre of evil, or, as he says, " the sin of Judah," just as in Samaria he sees " the transgression of Jacob " (i, 5). For him Zion is a town built with blood (iii, 10). And so in the name of the Lord he demands

[1] **XXXVI**, 254-5.
[2] i, 14, next to i, 15.

I

that this city be wiped out, and its Temple with it, because
of its mingled piety and wickedness :—

> " Therefore shall Zion for your sake be plowed as a field, and
> Jerusalem shall become heaps, and the mountain of the house as
> the high places of a forest " (iii, 12).

The difference is here clearly seen between this representative of the " devastated regions " and Isaiah, the
aristocrat of Jerusalem.

Did Micah, however, like his illustrious contemporary, see
any ray of hope beyond the approaching catastrophe, for
a converted remnant ? It has been maintained that he did.[1]
But the passages on which the assumption is based, and
which are taken chiefly from chapters iv and v of the book
of Micah are of doubtful authenticity.

III

HEZEKIAH'S REFORM

In his summary of the reign of Hezekiah, the compiler of
the book of Kings says :—

> " He removed the high places and break the pillars, and cut
> down the Asherah and brake in pieces (or melted) the brazen serpent
> that Moses had made ; for unto those days the children of Israel
> did burn incense to it ; and he called it Nehushtan." [2]

It is probable that this image of a serpent really
represented some Canaanitish god or spirit of healing, adopted
by the Hebrews when they had first settled in Palestine and
subordinated by them to Jahweh.[3] It is not known whether
this image had been transferred to the Temple,[4] as 2 Chron.
xxix, 16, might imply, or set up in a separate sanctuary,[5]
either in Jerusalem or in some other part of the country.
The destruction of this idol was not solely due to the influence
of the prophets, and it has been suggested that the King had
been induced to do away with it by the Old Jahwist party,
whose watchwords were the prohibition of all Canaanitish

---

[1] At the present time, for instance, by Hans Schmidt (**XXVIII,**
ii, 2², pp. 130, 147–154), who sees in Micah a faithful disciple of Isaiah.

[2] 2 Kings xviii, 4.

[3] Cf. **LVII,** 419, 498–9, 533, 587–8 ; cf. 124–5, 284.

[4] **LVII,** 498 ; **CXLI,** 279 ; **XXXVI,** 165.

[5] **LXVIII,** i, 393.

elements and the defence of Jahweh's exclusive rights to the worship of the Israelites.[1] Nevertheless, to explain Hezekiah's daring to attack a sacred object said to have been made by Moses himself, and to date from the days in the desert, it is necessary to take into account the influence, at least indirect, of those new prophets who were attacking all the religious institutions of the nation, even the most venerated, and who would not suffer any plastic representation of the divine. We have here, therefore, in all probability, evidence of an attempt, if only a tentative one, on the part of the prophets, to influence public authorities, and of a first effort on the part of those authorities to comply with their requests. And, in fact, Isaiah demanded, and foretold, the destruction of all gold and silver images (xxx, 22). If this theory is correct, the decree for the destruction of idols must have been proclaimed at one of the periods during Hezekiah's reign when he came under the influence of Isaiah and perhaps of Micah,[2] that is to say, when he was not actively engaged in anti-Assyrian policy as in 720, 713–711, 705–701. If Hezekiah's reforms are to be interpreted as a blow aimed at the religions of Assyria,[3] they would, on the contrary, have to be regarded as taking place at a time when the King was not being ruled by Assyria, that is to say, probably between 705 and 701, at which time he was in complete opposition to Isaiah.

As we have seen, the book of Kings also attributes to Isaiah measures of reform which were much more sweeping : the abolition of the high places, that is to say of all the sanctuaries of Jahweh except Jerusalem,[4] the destruction of raised stones, and of the sacred pole called an *asherah*. But it is probable that the Deuteronomic editor of this biography, in his enthusiastic admiration for Hezekiah, exaggerated his merits in this passage, and attributed to his attempted reforms the scope and influence which really belonged to those of his great-grandson Josiah.[5] We know, from a definite and

[1] **XXXVI**, 262.
[2] *Cf.* the traditions mentioned in Jer. xxvi, 18–19 ; 2 Kings xviii–xx.
[3] **LXVIII**, i, 392.   [4] Also 2 Kings xviii, 22 ; xxi, 3.
[5] This is the opinion of Wellhausen (**LXXXVII**, 255 ; *Prolegomena*, 5th ed., 26), Stade (**ZATW**, iii, 8*ff.* ; iv, 170 *ff.* ; **LXXXI**, i, 607), A. F. Puukko (**CLXIV**, 169 *ff.*), Otto Eissfeldt (**CXIII**, *ad loc.*), Gustav Hölscher (**XXXVI**, 165, 261), Hans Schmidt (**XXVIII**, ii, 2², pp. 9–10),

circumstantial account, that the latter introduced about 622 precisely the three measures described, while nothing in the text indicates that he had been in this respect forestalled by any of his predecessors : the king deplores the sins of his fathers without making any exception for any of them (2 Kings xxii, 13 ; *cf.* xxiii, 5) ; he destroys the high places built by Solomon, Ahaz, and the " kings of Judah ", but we are not told that these places of worship were destroyed by Hezekiah, or rebuilt by Manasseh (2 Kings xxiii, 12). It is, moreover, hard to believe that Hezekiah could have been more radical in his reforms than his contemporaries the prophets required him to be ; but neither Hosea, nor Isaiah, nor yet Micah, demanded the abolition of non-pictorial representations of divinity, such as the stelæ : it is the prophets of the seventh century who insist on this being done.

Since, however, it is plausible to suppose that the editor of Kings was enlarging on an event which had actually occurred, we may take it that Hezekiah anticipated in some way Josiah's reforms,[1] by abstaining, for instance, from rebuilding the provincial high places destroyed by the Assyrians in 701.[2] Such an attitude may have been suggested to him by the priests in Jerusalem, who, as was often the case in ancient times, considered as rivals the colleges of priests of other religious centres, and might quite sincerely regard the preservation of the only temple of the capital as a sign that God looked upon it with favour.

IV

THE SPREAD OF PROPHETIC IDEAS

Although the new prophets, Amos and Hosea, Isaiah and Micah, are essentially isolated figures, by the end of the eighth century their preaching was meeting with a good deal of response.   Isaiah had grouped around him a band of

Theodore H. Robinson (**LXVIII**, i, 392–3), Alfred Loisy (**LIX**, 199). The historicity of the abolition of the high places has, on the other hand, been upheld by Alexander Westphal (**XCI**, ii, 273–6, 285), Steuernagel (**CLXXXI**, 100), Rudolf Kittel (**CXLI**, 278–9), Arthur Robert Siebens (**CLXXVI**, 156, 170), Giuseppe Ricciotti (**LXXII**, 444, 473).

[1] **LXVIII**, i, 392.   [2] *Cf.* H. Schmidt (**XXVIII**, ii, 2², 155).

" disciples " (viii, 16). And as we have just seen, the King himself, Hezekiah, in his religious policy, probably took account of the suggestions of Isaiah and of Micah.

That the impression made on certain minds by some at least of the prophetic ideas was a profound one, may be seen from the literature of the period, which also makes it possible to give a certain number of details. The Jahwist and Elohist sections of the historical books include pages which were certainly written at the end of the eighth century, or during the first three-quarters of the seventh, with the intention of enriching, correcting, or interpreting ancient traditions in the light of prophetic principles.

To these belong, in the J source, the account of the intercession of Abraham on behalf of Sodom (Gen. xviii, 22b–33), a kind of philosophic dialogue which endeavours to solve a burning problem for the Judæans of the seventh and sixth centuries [1] : what will be the fate of the righteous in a guilty and condemned city ? The narrator is speaking of Sodom, but clearly thinking of Jerusalem. Will not Jahweh forgive the transgressions of the whole town for the sake of the few just men whom it contains ?

Pages of this kind are still more numerous in the E narrative : a new account of the institution of the elders is invented [2] : it is no longer said to be due to a suggestion made by Jethro to Moses, but is prescribed by Jahweh himself ; and the passage ends with this characteristic exclamation : " Would God that all the Lord's people were prophets ! "

In the scene where the covenant made by Joshua at Shechem is described (Jos. xxiv), we find once more the tragic seriousness with which the great prophets regarded the religious situation among their people, the almost impossible loftiness of the ideal which, according to them, Jahweh had set before those who believed on him (" Ye cannot serve the Lord ; for he is an holy God "), and the duty incumbent upon each individual of making a decision with regard to his moral and religious life, even if it should be contrary to his whole nation : " Choose you this day whom you will serve "—the gods of the land beyond the river or those of the Canaanites—

[1] Jer. v, 1 ; xxxi, 29–30 ; Ez. xiv, 12–23 ; xviii ; cf. Deut. vii, 10 ; Ex. xx, 5–6.
[2] Num. xi, 14–16–17–24b–30.

" but as for me and my house, we will serve the Lord." These
proud words, put into the mouth of Joshua, admirably express
what must have been the watchword of the disciples of the
prophets at the time of the great invasion of religions " from
beyond the Euphrates " in the reigns of Manasseh and Amon,
and during the minority of Josiah.

In short prefaces added to the accounts given of the
" Judges ",[1] an Elohist editor outlines a philosophy of the
history of this period which a subsequent editor of the
Deuteronomic school will only have to schematize and
generalize in order to set out the theory which everyone knows:
that mould with its four compartments into which he will fit
the refractory material of the old heroic tales of Israel's
turbulent youth : (1) the nation relapses into heathenism ;
(2) Jahweh sends conquerors to oppress it ; (3) the nation
repents ; (4) Jahweh raises up a saviour in the person of
a " judge ".[2]   It is the Elohist editor who is responsible
for this transformation of living history into a mechanical
morality.   It was, in fact, a rather broad application of
the ideas of the great prophets as to the absolute justice
of Jahweh, and the way in which he turned to account the
foreign invasions in order to chastise his people, a version
written with a view to popularizing the lesson they
contained.

An Elohist narrator composes a new version of the
institution of royalty which is violently hostile to the very
principle of monarchical government [3] : to demand a king
is to reject the sovereignty of God ; Jahweh ought to be the
only ruler of Israel, through the sole medium of those inspired
by him—as was the case, according to the narrator, in the
time of the judges.   We have here the development, in
narrative form, of the subversive political views at which the
prophet Hosea had arrived.[4]

Royalty is only to be tolerated if the sovereign obeys the
laws of God, the *toroth* which are conveyed to him by those
whom Jahweh inspires—such a ruler is Hezekiah, in his best

---

[1] Judges ii, 20, 21, 22, 23*b* ; iii, 1*a*, 3 ; ii, 13 ; parts of vi, 1–10,
and x, 6–16.
[2] Judges ii, 11*a* ; xii, 14–16, 18–19.
[3] 1 Sam. vii ; viii ; x, 17–25*a* ; xii ; xv.
[4] See pp. 93–4.

days, when he gives ear to the political advice of Isaiah : if he
does not do this, the man of God has the right to depose the
rebellious king and appoint his successor, and it is his duty
to do so—as Elisha and Elijah had done in the ninth century
when they substituted the house of Jehu for that of Omri.[1]
These pages show how convinced the group of prophets
already was that the power of the king was to be made use of
in order to realize an ideal which in their minds was
indistinguishable from the will of God himself.

This literature of prophetic inspiration which was
beginning to be written before 622 is seen at its best in the
decalogue, as it appears in Exodus (xx, 2–17) and in
Deuteronomy (v, 6–21), when it is pruned of the explanations
and commentaries which were certainly added later.[2]   It
had long been the custom in Israel to sum up in a list of ten
or twelve brief " words " the " law of Jahweh ",[3] that is to
say, the chief and most characteristic commands of the
national God, perhaps with a view to the admission of
foreigners to the ranks of the people of Jahweh (as, for
instance, the Canaanites who joined in their hundreds at the
beginning of the monarchical period [4]), when these formulæ
may have been recited by the converts.   Or perhaps they
formed part of the conditions of access to the temples and
were repeated by a priest in the course of certain ceremonies
of the cult.[5] The J source, and certainly the E narrative in its
first form (E [1]), each included one of these summaries of
Jahweh's commands : God himself was said to have communicated them to Moses on the holy mountain in the desert.[6]
These lists, like those used in various temples in ancient
Greece,[7] contained only such regulations and prohibitions
as concerned the *ritual* of the worship of a particular god,
and perhaps of a particular place sacred to this god.

---

[1] *Cf.* **LVII**, 408, 412–13.
[2] *Cf.* **LVII**, 365–6. In these pages we have summarized the reasons
which we consider to be definite proofs that the first decalogue was
composed in the seventh century.
[3] 2 Kings xvii, 26–7.   [4] K. Budde, **VI**, 96.
[5] Ps. xv ; xxiv, 3–6 ; cxviii, 20 ; Is. xxxiii, 14–17. *Cf.* S. Mowinckel,
CLVII, 141–155.
[6] Ex. xxxiv, 1–28, and xx, 19–21.
[7] e.g. the ritual of the Thasian Heracles, of which Chas. Picard
has made a study, **BCH,** 1923, pp. 241–273 ; *cf.* **RHR,** lxxxix (1924),
132–3.

One well versed in prophetic ideas, probably a priest, since the priests were the jurists of the time, recast these ancient summaries, preserving and developing certain elements, such as the commandments referring to monolatry, idols, and the day of rest, and rejecting all items having a direct bearing on sacrificial ritual, obviously because, according to the new prophets, who claimed to be the only authentic interpreters of the will of Jahweh, sacrifice was not essential to the worship of the God of Israel, if it had any place in it at all. On the contrary, he incorporated in the new version the teaching of his masters that the keynote of God's will for man was morality.

The " first decalogue " is unquestionably more deeply imbued with the spirit of the prophets than any of the codes which go to make up Jewish law, a fact which justifies the exceptional significance which the Deuteronomist school already attached to it (Deut. v), a significance which Judaism did not fail to recognize, and which the Christian church, with a sure instinct, has continued to acknowledge. The value of this summary of divine demands is in no way diminished by the fact that most of the commandments which it contains are to be found in Egyptian or Babylonian writings, in particular the declaration of innocence which the soul of a dead Egyptian was supposed to make to the gods, and in the inquiries of the Babylonian priest who sought to discover by what sin a victim of calamity had incurred his misfortune. For in these documents, moral failings are merged in a multitude of purely ritualistic or magical shortcomings, whereas the essential merit of the first decalogue is its realization that God's demands are essentially moral demands, and not its affirmation of the necessity for obeying the law, a necessity which all ancient religions had inculcated.

This does not mean that the first decalogue was a complete and adequate expression of the moral ideal of the great prophets.

In the first place, what God requires of the soul is a general attitude, to describe which they made use of such general terms as righteousness, piety, or faith. To adopt this attitude is man's supreme, indeed man's only duty. Now this obligation is entirely absent from the decalogue or is, at the most, broken up into a series of separate duties which could be observed without interrupting the even tenour of life.

Secondly, morality in the decalogue is presented in an almost exclusively negative form.

Thirdly, it partakes both of civil law, which can only condemn delinquents on the strength of their actions, and of moral law, which seeks to regulate motive : " Honour thy father and thy mother," " Thou shalt not covet." As far as the latter commandment is concerned, it must not be forgotten that, according to a conviction firmly established among many peoples, the mere fact of desiring to possess another's property, of casting envious eyes upon it—" the evil eye," as the Hebrew has it—even of praising it excessively, is of positive injury, for it attracts the jealousy of invisible powers :—

" He that blesseth his friend with a loud voice, rising early in the morning, it shall be accounted a curse to him." [1]

It is therefore comprehensible that a legislator of ancient times should have considered it a crime worthy of punishment. It is, nevertheless, more likely that if this commandment was based on some old statute the editor of the first decalogue interpreted it spiritually as a moral precept.

Fourthly, in the second commandment (against idolatry), and more particularly in the fourth (on the keeping of the Sabbath), the decalogue deals with the ritual element which the prophets had intentionally excluded from the number of God's requirements : Hosea and Isaiah placed the keeping of the Sabbath on the same level as the other religious observances.[2]

Thus the first decalogue, however lofty its inspiration may be, already contains a hint, as yet hardly perceptible, of the impoverishment of the prophetic ideal which must necessarily attend any attempt to translate into laws the divine will.

It is evident from these writings that a group of believers in the prophetic message was in process of formation, but that, under the influence of their surroundings, the teaching of the pioneers tended to become less spiritual and more accessible to the masses.

[1] Prov. xxvii, 14. *Cf.* the African saying quoted by A. Causse, **CVIII**, 117, note 3.　　[2] Hos. ii, 13 ; Is. i, 13.

CHAPTER IV

RELIGIOUS LIFE IN THE KINGDOM OF JUDAH IN THE SEVENTH CENTURY

I

PERIOD OF SYNCRETISM. REIGNS OF MANASSEH AND AMON. JOSIAH'S MINORITY

THE events of 701 made an impression on the mass of the population that was both deep and immediate. The Assyrians had ravaged the countryside ; Sennacherib had levied tribute grievous to be borne ; yet both these things were forgotten in the joy of watching the hurried departure of the besieging army decimated by plague, or, in other words, by the angel of Jahweh himself. It was this unhoped-for deliverance which invested the Temple with that unparalleled religious prestige which it had hitherto lacked, and which paved the way for the concentration of all worship in this one sanctuary. The town of Jerusalem also reaped from this event the reputation, which was to belong to it henceforth, of being the holy city, strong in the strength of its God, who would never allow it to be taken : when in 586 Jerusalem was besieged by the Babylonians, King Zedekiah asked Jeremiah if Jahweh would not again perform one of his miracles for his chosen people, and compel Nebuchadnezzar to raise the siege.[1] Another result of the check experienced by the Assyrians was to increase Judah's confidence in its national God. It is, moreover, very probable that it was national Jahwism, in the narrow traditional sense, that benefited from the reawakened fervour, and not, as has often been said, the severe moral teaching of the great prophets ; so at least the indignant denunciation of his people in the last prophecies of Isaiah would seem to imply.

This strengthening of belief in Jahweh did not last long.

---

[1] Jer. xxi, 2.

122

PLATE IV

[face p. 122

Banquet of Asshurbanipal and his Queen. Bas-relief in the British Museum

With the accession of Manasseh to the throne, a long period
of reaction set in,[1] which persisted for nearly three-quarters
of a century, and threatened not only to wreck the prophetic
movement, but also to distort the essential features of the
religion of Jahweh, even in its popular form. The book of
Kings might lead one to infer that this reaction was the result
of measures introduced by the king on his own initiative.
In reality these measures must have been primarily the
expression of a religious crisis which shook the nation to its
very foundations ; in which case Jeremiah and the author of
the book of Kings [2] were justified in their view that the king
had the support of the entire nation.

The inhabitants of Jerusalem who were saved from
disaster in 701 thought, no doubt, that Jahweh would soon
vouchsafe a final and supreme proof of his omnipotence by
breaking the yoke of Assyria once and for all. But this empire,
far from declining, attained under Esarhaddon (681–688)
and Asshurbanipal (668–626) a degree of power which it had
never known before. Judah's one hope of survival lay in
accepting the part of humble vassal to the master of the
world.[3]

How were the Israelites to account for such a state of
abasement ? Some, true to the explanation of misfortune
most usual in ancient times, thought that the national God
was angry with his people ; but when they found that the
means hitherto employed to appease Jahweh, such as
hecatombs of rams and " ten thousands of rivers of oil ",[4]
had no result, they persuaded themselves that some more
effectual appeal to divinity must be devised. Offerings of
sweet-smelling substances were, if not introduced, at least[5]
developed as a feature of the worship of Jahweh at this time ;
the use of incense is attacked for the first time by Jeremiah.[6]
To this method of reasoning must be attributed the alarming
rate at which, according to the unanimous testimony of the
writers of the time,[7] the custom of sacrificing children spread
throughout the land. The expression used in several passages

[1] Probably about 692 ; according to **CLVI** in 697–6.
[2] Jer. xv, 1–4 ; 2 Kings xxi, 10–15 ; xxii, 16–17.
[3] See pp. 38–9.   [4] Micah vi, 7.
[5] Cf. **LVII**, 504–5, 586–7.
[6] vi, 20 ; xli, 5.
[7] Micah vi, 7 ; Jeremiah, Ezekiel ; 2 Kings ; Is. lvii.

to describe this ceremony is " making one's son or one's daughter pass through the fire ", from which it might be thought that nothing more was meant than a kind of test or purification by fire, of the type with which one is familiar in Greece, at Rome, in India, and other countries.[1] The phrase was, however, a euphemism subsequently interpolated in the text.[2] What took place, as some texts expressly state, was a real holocaust, in which the little victim was consumed by the flames.[3]

According to several passages, the immolation was in honour of Baal or of Melek (the king)—a name which the Massoretes distorted into Molek (by giving it the vowels of bošeth, shame), and the Greek translators into Moloch. Other texts, however, show that it was Jahweh himself, invoked perhaps in this rite by the title of " king ", whom it was hoped to appease.[4]

Some have held that the custom of sacrificing children was borrowed from the Assyro-Babylonians[5] : the immigrants from Sepharvaim, whom after 722 the Assyrians settled in what had once been the land of Israel, used to make their children pass through the fire—so we read in 2 Kings xvii, 31—in honour of Adrammelek (Hadad had the title of Melek) and of Anammelek (Anu the king). But the settlers from Sepharvaim were much more probably Syrians, who came from Sibraim in the neighbourhood of Hermon,[6] and worshipped Hadad, the chief divinity of the district, and Anat-Melek, that is to say, the goddess Anat, the consort of this divine " king ". Among the Assyrians and the Babylonians the sacrifice of children seems, it is true, to have been very common.[7]

There is no reason to go outside Palestine in order to account for the prevalence of this barbarous custom in Judah in the seventh century. It had doubtless been practised

---

[1] Cf. **XLIX**, ii [6], 394, note 3 ; **CCXXVI**, 29–30 ; there may be an allusion to it in Is. l, 11.

[2] He‘ebîr " to make pass " instead of hib‘îr " to burn ".

[3] Deut. xii, 31 ; 2 Kings xvii, 31 ; Jer. vii, 31.

[4] Micah vi, 7 ; Jer. vii, 31 ; Ez. xx, 25, 26.

[5] **LXXXII**, 232–3, 244–6.

[6] Ez. xlvii, 16.

[7] **CXXIII**, 403 ; **CXXXVII**, i, no. 310, Rev. 10 ; no. 436, Rev. 8 ; no. 474, Rev. 4 ; **XCV**, 434 ; H. de Genouillac, **AI**, 1929, pp. 268-9.

both by the Hebrew ancestors of Israel,[1] and very extensively by the Canaanites, who formed a large proportion of the population.[2] Ever since the entry into Palestine it had never completely ceased : it was resorted to in desperate cases as a particularly efficacious method of appeal to divinity.[3] It is not surprising that it was made use of under the stress of the terrible ordeal of the seventh and sixth centuries. The horrible rites were once more celebrated—by Manasseh, among others (2 Kings xxi, 6)—no doubt in the very same place in which the Canaanites had previously performed them : it is hardly rash to suppose that the high place of Tophet in the valley of the Son of Hinnom, where the people of Jerusalem burnt their children in the seventh century, and which, more than any other, was to figure in men's minds in ages to come as a place of terror, the prototype of Gehenna,[4] had once been a pre-Israelite temple, with a reputation even then for human sacrifices.

The habit of resorting to rites, whether old or new, in order to turn away the wrath of Jahweh, was denounced by the prophets. A magnificent passage preserved for us in the book of Micah,[5] shows us Jahweh arraigning his people while he calls the hills to witness :—

> " O my people, what have I done unto thee ? And wherein have I wearied thee ? Testify against me."

And Jahweh reminds them of some of his benefactions. A conclusion somewhat in the manner of the final peroration must be supplied or understood in a similar arraignment to be found in the first chapter of Isaiah : why wilt thou force me to chastise thee thus unceasingly ? And the people reply by offering all the atonements by which it was then hoped to appease the anger of God : burnt offerings, calves of a year old, thousands of rams, ten thousands of rivers of oil, and human victims.

> " Shall I give my firstborn for my transgression, the fruit of my body for the sin of my soul ? "

The prophet replies :—

---

[1] See **LVII**, 330–1.   [2] See **LVII**, 102–3, 112–14.
[3] Judges xi, 30–40 ; 1 Kings xvi, 34 ; 2 Kings iii, 27 ; xvi, 3.
[4] A name derived from *ge' hinnom*, valley of Hinnom.
[5] vi, 1–8.

" He hath showed thee, O man, what is good : and what doth the Lord require of thee, but to do justly, and to love mercy, and to walk humbly with thy God ? "

This striking dialogue, which sums up so clearly the exclusively moral and religious nature of the response which the great prophets of the eighth century demanded—the justice enjoined by Amos and Micah, the mercy (ḥesed) dear to the heart of Hosea, the humble trust prescribed by Isaiah— might, as far as the question of time is concerned, belong to Micah, since the allusion to the sacrifice of children suggests that it dates from the reign of Manasseh. It is unlikely, how- ever, that the prophet of Moresheth was really the author, for the bitterness so characteristic of him is lacking. Instead we find that pathos, that note almost of tenderness, which is to characterize the men of the next generation, the generation of Jeremiah and Deuteronomy.

The Judæans as a whole, however, were not disposed to embark upon those moral reforms which a handful of prophets urged them to undertake. Side by side with those who sought to appease Jahweh by whatever means were considered most effective, there were others who were inclined to doubt the omnipotence of the ancient God of Israel. If he does not save his people, they said, it is not because he does not wish to do so, but because he cannot. The catastrophes which over- whelm us do not come from him, but from some other divinity, whose anger must be assuaged.

Manasseh " reared up altars for Baal " and made a graven image of Asherah,[1] that is, doubtless, he did homage to the local divinities of the land of Canaan, who were thought to be avenging themselves because they had been overlooked.

One at least of those still more ancient practices, observed by Hebrew tribes before ever the national religion existed, came into its own again and began to flourish exceedingly ; this was the worship of the dead, a custom which had never completely died out,[2] but which had hitherto been successfully opposed and kept in the background by the more enlightened followers of Jahweh. Manasseh, on the contrary, gave it official protection : " he dealt with them that had familiar spirits and with wizards." [3]

[1] 2 Kings xxi, 3, 7.   [2] 1 Sam. xxviii, 3–25 ; Is. viii, 19.
[3] 2 Kings xxi, 6.

But the gods to which men turned most hopefully were naturally the gods of the Assyrians, since misfortune apparently came direct from them, and since they rewarded their followers by making kingdoms obey them. For the man of " primitive mentality ", the best gods are the gods of the conquerors.[1] Manasseh " built altars in the two courts of the temple of Jahweh to all the host of heaven ", that is to the various divinities of the Assyrian pantheon, of which each was then associated with the name of a celestial body.[2] Josiah found in the Temple a chariot [3] dedicated to the Sun, and in the precincts of the Temple horses " given " to the same god by " the kings of Judah ".[4] There can be no doubt that the first of these kings had been Manasseh. It is true that the observance of these customs is not borne out by Assyrian documents as far as we know ; but the horse was for them the animal always associated with the sun : on the bas-reliefs of Maltai, Shamash is represented standing on a horse.[5] It is possible that the kings of Judah, like the Rhodians, the Spartans, the Persians, and the Massagetes, sacrificed these horses each year with the idea of renewing the team which drew the sun's chariot when the animals grew tired.[6]

Another rite which belonged to the worship of the sun, and which probably also went back to the reign of Manasseh, although it is only spoken of in the reign of Zedekiah,[7] consisted in raising a branch to the nostrils while adoring the sun as it rose.

The fact that these rites were celebrated in the temple of Jahweh and were thought by some to have been ordained by him [8] suggests that the God of Israel had been included in the number of astral gods of the Assyro-Babylonian religion.

By acting in this way Manasseh resigned himself to the religious attitude which, according to ancient ideas, became

---

[1] Cf. for example Pierre Loti, *Figures et choses qui passent*, Paris, Calmann-Lévy, 1898, 15th edn., p. 291.

[2] 2 Kings xxiii, 5.

[3] Read the singular, as in the Septuagint.

[4] 2 Kings xxiii, 11.

[5] Thureau-Dangin, *Les Sculptures rupestres de Maltaï*, **RA**, 1924, pp. 185 *ff*. ; René Dussaud, **RHR**, xci, 1925), 127.

[6] See the texts in Loisy, **LVIII**, 220.

[7] Ez. viii, 16.   [8] Deut. xvii, 3.

a vassal, and which made it incumbent on him to worship his master's god along with his own.[1] Ahaz would seem to have set him an example, when under the protection of Tiglath Pileser.[2] It was the general rule : the Canaanite princes, in the days of the Egyptian sovereignty, paid homage to the god of the king, whether the god was Amon or Atôn.[3] A Ninevite conqueror said of the vanquished : " I required them to sacrifice to the great gods of the Assyrians." [4]

The homage paid to the Assyro-Babylonian gods was not, however, only official. Some at least among them were the objects of private devotion. From many a flat-roofed house in Jerusalem, rising terrace-like one above the other, could be seen the smoke of sweet-scented offerings burnt in honour of the astral gods.[5] The worship of the " queen of heaven " was especially the vogue among the women. At the end of the century, under Jehoiachim, Jeremiah records indignantly that it is celebrated in the streets of the capital [6] ; and even in Egypt, the land of exile, Jewish women clung to its observance.[7] It may be taken as an established fact that this goddess was none other than Ishtar, not so much because of the title " queen of heaven " or " queen of heaven and the stars ",[8] which Ishtar shared with others,[9] as in view of the particular rite attacked by Jeremiah, which consisted in the presentation to Ishtar, as " queen of heaven " for the inhabitants of Jerusalem, of certain cakes, called in Hebrew *kawwân*, and in Assyrian *kâmanu* : it is the same word.[10] This form of worship must have been introduced or revived in the reign of Manasseh ; for the women, when admonished by Jeremiah, plead that the cult of the queen of heaven had been practised officially by the kings and leaders of Judah when the country was still prosperous (Jer. xliv, 17) ; and there is no doubt that the long reign of Manasseh did bring the kingdom material well-being, though not independence.

Manasseh's reign must also have witnessed, if not the

---

[1] Gen. xxiv, 3, 12–14, 21, 26–7, 31, 42–4, 48, 52, 56.
[2] 2 Kings xvi, 10–18. See p. 23.
[3] **LVII**, 158–162.   [4] **KB**, ii, 195.
[5] Zeph. i, 5 ; Jer. xix, 13 ; xxxii, 29 ; *cf*. 2 Kings xxiii, 12.
[6] Jer. vii, 18.   [7] Jer. xliv, 15–25.
[8] **XCV**, 425.   [9] e.g. with a Hittite divinity (**CX**, 73).
[10] **XCV**, 441–2.

beginnings, at least the development of the custom of the ceremonial mourning for Tammuz, the Babylonian god of the vegetation that dies each year, a custom observed by the women of Jerusalem in the time of Ezekiel (viii, 14), which must have become merged into some of the ancient Canaanite cults showing similar features [1] ; the worship of Naaman, one of the names or prototypes of Adonis,[2] is recorded in Judah in the time of Isaiah.[3]

This syncretism was apparently energetically opposed by the prophets, and even by some supporters of the old popular beliefs. Nevertheless, the bloodthirsty persecutions which tradition attributes to Manasseh—he is said, for instance, to have put Isaiah to death by having him sawn asunder [4]—are not well attested : 2 Kings xxi, 16, may be intended to condemn in general terms all miscarriage of justice, and Jeremiah ii, 30, may be an allusion to the massacres of the prophets which are laid to the door of Ahab.

The secret of the prolonged success of Manasseh's religious experiment was that to all appearances, instead of subordinating the God of Israel to the Assyrian divinities, or of placing him on a footing of equality, he gave Jahweh the highest place in his pantheon. It may be that the title " God of heaven " was beginning to be applied to Jahweh in Manasseh's day,[5] if so, he would seem to have identified Jahweh with Anu, the supreme divinity in the celestial hierarchy of the Mesopotamians.[6] This would prove that the worshippers of Jahweh, even those most susceptible to foreign influence, were already conscious, as a result of the preaching of the prophets, of the exceptional value of their religion.

---

[1] See the myths of Moth, Aleyin, Baal, and Naaman in the poems of Ras Shamra, SY, xii (1931), 193–24, 350–7 ; xiii (1932), 113–163 xiv (1933), 128–151.

[2] Cf. R. Dussaud, RHR, civ (1931), 377–400.

[3] Is. i, 29 ; xvii, 11.

[4] The Ascension of Isaiah, ch. ii–v (Latin translation by August Dillmann (1877), French by René Basset (Les apocryphes éthiopiens trad. en franc., Paris, 1894), English by R. H. Charles (The Ascension of Isaiah, London, Black, 1900), German by Georg Beer, Die Apokryphen und Pseudepigraphen des A.T., Tübingen, Mohr, 1900, pp. 124–7) ; cf. Heb. xi, 37.

[5] Previously used only in Gen. xxiv, 3, 7.

[6] CV. But see H. Gunkel, Genesis³, 251–2.

Thus the Judæan community adapted itself progressively to the humiliating circumstances of Assyrian domination,[1] by setting itself to admire and to imitate the sometime enemy. Foreign modes of dress were adopted,[2] Assyrian literature was studied. It was probably at this time that the story of the flood was interpolated in the Jahwist version, which did not originally contain it.[3] While other Oriental traditions, when taken over by the Hebrews, had as a rule been extensively remoulded by the genius of Israelite folklore, and had an unmistakably Palestinian air about them, the story of the flood follows so closely its Assyro-Babylonian models that it is obviously a piece of literary and scholarly plagiarism. It is all the more significant that the Hebrew narrator should have systematically eliminated from it the polytheistic background and given additional prominence to its moral bearing.

II

REVIVAL OF PROPHETIC OPPOSITION. ZEPHANIAH. BEGINNING OF JEREMIAH'S CAREER

Since the beginning of the seventh century the humiliation of Judah beneath the yoke of Assyria had been the cause of the undermining of religious belief. Since the middle of the reign of Asshurbanipal, however, the power of Nineveh had weakened visibly. Egypt had freed itself about the year 645 ; Babylon became independent on the death of Asshurbanipal (626), and soon attacked Asshur and Nineveh, the very heart of the empire, which on the east was being repeatedly attacked by the Medes. So great was the disorganization that hordes of barbarians from the north, Scythians and Cimmerians, forced the frontiers and overran the entire country, looting as they went ; one of these tribes is known to have sacked Ashkelon in Palestine and did not stop till it reached the frontiers of Egypt.

Nevertheless, the majority of the population of Judah seem to have been slow to realize the meaning of these upheavals, or to see in them a sign of the ultimate downfall of Assyria, and a proof of the superiority of the god of their

---

[1] Cf. **XLIX**, ii [6], 395.   [2] Zeph. i, 8.
[3] See **LVII**, 563.

PLATE V

Deportation of a conquered people. Bas-relief from the palace of Asshurbanipal at Nineveh. (In the Louvre, no. 65.)

fathers over the gods of the foreign tyrants. Finally, however, a revival of religious and political nationalism did take place— as the reforms of Josiah (622), and the prophecies of Nahum (about 612) bear witness—but not till several years after similar movements in Egypt and Babylonia. All the more did the leaders of the nation endeavour to counterbalance Assyrian power, as Hezekiah had done before them, by throwing in their lot with the Egyptians, who had just shaken off the yoke.[1] Life in Judæa, as we find it reflected in the book of Zephaniah (between 640 and 662) and the first prophecies of Jeremiah (after 627), had become so ingrained with Assyrian views, both political and religious, and so attuned to habits of obedience that men continued to prostrate themselves on roofs before the astral gods, to call upon the name of Baal, to swear by Milcom as well as by Jahweh, whose power some doubted [2]; and foreign fashions were as popular as ever.[3] And since they were persuaded that in so doing they were not offending the god of Israel, Jeremiah was hard put to it to convince Jerusalem, by all the resources of indignant eloquence at his command, that it was a sin against God to associate him with other divinities,[4] or to appeal for help from Egypt, and that to do so was to be doomed to disappointment, just as Ahaz had been disappointed when he trusted in Asshur. They were unmoved by the logic of events [5]: they counted on the strength of their fortresses—which to troops of barbarian horsemen were, in fact, impregnable—and on their gold, with which, like Pharaoh, they could bribe their assailants to retreat.[6]

But in the midst of this easy-going and short-sighted generation the voice which had been silent for three-quarters of a century, the voice of prophecy, is heard once more. Zephaniah, who probably was of royal descent (for, contrary to custom, the preface to his book traces his genealogy back to the fourth generation, evidently because his great-great-grandfather was King Hezekiah), and Jeremiah, who was the son of a priest of the village of Anathoth, were fully aware of

---

[1] Jer. ii, 18, 36–7. Passages certainly before 616, at which date Egypt had become the ally of Assyria.
[2] Zeph. i, 12.   [3] Zeph. i, 4–5, 8.
[4] Jer. ii, 23–8, 35.   [5] Zeph. iii, 6–7.
[6] Zeph. i, 16, 18.

the decisive importance of the events which were making of Asia a shambles. Zephaniah foretold that Nineveh would be laid waste, that it would become a desert and the home of wild beasts, a place of wandering herds (ii, 13–14), and claimed that Jahweh was the cause of this destruction, which, however, seemed to him only a minor result of the catastrophe he foresaw. For the enemy which was to overwhelm the towns of Philistia, distant Ethiopia, and Nineveh, was also to overwhelm Judah. He could almost hear beforehand the cries of anguish from the country round about Jerusalem (i, 10–11), and could see Jahweh, lamp in hand, searching Jerusalem, house by house, in order to exterminate the last of the inhabitants.[1] Jeremiah is more precise in his details about the nationality of the invaders, who are to be instruments of the justice of God : they will come from far, they will be an ancient and warlike people (v, 15), speaking an unknown language and inhabiting a northern country (i, 15), they will be horsemen and archers (iv, 13, 29 ; v, 15, 16). From his description it is easy to recognize the Scythians. Both Zephaniah and Jeremiah, who had doubtless witnessed, in horror and dismay, the raid in which the hordes from the extreme north had swept across Palestine, were convinced that these invasions would be repeated, and that Judah would this time fall a prey to the barbarians, in common with all the kingdoms of the civilized East, as a punishment for her sins.

The burden of their prophecies echoes the sinister warnings of Amos, Hosea, and Micah, and they are no less scathing. But there is a spaciousness about them which does not appear in those of their eighth-century predecessors : the whole world is to be involved in the judgment, that world with which Judah had become better acquainted since, as vassal of Assyria, it had been drawn in spite of itself into the vortex of world politics.

Zephaniah even goes so far as to endow the " day of the Lord " with the proportions of a cosmic cataclysm :

" I will utterly consume all things from off the face of the ground, saith the Lord . . . the fowls of the heaven and the fishes of the sea."

It was from a passage in his book that the medieval

[1] i, 12. It is on account of this passage that medieval artists represented the prophet as carrying a lantern.

church took the theme of the famous hymn on the Last Judgment : *Dies irae dies illa* (i, 15). Poetic hyperbole must, however, be fully allowed for in the language of the prophet. In any case, what he expects is an enemy invasion (i, 10–12, 16–17), not an upheaval of the elements. Certain features of the picture may be due to its having been touched up afterwards. Even so, it is obvious that the catastrophe envisaged by Zephaniah was a " world " catastrophe.

Another new characteristic of his message, and of Jeremiah's too, is that they attach as much importance to the crime of worshipping " other gods " as to sins of a purely moral order. They could scarcely do otherwise, faced as they were with the flood of syncretism in which, since the reign of Manasseh, Judah had been submerged. But their action had far-reaching consequences, for it obliged the great prophets of the seventh and sixth centuries to stress the importance of a reform of religious observances in a way which their predecessors, preoccupied almost exclusively with questions of morality and the spiritual life, had not thought necessary. On the other hand, it made the representatives of the new prophecy appear in the somewhat unexpected guise of champions of the national religion. Was it not they who raised the banner of revolt against the astral gods of the oppressor ? This consideration was one reason for the comparative success of the attempt made at this time to give legal expression to the wishes of the prophetic group.

CHAPTER V

JOSIAH'S REFORM

I

CUSTOMARY LAW AND THE TORAH BEFORE THE REFORM

LIFE in ancient Israel, as was the case among all the peoples of antiquity, was ruled by customs handed down from father to son.[1] What " is done " or " not done " in Israel,[2] was the standard according to which differences between individuals were settled by the sheikhs of the clans, the elders of the towns, the kings, and the royal judges.

When a case arose for which there was no precedent, or the dispute involved some particularly obscure point, the judgment of God was invoked, that is to say, a detailed explanation was laid before the priest of the temple of Jahweh nearest to hand ; the priest, when he had consulted God, gave sentence ; the sentence had only a moral authority, but that authority was supreme. Sometimes he indicated the culprit by a kind of drawing of lots—*urim* or *thummim* [3]— sometimes he put the accused through an ordeal [4] or administered the oath, originally in itself a kind of ordeal, for it was thought that God—or in more ancient times the magic power of the curse—would not fail to strike down the perjurer ; or else he assessed the damages or determined the nature of the penalty. This sentence of the priest was what was called *torah*, a word which, according to the most probable etymology, meant " throwing ", " casting of the lot ", hence " oracle ".

To settle thus, by an appeal to God, all litigation which arose among Israelites had been, according to tradition, one

---

[1] *Cf.* **LVII**, 552.
[2] Gen. xx, 9 ; xxix, 26 ; xxxiv, 7 ; 2 Sam. xiii, 12 ; *cf.* Deut. xxii, 21 ; Judges xx, 6, 10 ; Jer. xxix, 23.
[3] Jos. vii ; 1 Sam. xiv, 36–45 ; *cf.* **LVII**, 344, 348, etc.
[4] Num. v, 11–31 ; *cf.* **LVII**, 244–5.

of the principal tasks of Moses, the first priest of the national religion.[1]

As it was essentially a divine command given with a special new or difficult case in view, the *torah* was by its very nature oral, living, and unfinished, a never-failing source of inspiration for Israelite law. It remained so until the time of Ezra, in spite of the limitations which increased with the growth of writing : the priests are " those that handle the law " [2] ; in *their mouth* is the *torah* [3] ; if God withholds his instructions the *torah* " perishes from the priest " [4] ; when they are deported, " the law is not." [5]

In ordinary cases the customs of their fathers, with, in exceptional circumstances, a priestly sentence to supply the deficiencies, or, at times, correct the harshness of the law of custom—these two means of solving judicial or religious difficulties were deemed sufficient for the needs of the social fabric of ancient Israel. In addition to the laws prescribed by tradition, and the above-mentioned oracles, the older books tell us of a few rare edicts on the part of leaders or kings, the " statute and the ordinance " given by Joshua,[6] David's decree regulating the sharing of pillage [7] ; to these may be added the decree instituting the days of mourning for Jephthah's daughter (Judg. xi, 40). When the need was urgent the leader called for an oath from those whom the new statute was intended to bind : this was called a " covenant ".[8]

It is hardly necessary to say that writing was not indispensable, either for the promulgation of the law of custom or for the revelation of *torah*. Thus it is not surprising that Israelite literature before Josiah's reform should contain so few legislative texts : the second decalogue (Ex. xxxiv, 14–26), the so-called " book of the covenant " (Ex. xx, 22–3, 19), a few brief instructions for the observance of the Passover (Ex. xii, 21–3), or for unleavened bread, and the offering of the first-born (Ex. xiii, 3–16), the first decalogue (Ex. xx, 2–17). On the contrary, it is surprising that at so early a

[1] Ex. xviii, 13–19, 21–6.   [2] *Tophese hat-torah*, Jer. ii, 8.
[3] Mal. ii, 6 ; *cf.* Hagg. ii, 11–13.
[4] Jer. xviii, 18 ; Ez. vii, 26.   [5] Lam. ii, 9.
[6] Jos. xxiv, 25–6.   [7] 1 Sam. xxx, 23–5.
[8] Jos. xxiv, 25–7 ; 2 Sam. v, 3 ; Jer. xxxiv, 8–10, 18 ; *cf.*
LVII, 364.

period certain laws should have been written down, and one wonders why the ink and the reed should have been resorted to in these particular cases.

One of the reasons, no doubt, was that among those judges and priests whose duty it was to declare the law there began to be grave differences of opinion as to the real nature of national custom. There were Israelites who thought themselves justified in worshipping graven images, especially when made of gold or silver—Gideon, for instance,[1] and Micah,[2] David,[3] and Jeroboam the First [4]—in using altars with steps leading up to them,[5] ornamented with carved horns at the corners [6] or made of bronze.[7] The second decalogue and the so-called book of " the covenant " protest against this interpretation of " the law of Jahweh ", in a statement evidently of hostile intent, that Moses had received a divine *torah* forbidding " molten gods ",[8] altars not made of clay or of rough stones, and altars with steps.[9]

The prophet Hosea accuses the priests of his day of having " forgotten the law of God " and rejected the " knowledge " (of God), that is to say of having ceased to instruct their followers in the knowledge of the real will of Jahweh.[10]

Conflicting tendencies of this sort could only be reconciled by resorting to the written word, and an attempt was made, particularly from the eighth century onwards, to fix in writing the authentic tradition of Israel as seen from various points of view, in other words to have a permanent record of the real will of Jahweh.

Hosea apparently alludes to *toroth* written down in his day, and considered by him to be an expression of the divine will, when he speaks of Jahweh as saying :—

" Though I write for him my law in ten thousand precepts,[11] they are counted as a strange thing." [12]

Isaiah, for his part, calls down curses on some of his con-

---

[1] Judg. viii, 24–7. [2] Judg. xvii–xviii.
[3] 1 Sam. xix, 13–16. [4] 1 Kings xii, 28–30.
[5] 1 Kings, i, 53 ; xii, 33.
[6] 1 Kings i, 50–1 ; ii, 28–34 ; Am. iii, 14.
[7] 1 Kings viii, 64 ; 2 Kings x, 14–15 ; Ez. ix, 2.
[8] Ex. xxxiv, 17. [9] Ex. xx, 24–6. *Cf.* **LVII**, 501–3.
[10] Hos. iv, 5. [11] Read *ribbo torothay.*
[12] Hos. viii, 12.

temporaries, because they have made laws which in his eyes uphold the strong at the expense of the weak :—

> " Woe unto them that decree unrighteous decrees, and to the writers that write perverseness : to turn aside the needy from judgment, and to take away the right of the poor of my people, that widows may be their spoil, and that they may make the fatherless their prey ! " [1]

It is natural that jurists who had been won over to the ideals of the prophets should have wanted to intervene in the dispute and to define the essentials of Jahwistic, and consequently of Mosaic, law, both religious and civil. They were not concerned merely with an academic controversy about a historical point. Given the practical importance of the torah, the orientation of the whole religious and social life of the nation was at stake. This was the way, then, in which the first decalogue probably first saw the light. The same causes led to the great attempt made, in the name of the authentic tradition of Moses, to bring about a general reform of national life in the reign of Josiah.

II

JOSIAH'S REFORM.   DISCUSSION OF THE ACCOUNT IN THE
BOOK OF KINGS

This is what we are told in the second book of Kings (ch. xxii and xxiii).

In the eighteenth year of King Josiah, therefore probably in 622–621, Shaphan, the king's scribe and the head of a family which for several generations protected the great prophets, went to the Temple to empty the collecting-boxes of the money contributed to the fund for the repair of the building. The priest Hilkiah said to him : " I have found the book of the law in the house of the Lord," and handed him the book. Shaphan read it, and when he had rendered account to the king of the financial errand with which he had been entrusted, he read it to the king. Josiah gave signs of the most intense distress, he rent his garments and sent to inquire of the prophetess Huldah—

> " For," he said, " great is the wrath of the Lord that is kindled against us, because our fathers have not hearkened unto the words

[1] Is. x, 1–2.

of this book, to do according unto all that which is written concerning us."

As a result of the inquiry Josiah decided to proclaim the newly discovered torah as the law of the kingdom ; he assembled all the people and, according to the usual procedure, made a covenant with them before Jahweh, that is to say, he called upon his subjects to swear to abide by the requirements of the code.

He then embarked on a series of measures, evidently necessary for the carrying out of the law.

(1) The Temple was purified. Not only was a clearance made of such sacred objects as were specifically foreign, like the altars of the astral gods, but also of objects which had long been enthroned in many of the shrines of Jahweh— an asherah, or sacred pole, and a house reserved for the Temple prostitutes [1] ;

(2) The king abolished all the high places of Judah, that is to say, all the sanctuaries of the kingdom intended for the worship of Jahweh, with the sole exception of the temple of Jerusalem. The priests of the holy places which were closed were obliged to come and live in the capital, but were not authorized to officiate at the altar of the Temple [2] ;

(3) All places of worship and all emblems, whether heathen or reputed to be heathen, in Jerusalem and the surrounding country, were destroyed or profaned : the high-place of the satyrs which was at one of the gates of the city, the altar in the valley of Hinnom, on which children had been burnt, the chariot and the horses dedicated to the Sun, the high-places built by Solomon on the Mount of Olives [3] in honour of various foreign divinities, the steles, and sacred posts.[4] The reform was extended—perhaps not till later, it is true—to include the land which had once been the kingdom of Israel [5] ;

(4) Josiah celebrated at Jerusalem a Passover such as had not been seen since the time of the Judges [6] ;

[1] 2 Kings xxiii, 4, 6, 7.
[2] 2 Kings xxiii, 8a, 9.
[3] The correct reading may be *har ham-mishah* " mount of oil ", according to LXX, Vet. Lat., Targ., instead of *har ham-mashith* " mount of the Destroyer " (2 Kings xxiii, 13).
[4] xxiii, 8b, 10–14.   [5] xxiii, 15–20.
[6] xxiii, 21–3.

(5) Finally he prohibited necromancers, *teraphim,* and idols of every description.[1]

The tale is so sober, so devoid of the miraculous, so full of concrete and precise detail, that it seems impossible to see in it only a legend of later date, as did Seinecke, E. Havet, G. d'Eichthal, Maurice Vernes, and, to some extent, Louis Horst. To do so it would, moreover, be necessary to set aside the testimony of Jeremiah, who tells us that he " proclaimed all the words of this covenant " in the towns of Judah and the streets of Jerusalem (Jer. xi, 1–8), who quotes Deuteronomy (xxxiv, 9), and frequently alludes to an attempt at reform in Judah (iii, 10 ; iv, 3–4 ; viii, 8), that of Ezekiel, who takes for granted that it is an act of impiety to frequent the " high places " (Ez. xx, 27–9), or to " eat upon the mountains " (xviii, 6, 11, 15 ; xxii, 9), and that of the editors of the book of Kings, whose estimate of all the rulers is based on the degrees of fidelity they show to the principles of Josiah's reform.

Some more recent critics, while regarding the narrative as on the whole historically accurate, feel unable to admit the historicity of the chief measure of reform attributed to the king, the centralization of all worship in the Temple, on the ground that in the seventh century it would have been impossible to carry out. According to Hölscher [2] who is supported by Spiegelberg,[3] F. Horst,[4] Alfred Loisy,[5] this Utopian idea can only have been engendered in the unpractical brain of a dreamer like Ezekiel during exile. According to Kennett,[6] whose opinion is shared by Stanley A. Cook,[7] Binns,[8] and Burkitt,[9] the centralization of worship was a necessity imposed upon the Jews who remained behind in Palestine at the time of the deportation, and can only have arisen at that time and in that place.

These interesting theories are founded on the very doubtful axiom that the centralization of worship, since it was Utopian, chimerical, and impracticable in the time of Josiah, could not have been decreed then. Granted that the measure was violently revolutionary and bound to encounter almost

---

[1] xxiii, 24.   [2] **CXXV.**   [3] **CLXXIX.**
[4] **CXXVI.**   [5] **LIX³,** 200–5.   [6] **CXXXIX.**
[7] **JTS,** xxvi (1925), 162 ; CAH, iii, 406–7, 481–3.
[8] **CIII.**   [9] **JTS,** xxii (1920), 44–51.

insurmountable obstacles, it is difficult to see why doctrinaire idealists, as impatient of compromise as all the followers of the great prophets, should not have demanded the reform and attempted to put it in practice as early as the seventh century, especially as we know, and Hölscher admits, that Ezekiel and his disciples, the priestly lawgivers, insisted on its being carried out fifty years later, along with many other religious and social Utopian ideas, all as impracticable as, for instance, the jubilee.

The narrative of the book of Kings must, we take it, be substantially correct. Then there is the question of whether it has reached us intact in its original form.

Some scholars have recently come to the conclusion that the narrative is really two narratives woven together,[1] and that one of them is concerned, wholly [2] or in part,[3] with an incomplete, preliminary reform carried out by Josiah in the twelfth year of his reign, as is indicated by the book of Chronicles.[4] But the evidence in support of the existence of two such parallel accounts is insufficient or even doubtful. As to the reform of the twelfth year, it is more than doubtful whether it can ever have taken place : the editor of Chronicles, unable to understand how the devout Josiah could have reigned for eighteen years without putting an end to infringements of the law, antedated the reforms by six years, making them synchronize with the young king's attainment of his majority, which took place at twenty years of age. The reforms which the king is supposed to have carried out in this twelfth year are, moreover, so sweeping that one wonders what improvements could still have been possible at the time of the discovery of the torah.[5]

It will be sufficient, in reviewing the narrative in the book of Kings as it now stands, to remember that some points of the original story have been touched up, for instance, Huldah's reply to the messengers sent by Josiah.   In the present state

---

[1] **CLXI ; CII ; CLXXII.**

[2] According to Hans Schmidt ;   *cf.* F. X. Kugler, *Von Moses bis Paulus*, 1922, pp. 139–141.

[3] According to Oestreicher.   [4] 2 Chron. xxxiv, 3–7.

[5] It is contrary to the data afforded by both Kings and Chronicles to attribute the abolition of astral worship to the reform of the twelfth year, and the prohibition of Canaanitish rites to that of the eighteenth (**LXXII**, 469).

of the text the prophetess is said to have declared that there
was no way of averting the wrath of Jahweh, that the evil
foretold would come upon this place, but that the king, having
humbled himself and wept before Jahweh, should not see the
disasters, but should be gathered to his fathers in peace, that is
to say his end would be peaceful. If this had really been
Huldah's answer, Josiah would scarcely have attempted a
radical reform, since he would have been assured beforehand
that his efforts would be in vain, and also that it was only after
him that the deluge was to come. In the original story, it may
be conjectured that the prophetess urged the king to use all his
authority to ensure the observance of the new *torah*, promising
him, if he succeeded, not only a happy end to his reign—a
promise which must be authentic, for, as it turned out,
Josiah's end was very different, and he died a violent death
at Megiddo—but also the pardon of Jahweh for his people.
In Huldah's reply, as we have it, there must therefore be a
nucleus of fact (2 Kings xxii, 18–20*a*) ; and the rest (v. 15–17)
must have been added or altered after the catastrophe of 586.

In the same way, the conclusion (xxiii, 25–7) must
certainly have been composed after the destruction of
Jerusalem.

Hölscher has tried to prove that the account of the chief
measure of reform, ordering the defilement of the high-places
and forcing the priests who had belonged to them to go to
the capital (xxii, 8*a*, 9, 10) should be included in the list of
subsequent additions. It is true that at this stage of the
narrative there is a certain amount of confusion, but not
more [1] that is characteristic of oriental historiographers : the
mustering of the priests at Jerusalem is, like the events
related in the preceding and following verses, part of the
reforms connected with the capital.

Besides, it goes without saying that the reforms
enumerated were not carried out either all on the same day
or necessarily in the order indicated. It may not have been
possible to extend them to the Assyrian province which
had once been the kingdom of Israel (xxiii, 15–20) much
before the date of the fall of Nineveh (612) ; and it is quite
likely that the compulsory concentration of the priests of

---

[1] With the exception of v. 8*b*, which is obviously historical but must
have been transposed.

the high-places in Jerusalem may only have been decreed after a first and more generous attempt at control had failed.[1]

Some of the king's reforms, especially the abolition of the provincial sanctuaries, were bound to meet with vehement opposition from the numerous people whose interests were attacked. For having tried by his preaching to bring his compatriots to see the error of their ways, Jeremiah was threatened with death by the people of Anathoth,[2] who were probably enraged by the destruction of the high-place of their village. There seems, however, to have been a cessation of hostility, at least temporarily, partly, no doubt, because of the weight lent to the code by the use of the name of Moses, partly owing to the personal reputation of the king, who was known to sympathize heartily with the reformers, probably also on account of a threat of Scythian invasion, which was a sign of the wrath of Jahweh, and lastly because of the patriotic aspect of the reforms, which were tantamount to a solemn declaration of independence with regard to Assyria and the gods of Assyria.[3]

III

THE TORAH OF JOSIAH

A number of new, and for the most part widely divergent, theories about the book of torah discovered in the reign of Josiah, its character and its age, have been propounded in the course of the last few years. The ensuing discussions seem to us to have confirmed rather than shaken the opinion which has prevailed among critics since the beginning of the nineteenth century, namely that the text of this code has been preserved for us in Deuteronomy, of which it forms the original nucleus. It was drawn up in the course of the seventh century, between 692 and 622.

[1] See below, p. 143–4.
[2] Jer. xi, 18–23.
[3] See above, p. 42.

APPENDIX : IDENTITY OF THE CODE DISCOVERED IN THE
REIGN OF JOSIAH
DATE OF ITS COMPOSITION

1. Josiah's Reforms and Deuteronomy

That there is a close and organic relation between the reforms
carried out by Josiah and the collection of laws and exhortations
which constitute the major part of the present book of
Deuteronomy [1] is so evident that all critics may be said to be agreed
about it.

The measures of reform undertaken by the king all form part of
those prescribed by the code, and some are not prescribed elsewhere : the offering of worship in one place and only in one, namely
that which " Jahweh will choose from among all the tribes when he
has given rest unto Israel and freedom from all his enemies "—a
periphrasis for the temple of Jerusalem which could hardly be
clearer, seeing that the words are put into the mouth of Moses ;
the destruction of all the other temples in Palestine ; the prohibiting
of the worship of all other gods, especially those of the Canaanites, on
the one hand, and of the " host of heaven " on the other,[2] that is to
say, of the astral gods of the Assyrians ; the ban on certain customs
and objects having heathen associations—in particular, the sacred
stelæ and posts (asherah),[3] prostitution in honour of the divinity,[4]
and the sacrifice of children [5] ; the celebration of the Passover
at Jerusalem only [6] ; the suppression of necromancy [7] and the
abolition of idols.[8]

There is therefore an evident connection between the measures
of reform decreed by Josiah and the laws which we can read for
ourselves in Deuteronomy. The most natural explanation of this
connection is that Deuteronomy is, wholly or in part, the identical
book of torah, the reading of which, according to the book of Kings,
made the king decide to carry out his reforms.

And it is, a priori, extremely probable that the code adopted by
Josiah, which became the law of the land in 622, was carefully
preserved, and that, in consequence, it was included in the great
collection of the laws of Israel which form the Pentateuch. The
names used to denote the torah of Josiah are among those given
to Deuteronomic law. The influence of Deuteronomy is manifest
among those authors who come after Josiah's reforms, as, for
instance, Jeremiah and the editor of the book of Kings : they allude
to it and even quote it expressly.[9]

There are certainly differences of detail between Josiah's reforms
and the laws laid down in the Deuteronomic code. According
to the latter, the Levite living in the country—that is to say the

---

[1] Ch. i–xxx. Chaps. xxxi–xxxiv, which contain the end of the
biography of Moses, must, of course, be excluded.

[2] Deut. iv, 19 ; xvii, 3.

[3] Deut. xvi, 21–2 ; cf. xii, 3, etc.   [4] Deut. xxiii, 18–19.

[5] Deut. xii, 29–31.   [6] Deut. xvi, 2, 5–7.

[7] Deut. xviii, 11.   [8] Deut. xii, 3, etc.

[9] Jer. xxxiv, 1–12 (cf. Deut. xv, 14) ; 2 Kings xiv, 6 (cf. Deut.
xxiv, 16).

priest of one of the high-places which are to be destroyed—may be left free to come to the central temple—to Jerusalem—or not, as he chooses : if he comes, " then he shall minister in the name of the Lord his God, as all his brethren the Levites do, which stand there before the Lord. They shall have like portions to eat." [1] Josiah, on the contrary, " brought all the priests out of the cities of Judah . . . Nevertheless the priests of the high-places came not up to the altar of the Lord in Jerusalem, but they did eat unleavened bread among their brethren ".[2] But it is easy to understand how, in this respect, the king was led to depart from the regulations prescribed by the torah : he tried, perhaps, at first to adhere to them strictly, but then the priests who were no longer allowed to officiate, remaining where they were, became the prime movers in resisting reform, and continued to practise the forbidden rites in secret. That being so, the step taken by the king is explained, and we can see why he insisted on their coming to the capital, providing them with a means of subsistence, but depriving them of their priestly functions, both as a disciplinary measure and because pressure was brought to bear on him by the Temple priests, who were loath to share their rights and their wealth with a mass of intruders.

An immense majority of critics, especially since De Wette's detailed demonstration [3] of the thesis, have echoed Athanasius, Chrysostom, Jerome, Procopius, Hobbes, Le Clerc, and Voltaire, in identifying the book discovered in the reign of Josiah with Deuteronomy.

There is, however, another interpretation of the undeniable relationship between the improvements ordained by Josiah and the laws of Deuteronomy, namely that it was not the code which caused the reform, but the reform which resulted in the drawing up of the code : Deuteronomy would then be a summary of the king's decrees.[4]

Siebens supports this theory by stating, as a principle of legal history in general, that a code is always the consequence, and never the cause, of a reorganization of the law of a nation.

It is true that, if complete and instantaneous success is to attend their application, laws must be a reflection of a radical change in customs and ideas. But there have been in the past, and still are, a large number of laws which do not answer to this definition in the least, and which, however various and widespread the manner of their promulgation, in practice remain, or become, almost a dead letter. This is what seems to have happened to many of Josiah's reforms, in particular the law of centralization, which ceased to be observed when the king was no longer there to enforce it. The feeling of the masses was certainly against it, for they were strongly attached to their local temples, and it was only because of the upheavals caused by the deportations that it succeeded in the following century. Josiah's reforms were " an ecclesiastical revolution carried out by the leaders ".[5]

---

[1] Deut. xviii, 6-8.   [2] 2 Kings xxiii, 8a, 9.   [3] **CLXXXVII.**
[4] This view of the whole of the Deuteronomic code has been maintained by Cullen (**CXI**), and for a considerable part of it perhaps by Vatke (**CLXXXIII**) and by Siebens (**CLXXVI**).
[5] **XCI**, ii, 298.

There is, then, it seems, no cogent reason to doubt that it was really provoked by the discovery of a book of torah, which book is to be found in Deuteronomy.

It is much more difficult to say what elements of Deuteronomy were contained by the book in question.

It has been thought that its contents were confined to the legislative parts of the Biblical Deuteronomy.[1] An improbable theory, if the impression made upon the king by the reading of the book is to be explained. His dismay is only comprehensible if it included, like the present Deuteronomic code, terrible curses upon the nation if it was disobeyed. In the same way the code of Hammurabi and the Code of Holiness (Lev. xvii–xxvi) end with imprecations.

The book of torah, on the other hand, being from the very beginning presented in the form of a discourse delivered by Moses, also had to contain an introduction explaining the circumstances which led the founder of the nation to utter it.

Some critics have in consequence admitted that the original Deuteronomy must have contained, in addition to the code (ch. xii–xxvi), one of the two preambles, and one of the two perorations which now compose its framework.[2]

But the problem is more complex. In each of the introductions and in each of the conclusions, as in the code itself, there are discrepancies and repetitions which show that several hands have been at work on it. The law of the centralization of worship is even repeated three times.[3]

The explanation which seems to keep most closely to the facts is that immediately after the king's intervention, a whole army of well-meaning propagandists, recruited among the disciples of the prophets, set to work, in Jerusalem and throughout Judah, to " publish the words of this law ", to expound its nature and intention, define its scope, and impress upon all whom it concerned the necessity of observing it. Jeremiah was one of those who preached reform, and it is through him that we have become acquainted with this interesting movement.[4] Now each of these propagandists must have had his own copy, written or oral, of the torah he meant to preach. Each made his own comments upon it, varying them according to his public. The " book of the covenant " of Josiah thus speedily became the most widely copied book in all Hebraic literature,[5] and the most copiously furnished with glosses and explanations. It would be natural that, later, someone wanting to have a final version of the Deuteronomic torah—perhaps with a view to incorporating it in the classical collection (JE) of traditions about Moses—should have fused together all the parallel versions of the law which he was able to procure, taking good care to lose nothing. Thus chapters 1 to 30 of Deuteronomy would, as far as

---

[1] Ch. xii–xxvi.   So Vater (**CLXXXII**, iii, 461), Wellhausen (**LXXXIX**, 194–5).

[2] Ch. v–xxvi, xxvii, 9–10 ; xxviii, according to A. Westphal, **XCI**.

[3] xii, 4–7, 8–12, and 13–19.

[4] Jer. xi, 1–6, 18–23. Duhm has contested the originality of this passage, also Hölscher, Kennett, Mowinckel, but Theodore H. Robinson, among others, defends it (**LXVIII**, 1, 427–8).

[5] Cf. Jer. viii, 8.

essentials are concerned, have sprung from the union of several editions.[1]

Many ingenious attempts have recently been made to disentangle and reconstruct these various editions,[2] but no convincing results have been obtained. The task was a particularly delicate one, for the different versions disseminated by the propagandists must have closely resembled each other, both in style and in matter. For the present it would be well to abstain from any effort to distinguish them, or to define precisely the original contents of the book found in the reign of Josiah.

To distinguish certain additions which seem to have been inserted at a later date is a less difficult task.[3]

2. Date of the Redaction of the Code of Josiah

At what period had the original Deuteronomy been drawn up, which most critics identify with the book of torah found in the Temple ?

Some of the many theories propounded, which have increased in number during the recent discussions, may be ruled out : the code cannot date back to Moses, either wholly [4] or in part,[5] nor, as far as essentials are concerned, to the Mosaic period,[6] nor to the first days of the monarchy in Israel.[7]

The narrative in the book of Kings does not say, as Naville alleged, that the book was found *in the foundations* of the Temple, nor even at a time when the building was being repaired ; nor does it suggest that the manuscript could only have been read by a professional scribe, an inference which led Naville to conclude that the code was written in archaic characters, or even in a language unknown to the ordinary run of Judaeans at the time, therefore in Babylonian. On the contrary, the narrative implies that Hilkiah had already read it before giving it to the scribe, since he says to him : " I have found the book of the Law."

To follow Welch's example, and interpret the Deuteronomic law about the place of sacrifice as a purely *regional* concentration of the worship of Jahweh in the *principal* high places, and to say that

[1] This is the opinion, for instance, of Cornill (**X**), Budde (**VI**), Puukko (**CLXIV**), Hempel (**CXXI**), Steuernagel (**CLXXXI**), Eissfeldt (**XX**, 251–268).

[2] In particular by Puukko, Hempel, and Steuernagel.

[3] e.g. certainly iv, 41–3 ; x, 6–7 ; xxvii, 4–8 ; 11–26 ; probably all or part of xiv, 1–21 ; xv, 4–6 ; xvii, 18–20, etc. According to Siebens the civil laws in their entirety (ch. xix–xxv) at first formed an independent codification of the Judaean law of the seventh century. This theory entails serious objections : these laws are characterized by the rhetorical style and the religious exhortations to be found in the ritual regulations of Deuteronomy ; they are also said to have been uttered by Moses. The law about the cities of refuge (xix, 1–13), which secularizes the law of asylum, is organically connected with the abolition of provincial temples ordered by Josiah.

[4] **CLXVI** ; **CLXII** ; **CLXXXVIII** ; **CLXXXIX**.
[5] **CLIX** ; **CLX**.   [6] **CLI**.
[7] **CXLII** ; **CXLI** ; **CLXXXV**.

this concentration took place long before the seventh century,[1] is, on the other hand, arbitrary. Such a theory has no foundation in fact, for in the seventh century men still worshipped " upon *every* high hill and under *every* green tree ".[2]

Nor can it be maintained that, according to Deut. xii, 14, when Moses commanded that sacrifices should only be offered " in the place which the Lord shall choose in one of thy tribes " he meant to approve of the multiplication of high places, provided that they had been chosen by God and not by man.[3] Oestreicher quotes a similar phrase (xxiii, 16) with regard to fugitive slaves, but it does not justify the conclusions he draws. The fugitive slave is to be left free to choose his place of residence, but he will naturally only live in one place at one time. According to the lawgiver, it is to be the same with Jahweh.

The fact that he prohibits a multiplicity of places of sacrifice, that he condemns in principle all graven images, that he presumes that the monopoly of the " Levite priests " is established, proves that Deuteronomy must belong to a period after the editing of the collections J and E ; by ordering the destruction even of standing stones (*maṣṣeboth*), he shows himself in advance of Isaiah. He makes a clear allusion to the reign of Solomon (xvii, 16–17). He combats the worship of the astral gods.[4] His style is akin to that of the prophets of the seventh century, Jeremiah in particular.

His conception of the law is no longer the ancient idea of θεσμός, a sacred axiom which owed its authority to the simple fact that it expressed the custom of the forefathers or emanated from the god, but the much more modern νόμος, which admits of modification and therefore seeks to recommend itself to the reason, basing its authority on what is rational, just and useful.[5]

Although such a code could not, apparently, have been drawn up before the seventh century, it seems unlikely, as we have seen,[6] that it can have been composed after Josiah's reform.[7] The period of the exile[8] would be especially ill-suited, for Deuteronomy is legislating for a nation which still can be called a State, which has a king, armies, and diplomatic relations with the neighbouring States.[9]

That being so, the code found in the Temple must have been drawn up in the century which preceded Josiah's reforms. An opinion which has met with a good deal of support is that it was written in the reign of Hezekiah, before[10] or after[11] the reforms enacted by him. But as we have shown, there is good reason to

---

[1] **CLXXXV.**

[2] Jer. ii, 20 ; iii, 6, 32 ; xvii, 2 ; Ez. vi, 13 ; xviii, 6, 11 ; xx, 28 ; Is. lvii, 7 ; lxv, 7 ; *cf.* 1 Kings xiv, 23 ; 2 Kings xvi, 4 ; xvii, 10 ; Deut. xii, 2.

[3] **CLXI.**   [4] iv, 19 ; xvii, 3.

[5] See the excellent study by Antonin Causse, *La transformation de la notion d'alliance et la rationalisation de l'ancienne coutume dans la réforme deuteronomique*, **RHP**, xiii (1933), 1–29.

[6] pp. 164–5.   [7] Cullen, Siebens (part of the code).

[8] Hölscher, Loisy, Kennett, etc. See pp. 139–140.

[9] xvii, 14–20 ; cci, 23, 10–15 ; xxiv, 5 ; *cf.* Causse, **RHP**, xiii, 4.

[10] Westphal, Sellin, König, Steuernagel.

[11] Siebens, **CLXXVI**, 91–6, 178, 239–0.

doubt that the centralization of worship was included in those reforms [1]; and besides, how could a book which had created so great an upheaval disappear so completely that, eighty years later, all that was left of it was a single copy forgotten in a vestry?

According to Oesterley and Theodore Robinson,[2] Deuteronomy was composed by a disciple of the prophet Hosea in *northern Israel* with a view to the concentration of the worship of Jahweh at *Bethel*, and not at Jerusalem. They base their argument on the close relationship between the book in question and the Elohist document, which is generally considered to be Ephraimite. But in the seventh century, what had once been the kingdom of the north, was no longer a State governed by a king and capable of arming, but an Assyrian province. It may, however, be possible, as we have seen, to date the composition of the code in the previous century.

It would be more likely that the code was drawn up in the reign of Josiah himself,[3] a little before the reforms were inaugurated, and with a view to that event, whether by means of a " pious fraud "[4] or with avowed intent. For Hilkiah's announcement that he found the book in the Temple may have been meant simply as an indication that he guaranteed its divine origin, just as in Egypt when a book had been composed it was said to have been found in the Temple at the feet of Thoth, the revealer of books.[5] Or the whole episode of the discovery of a torah, ready made, may be a legendary embellishment of the original story.[6]

Still another conjecture is possible.[7] The long reign of Manasseh cannot have been a period of easy and unbroken victory for paganizing syncretism. There must have been times when the people, perhaps under the threat of some new calamity, sought in their bewilderment unauthorized means of regaining the goodwill of the God of their fathers, and gave ear to those who preached the acceptance of prophetic ideals.[8] At such times it would have been possible for reformers to draw up a programme which might be successful in restoring Mosaic Jahwism in what seemed to them its pure and unadulterated condition. Speedily convinced of the hopelessness of an attempt to enforce their ideals, they may have deposited their project of legislation in some hidden corner of the Temple, where it remained, forgotten, until Hilkiah found it, either by chance or as the result of a deliberate search [9]; both Shaphan and Hilkiah seem, as a matter of fact, to have some vague idea of its existence, since Hilkiah says : " I have found *the* book of the Law."

Everything points to the original Deuteronomy having been composed between 692 and 622.

[1] pp. 114–16.
[2] *An Introduction to the Books of the O.T.*, 1934, pp. 57–60.
[3] Schrader, Nöldeke, Graf, Wellhausen, Kuenen, Reuss, Dillmann, Stade, Cornill, Budde, Marti.
[4] Renan, Stade.   [5] Maspero, Budde (**VI,** 109).
[6] Marti, **XLVIII,** 1[3], 239.
[7] Ewald, Riehm, Valeton, Ferd. Montet (*Le Deut. et la question de l'Hexateuque*, Paris, Fischbacher, 1891), G. Wildboer (*Die Litt. des A.T. nach der Zeitfolge ihrer Entstehung*, Göttingen, Vandenhoek and Ruprecht, 1895), Peake (*Rel. of Israel*, 1908, p. 84).
[8] Mi. vi, 6–8, see pp. 124–8.   [9] **LXXXII,** i, 261.

IV

NATURE OF THE REFORM UNDER JOSIAH

If the old legal adage *Is fecit cui prodest* is to be trusted, it is among the priests of Jerusalem that the promoters of Josiah's reforms must be sought. They were its chief beneficiaries. By abolishing all the temples of Jahweh which had hitherto competed with their own, by forcing all the inhabitants of the kingdom to come to the one central place of worship, there to offer their sacrifices, pay their dues, celebrate their festivals and ask for oracles, by even going so far as to penalize those who refused to submit to the judicial sentences pronounced by the ministers of the house of Jahweh,[1] the new code assured the priests of the capital of an immense increase in prestige, income, and power.[2]

But though the priests who drew up the code did not forget the interests of their corporation, they also showed themselves to be convinced partisans of the principles proclaimed by the great prophets : that there were such men among the priests of the seventh century, men who sympathized with the new ideas, the names of Jeremiah and Ezekiel amply prove.

In one sense Josiah's reforms were a vigorous attempt to put into practice the aspirations of the great prophets, and to formulate in legal documents the demands of Jahweh as revealed by the prophets since the eighth century.

The struggle against the worship of strange gods and the continued observance of rites held to be pagan, with which the Deuteronomic legislators are chiefly concerned, had been, especially since the reign of Manasseh, one of the watchwords of the prophets, another side of whose preaching is also reflected in the code, namely in the large proportion of laws intended to promote justice and goodwill among the various sections of the nation, which, according to the prophets, could not hope for salvation without them. A number of laws are designed for the protection of the poor, of women, slaves, and foreigners, among whom is usually included the

---

[1] Deut. xvii, 12–13.
[2] According to Adalbert Merx, Deuteronomy has a better claim than " the law of the Tabernacle " to the title of a " priestly writing " (**CLV**).

provincial Levite whom the abolition of the high-places at
which he officiated has deprived of a livelihood. The lawgiver aims at mitigating the horrors of war. He interprets
in a spiritual manner ancient customs whose origin was in
reality derived from animist, idolatrous or magical beliefs,
but in which, however, he finds the occasion for actions inspired
by the finest feeling.[1] Such are the exemptions from military
service which were originally dictated by fear of demoniacal
or magical influences,[2] and the command that the bird whose
eggs or whose young are taken is to be spared.[3] The restriction against picking up the forgotten sheaf of corn, or gathering the very last of the fruits of the olive-tree or the vine, is
likewise not to be explained by the fear of driving away the
spirit of fertility from the field or the plant but sprang from
the desire to leave the poor something to glean.[4] The seventh
day is to be a day of rest, not because it is an unlucky day
for certain kinds of work, but because slaves and cattle must
be assured of rest.[5] The signs of Jahweh worn on the forehead
or the hand,[6] the tassels at the four corners of the cloak,[7] are
there to remind the Israelite that it is his duty to obey the
commandments of his God.[8]

There is one cardinal point, however, on which those of
the prophets and their followers who rallied to the
Deuteronomic reforms departed from one of the fundamental
principles of the pioneers. The latter had been unanimous
in their denial of the value and efficacy of sacrificial ritual,
in which all their fathers had believed, but which they decried,
proclaiming their conviction that these practices formed no
part of God's real requirements, for Jahweh demanded justice,
mercy, and faith, not burnt-offerings. But Deuteronomy
implicitly sanctioned them by the very fact of reforming the
Temple worship. By insisting that Jahweh desired that
worship should be celebrated in a particular place, it taught

---

[1] Cf. A. Causse, **RHP**, xiii (1933), 289–323.
[2] Deut. xx, 2–9 ; cf. **LVII**, 341–2.
[3] Deut. xxii, 6–7 ; cf. **LVII**, 246.
[4] Deut. xxiv, 19–22.
[5] Deut. v, 14–15 ; cf. **LVII**, 508–511.
[6] Cf. **LVII**, 368, 375–7.
[7] Deut. xxii, 12 ; cf. Numb. xv, 38–9.
[8] Deut. vi, 8 ; xi, 18. See also the interpretation of the old rites,
Deut. xxi, 1–9, 22–3.

ipso facto that Jahweh desired that worship should be cele-brated. Thus, into the very centre of the spiritual religion which the prophets had hoped to build up, a wedge of popular belief was driven : the belief in the Temple of Jerusalem and its ritual. The reformers of 622 did what Mahommed was also to do, when he embodied in his monotheistic religion the ancient heathen cult of the black stone of the Kaaba of Mecca.

In order to understand the first beginnings of the Deuteronomic reforms and in particular that of the centralization of worship, we must take into account not only the aims of the priesthood and the influence of men like Amos and Isaiah, but also a third factor, whose origin dates back far beyond the great prophetic movement of the eighth century, namely the bias against the Canaanites. When they first settled in Palestine the Israelites took over, as we know, the high-places of the land of their adoption, their sacred objects and their rites, consecrating them anew to the service of their God, Jahweh [1] ; in each temple the names given to the former local deity were used for Jahweh, so that the God of Israel seemed about to be dissociated into several more or less distinct entities : the " God of Dan ", the " Patron of Beersheba ", the " Jahweh of Hebron ", and so on,[2] just as, among the neighbouring peoples, the Ishtar of Arbela was distinguished from that of Nineveh, or Anat ašr ba'al (of the temple of Baal ?) from the Virgin Anat.[3]

This incursion of heterogeneous elements into the austere religion of their fathers was soon felt, in certain quarters in Israel, as a deviation from the true path. In the ninth century the Rechabites advocated the return of the whole nation to the desert and called upon the people to throw off the shackles of civilization. The old codes at least, the second decalogue and the book of the covenant, prohibit the use of gold and silver images, as too luxurious, and of carved and raised altars. The narrators J and E idealize the days of the fore-fathers.[4] This somewhat vague longing to purify worship by eliminating Canaanitish elements must surely have lasted on into the eighth century, for some of the great prophets,

[1] See p. 74. [2] *Cf.* **LVII**, 472–3.
[3] In the poems of Ras Shamra (**II**, 9, 14, 27, 30, etc.).
[4] *Cf.* **LVII**, 476–7, 485–7.

Hosea and Isaiah, made room for it in their preaching. And it was doubtless in this diluted form, easily intelligible and accessible to the masses of the people, that many of their disciples assimilated the new teaching, the full purport of which was beyond them.

It was on this lower plane of the prophetic movement that the originators of the idea of the concentration of worship in Jerusalem must have worked. Since the high-places which had once been Canaanite were incurably infected with ritual foreign to the true religion of Jahweh, they were to be destroyed. This radical attitude can be seen among the Wahabis of modern Islam with regard to the saints or *welis* : interpreting the respect paid to them as an infringement of the principle of the Koran that Allah is the only *weli* (protector), and a return to paganism, they ruthlessly destroy the tombs of even the most holy persons.

The Temple of Jerusalem had no such associations. Nothing about it was reminiscent of Canaan. On the contrary, everything recalled a specifically Israelite period of national history, the glorious reigns of David and Solomon. Moreover, it was easier to supervise worship when concentrated in one place, and to preserve it from any new heathen contacts. And finally there was the great advantage that in future any dissociation of the God of their fathers could be forestalled : " Hear, O Israel, the Lord our God is one Lord." [1] This formula was no doubt the expression of " monojahwism " [2] before it was interpreted as that of monotheism.

The nationalism which viewed the stranger with hostility has also left its mark on the civil and moral clauses of the Deuteronomic code. Properly speaking, the Israelite's only duties are his duties to " his neighbour ", that is to say his compatriot.[3] Here is evidence of an exclusiveness which neither ancient Israel nor the great prophets had known to anything like the same degree.

Of these three tendencies—sacerdotal, prophetic, and anti-Canaanite—the second seems to have predominated among the devotees and propagandists of reform. The commentaries which now form the framework of the code itself

---

[1] Deut. vi, 4.   [2] *Cf.* C.
[3] For instance, Deut. xxiii, 20–1 ; xxiv, 7. (On the other hand, see Ex. xxi, 16.)

(Deut. i–ii and xxvii–xxx) are inspired by religious and moral ideals of great purity and loftiness, to which their progressive attitude to the suppression of idols, their idea of Israel as the chosen people, and the spirit which sums up the Law in the phrase " Thou shalt love the Lord thy God with all thy heart " are sufficient testimony. Here for the first time appears the motto of theoretical monotheism : " Jahweh, he is God : there is none else beside him." [1] These developments, rather prolix and monotonous as they may seem to us, however novel they were when they first appeared, and these ardent exhortations, couched in such simple language that everyone could understand them, must have done more than the most audacious and inspired flights of the prophets to popularize the new teaching and to instil into the masses the conception that the religion of Israel was a unique religion, essentially different from all others.

V

CONSEQUENCES OF JOSIAH'S REFORM

Josiah's reforms did not bring about that result for which the promoters chiefly hoped, namely the preservation of the last of the Israelite states from destruction. On the other hand, certain unlooked-for consequences emerged which we shall be able to trace in the centuries that followed. Let us point out a few of these.

The division of the priesthood into two castes was hastened : an upper caste, formed by the priests at Jerusalem, and a lower caste, composed of those who had once officiated in high-places ; here may be seen in embryo the classification of Jewish clerics into priests and Levites.

The fate of prophecy was sealed when, side by side with the living word of the messenger of Jahweh there appeared a new authority, that of the written word, which very soon was thought to convey the final will of God in its entirety : " Ye shall not add unto the word which I command you, neither shall ye diminish from it," we read in Deuteronomy itself.[2] And Jeremiah already encountered men who refused to believe

---

[1] Deut. iv, 35, cf. 39.　　　　[2] Deut. iv, 2.

him, saying : " We are wise, and the law of the Lord is with us." [1]

The reforms profoundly modified the function, and even the character of ritual, by breaking the bonds which in Israel, as elsewhere in ancient times, had united it with the multifarious events of everyday life : henceforth, except for a few days in the year, the days of the great festivals, the sacrificial rite disappears from the lives of all Jews who do not inhabit the capital. The piety of multitudes of the faithful must find a new outlet—the worship of the synagogue.

In a more general way the reforms of Deuteronomy influence the entire subsequent trend of the religious history of Israel down to our own time : they may rightly be said to have created " Judaism " in so far as they initiated that fusion of prophetic ideals with the rites and traditions of popular religion which is characteristic of the new aspect of Jahwism after the exile.

Finally, Josiah's code was the first stratum of the torah in the Jewish sense, that of a written formula of the will of God, considered as final and sufficient. It was at the same time—and here its historical significance is still more momentous—the nucleus of the Bible, regarded as the divine norm of life. It was after 622 that Israel began to be the people of the Book.

<hr />

[1] Jer. viii, 8.

CHAPTER VI

THE LAST YEARS OF THE KINGDOM OF JUDAH

I

THE END OF THE REIGN OF JOSIAH. JEREMIAH'S ESTIMATE OF THE REFORMS. REVIVAL OF NATIONAL JAHWISM : NAHUM

WHEN King Josiah began his work of reform, Jeremiah, as we have seen,[1] apparently supported it resolutely, making it the burden of his preaching in the towns of Judah.[2] But it did not take him long to realize that the improvement resulting from the king's decrees was on the surface, and only served to nourish illusions. By observing a few of the laws dealing with externals, such as the centralization of worship, men were to be able to pay off all their debts to Jahweh, though morally the last state was the same as the first. Or, to make use of the prophet's own imagery, the thorns had not been removed before the seed was sown, and the field had not been thoroughly ploughed.[3] The possession of a written torah constituted a pretext for rejecting the " word of the Lord "—that is to say, the message delivered verbally by the prophet—and with it the real " law of the Lord ", those things which he had always required of his followers.

> " Yea, the stork in the heaven knoweth her appointed times [4] ; and the turtle and the swallow [5] and the crane observe the time of their coming, but my people know not the ordinance of the Lord. How do ye say : We are wise, and the law of the Lord is with us ? But behold, the false pen of the scribes hath wrought falsely. The wise men are ashamed, they are dismayed and taken : lo, they have rejected the word of the Lord ; and what manner of wisdom is in them ? " [6] " And yet for all this her treacherous sister, Judah, hath not returned unto me with her whole heart, but feignedly, saith the Lord." [7]

[1] p. 145.
[2] Jer. xi, 2–6.
[3] iv, 3–4.
[4] Read mô'adâh (lxx).
[5] Read wesus 'âgur (LXXL).
[6] Jer. viii, 7–9.
[7] Jer. iii, 10.

And so, even in the reign of the king responsible for the reforms, Jeremiah returns to his task of warning the nation that the final catastrophe is inevitable.[1]

But he was to be almost the only one to judge the moral and spiritual condition of the nation with so much discernment and to foresee the worst. Most of the prophets, the priests, and the masses of the population were entirely optimistic,[2] evidently convinced that, thanks to the reforms introduced by the king and accepted by the nation, Jahweh had become reconciled to his people and had finally revoked the threats of which his prophets had once been the mouthpiece.

For about twelve years, the course of events seemed to favour the optimists and belie the sombre presentiments of Jeremiah. Taking advantage of the increasing weakness of Assyria, Josiah succeeded in extending his power to include the former northern kingdom, and in bringing it within the scope of his reforms,[3] thus uniting once more Israel and Judah beneath the sceptre of David.

What was more, Nineveh itself finally fell in 612.[4] The excitement aroused in Judah by such an event, as also no doubt in all the other populations which had been forcibly incorporated in the Assyrian empire, can well be imagined. The little book of the prophet Nahum rings with it.

Until 1923, when the chronicle of Nabopolassar was published, there was great divergence among the critics as to the date of this short work : some dated it 660, others about 650, others again between 647 and 625,[5] others about 625, others about 606, the date at which the town was supposed to have surrendered.

It seems very probable that the events to which the Jewish writer alludes are the same as those related in the Babylonian chronicle, namely the events which preceded or took place at the siege of 612. For Nahum says that, before the Assyrians were imprisoned in their capital, all their

---

[1] Jer. iv, 4 ; viii, 9–13.
[2] See Jer. xxvi, particularly vv. 7–9, 11, 16. The scene takes place the year after the death of Josiah.
[3] 2 Kings, xxiii, 15–20 ; cf. Jer. xli, 4–5.
[4] See p. 43.
[5] According to Ricciotti (**LXXII,** 469) it was composed early in the reign of Josiah.

fortresses had been captured, the gates of the land set wide open unto their enemies, and that the fire had devoured their bars (3, 12). The strongholds of Tarbiz and Asshur are meant, which were taken by Cyaxares two years before Nineveh. Nahum must have composed these impassioned lines either when he heard that the " bloody city " as he calls it, had fallen, or perhaps during the siege as a triumphant forecast of the issue, which was to be fatal to the Assyrians.[1]

In two pictures, full of colour and movement, and ranking among the most brilliant examples of Hebraic literature, he depicts the failing courage of the Assyrian warriors, who have become as weak as women, the vain exertions of the besieged, and finally the fall of the city, which draws from him a pæan of victory.

These poems express with moving sincerity the feelings of relief with which the populations of Asia greeted the overthrow of the rulers who for centuries had preyed on them, robbed them, held them to ransom, deported them. In them burns the long repressed indignation of the patriot, his humiliation at having for so many years seen his leaders tremble at the arrogant voices of the great king's envoys :

" The voice of thy messengers shall no more be heard." [2]

On the other hand, it must be admitted that the prophet who wrote these pages did not rise above the point of view of the national Jahwism of tradition. Not a single word implies that Judah deserved the misfortunes which had overtaken it, Judah appears only in the light of a victim unjustly despoiled by a proud and cruel Nineveh. Jahweh intervenes, not as a judge, but as a combatant : he is avenging himself on the city from which " went forth "—in the time of Sennacherib, for instance—" one that imagineth evil against the Lord," that is to say, against the people and the sacred city of the God of Israel.[3]

Some critics have thought that Nahum was an Israelite from the north, who had been deported into Assyria,[4] and that his birthplace, Elkosh, may be looked for at Alkosh, a village situated a two days' march to the north of the ruins

---

[1] As Th. H. Robinson thinks (**LXVII**, 217).
[2] Nah. ii, 13.   [3] Nah. i, 11.
[4] See **LII**, 150 ; **LXIV**, 173.

of Nineveh. But nothing in the book authorizes one to suppose that it was written by a descendant of the Israelites in the narrower sense ; the author speaks only of Judah and breathes no word of those who had been deported from the northern kingdom. Besides, the tradition identifying Elkosh with the Turkish village of Alkosh only makes its appearance in the sixteenth century. Evidence much earlier than this gives Galilee [1] as Nahum's birthplace, but it is also thought that he may have come from the neighbourhood of Beit Djibrin [2] in that south-west corner of Judah so often traversed by Assyrian armies.[3]

It is therefore probable that Nahum was writing in Judah about 612, therefore after Josiah's reforms.[4] If so, his book shows that he was far from adopting the attitude of Jeremiah at the time : he must have belonged to that group of prophet patriots who, although for the most part they supported the king's reforms, had in practice reverted to the national Jahwism which preceded the prophetic movement of the eighth century. Jahweh, in fact, according to them, was now reconciled with Judah, and his cause was the cause of his chosen people.[5]

II

Religious Life under the Four Last Kings of Judah

The tragic end of the reformer king at Megiddo (609), which was to be followed by an unprecedented series of disasters, rudely shattered the splendid dream of national greatness and security in which the patriots of Judah had been living.[6] A religious crisis followed, which resembled that to which the triumphs of Assyria had given rise in

---

[1] Jerome.   [2] Pseudo-Epiphanius, *Vitae Prophetarum*, 17.
[3] *Cf.* **XXXVI**, 264.   [4] *Cf.* Guthe, **XXXIV**, ii⁴, 66.
[5] In its present form the book is composed of the prophecies of Nahum with an incorporated fragment of an alphabetic psalm (i, 2–10) and various slight additions, recognizable from the fact that Judah and not Nineveh is apostrophized (i, 12 (?) and 13 ; ii, 1, 3) ; in these extraneous passages the role of Jahweh in the destruction of Nineveh is emphasized, and a more religious tone given to the book ; but the moral element is equally lacking in them. With regard to this question, see Paul Humbert (**CXXX, CXXXIII, CXXXV**), Guthe (**XXXIV**, ii⁴), Sellin (**LXXIX**).
[6] *Cf.* pp. 43–50.

the time of Manasseh. The situation went from bad to worse.

Those who had accepted the reforms grudgingly, because the repudiation of time-honoured practices seemed to them nothing less than dangerous sacrilege, relapsed into their former transgressions, and did so all the more eagerly that their rulers, while officially refraining from revoking the Deuteronomic laws—which were theoretically still in force at the time of the siege of 586[1]—turned a blind eye whenever its religious clauses were violated. The compiler of the book of Kings, who must have been well-informed, accuses them all, even Jehoahaz and Jeconiah, each of whom reigned only a few months, of having " done evil in the sight of the Lord " : in religious matters, therefore, they must all have forsaken the path traced out for them by Josiah.

In the reign of Jehoiakim there were in the streets of Jerusalem and the cities of Judah, men, women, and children who offered up cakes to the Queen of Heaven.[2] In the time of Zedekiah, women could be seen sitting at the gate of the Temple and weeping for the god Tammuz [3] and men actually standing beside the altar of Jahweh and worshipping the rising sun with a branch in their hands.[4] In one of the rooms adjoining the sanctuary, elders of the land burnt incense with much mysterious ceremonial, in front of figures of animals traced upon the walls [5] : according to some [6] these were Babylonian rites practised by politicians who wished to ingratiate themselves with the authorities of the moment ; others [7] think they were Egyptian—there was a strong pro-Egyptian and anti-Babylonian party among the nobles of the kingdom; according to a third theory [8] they were a revival of the worship of very ancient theriomorphic Hebrew deities, because the text notes that this homage was paid to " all the idols of the house of Israel " (viii, 10). But these words are open to the suspicion of being a later addition, not necessarily in conformity with Ezekiel's mode of thought. The use of incense and of figures carved upon the walls,

[1] Jer. xxxiv, 8–9. [2] Jer. vii, 18 ; xliv. *Cf.* p. 128.
[3] Ez. viii, 14. *Cf.* p. 129.
[4] Ez. viii, 16–18*a*. [5] Ez. viii, 7–13.
[6] Gunkel, Kraetzschmar (**HK**, *Ez.*), Jeremias (**XLV**), Loisy (**LIX**[3])
[7] Smend (**KEH**, *Ez.*), Bertholet (**KHC**, *Hes.*).
[8] Toy, Davidson.

the performance of the rites in the dark, inside a building and not upon a high-place, all seem to point to the improbability of a Hebrew origin.

Many of these partisans of a return to syncretism no doubt attacked the reforms openly as being the cause of the nation's misfortunes ; such at least was the line of reasoning adopted by certain Jewish emigrants after the final catastrophe :

> " We will certainly perform every word that is gone forth out of our mouth, to burn incense unto the queen of heaven and to pour out drink offerings unto her, as we have done, we and our fathers, our kings and our princes, in the cities of Judah and in the streets of Jerusalem : for then had we plenty of victuals, and were well, and saw no evil. But since we left off . . . we have wanted all things, and have been consumed by the sword and by the famine." [1]

Others who had, on the contrary, retained their faith in Jahweh, and were convinced that all their misfortunes were sent by him in his anger, followed the example of Manasseh's contemporaries, and tried to find some means of forcing God, as it were, to renew his favours, which should be more effective than the traditional rites. It was apparently with this end in view that many Jews, to the great indignation of Ezekiel, " ate with the blood," [2] that is to say consumed, in their burnt-offerings, not only a part of the flesh of the victim but also some of the blood, evidently in the hope that by such communion in both kinds a bond between them and the deity would be established which nothing could break, a bond much closer and more lasting than that established by traditional custom in Israel, which regarded all the blood, that supernatural fluid, as the object of a sacred taboo.[3] The setting up of a " covenant of blood " with the divine was a reversion to a very ancient practice,[4] of which traces still survived, not only in the ritual of ancient Israel,[5] but in Judaism as well.[6]

The same need for a more energetic appeal to the deity probably explains the increasingly large part played by expiatory rites in Jewish worship, the development of which

---

[1] Jer. xliv, 17–18.
[2] Ez. xxxiii, 25 ; cf. Lev. xix, 26. See, however, p. 209, n. 8.
[3] 1 Sam. xiv, 31–5 ; Deut. xii, 15–16, 22–3 ; xv, 22–3.
[4] LVII, 323–4.   [5] Ex. xxiv, 6, 8.
[6] Ex. xxix, 20 ; Lev. viii, 23 ; xiv, 14.

THE LAST YEARS 161

can be seen in the legislation of the period of exile, as well as
in that of Ezekiel, and in the Holiness Code and the Priestly
Code.[1] It is probable that the ritual of these ceremonies
was extremely ancient [2]; they seem to have played only a
very minor part in the worship of ancient Israel, however,
for they are never mentioned in the old texts. Their extraordinary popularity must date from the troubled years
before the fall of Jerusalem.

Men's minds were full of the utmost uncertainty and
dismay. Some wondered if Jahweh had not forsaken the land.[3]
Others dared to argue that he was unjust. When certain
prophets, like Jeremiah,[4] saw in present ills a well-deserved
punishment for the sins of Manasseh, they replied ironically
" The fathers have eaten sour grapes, and the children's
teeth are set on edge," [5] and added " The way of the Lord
is not equal ".[6] The protest was a symptom, showing how
profoundly shaken was the old belief in the solidarity of the
group, whether tribal or national, that belief which was the
keystone of the organization inherited from nomadic times,[7]
revealing too the progress already made by individualism.

Another attitude was, however, predominant, especially
among the spiritual leaders of the people, the priests and the
prophets. With a stubbornness little short of heroic they
persisted in the optimistic outlook caused by Josiah's reforms.
In spite of repeated disasters they remained convinced that
peace had been made between Jahweh and his people, and
they shut their eyes to the fact that the torah was being more
and more gravely violated, both with regard to its religious
precepts and its civil laws. Since Judah possessed the Temple
of Jahweh [8] and the law of Jahweh,[9] they persuaded themselves that all was well between the nation and God, and that
the future might be awaited with confidence, since the
calamities of the present could be nothing but a passing
trial and the prelude to a glorious recovery. And the prophets,
who were almost all of the same mind, foretold that the
hour of reprisals was at hand. Thus in 594–93, four years

---

[1] See below, pp. 258–62, 263, 293–6. [2] **LVII**, 322–3.
[3] Ez. ix, 9. [4] Jer. xv, 4.
[5] Jer. xxxi, 29 ; Ez. xviii, 2. [6] Ez. xviii, 25.
[7] Cf. **LVII**, 221–4, 453–462 ; Causse, **RHP**, x (1930), 24–60.
[8] Jer. vii, 4. [9] Jer. viii, 8.

M

after the exile of Jeconiah, a prophet named Hananiah declared to the inhabitants of Jerusalem :

> " Thus speaketh the Lord of hosts, the God of Israel, saying, I have broken the yoke of the king of Babylon. Within two full years will I bring again into this place all the vessels of the Lord's house . . . with all the captives of Judah that went to Babylon." [1]

Other prophets fostered the same hopes among the exiles.[2] As late as 586 they were still expecting Jahweh to perform a miracle which should liberate them [3]; and this state of feverish anticipation certainly goes a long way to explain the insensate revolts of the Judaeans against the gigantic empire of the Chaldeans, and the stubbornness of their resistance : a temerity which is doubtless not without its heroic side, but which was inspired by the gravest illusions, both moral and political.

Very different was the attitude adopted by Jeremiah and by a few other exceptionally clearsighted individuals in the spiritual crisis in which Judah was involved. In Jeremiah's eyes the disasters overwhelming the land were only the fulfilment of those threats which all true prophets before him [4] had uttered on Jahweh's behalf, and which he himself had pronounced at the beginning of his career [5] : they were a punishment for all Judah's sins, especially for the celebration of heathen rites, officially authorized during the reign of Manasseh,[6] and again tolerated by Jehoiakim and Zedekiah, for the shallow hypocrisy with which Josiah's reforms were carried out, for the violation of the covenant made in 622,[7] for innumerable crimes against the rights of the poor, whose very existence was imperilled.[8] Nothing less than a genuine and fundamental change of conduct and of heart [9] could prevent the still more devastating catastrophe which the prophet foresaw was about to happen.[10]

Soon after the disaster of Megiddo (609), probably very early in the reign of Jehoiakim, when the new king had not yet returned from Riblah to his capital, Jeremiah, standing

---

[1] Jer. xxviii, 1–4.   [2] Jer. xxix, 8–9, 21–32.
[3] Cf. Jer. xxi, 2.   [4] Jer. xxviii, 8.
[5] Jer. xxxvi, 2–3.
[6] Jer. vi, 31 ; xv, 1–4 ; 4b, however, has been suspected of being an addition. Cf. H. Schmidt, **XXVIII**, ii, 2², 270.
[7] Jer. xxxiv, 8–22.
[8] Jer. vii, 8–11 ; cf. ii, 34 ; v, 1, 25–9 ; etc.
[9] Jer. iv, 4.   [10] Jer. xxxvi, 7 ; xviii, 1–12.

in the court of the Temple, declared that the Temple would
soon be overthrown, as that of Shiloh had been, and that the
town would be destroyed. He was almost torn in pieces by
the priests and the prophets, as well as by the people [1];
and was only saved by the intervention of some of the officers
of the king, in particular Ahikam, a son of Shaphan, the
scribe of Josiah,[2] and by elders who invoked the precedent
of Micaiah.[3]

Another prophet, Uriah of Kiriath-jearim, having
" prophesied against this city and against this land according
to all the words of Jeremiah ", took refuge in Egypt, was
handed over to Jehoiakim by his suzerain, the King of Egypt,
put to death, and his body thrown into the graves of the
common people.[4]

As soon as the news of the victory of Nebuchadnezzar
at Carchemish (605) reached Jerusalem, Jeremiah realized
that the Chaldeans were the enemies of the north whose
coming he had persistently foretold since the days of the
Scythian invasions, earning for himself much sarcasm by
so doing.[5]

He had a vision in which it seemed to him that Jahweh
commanded him to cause Judah and all the nations about
to be conquered by the king of Babel to drink at his hand the
cup of the fury of the Lord.[6]

Another day he called together several of the elders of
the people and of the priests, bought a potter's earthen bottle,
and went with them to one of the gates of the town, which
seems to have been called the gate of the Potsherds or the
Pottery gate. There he solemnly broke the vessel, saying :

> " Thus saith the Lord of hosts : Even so will I break this people
> and this city, as one breaketh a potter's vessel that cannot be made
> whole again. Thus will I do unto this place." [7]

Then, going into the court of the Temple, he related and
explained to all the people the symbolic gesture which God
had commanded him to perform. The priest, who was the

---

[1] In v. 16 of ch. xxvi, where the people seem to defend the prophet,
contrary to what appears in vv. 7–9 and 24, the reading should be :
" The princes said to all the people and to the priests," etc. ('el kol ha' am
we'el), and not " The princes and all the people said to the priests ".

[2] See p. 137.

[3] Jer. vii, 1–15, and xxvi, 1–19, 24. Cf. pp. 111–113.

[4] Jer. xxvi, 20–3.   [5] Jer. xv, 15 ; xvii, 14–18 ; xxv, 3–4.

[6] Jer. xxv.   [7] Jer. xix, 11a, 12a.

chief officer of the Temple and who was entrusted with the
supervision of the Temple prophets,[1] one named Pashhur,
had him beaten with rods and put in the stocks until the
next day, no doubt regarding the prophet's gesture as something more than a symbol, or concrete expression of an
opinion, namely a kind of spell which might bring upon
Jerusalem the most dire results : when they wanted to curse
the enemies of the Pharaoh, and to compass their death,
the Egyptians wrote each name separately on vases which
were then broken.[2]   Among the Hittites it was a grave
offence, punishable by a fine or even death, to indicate a
man by name while killing a serpent.[3]   In the same way
Jeremiah had done positive harm to the city by identifying
it with the broken vessel.

Outraged by this wilful misunderstanding of the commands of God, the prophet informed Pashhur that he would
end his days in exile.[4]

A little later there was a still more impressive scene.
Deprived of the right to enter the Temple—no doubt by
the priestly overseer,—he dictated to his disciple, the scribe
Baruch, all the prophecies uttered by him since the beginning of his career, and told him to go into the Temple and
read the scroll before all the people assembled for a fast.
The burden of this summary of twenty-three years of
preaching was the urgent appeal : " Return, every man,
from your evil way,"—otherwise the misfortunes so long
foretold would not fail to come to pass : " The king of
Babylon shall certainly come and destroy this land." [5]
Baruch read this threatening document in a room of the
temple belonging to Gemariah, another of Shaphan's sons.
Then the roll was brought before the king Jehoiakim, who,
after glancing through it, cut it in pieces and threw the
pieces on his brazier.   Jeremiah and Baruch only escaped
death by hiding themselves.[6]

It was at this time that the anonymous prophecy of the
avenging onslaught of the Chaldeans must have been uttered,
which has been preserved for us in the book of Habakkuk,[7]

[1] Jer. xx, 1–6 ; cf. xxix, 26.   [2] CLXXV.
[3] Hittite Code, § 170 (CXXIX, 130–1).   [4] Jer. xix, 1–20, 6.
[5] Jer. xxxvi, 3, 7, 29.   [6] Jer. xxxvi.
[7] Hab. i, 5–10, and perhaps vv. 14–17, in their original form.

the prophet, who seems to have lived in exile about the year 550, having used the prediction as the theme of his mournful reflections on the triumph of proud nations.[1] A prophecy foretelling the coming of the Chaldeans must necessarily, like similiar prophecies by Jeremiah, date from before 602, at which time approximately the new conquerors invaded the land. Perhaps—who can tell ?—the book of Habakkuk was the work of the ill-fated Uriah of Kirjath-jearim, who died the death of a martyr in the reign of Jehoiakim.

Once the King of Babylon had in fact reached Jerusalem and subjugated Judah, Jeremiah set himself the task of preaching submission to Chaldean supremacy, of instilling the need for a humble acceptance of the chastisement with which Jahweh had smitten his erring people ; it was an ungrateful task, and one most repugnant to his patriotic soul, but though it meant that he was openly at variance with the almost unanimous feeling of his fellow-countrymen, he did not flinch from it.

In the year 593, the fourth of Zedekiah's reign, Jerusalem was in a state of effervescence : envoys from the kings of Edom, Moab, Ammon, Tyre, and Sidon were holding council in the capital of Judah with a view to a general revolt against the Chaldeans. Jeremiah appeared before the ambassadors with a yoke on his neck and charged them to deliver to their masters a message from Jahweh,[2] which he repeated for Zedekiah's benefit. The gist of it was : Put your necks under the yoke of Nebuchadnezzar. The yoke is not merely a man's yoke, but it is a God, the mightiest God of all, who lays it upon you.

As Jeremiah continued to go about the streets wearing his ill-omened yoke, one of the prophets who were opposed to him, Hananiah, in the course of an ecstatic trance which increased his strength tenfold, seized the heavy piece of wood and broke it, saying : " Thus speaketh the Lord of hosts, I have broken the yoke of the King of Babylon." Jeremiah's first words, on hearing Hananiah's prophecy

---

[1] This at least seems to us the most natural explanation of the composition of this enigmatic little book ; cf. pp. 232-6.

[2] And not to carry yokes to them, as the Massoretic text suggests (Jer. xxvii, 3) ; read *wesillaḥtâ* (LXX[L]) " and thou shalt send (a message) ", and not *wesillaḥtâm* " and thou shalt send them " (the yokes).

were : " Amen : the Lord do so : the Lord perform thy
words which thou hast prophesied." He may have hoped
that God meant to revoke his sentence. But a short time
afterwards he received a new revelation. Jahweh would
substitute a yoke of iron for the yoke of wood. As for
Hananiah, for having " made the people to trust in a lie "
he would die within the year.[1]

The state of patriotic ferment had spread to the Jews
exiled in Babylonia with Jeconiah. Several prophets had
arisen among them who foretold an immediate return to
Palestine. The Chaldean police got wind of the movements
among them, several " elders " were arrested,[2] and the
seditious prophets were searched and threatened with being
burnt alive.[3]

Taking advantage of an expedition, composed of some of
Zedekiah's nobles, which was then setting out for Babylon,
apparently with the object of conveying expressions of
the king's loyalty to his overlord, Jeremiah confided to
two officials who were in sympathy with his views a letter
intended to calm and reassure the exiles.   He exhorted
them to build houses and plant gardens in Babylon, to
marry and give in marriage, and to pray for the country
which for the time being was their home, for their sojourn
in it was to be a long one. As for the prophets who are
deceiving them, Jeremiah foretells that they will fall into the
hands of the King of Babylon, who will put them to death.[4]

And when, finally, the last rebellion broke out, while
Jerusalem was being besieged by Nebuchadnezzar (587–586),
with unwearying insistence Jeremiah counselled everyone,
the king and those in authority no less than the humble,
to surrender to the Chaldeans. For this apparently un-
patriotic attitude, which was even tantamount to sacrilege
according to the ideas of the time, though it was the only
attitude in keeping with his clear perception of his country's
true interests and God's real demands, the old prophet was
arrested on the suspicion of intending to desert to the
enemy. In spite of the intermittent protection of the king,
the weak Zedekiah, who often consulted him in secret, but

---

[1] Jer. xxviii.
[2] Jer. xxix, 1 (MT) speaks of the " *residue* of the elders of the
captivity ".
[3] Jer. xxix, 22.   [4] Jer. xxix.

was terrorized by his ministers, Jeremiah was thrown into prison and then cast into a cistern, where he would have perished but for the assistance of an Ethiopian eunuch.

After the fall of Jerusalem (586) and the deportation of all the chief men of the city, he stayed in the country, at Mizpah, in the house of Gedaliah, a grandson of Shaphan, who had been appointed governor by the Chaldeans and who courageously endeavoured, no doubt in agreement with the prophet, to reconstruct a nucleus of the Jewish nation which would still loyally submit to Chaldean rule. Owing to the assassination of Gedaliah by the Jewish prince Ishmael, the attempt failed, and Jeremiah was involved against his will in a flight to Egypt, where the fugitives, or some of them, settled at Tahpanhes, the modern Tell Defenneh, in the Delta. The prophet warned them that they were not out of Nebuchadnezzar's reach ; he even laid down the foundations of the throne which the King of Babylon would soon erect in front of the Pharaoh's palace.[1] To his great grief, he witnessed a revival among the exiles of the worship of the Queen of heaven, who was apparently regarded by the women who prayed to her as the feminine counterpart of Jahweh, as was the case with Anat Jahu who was worshipped by the Jews of Elephantine in the fifth century [2]; this at least is to be inferred from the fact that one of the most terrible threats which he could utter against those who practised or tolerated this cult is that they would no longer be allowed to *name the name of Jahweh* [3] ; they must therefore have declared themselves faithful to the God of Israel while they were associating him with other deities.

The last that we know of Jeremiah's career shows us this valiant fighter grappling with this latest difficulty.[4]

III

WORK AND PERSONALITY OF JEREMIAH

In his struggles to save his people, the prophet was to all appearances vanquished. In reality it was to him more than

---

[1] Jer. xliii. Nebuchadnezzar, in fact, made an expedition into Egypt in 568 ; *cf.* p. 180.

[2] See pp. 307–8.   [3] Jer. xliv, 26.   [4] Jer. xliv.

to anyone else that Judah owed its ability to survive the misery of exile. By repeating with indefatigable zeal the unwelcome tidings of the wrath to come, as the prophets of the previous century had done, he made it possible for the nation to see in the disaster, when it did come, the just and deliberate hand of God instead of interpreting it as a proof of the superiority of the gods of the stranger. If Judah had known only such prophets as Hananiah, the nation would have been so taken by surprise and so bewildered by apparently undeserved misfortune that it would almost certainly have lost its faith in a national God, and, like northern Israel, have become merged in the surrounding mass of paganism.

Still more fruitful for the centuries to come was the personal influence of Jeremiah, in the richness, the intensity, the dramatic grandeur of his religious life. By nature, in spite of appearances, gentle, tender-hearted and timid, on him was laid the task of proclaiming death to all that he loved. In the same breath in which he foretells the final overthrow of Jerusalem, he intercedes for the guilty.[1] Though at God's command, and in order to foreshadow in his own life the misfortunes which will overtake the country, he abstains from marriage and the joy of sons and daughters, though he will neither take part in festivities nor in mourning,[2] though outwardly he is as insensible as a brazen wall,[3] he shrinks from danger and from threats ; when he is taunted and accused of loving neither his country nor the religion of his fathers, he suffers so cruelly that he curses the day when he was born.[4] When God delays the execution of the threats he has put into his mouth, he is tormented by the thought that Jahweh may have deceived him.[5] When he is on the point of forsaking the work entrusted to him, the divine voice which never ceases to echo in his soul recalls him with an urgency he cannot gainsay, and he takes up the fight again :

" O Lord thou hast deceived me, and I was deceived : thou art stronger than I and hast prevailed. I am become a laughing-stock all the day, every one mocketh me. For as often as I speak, I cry out : I cry, Violence and spoil : because the word of the Lord is

---

[1] Jer. xiv, 7–9 ; *cf.* xviii, 20.   [2] Jer. xvi, 1–9.
[3] Jer. i, 18 ; xv, 20.   [4] Jer. xx, 14–18 ; *cf.* xv, 10.
[5] Jer. xv, 18.

made a reproach unto me and a derision all the day. But if I say I will not make mention of him,[1] nor speak any more in his name, then there is in mine heart as it were a burning fire shut up in my bones, and I am weary with forebearing, and I cannot contain." [2]

Others before Jeremiah must have known inward conflicts of his kind, at least to some extent [3] ; but they took care not to give a detailed account of them, probably because it seemed a weakness on their part to complain and to be reluctant to carry out God's commands. It is something quite new and original that Jeremiah should have put in writing and included in a prophetic book all these bitter intimacies about his private life, as well as the prayers in which he held personal converse with God of a kind which, for the time being, restored his balance and his peace of mind. It had certainly long been the custom for the Israelites in the supplicatory psalms—a form of expression with which they, and the Babylonians before them, must have been familiar at a very early date—to bewail their sorrows before God, and in the canticles of thanksgiving to recall the lamentations, or even the doubts, which they had uttered in the time of distress. And in this part of his work Jeremiah may have been inspired by the traditional language of hymnology.[4] But he analyses, much more deeply than they did, his secret griefs, and his outpourings are entirely unpremeditated. It may justly be said that he wrote the first book of Confessions. He has laid bare a whole new world of religious thought, the world of spiritual conflict, of struggles between nature and a higher call. In these experiences lay revelations of truths new to the mentality of the day, truths whose full bearing Jeremiah himself probably did not grasp. For they showed that not only may there exist a religious relation between the nation and its God, but also one between God and the individual, even when the bond between God and the nation is broken. They also proved that those who are unhappy may, in spite of, even because of, their sorrows, enter into more intimate communion with God than those who are

---

[1] Read 'azkîrennu (LXX).

[2] Jer. xx, 7-9 ; cf. xi, 18 ; xii, 1-6 ; xv, 10-21 ; xvii, 15-18 ; xx, 10-18.

[3] Amos, for instance, vii, 2, 5 ; cf. Ex. iii, 11-12 ; xxxii, 31-2 ; 1 Sam. xv, ii, 35 ; 1 Kings xix, 4.

[4] Cf. Mowinckel, LXVI, passim, e.g. V, 93, note 4 ; VI, 23.

accounted happy in the eyes of the world : misfortune therefore was not necessarily a sign of divine disapproval.

But, though in private Jeremiah discovered and practised
a more individual and more spiritual religion, he did not make
it the subject of his teaching in public. In his preaching,
however, there are traces of the same tendency to give to
religion an inward direction.

Guided on his resolute course by the same spirituality
which had characterized men like Amos and Hosea, he
declares once more, after the compromises of the Deuteronomic reforms, that sacrificial ritual is not included in the
demands of Jahweh, and has no power to take away sins.[1]

What he considers indispensable is the circumcision of
the heart, the return of *the heart* to the Lord.[2] According to
him, the chief of all sins is hardness—that is to say, stubbornness—*of heart*.[3]

The higher his ideal, the more clearly he realizes that,
humanly speaking, it is unattainable. For Judah is so
enslaved by vicious habits that reform is impossible :—

" Can the Ethiopian change his skin or the leopard his spots ?
Then may ye also do good that are accustomed to do evil." [4]

And yet, Jeremiah is convinced that one day the nation
will come into its own again. In the last days of the siege,
when the Chaldeans were on the point of taking possession
of the town, he bought from one of his cousins a field at
Anathoth, for the Lord had said to him " Houses and fields
and vineyards shall yet again be bought in this land ".[5] He
maintained, however, that the recovery must be brought
about by a sincere and profound change of heart.[6] How was
that possible, since Judah was incapable of reform ? His
answer was the same as the answer with which Jesus solved
a similar problem [7] : God himself would give his rebellious
people hearts capable of knowing him [8] and would put
his law into their minds.[9] In fact the prophet foretells a
new covenant of the future, whose precepts shall not be

---

[1] Jer. vii, 22–3 ; ii, 15 (LXX). See pp. 66–7.
[2] Jer. iv, 4, 14 ; xvii, 5.
[3] Jer. vii, 24 ; ix, 13 ; xi, 8, 13, etc.; *cf.* v, 23.
[4] Jer. xiii, 23.   [5] Jer. xxxii, 15.
[6] So xxix, 13.   [7] Mark x, 27 ; John iii, 5–8.
[8] Jer. xxiv, 7.   [9] Jer. xxxi, 32.

written in a book—like Deuteronomy—but in the heart of every man, when the authority that rules from without shall have given place to the authority that rules from within.[1]

Jeremiah's idea of God is indeed a lofty one. Not only does God know all, see all, hear all,[2] but he is present everywhere.[3] The prophet does not go so far as to deny the existence of any other gods.[4] But he describes their impotence in terms so sweeping that it is hard to see what divine attributes he has left them : they " cannot save ",[5] they are " broken cisterns ",[6] he calls them " vanities " and " falsehood ",[7] and says they are " no gods ".[8]

Of all the prophets of Israel, Jeremiah understood most clearly the " religion of the spirit ".

[1] Jer. xxxi, 31–4.
[2] Jer. viii, 6 ; xvii, 9–10 ; cf. xi, 20 ; xvi, 17 ; xx, 12 ; xxxii, 19.
[3] Jer. xxiii, 23–5.   [4] See, for instance, xvi, 13.
[5] Jer. ii, 8, 11, 28 ; xi, 12.   [6] Jer. ii, 13.
[7] Jer. ii, 5 ; viii, 19 ; xiii, 25 ; xviii, 15.
[8] Jer. ii, 11 ; v, 7.

THE BEGINNINGS OF JUDAISM

BOOK I

THE HISTORICAL BACKGROUND

CHAPTER I

THE EXILE

I

THE JEWS SPLIT INTO THREE GROUPS. THEIR POLITICAL AND ECONOMIC CONDITION

AS a result of the events which characterized the end of the kingdom of Judah, the population was split up into three groups, each of which was henceforth to live under entirely different conditions : the group of exiles deported to Babylon, the Jews who were allowed by the conquerors to remain in Palestine, and finally a diaspora consisting of those who, for diverse reasons, chief of which was the desire to escape the catastrophes in which the country was involved, settled abroad.[1]

Some took refuge in the northern and western lands and some in those to the east and south,[2] and even further[3]; while many settled in Egypt.[4] Some of them, no doubt, hoped at first that they would be able to return to their own land,[5] and only awaited a favourable opportunity.[6] But most of them lost no time in adapting themselves to the conditions of their new home. To such belonged the Jewish colony of Elephantine in Upper Egypt, whose existence has been

[1] Jer. xl, 11–12.　　　　　[2] Is. xliii, 5–6 ; xlix, 12.
[3] Is. xlix, 22–3 ; lx, 4 ; lxvi, 19–20.
[4] Jer. xli, 17–44, 30, sp. xliv, 1, 15 (gloss).
[5] Jer. xliv, 28.　　　　　[6] Jer. xl, 11–12.

revealed to us by Egyptian papyri of the fifth century, and their curious social organization described. They were a military colony playing an official part in the life of the country, and had for several generations become so thoroughly established that they had built a temple to their God Jahu (Jahweh).[1]

That part of Palestine which had formed the kingdom of Judah was not, as certain passages might lead one to believe, so ravaged and laid waste by the Chaldeans after 586 that even animals could not live in it,[2] nothing being left but ruined towns [3] and uncultivated land [4]; such descriptions belong to rhetoric and poetic hyperbole. The deportations of 597, 586, and 581 only took away 4,600 men (3,023 + 832 + 745), if the most detailed statistics are to be believed.[5] Supposing that this figure represents the men capable of bearing arms, the exodus would amount to about 20,000 souls. As the population of Judah, before 586, must have been at least 90,000—reckoning thirty inhabitants to the square kilometre over a territory of about 1,200 square miles [6] —it may be estimated that three-quarters of the total number of Judæans remained in the country, even allowing for the emigration of some of them to Egypt and other countries. Guthe thinks that the exiles formed only an eighth of the whole population.[7] We have Ezekiel's word for it that the inhabitants of the " waste places in the Land of Israel " outnumbered those who had been carried into captivity.[8]

The book of Kings expressly states, moreover, that " the captain of the guard (Nebuchadnezzar's guard) left of the poorest of the land to be vinedressers and husbandmen ",[9]

---

[1] See below, pp. 304–12.

[2] Jer. ix, 10 ; xxxii, 43 ; xxxiii, 12–13 ; xliv, 2.

[3] Is. xliv, 26 ; xlv, 13 ; xlix, 8, 16–21 ; lii, 9 ; liv ; lviii, 12 ; lx, 10, 15 ; lxi, 4 ; lxii, 4 ; lxiv, 9–10 ; Jer. xvii, 26 ; xxii, 4–5, 8–9 ; Ez. xxxviii, 12 ; Zech. vii, 7 ; Lam. i, 4 ; etc.

[4] Lev. xxvi, 31–5, 43 ; Ez. xxxvi, 33–8.

[5] Jer. lii, 28–30. 2 Kings xxiv, 16, places the figure at 8,000 exiles for the first deportation ; while 2 Kings xxiv, 14, gives 10,000, not including the blacksmiths and locksmiths, that is to say the workmen capable of making arms.

[6] **XLIX**, iii, 2, 1929, pp. 344–5.

[7] **XXX²**, 255–6.   [8] Ez. xxxiii, 24.

[9] 2 Kings xxv, 12. The translation of the last word is conjectural. *Cf.* Jer. xxxix, 10 ; lii, 16.

and in fact we find the governor exhorting them to " gather wine, and summer fruits and oil "[1] in the very year that the Temple was destroyed. Although some still tried to hold out, keeping to the caves and hiding-places of the mountains, others had made homes for themselves in the ruins of the the cities, and others again were scattered about the country-side.[2] That only the poor, or as another passage puts it,[3] those " which had nothing ", were allowed to remain behind, is a statement which must not be taken too literally, for among those who were not deported were men of standing like Gedaliah and Jeremiah, and members of noble families like " the king's daughters ".[4] Later still, the Jewish population of Palestine seems to have included priests [5] and elders.[6]

The country was made into an organized administrative district by the Chaldeans, so that when the exiles returned, they found Judah already a province, or, more literally, a " judicial district " (medînâh), in which they were quartered. Immediately after the destruction of the State the conquerors had placed at the head of the district a governor, the Jew Gedaliah, with a small Chaldean garrison.[7] Far from there being any suspension of life owing to the national catastrophe in what had once been the land of Judah, vitality was not long in recreating the conditions indispensable to existence.

The lot of the survivors, however, was anything but a bed of roses. The territory belonging to Judah had been so reduced, that when the captives returned, the medînâh no longer included either Hebron or the Negeb, which were in the hands of the Edomites, while Beth-zur and Tekoah marked the limits of Jewish possessions to the south.[8] The Calebites, the Jerahmeelites and the Rechabites, tribes which were old allies of Judah, had been driven back towards the north ; the Calebites, for instance, had been forced to withdraw from Hebron to Bethlehem.[9] It was probably in 586 that the Edomites, taking advantage of Judah's misfortunes, had thus laid hands on the southern part of the kingdom,

[1] Jer. xl, 10.   [2] Ez. xxxiii, 27.
[3] A later one, no doubt : Jer. xxxix, 10.
[4] Jer. xli, 10 ; xliii, 6.   [5] Lam. i, 4.
[6] Lam. ii, 10.   [7] Jer. xl–xli, especially xli, 3.
[8] The former about 13 miles, the latter 17 miles from Jerusalem.
[9] Cf. 2 Chron. ii, 4.

and that the Chaldeans, whose allies they had become, had sanctioned the annexation. This would explain the virulent and indignant language in which all the Jewish writers of the period condemn the disloyal attitude adopted by Edom in " the day of Jerusalem ".[1] Ezekiel names them as the nation which has usurped the land of Jahweh.[2]

The fifth Lamentation, composed apparently in the course of the second generation in Palestine,[3] gives a very sombre picture of the life of Judaeans at the time. Many of them, dispossessed by strangers, were reduced to paying for the water they drank and the wood they burnt, since they no longer had free access to their cisterns or their communal thickets.[4] Conditions remained insecure, at least in the neighbourhood of the desert.[5] The depression was general. Some had even followed the emigrants to Egypt or to Assyria —which doubtless means Syria—in order to have enough to eat.[6] Even admitting that the poet may have lent a dramatic colour to the situation by speaking of individual cases of distress as if they were general, the fact remains that the comparatively large number of Jews who had remained in Palestine seem to have eked out a miserable livelihood, and that being now without leaders [7] they accepted humiliation with a listlessness which gave little hope of future recovery.

The third group was composed of those who were led captive by the Chaldeans into Babylonia in 597, 586, and 581. Certain passages from the prophets or the poets of the time might lead one to form quite a wrong idea of the fate which befell them, especially the references to captivity,[8] to prisoners chained in dungeons or shut up in dark and gloomy jails.[9] But these are figures of speech. Only a few of the vanquished, like Zedekiah, the rebellious and perjured vassal,[10] were kept in chains for the rest of their lives, or imprisoned for a time, like Jeconiah, Zedekiah's predecessor.[11] As for

---

[1] Ps. cxxxvii, 7 ; Lam. iv, 21-2 ; cf. i, 17 ; Ez. xxv, 12-14 ; xxxv–xxxvi; Mal. i, 2-5.

[2] Ez. xxxvi, 5.   [3] Lam. v, 7.

[4] Lam. v, 4.   [5] Lam. v, 9 ; cf. Jer. xli.

[6] Probable meaning of Lam. v, 6.

[7] Lam. v, 8 ; " Servants rule over us."

[8] Lam. i, 5, 18 ; Is. lii, 2 ; Jer. l, 33 ; Ps. cxxxvii, 3 ; Ezr. ix, 7, etc.

[9] Is. xlii, 7, 22 ; cf. Lam. iii, 24.

[10] 2 Kings xxv, 7 ; Jer. lii, 11 ; cf. Ez. xvii, 11-21.

[11] 2 Kings xxv, 27-9 ; Jer. lii, 31-3.

the rank and file of the exiles, to judge from a bas-relief depicting a deportation scene, though the men were tied to each other in couples by the wrist to prevent them from escaping during the journey,[1] the women were allowed to march unshackled ; baggage and bags of money, beasts of burden and waggons for the transport of household goods and children were all permitted.[2] Once they had reached their destination, the deported Jews were obliged to settle in the villages assigned to them as a place of residence. We know the names, if not the exact position, of many of these places.[3] Tel Abib, Tel Harša, Tel Melaḥ,[4] Kasiphia, perhaps Kerub Addan and Immer.[5] The first was not far from Nahar Kebar, that is, the Grand Canal, the *nâru kabaru* mentioned in Babylonian contracts,[6] to-day the Shatt en-Nil, drawn from the Euphrates, which watered the town of Nippur, the modern Nuffar, in one of the most fertile regions of Babylonia [7] ; the very name of the village serves to identify it : in Babylonian it was doubtless called Tel Abubi, " the mound of (i.e. emerging from) the flood," but the Jewish colonists had Hebraized it into Tel Abib, the mound of corn.

Land was allotted to them, which they were expected to cultivate at their own expense : Jeremiah, it will be remembered, in the letter which he wrote them soon after 597, said : " Build ye houses and dwell in them ; and plant gardens and eat the fruit of them." [8] They were allowed to correspond with their compatriots in Palestine, even when they expressed disapproval of those who advocated submission to Babylon.[9]

As in the days when they lived in Palestine, they looked for guidance to their " elders ", that is to say the men of standing among them, whom on several occasions we find

[1] *Cf*. Jer. xl, 1, 4.
[2] Louvre, bas-relief no. 65, of the palace of Asshurbanipal at Nineveh. See pl. v. *Cf*. Edmond Pottier, *Catal. des Antiqu. assyr.*, Paris, Musées nationaux, 1924, pp. 98–9.
[3] Ezr. ii, 59 ; viii, 17 ; Neh. vii, 61 ; Ez. iii, 15.
[4] *Cf*. perhaps Malaḥanu, mentioned in the documents of Murachu the younger, of Nippur˘ (CCVII, ix, no. 68, 6 ; 91, 4, 6).
[5] Ezr. ii, 59.
[6] Hilprecht, CCVII, ix, *cf*. J. Peters, *Nippur*, 1897, ii, pp. 106, 192 ; XLV, 347–8.
[7] Berossus, in Josephus, *c. Ap.*, i, 19, § 137–8.
[8] Jer. xxix, 5.
[9] Jer. xxix, especially vv. 24–9.

N

conferring on their behalf with the prophet Ezekiel.[1] They lived in families, and were free to give their sons and their daughters in marriage as they wished [2]; they were doubtless grouped in clans, or the poorer people may have been grouped according to the village in Palestine from which they had come ; for, according to Ezra ii, and Nehemiah vii, it is thus that they seem to have been divided when they returned to their native land.[3] All that was lacking, therefore, to complete their traditional social structure was a king and his ministers. And it is quite possible that Jeconiah, when after twenty-seven years of exile he was restored to favour,[4] received the title of " prince (nâsî) of Judah ", which in any case was borne by his son Sheshbazzar,[5] before he was appointed governor (pehah) of " the province ". From the point of view of religion, it was of the utmost importance that the exiles were not deprived of corporate life, for it enabled them to bring up their children to respect and to observe the traditions of their forefathers.

It is evident, then, that the exiles were neither treated as slaves nor even reduced to a state of serfdom ; they were merely the victims of forced transplantation, or a kind of internment, which certainly entailed much mental suffering, but did not necessarily mean that materially they were worse off—their circumstances might indeed in some cases be improved. It is possible to understand how an Assyrian officer, when addressing the besieged, could speak of the deportation as if it were a most attractive prospect :—

> " I will take you away to a land like your own land, a land of corn and wine, a land of bread and vineyards, a land of oil olive and of honey, that ye may live and not die." [6]

The object of the kings of Assyria and Babylonia in adopting the system of the deportation of the vanquished seems to have been twofold. On the one hand, they wished to deprive the rebel nation of the power to resist, by removing all its best men at one blow, by decapitating it, in fact. But on the other hand, they intended to turn the talents of this picked body of men to good account by using them for the benefit of the empire ; and for this reason they made their

[1] Ez. viii, 1 ; xiv, 1 ; xx, 1, 3.   [2] Jer. xxix, 6.
[3] But see below, pp. 190–3.   [4] 2 Kings xxv, 27–30.
[5] Ezr. i, 8.   [6] 2 Kings xviii, 32.

circumstances such as they could accept. They used these picked settlers chiefly to repopulate a devastated area—this seems to have been the case with the Israelites sent to Media in the eighth century—or to keep in check a nation or tribe which had been recently subdued, in which case, when they had been settled in the midst of the defeated tribe, they were sometimes allowed privileges which placed them on a superior footing : to this category belong the parties of Syrians, Babylonians, Elamites, and Arabs deported by the kings of Assyria into the country which had once been the kingdom of Israel ; such men, we are told " ate the salt of the palace ".[1]

We do not know Nebuchadnezzar's reason for choosing the region of Nippur as the place of settlement for the exiled Judæans, but it is clear that the first of his aims was fully realized, for, during the four centuries which followed, Judah did not make a single attempt, as far as we know, to recover its political independence by force.

On the other hand, the relatively liberal terms granted to the exiles explain to some extent the persistence among them, even in a foreign land, of a lively national sentiment and a deep attachment to their religion, for they lived in the closest contact with each other and were at liberty to observe their own customs. Once the first feelings of dejection had worn off, their spiritual leaders had little difficulty in awakening in their minds the firm hope of seeing their nation revived and restored in a new form.

Conscious that in their midst were all the men who were the real backbone of the nation—the court, with the high officials of the kingdom, the army, nearly all the priests, and the craftsmen, were in Babylonia—they viewed with contempt the rabble which had remained behind in Palestine,[2] and considered that they by themselves were the true Israel,[3] the nucleus of the future nation of Jahweh.

Moreover, they had at their disposal ways and means which justified a confident outlook such as were denied to their compatriots in the Holy Land—they were rich. The Jewish colonies in Babylonia rapidly became very prosperous. In

---

[1] Ezr. iv, 14.   [2] Ez. xxxiii, 24–9.
[3] Jer. xxiv ; Lam. i, 3 ; Ez. ii, 3 ; iii, 1, 4, 7 ; xi, 15–21 ; xii, 6, 9 ; xvii, 2, etc.

the course of the century which witnessed the restoration they sent repeatedly considerable sums for the Temple or to assist the community [1] ; Ezra alone brought with him over £300,000 in gold and silver.[2] The Jewish settlements of the East included at that time among their members, besides well-to-do agriculturists, a large number of rich merchants and even persons in high position at the court.[3]

Of the three sections of the Jewish world of the day—the Jews of the dispersion, those who stayed in Palestine and those who went to Babylonia—the last-named evidently had the most vitality and were the best fitted, even from the purely political and economic point of view, to play the chief part in the event of a restoration. For this reason alone it seems, *a priori*, hardly necessary to reject the testimony of tradition and, with Kosters, for instance, credit the Jews of Palestine with having brought about the recovery.

II

Rise and Fall of the Neo-Babylonian Empire

During the whole of the latter part of Nebuchadnezzar's long reign (605–562), nothing seems to have happened which could have justified the Jewish patriots' hopes of recovery. In 581 the King of Babylon inflicted a crushing defeat on two of the former allies of Judah, Ammon and Moab.[4] Tyre had also taken part in the revolt, and for thirteen years Nebuchadnezzar besieged it.[5] It is true that, as Ezekiel [6] tells us, he " had no wages " from the town, whether because the fortified island was able to defy him successfully,[7] or because he was obliged to grant the city honourable terms of capitulation and to abstain from sacking it.[8] In any case,

---

[1] Ezr. ii, 68–9 ; Neh. vii, 70–2 ; Zech. vi, 9–15.

[2] Ezr. viii, 26–7.

[3] See below, pp. 194–6, 297–9.

[4] At least according to Josephus, *A.J.*, x, 9, 17, § 180.

[5] 586–574 (598–586 according to **CCVIII**, 20–4) ; *cf.* Josephus, *A.J.*, x, 11, 1, according to Philostratus ; *c. Ap.*, i, 21, according to Phenician sources ; **XCV**, 132.

[6] Ez. xxix, 18 (571).

[7] Smend, **KEH**, Ezr. ², 234–5 ; **LII**, 160.

[8] Scaliger, Hugo Grotius, Oesterley (**LXVIII**, ii, 11–12) ; *cf.* Unger, **ZATW**, 14 (1926), 314–17.

in 568 the King of Babylon was powerful enough to attack the Pharaoh Amasis and invade Egypt.[1]

Nebuchadnezzar's son, Amel Marduk, the Evil-merodach of the Bible, in the very first year of his reign (562), released Jeconiah, the exiled King of Judah, from prison, spoke kindly to him, set him on a throne and henceforth fed him at his own table. This occurrence, which is circumstantially related in the Book of Kings [2], evidently aroused great hopes among the Jews,[3] who thought that through the generosity of their conquerors the state and the royal house were about to be restored to the land of their fathers. Such hopes were not as insane as they may seem ; a few years later, two princes of Tyre, Mer Baal and Hiram III, were successively brought back from Babylonia (in 556 and 552), evidently with the authorization of the Chaldean ruler of the time, and became kings of their city.[4] But Amel Marduk died in 560 at the hand of the assassin Nergal-šar-uṣur, the Neriglissar of the Greeks,[5] and the cherished dreams of the Jews vanished into thin air.

Their one hope of liberation was now the dissolution of the Chaldean empire. Signs of its disruption became increasingly frequent : there were repeated changes of ruler, and even of dynasty : Neriglissar only occupied the throne for seven years : his son, Labaši Marduk, was put to death by Nabonidus (555–539), after reigning only a few months. During the first years of his reign, Nabonidus had to crush a revolt of his Syrian vassals (554–553) and to fight the prince of Teima in the land of Edom (552). He soon made himself very unpopular with the inhabitants of Babylon, his capital, and in particular roused the antagonism of the priests, in spite of his fondness for sacred archæology and the building of temples. For eight years (552–544) he lived in the oasis of Teima, where he built himself a palace, leaving to his

---

[1] The historicity of this campaign (foretold by Ez. xxix, 19–21), long disputed because the facts given by the Greek authors are vague and contradictory, is established by a fragment of Babylonian annals published by Pinches (**TSBA**, vii (1882), 218–225 ; **KB**, iii, 2, pp. 140–1 ; cf. **CXCIV**, 156 ; **LXVIII**, ii, 12.

[2] 2 Kings xxv, 27–30.

[3] As is seen from 1 Kings viii, 50, written in exile.

[4] Josephus, c. Ap., i, 21, § 158 ; cf. **XCV**, 132.

[5] An officer under Nebuchadnezzar, Nergal-šar-eṣer is mentioned in Jer. xxxix, 3, 13. Cf. **LXVIII**, ii, 13.

son Bel-šar-usur (the prototype of the Belshazzar of the Book of Daniel) the task of governing, and rendering impossible by his absence the celebration of the great Babylonian festival of the New Year [1] : it is evident that his unpopularity had something to do with his forsaking the capital, but whether as cause or effect it is hard to say.

To internecine dissensions were soon added threats of increasing gravity from the outer world. The Medes, who had become neighbours of the Babylonian empire on the east since the spoils of Nineveh had been divided up, had as their vassals the Persians, a nation of horsemen who had barely emerged from the nomadic stage to adopt an agricultural mode of life in their native Anshan ; Cyrus, their leader, rebelled against his suzerain Istamagu (Astyages). Astyages' army mutinied and he was dethroned (550–549). Nabonidus, who had at first seen fit to support the rebellious vassal, soon grew alarmed at the ambitions of the new king of the Medes and Persians. He allied himself with Egypt, Sparta, and Crœsus, King of Lydia, against Cyrus. Crœsus attacked Cyrus, but was defeated (547–546).

Nothing definite is known about the six years which followed.   In 539 Cyrus was at war with Nabonidus, from whom he had already wrested the province of Gutium to the east of the Tigris.[2] In the month of Tishri (October) he seized Opis and Sippar, the two strongholds commanding the wall which connected the Tigris with the Euphrates.   On the 16th, Gobryas, who was at the head of the Persian troops, captured Babylon without striking a blow, and took Nabonidus prisoner.   On the 3rd of Araḥsamma (November), Cyrus made a ceremonial entry into the capital over branches spread for his progress.

> " All the people of Babylon, all Sumer and Akkad, the great men and the governors, bowed down before him, kissed his feet and rejoiced in him as king." [3]

[1] *Cf.* the Persian verse narrative of Nabonidus published by S. Langdon (**CXLIV**) and the chronicle of Nabonidus edited by G. Pinches, **TSBA**, vii (1882), 139 *ff.* ; *cf.* **XCIV**, 154–5 ; **CCIV** ; **CCXLV**, pl. xii *ff.*, translated by Pinches, *op. cit.*, Winckler, *op. cit.*, Schrader (**KB**, iii, 2, 128 *ff.*), Hagen, *op. cit.*, Sidney Smith, *op. cit.*, 216 *ff.*, Ebeling (**XXVII**, i, 366–8).   See also Dougherty, *Nabonidus in Teima*, **JAOS**, 42, pp. 305–316.

[2] Cyrus Cylinder, 13.

[3] Cyrus Cylinder, 18.

Cyrus gave out that he was Marduk's chosen instrument of deliverance for his city Babylon, and that the god had delivered Nabonidus into his hands because he feared him not.[1]

In the provinces, the rule of the Persians was substituted for that of the Chaldeans without resistance.[2]

[1] Cyrus Cylinder, 10–12, 15, 17.
[2] Cyrus Cylinder, 28–30 ; inscription from Ur published by Gadd and Legrain, **CC,** no. 194, p. 58.

CHAPTER II

THE JEWS UNDER PERSIAN DOMINATION

THE REIGN OF CYRUS. RETURN OF THE FIRST BODY OF
EXILES TO JUDAH. CAMBYSES

THE policy introduced by Cyrus was something quite new in
the East. The empire founded by him was not, like
those of his predecessors, a robber state, which exploited
conquered nations solely for its own benefit. The Achæmenid
ruler presented himself to his subject peoples as a liberator ;
he respected their customs, honoured their gods, and granted
their leaders a share in the administration of their province.
Privileged posts in the empire were, it is true, reserved for
Persians, from among whom he recruited his ministers and
satraps ; he also kept a watchful eye on the maintenance of
order in the provinces, garrisoning them with Persian troops,
increasing the number of strategic roads radiating in all
directions from Susa, and creating here and there domains
belonging to the crown. But the lieutenant-governors were
often natives of the place ; local systems of government,
for instance the tyrannies in the Greek cities, were preserved.
The satraps were closely supervised by *missi dominici* who
were called " the king's eye ".

Cyrus had from the first signalized this change of policy by
his treatment of Babylon itself, the enemy capital, which he
neither burnt nor pillaged [1]—thereby causing bitter disappointment, no doubt, to many Jews who, on the strength
of predictions uttered by their prophets,[2] had looked forward
to a general massacre of their oppressors and hoped that the
accursed city would be razed to the ground. The temple
of Marduk was left completely untouched by the Persian
troops, and the New Year festival was celebrated there according to custom.[3] Cyrus treated the other towns of the conquered
countries and their inhabitants with the same generosity,

[1] *Cf*. Max Haller, **XXVIII**, ii, 3², pp. 5–6.
[2] Is. xiii–xiv ; Hab. ii.
[3] Chronicles of Nabonidus, iii, 16–18.

and restored to the different cities of Assyria and Babylonia the statues of their gods, which Nabonidus had assembled in the capital when the invasion began.[1] He gathered together the scattered inhabitants of the land of Gutium beyond the Tigris and restored them to their homes.[2]

It is therefore, quite in keeping that he should have given orders for the deported Jews to be brought back to Palestine, authorized the rebuilding of the Temple of Jahweh at Jerusalem, and the return of the sacred vessels removed by the Chaldeans. In order to explain this gesture of his, it is unnecessary to suppose, as Josephus did, that Cyrus was acquainted with the prophecies of the Second Isaiah which foretold his victories, and looked to him to liberate Israel and restore the worship of Jahweh,[3] or to agree with the theory, upheld by many modern critics, that the king felt particularly sympathetic towards the Jewish religion, because its doctrines were akin to those of his master Zarathustra, the great reformer of Iran. The measures adopted by Cyrus in his dealings with the Jews were merely the application to an individual case of the general principles of his policy. It was moreover obviously to his advantage to settle on the southern borders of his empire and in close proximity to Egypt a population on whose help he could count, because it was indebted to him.

There is therefore no reason to doubt that the conqueror of Babylon did in fact issue an edict in favour of the Jews and of their Temple, or to be as sceptical as Kosters is [4] about the restoration of exiles to Judæa under Cyrus, or to agree with him in attributing to the Jews who had remained in Palestine the first attempts to bring about a national recovery, and above all to rebuild the Temple.

On the other hand, it must be remembered that we have almost no exact or certain information about these events. In the account given in the beginning of the book of Ezra (i, 4) there are evident traces of improbability and confusion. The text of the edict of Cyrus is given twice over (i, 2-4, and

---

[1] Cyrus Cylinder, 30–32, cf. 9–10.
[2] Cyrus Cylinder, 32.
[3] Josephus, *A. J.*, XI, i, 2, §§ 5, 6.
[4] *Het Herstel van Israel in het Perzische Tijdvak*, Leiden, 1893 (German transl. by Basedow, 1895). *Cf.* A. C. Welch, **ZATW**, 1930, pp. 175–187.

vi, 3–5), and the two versions of the same rescript differ so much in their form and even in their contents, that the second cannot be considered as an epitome of the first : one at least of the two must have been composed inde- pendently by a Jewish editor who was trying to reconstruct the edict in its original form, much as Livy reconstructed the speeches which must have been uttered by the persons of his narrative. The first form is especially suspect, for, what- ever consideration Cyrus may have shown to the religious beliefs of the nations he conquered, it is hard to believe that he ordered his non-Israelite subjects to make volun- tary offerings for the benefit of the temple of Jerusalem, and to bring presents of gold and silver, of goods and of beasts to the Jews about to return to Palestine ; and besides, even supposing that, when they drew up the rescript, the royal scribes had in mind some petition framed by Jews in Babylonia, it is hard to admit that they can have followed Jewish terminology so closely that they described the exiles as " the remnant of the people of Jahweh ", " sojourning " as guests in a strange land.

The book of Ezra gives a detailed account of the solemn ceremony which took place when Zerubbabel and the high priest Jeshua laid the foundations of the temple in the second year after their arrival at Jerusalem.[1] But it is clear from the evidence of Haggai, a prophet who was alive at the time of the events described, that on the twenty-fourth of the ninth month of the second year of Darius—and therefore eighteen years later—" not a stone was laid upon a stone in the temple of the Lord " and that the temple was founded on that day.[2]

Elsewhere in the book of Ezra, moreover, the founding of the Temple in the reign of Cyrus is attributed to someone else, namely Sheshbazzar, governor of Judah.[3]

In one place we are told that, from that day until the reign of Darius, building operations had continued uninter- ruptedly,[4] and in another that work was suspended until the second year of his reign.[5]

[1] Ezr. iii, 8–13.
[2] Hag. ii, 15, 18. This is the natural meaning of the text ; the alternative interpretation given by R. Kittel (**XLIX**, iii, 2, 429–432) is improbable.   [3] Ezr. v, 14–16.
[4] Ezr. v, 16.   [5] Ezr. iv, 24.

The editor attributes this suspension of work to the influence of intrigues on the part of the " people of the land ", " enemies of Judah and Benjamin ", that is to say, those who were later to be known as the Samaritans, who bribed the advisers of Cyrus, Ahasuerus (Xerxes) and Artaxerxes. Here the confusion is self-evident. The narrator knew so little about the succession of the kings of Persia that he imagined Xerxes, who reigned from 486 to 465, and Artaxerxes the First (465–424) to have occupied the throne in the interval between Cyrus (549–529) and Darius the First (521–486). The very contents of the official documents which he quotes in support of his statements reveal his mistake, for there is no question in them of the building of the Temple, but of the walls[1]—that is to say the ramparts of Jerusalem— a matter which was heatedly discussed, and finally settled, under Artaxerxes the First (445).

The account of the first stages of the restoration of Judah [2] is a personal attempt at historical reconstruction made by the writer to whom we owe the history of Judah, on a larger scale, which is now represented by the books of Chronicles, Ezra and Nehemiah. He must have lived after Alexander at the earliest,[3] therefore at least two hundred years later than the restoration, and there are traces of his style and his ideas everywhere in this account. He based it on such documentary evidence as he could obtain—which seems to have been little enough—and he interpreted this evidence in the light of his somewhat scanty general knowledge of the history of the period, supplemented by those pious *a priori* statements of which he shows himself so fond in the book of the Chronicles. He was persuaded, as most people were in his day, that in the first few months after their captivity was at an end the exiles returned in a body to Palestine, that they formed by themselves the entire Jewish community of Judæa, that the sharp cleavage between Jew and Samaritan which existed in his own time actually went back as far as the reign of Cyrus, that the first and most ardent desire of those who were repatriated must have been

[1] Ezr. iv, 12–16, 21.
[2] Ezr. i–iv.
[3] He mentions " Darius the Persian ", that is Darius III, the adversary of the Macedonian conqueror (Neh. xii, 22). *Cf.* p. 7.

to rebuild the Temple and to celebrate in it the feasts prescribed by the law, etc.

Here are those details of his narrative which seem the
best substantiated and the most deserving of preservation ;
to begin with, Cyrus's edict, in the form in which it is reproduced in chapter 6 (vv. 2–5) :—

> " A record : In the first year of Cyrus the king, Cyrus the king
> made a decree ; Concerning the house of God at Jerusalem, let the
> house be builded, the place where they offer sacrifices.[1] The height
> thereof threescore cubits, and the breadth thereof threescore
> cubits [2] ; with three rows of great stones and a [3] row of new
> timber : and let the expenses be given out of the king's house :
> and also let the gold and silver vessels of the house of God, which
> Nebuchadnezzar took forth out of the temple which is at Jerusalem,
> and brought unto Babylon, be restored, and brought again unto
> the temple which is at Jerusalem, every one to its place, and thou
> shalt put them in the house of God." [4]

If the roll containing this rescript was found in the time
of Darius, in the archives of Ecbatana in Media, as we are
told,[5] we may infer that Cyrus came to the above-mentioned
decision in the course of the summer which followed the
taking of Babylon (538) ; for Persian sovereigns were in the
habit of spending the hot season first at Susa, and then at
Ecbatana in the Median mountains.[6]

The sacred vessels were transferred by the treasurer
Mithredath to one Sheshbazzar,[7] which is a Babylonian name,
a man who is described as " prince (nasi) of Judah " [8]
appointed by Cyrus pehah,[9] that is to say governor of
Jerusalem, pehah being the Assyrian title [10] distinguishing
satraps and their lieutenants. This Sheshbazzar must not
be identified, as has often been done, with Zerubbabel, for

---

[1] Read *we'eͫͫôhî*.
[2] The text is confused : the length is missing. The prescribed
dimensions were no doubt those of the temple of Solomon, length
60 cubits, width 20, height 30 (1 Kings vi, 2).
[3] Read *had*. The text mentions *new* wood.
[4] It is not clear to whom this order is addressed. The text must
be more or less corrupt.
[5] Ezr. vi, 2.
[6] Xenophon, *Cyropœdia*, viii, 6, 22 ; *cf. Anabasis*, iii, 5, 15.
[7] Variants : Sanamassar, Sanabassar, Sasabassar. This name
corresponds to the Babylonian Sin-bal-uṣur " may Sin protect the
son ! " or Šamaš-bal-uṣur " may the Sun protect the son ! "
[8] Ezr. i, 8.   [9] Ezr. v, 14.
[10] Abbreviation for *bel piḫâti* " Lord of a province ". *Cf.* Schrader
XCV², 186.

it is extremely unlikely that a Jew would have had two
Babylonian names. He was probably a son of King Jeconiah,
who figures in one of the genealogies of the book of Chronicles
as Shenazzar.[1] If so, Cyrus chose a descendant of David,
a member of the former royal house, to be his first governor
of the province of Judah. Herodotus [2] says it was

> " Customary for the Persians to respect kings' sons, and to
> restore to them their power and their crown, even though their
> fathers had rebelled."

We do not know the precise date, though it must have
been before 520, at which Sheshbazzar relinquished his
functions, nor the circumstances which caused him to resign,
but it was a descendant of David who was appointed in his
stead, Zerubbabel, the son of Shealtiel and grandson of
Jeconiah, therefore a nephew of the first *peḥah*, if the proposed
identification is correct.

It is *a priori* very probable that a certain number of the
exiles took advantage of the permission granted by
Cyrus and returned to their country, some with Sheshbazzar,
others with Zerubbabel—for it appears likely that these
two did not arrive at the same time—others later. But it is
certain that repatriation was far from being general, for we
know from subsequent history that a numerous, rich, and
influential colony of Jews remained behind in Babylonia,
and that later on more members of this colony returned to
Palestine.[3] The reason for their remaining behind is obviously
correctly explained by Josephus [4] :

> " Many stayed in Babylon because they did not wish to forsake
> their possessions."

In order to leave the country, the well-to-do Jews of
Mesopotamia would have been obliged to sell lands or stock-
in-trade for a mere nothing, or to give up lucrative positions
and begin life over again in a poor country, one which was
comparatively infertile, inhabited by others, and known to
most of them only through stories told them by their fathers.
Not all had sufficient self-abnegation to make such sacrifices
for the sake of their faith : many, no doubt, hoped to make
them when times were better, and for the present confined

---

[1] 1 Chron. iii, 18.   [2] iii, 15.
[3] With Nehemiah, for instance, and with Ezra.
[4] *A. J.*, XI, i, 3, § 8.

themselves to assisting, both by their sympathy and their gifts, those who had the courage to leave their new home for their former one, just as the Israelites of France, England, or the United States did, after the Balfour declaration allowing Jews to settle once more as a nation in Palestine.

The first years were years of struggle for the repatriated Judæans. It must have been no easy matter to portion out the land among those who had remained in Palestine and those who had returned from exile. As a result of drought, blight attacked the corn, and the first crops were poor : even the grain in the granaries was spoilt.[1] The returning exiles were obliged to build themselves habitations among the ruins of the former buildings. And when the armies of Cambyses (529–522), son and successor of Cyrus, passed near the borders of Judæa on their way to conquer Egypt (525), there must have been the usual accompaniments to events of the kind— requisitions, forced labour, looting, perhaps a levying of troops.

It is not hard to understand that during the first eighteen years of the Persian domination, the Palestine Jews, living as they did from hand to mouth, could hardly have had either the time or the means to rebuild the Temple. It is true that Cyrus had promised to defray the expenses " from the king's house " ; but that doubtless meant that the necessary sums would be deducted from the amount realized by the taxation of the province, an amount which, during the lean years, cannot have left any surplus available.

APPENDIX.   LIST OF THE JEWS WHO RETURNED FROM EXILE IN EZRA ii AND NEHEMIAH viii

If the list of those who returned with Zerubbabel and Jeshua, which is twice reproduced by the Chronicler, is to be trusted, we have circumstantial information as to the number of those who were repatriated in the first instance, and the way in which they were settled in Palestine.[2] According to this document, the first instalment comprised 42,360 men,[3] to which figure must be added

[1] Hag. i, 9–11 ; ii, 15–19.
[2] Ezr. ii and Neh. vii, 6–73a.
[3] Ezr ii, 64 ; Neh. vii, 66. This figure is not absolutely certain, for if the numbers given in detail in the body of the list are added together the total is considerably less : 29,818 units according to ch. ii of Ezra 31,089 according to Neh. vii ; 30,142 according to the version which has survived only in the Greek (1st Book of Esdras in the Septuagint).

7,337 slaves of both sexes, and 200 or 205 " singing men and singing women ". Those included in the list are called " children of the province " (medînâh) : they are grouped in villages (those at least whose family-connections are not too numerous), and we are told that they returned " every one unto his city ".[1] From this it has been deduced that the exiles were obliged by the authorities to settle within the confines of the " judicial province " (medînâh) of Jerusalem, that is to say, within a radius of some 20 miles from the ruins of the capital, and that each was given land in the district from which his family originally came, though we are told nothing about the arrangement made with the occupants of the soil.[2]

There can be no doubt that this list is of very early origin, as is proved by the fact that the laymen are placed *before the priests*, and the singers not yet numbered among the Levites.[3] But was the editor of the book of Ezra-Nehemiah aware of its real date and scope when he reproduced it ? The question is debatable and has been much debated. The view that he was aware of them finds support in such details as the minute proportion of Levites contained in the list—74 against over 4,000 priests : for of all the exiles the Levites who had settled in Babylonia must have felt least tempted to return to Palestine, where, in view of the new ideas advocated by Deuteronomy and Ezekiel, they would find that their functions had become purely subordinate. Then there are the statistics as to the animals owned by the exiles, which figure at the end of the list : only beasts of burden are mentioned, horses, mules, camels, and asses, all of them more suited to travellers than to settled farmers.

In favour of the above contention, there is also the incident of the priestly family of Hakkoz, the members of which were temporarily excluded from the priesthood because they could not produce a genealogy establishing their claim to the office [4] ; as, in the time of Ezra and Nehemiah, a high ecclesiastical dignitary belonged to this family,[5] it has been concluded that in the interval between 538 and 445 it had made good its claim.[6]

On the other hand, various indications incline one to the belief that the list in question was, in its original form, a census of all the pure-blooded Jews living in the province of Judah towards the time of Nehemiah, or even later.[7] The very numbers contained in the census give cause for reflection. How can one believe that the colony of Jews deported to Babylonia, which in 581 [8] amounted to 4,600 adult males, could have increased and multiplied to such an extent in less than fifty years that it was able to send to Palestine a body of 42,360 men without even then exhausting its resources ? This figure is exclusive of women, children, and 7,337 slaves. If they are added a total of at least 100,000 is reached, that is to say,

---

[1] Ezr. ii, 1, 70.   [2] **LII**, iii, 2.

[3] See Hölscher, **XLVIII**[4], ii, 504.

[4] Ezr. ii, 61-3 ; Neh. vii, 63-5.   [5] Ezr. viii, 33 ; Neh. iii, 4.

[6] *Cf.*, for instance, **XLIX**, iii, 2, p. 337.

[7] Hölscher (**XLVIII**, 504), Torrey (**CCXLVII**), Mowinckel, Oesterley (**LXVIII**, ii, 46, note 2).

[8] See p. 173-4.

exactly the figure which is supposed to represent *the entire population* of the province of Judah.[1]

The fact that one at least of the Jewish clans mentioned in the list has a Persian name : Bigwai, i.e. Bagôhi, must also be taken into account, for though the adoption of an Aryan name is comhensible enough after a century of intercourse between Jews and Persians, it would be much more difficult to explain in the very year that Babylon was conquered by Cyrus.

Another embarrassing consideration, if the list is really a list of immigrants, is the curious coincidence that localities from which the exiles are said to have originally come are all in the immediate neighbourhood of Jerusalem. How is it that among all those who came back there is not a single descendant of Judæans who had inhabited Hebron, the Negeb, or the south-east part of Judah ? Must we suppose, as Rudolf Kittel does,[2] that even before the first deportation in 597 Nebuchadnezzar had already reduced the kingdom of Judah till its frontiers were those of the Persian province of the name ? The conjecture is uncalled for. A more plausible theory is that Cyrus only allowed those Jews to return to Palestine whose ancestors had inhabited the limited area included in the *medînâh* ; but is such a restriction likely to have been made ? No such difficulty arises if, on the contrary, the statistics refer to the " children ", that is to say, the inhabitants " of the *medînâh* ", and indicate the number of " men " (not of noble family) in each locality.

The term *qahal*, used once by the author of the list,[3] would not be suitable to describe a batch of immigrants : the *qahal* is the aggregate of the members of the nation who have the right to take part in worship.

The desire to exclude from it all those who were not of purely Jewish race was one which was ever present to the minds of the men of Nehemiah's time. The temporary exclusion of the family of Hakkoz may have taken place at some date before or after the dispute between Nehemiah and Ezra, and a priest of this group, or even in the interval between their several encounters with such a man.

A few remaining details can be explained by the suggestion that the editor of the Chronicles, persuaded that this document was a roll of immigrants in the time of Cyrus, added a few touches here and there to complete the picture of this glorious homecoming ; the names of the twelve leaders,[4] the inventory of the beasts of burden,[5] perhaps the list of the slaves and the itinerant musicians,[6] and finally that of the offerings brought by the immigrants.[7]

In view of its doubtful nature, it is not wise to use this list in reconstructing the events which immediately followed upon Cyrus's generous action.

[1] See p. 174.　　　[2] **XLIX**, iii, 2, 241–2.　　　[3] Ezr. ii, 64.
[4] Ezr. ii, 2.　　　[5] Ezr. ii, 66–7.　　　[6] Ezr. ii, 65.
[7] Ezr. ii, 68–9.

II

DARIUS THE FIRST (521–486).   THE REBUILDING OF THE
TEMPLE

The defeats suffered by Cambyses in Egypt, followed by his death, whether intentional or accidental,[1] were the signal for a violent upheaval which threatened to bring about the final disintegration of the Persian empire. A magus imposter, who managed to pass himself off as Bardiya (Smerdis), the son of Cyrus, who had been secretly put to death by his brother Cambyses, succeeded, even during the latter's lifetime, in making his authority felt in nearly all the provinces. A relative of Cyrus, Darius, son of Hystaspis, put him to death and had himself proclaimed king (September–October, 522). But he had to crush a revolt led by a certain Atrina in Susiana, and another under a Babylonian, Niddintubel, who claimed to be the son of Nabonidus, Nebuchadnezzar III (December, 522). Fresh rebellions broke out in Susiana, Media, Armenia, Sagartia, Parthienis and Hyrcania, in Persia and in Babylonia. Darius had to fight nineteen battles before his nine rivals were subdued. He seems to have been master of the situation by April, 520.[2]

As we shall see when we trace the history of the Jewish religion, these disturbances had important repercussions in the little colony of Jerusalem. Two prophets, Haggai and Zechariah, hailed them as signs of the imminent overthrow of the pagan empires and of the beginning of the Messianic era. They thus provoked a revival of faith and religious

[1] Intentional according to the inscription of Behistun, accidental according to Herodotus : cf. **CCIX**, 59 ; **LXVIII**, ii, 66.

[2] Opinions differ widely as to the chronology of these events, because Darius, in his inscription at Bisutun (Behistun), gives the month and the day of the month, but not the year, in which each of his victories was won. It has been thought that they should be spread over four (**LXVIII**, ii, 67), seven (**CCIX**, 64), or even nine years. It is more likely that they all took place " in the same year " (Persian text, col. iv, 1. 4–5), the " first year of his reign " (April, 521–April, 520), adding only the last five months of " the year of his accession to the throne " (October, 522–March, 521), and the first days of the second year of his reign ; cf. **CAH**, iv (1926), 173–180, 662 ; **XLIX**, iii, 446 ; **CCXIII**, pp. xxxvi–xxxviii.

zeal which found an outlet in the rebuilding of the Temple
(520–515). Darius, moreover, encouraged the undertaking.
Not only was he an intrepid warrior, he was also a wise
statesman, and he continued the policy of liberality which
Cyrus had observed with regard to subject peoples, showing
himself particularly lenient towards their religions, their
temples, and their priests. Contemporary documents show
that he followed this policy in his dealings with the Egyptians
and with the Greeks of Asia Minor as well as with the Jews.[1]

III

Gradual Decay of the Persian Empire

Xerxes the First (485–465), son of Darius the First and
grandson of Cyrus by his mother Atossa, subdued the
rebellious Egyptians soon after his accession to the throne ;
it may have been on his way to Syria that he received an
accusation against the inhabitants of Judah and Jerusalem,
made, we are told, " in the beginning of his reign." [2]

Babylon was the next to rebel, and it was only thanks
to the military genius of his son-law, Megabyzus, that he got
the better of this stubborn insurrection. He razed the walls
of the rebellious town, destroyed the great temple of Marduk,
and carried away the golden image of the god. The
humiliating check inflicted on him by the Greeks is well
known. Xerxes was much more absorbed by intrigues of the
harem than by politics, a characteristic which must have
struck the Jews, for the historical romance of Esther perpetuated it in the person of Ahasuerus,[3] whose reign forms a
background to this bloodstained tragedy, which is not in
other respects in keeping with the actual history of the time
as we know it.

Artaxerxes the First, surnamed Longimanus (464–424),
had first to avenge the death of his father and his two
brothers, assassinated by the satrap Artaban. In 460 he
lost Egypt, which was wrested from him by the native
prince Inaros, and only regained it in 454 with the help of

---

[1] *Cf.* **CCXXVII**, 19–21, 64, 71 ; **CXCV**, 26–7.   [2] Ezr. iv, 6.
[3] Latin transcription of the Hebrew Aḥašweroš, which in turn represents the Persian Ḥšiarša, which became in the Greek Xerxes.

Megabyzus. But Megabyzus, his deliverer, then viceroy of Syria, annoyed at a breach of faith, revolted and imposed conditions. The king also became involved in a struggle against the Greeks, who defeated him at Salamis in Cyprus. As a ruler, Artaxerxes the First was weak, easily influenced, and eccentric, as can be seen from his dealings with the Palestine Jews : first he gave orders that the rebuilding of the ramparts of Jerusalem should be suspended,[1] and then he sent Nehemiah, his cup-bearer, with instructions that the work was to be completed.[2]

After reigning only a few months, Xerxes II was killed by his half-brother Sogdianus, who in his turn was assassinated by another half-brother, who took the name Darius II on becoming king (423–405). His reign was marked by new disorders, in particular by a revolt of the sons of Megabyzus in Syria, and disturbances in Egypt, which seriously affected the military colony of Jews in Elephantine.[3]

We possess firsthand documents of this period, or, to be precise, of the reigns of Artaxerxes I and Darius II, which throw light on the condition of the Jewish settlements in Babylonia. In May, 1893, the American expedition sent by the university of Pennsylvania discovered at Nuffar (the ancient Nippur), a room containing 730 tablets covered with cuneiform signs : these were the archives—contracts, bills of exchange, receipts—of the great trading concern directed by the sons and grandsons of Murachu of Nippur.[4] Now among the clients, agents, employees or rivals of the firm, and also among the witnesses who countersigned contracts with their seal or a nail-print, there is an unusually large proportion of obviously Jewish names—for they contain the name of Jahweh in the form Jahu, Jama (Jawa), or Ja—and of others which are probably Jewish because they are reproduced, exactly or approximately, in the books of the Bible—especially in Ezra and Nehemiah—and also in the Elephantine papyri. The inference is that the Jewish population in the district round Nippur was still large, as it

---

[1] Ezr. iv, 8–23.   [2] See below, p. 300.
[3] See below, pp. 309–12.
[4] These tablets were nearly all published and to a great extent translated by Hilprecht and Clay in 1898, 1904, and 1912 (CCVII). They have been studied by Kohler and Ungnad (1911), Ebeling (1914), Causse (VIII, 67), and Sidersky (REJ, 1929, pp. 177–199), and others.

had been in the days when the exiles were settled on the banks of the " great canal ", at Tell Abib and at Tell Melah.[1]

To judge from these documents, the majority of the Jews of Babylonia must have been cultivators of the soil, either as farmers or as landowners. They pay their dues with dates, barley, beer, sheep and flour.[2] Some pledge a field planted with trees or tilled for corn.[3] Others—partners apparently— rent a canal (for irrigation), two fields and three towers.[4] When Jeremiah exhorted the exiles of 597 to plant gardens, he was referring to what was already their chief occupation.[5]

Others had administrative posts, especially in the finance department : one is an inspector of taxes levied on the Sin canal and agent for the keeper of the seal [6] ; another, a servant of the keeper of the seal, is entrusted with the receipt of taxes levied by a revenue officer [7] ; another is governor of the treasury for the inhabitants of Susa.[8]

Some engage in trade, whether as employees or even, it seems, as owners of firms, as for instance Piliyama (Pelaya), who specialized in the farming of taxes.[9]

This settlement of Jews in the East, living as it did in the richest province of the Persian empire—Chaldea paid 1,000 talents of silver in taxes—must have been amply provided with the good things of this world. There is frequent mention of dues amounting to 40 or 50 kurs (30 to 36 hectolitres) of dates ; they even reach as high a figure as 2,155 kurs (more than 2,500 hectolitres). This being so, it is easy to understand the influence which these men of substance were supposed to exercise, and did in fact exercise over their poor relations in the Holy Land, whose decisions they more than once dictated.

These commercial documents tell us nothing directly about the state of religion among the Eastern Jews. The existence of Persian, Babylonian, Aramean, and Hebrew names, side by side in the same families, might tempt one to infer that a certain amount of syncretism prevailed among them. It is, however, a rare occurrence for the son of a man

[1] See above, p. 177.
[2] **CCVII**, x, 92.
[3] **CCVII**, x, 8.
[4] **CCVII**, ix, 45.
[5] Jer. xxix, 5.
[6] **CCVII**, ix, 14 and 15.
[7] **CCVII**, x, 60.
[8] **CCVII**, x, 65.
[9] **CCVII**, ix, 15.

with a Hebrew name to have a Babylonian one.[1] It happens much more frequently that the father has a Babylonian or Persian name, and the son a specifically Jewish one. Such cases may be those of heathen families which had been converted, but no doubt the explanation more often is that Jewish slaves or servants, whose master, according to custom, had given them a native name,[2] having won their freedom or an independent status, had proclaimed their fidelity to their nationality or their religion by giving Jewish names to their children.

On the death of Darius II (405), there was a rising in Egypt and the Egyptians regained their independence. They remained independent for sixty-eight years, during which period they had their last succession of national sovereigns.

The new King of Persia, Artaxerxes II, surnamed Mnemon (404–359), armed with the intention of reconquering the lost province ; but a revolt led by his brother, Cyrus the younger, obliged him for the time being to relinquish his intention. Artaxerxes defeated the rebel and killed him, but the extraordinary adventure of the Greek mercenaries whom Cyrus had hired, and the famous " retreat of the ten thousand ", who were able to march unscathed across the entire empire as far as the Black Sea, showed how greatly the strength of this vast assemblage of peoples was undermined.

Artaxerxes II made two attempts to invade Egypt (374 and 361), but failed. The Pharaoh Tachos even succeeded in occupying southern Syria, and following the time-honoured tactics of Ramses II, Necho, and Hophra, he undertook to " defend Egypt on the Lebanon "[3] by joining forces with the western satraps, then in revolt. He was assassinated, and his successor withdrew his Egyptian troops.

In the reign of Artaxerxes II, then, the territory in the neighbourhood of Palestine was in a continual state of disturbance. And it is easy to understand why the king, in order the better to assure himself of the loyalty of a population just on the other side of his own frontier, should have lent a willing ear to those Babylonian Jews who were desirous of tightening up the general organization of the Jewish community at Jerusalem. As we shall see,[4] there is good reason to

---

[1] CCVII, x, 64 ; N.S. 12.   [2] Cf. Dan. i, 7.
[3] XLIX, iii, 665.   [4] Pp. 296–304.

think that it was in the seventh year of the reign of
Artaxerxes II (398) that Ezra was sent from Babylon to
Judah to reform the country in accordance with the law
which he brought with him, and not in the seventh year of
Artaxerxes I (458), as the present sequence of the chapters
in the books of Ezra and Nehemiah might suggest.[1]

There is no proof that the Palestine Jews forsook their
policy of submission to the great king and intrigued with his
enemies, unless an anecdote related by Josephus [2] is capable
of this interpretation. Bagoses, he says, strategus to
Artaxerxes II,[3] promised Jesus (Jeshua), the brother of the

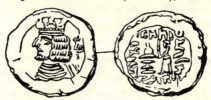

Fig. 2. Coin of Artaxerxes II (after Ricciotti,
Storia d'Israele, *II*, p. 163, S. E. I., Turin).

high priest Joannes (Johanan), that he would make him
chief priest. In the course of a quarrel with his rival, Johanan
killed him in the Temple itself. On this occasion Bagoses
profaned the Temple by forcing an entrance, and punished
the Jews by imposing a fine of fifty drachmas per lamb
sacrificed, which they were obliged to pay for seven years.
As Johanan was the high priest to whom the Elephantine
Jews wrote in 410, under Darius II, the strategus Bagoses
is certainly to be identified with Bagohi (Bagoas), who was

then governor (*peḥah*) of Judah, to
whom they again applied in 410 and
407.

Artaxerxes III Ochus (358–338)
was confronted with a new revolt

Fig. 3. Coin of Artaxerxes
III (after Ricciotti *Storia
d'Israele*, *II*, p. 35, S. E. I.,
Turin).
in the west, under the leadership
of the satrap Artabazus, which he
suppressed, but failed in an attempt
against Egypt. Renewed disturbances in the western part
of the empire ensued. Artaxerxes then defeated Tennes,

---

[1] Ezr. vii, 8.   [2] *A. J.*, XI, vii, 1, § 297–301.
[3] The word " two ", ἄλλος, is, nevertheless, lacking in several
manuscripts.

King of Sidon, also Cyprus and Phenicia, and reconquered
Egypt, whose national religion he treated with contempt.
This time the Jews may have joined the rebels and been
involved in their overthrow ; certain texts, it is true, make
somewhat vague allusions to a deportation of Jews into
Hyrcania (on the borders of the Caspian Sea) at the time
of Ochus' campaign in Egypt,[1] and also refer to one
Artaxerxes who attacked Hierichus (Jericho ?), said to
have been the capital of the Jews after the destruction of
Jerusalem.[2]

Artaxerxes III was poisoned, with his elder sons, by the
eunuch Bagoas, who also got rid of Arses, whom he himself
had set on the throne. But Darius III Codomanus (338–331)
had the murderer put to death.

In 336, his States were invaded by Alexander, king of
Macedonia. After a series of brilliant victories the youthful
conqueror secured possession of all the provinces. The
Persian empire, its strength having been slowly sapped by
internal dissension, the weakness of its rulers, the ambition
and cupidity of its satraps, and the increasing use of mercenary
troops, finally collapsed.

The two centuries of its existence had been on the whole
favourable to the Jews. Except during the latter years,
they had enjoyed the blessings of peace, and had as a rule
been kindly treated by the central power.

[1] Eusebius, *Chron.*, ed. Schoene, ii, 112.
[2] Solin, xxxv, 4.

CHAPTER III

THE JEWS UNDER GREEK DOMINATION

IT was in 332, when Alexander was laying siege to Tyre and Gaza, that Jerusalem was obliged to open its gates to this new master. According to Josephus, the submission was made in dramatic conditions. When first called upon to surrender, the high priest Jaddua refused, not wishing to break faith with Darius. Incensed, Alexander marched against the Jewish capital, bent on avenging the insult. But the priests and all the people came out to meet him in a solemn procession; and Alexander was so impressed that he forebore to carry out his intentions, and even prostrated himself before the high priest, because he recognized in him a celestial visitant whom he had seen in a dream, and who had foretold his victories. Alexander exempted the Jews from taxation every seven years, as the Sabbatical year came round.[1] This is a tendentious legend. In reality, the Jews of the time knew no such scruples of fidelity towards defeated masters. Resigned to pagan domination, they watched with indifference, or with secret satisfaction, the overthrow of one empire by another.

Alexander died in 323. Each of his Macedonian generals tried to carve themselves a kingdom from the vast territories over which their master had ruled. The more fortunate among them even aimed at restoring, for their own benefit, the universal monarchy created by the conqueror. There ensued a state of war which continued for centuries almost without interruption, the dagger, gold, and the basest of intrigues playing almost as important a part in it as armed force. Nevertheless, the struggles were no obstacle to the fulfilment of the great plan conceived by Alexander. On the contrary, by destroying the last vestiges of the old system of nationalities, they paved the way for the advent of Hellenic civilization in the East.

[1] *A. J.*, XI, viii, 4–5, § 325–339.

By sheer force of circumstances, Syria, of which Judæa formed a part, found itself the bone of contention between the two principal kingdoms which had been carved out of the empire of Alexander, the kingdom of the Ptolemies or Lagids, and that of the Seleucids. Ptolemy the First, son of Lagus, annexed Egypt immediately after the death of his master, and his descendants succeeded in keeping possession of it. On the other hand, in the valleys of the Tigris and Euphrates a powerful State came into existence whose rulers were members of the family of Seleucus I Nicator, who seized Babylon after the battle of Gaza in 312, which year marks the beginning of the Seleucid or Greek era, and

Fig. 4. Coins of Alexander the Great (after Ricciotti *Storia d'Israele*, II, p. 51, S. E. I., Turin).

was for long used as a point of reckoning in the East.[1] This state was the natural successor of the Assyrian, Chaldean, and Persian empires ; and the same reasons which had led these empires to vie with ancient Egypt for the possession of Syria, now led the Ptolemies and Seleucids to quarrel for possession of the Asiatic provinces of the extreme south-west. It was in fact a matter of urgent necessity that the state which ruled over the Tigris and Euphrates should occupy that part of the Mediterranean coast which lay nearest, so that contact with the Greek world might be maintained, and for this reason the Seleucid sovereigns established first at Seleucia and then at Antioch, the capital of their empire in that

[1] Used for instance in the first book of the Maccabees.

region, which received the name of the kingdom of Syria. Egypt, on the other hand, could not allow a rival power to establish itself at the very entrance to the valley of the Nile.

The struggle continued with varying fortunes. Speaking generally, it may be said that from 320 to 198 the Ptolemies most often had the upper hand in Palestine, and that from 198 to 168 the land undoubtedly belonged to the Seleucids.

The Jews do not seem to have suffered much from the frequent change of rulers. It was Samaria, the chief town of the province, which bore the brunt of reprisals. Nevertheless, Josephus recounts that Ptolemy I seized Jerusalem one Sabbath day and led many of the inhabitants captive into Egypt.[1]

On the whole, especially under Egyptian domination, the Jews seem to have enjoyed a good deal of liberty, and even favour, at the hands of their rulers. The dissemination of the Jewish population throughout the ancient world made great strides at this time, for they were allowed right of entry into the whole of the Greek world. Finding the Jews capable of assimilating Greek culture, however conservative they might be in the domain of religion, and knowing them to be brave and reliable soldiers, the kings encouraged this emigration. According to Josephus, Antiochus III the Great, transported two thousand Jewish families from Babylonia to Phrygia and Lydia to hold the country.[2] Demetrius I demanded thirty thousand men from the high priest Jonathan, to man the strongholds of his kingdom and to be his own personal guards.[3]

In several towns, notably in the new cities founded by the Seleucids and the Ptolemies, in which colonists were in great demand, the Jews obtained, either the freedom of the city pure and simple,[4] or possibly a special statute [5] which

[1] *A.J.*, XII, i, 1, §§ 4–7 ; *c.Ap.*, i, 22, § 186 ; *cf. The Letter of Aristeas* iv, 12–14.

[2] *A.J.*, XII, iii, 4, § 147–153. The authenticity of this rescript has been contested ; *cf.* **XLVI**, iii, 80.

[3] *A.J.*, XIII, ii, 3, § 53.

[4] The Jews declared in the most positive way that it had been conferred upon them at Antioch (*A.J.*, XII, iii, 1 ; *B.J.*, VII, iii, 3 ; v, 2) and at Alexandria (Philo, *In Flacc.*, § 44, M. ii, 598 ; Josephus, *c. Ap.*, ii, 4, § 35 ff. ; *B.J.*, II, xviii, 7, § 487–8 ; *A.J.*, XII, i, 1, § 8 ; **XIV**, x, 1, § 188 ; **XIX**, v, 2, § 281 ; vi, 3, § 306). The legitimacy of this claim has been energetically defended by Jean Juster (**XLVII**, ii, 7–11) ; see also **LXXV**, iii [4], 122–4 ; **CCXXIX**. Serious objections have been

gave them rights almost equivalent to the citizens of the most privileged class, namely " the Macedonians ", as they were called in Egypt.[1]

raised by Theodore Reinach (**XLVI**, *ad A.J.*, XII, i, 1 ; XIV, x, 1), Wilcken, Schubart. *Cf.* Perdrizet, **REA**, 1910, pp. 218 *ff.* ; H. J. Bell, **CXCIII**, 10 ff. ; William Lods, **REG**, 36 (1923), pp. 341–2, and **CCXXII**, 20–5 ; Pierre Jouguet, **CCXI**, 399.

[5] The δικαιώματα which Julius Cæsar confirms for the Jews of Alexandria on his stele (*C. Ap.*, II, iv, 37), and the οἰκία which were recognized by Claudius in his letter (Lond. Papyrus, 1912).

[1] This solution, which is proposed by William Lods, **CCXXII** would explain both the affirmative statements of the Jews and the denials of their opponents.

BOOK II

THE RELIGION OF ISRAEL

DEVELOPMENT IN ISRAEL OF A NEW RELIGIOUS TYPE : JUDAISM

THE national catastrophe of 586 had grave and far-reaching effects on the state of religion among the Jewish population. The most important may be summed up as follows : (1) Some at least of the teaching of the prophets which had hitherto met with little response from the masses is at last being assimilated. (2) Their preaching is itself in process of adaptation to the new conditions. Although some of the seed sown by the pioneers of the movement reaches maturity, it nevertheless in many respects shows an increasingly close resemblance to the national traditional religion. On the other hand, the prophet no longer seems to have that complete confidence in his message which endowed the sayings of his predecessors with supreme authority. The inward flame which had inspired the movement until now is growing dim, and may soon be extinguished. A general lowering of the prestige of pneumatic phenomena and their increasing scarcity throughout the Jewish nation is no doubt partly responsible for this. (3) On the other hand, there is a strong tendency to put into the form of laws the requirements of religion, and to codify in minute detail its institutions and traditional rites. The reign of written law as the normal basis of Judaism has begun. (4) When the Jewish social fabric is reconstituted, it is no longer organized on the lines of a State, but of a kind of Church, a community at once national and religious. (5) A body of doctrine takes shape among the Jews : the intellectual element is given a place in religion which it had never previously occupied in the life of any community of ancient times.

These various consequences of the political upheaval which marked the beginning of the sixth century only manifested themselves gradually in the course of a long period of evolution, which was not uniformly progressive, but marked also by relapses and divergences. In our effort to follow its course, we shall find that, though religion was certainly influenced by outward events, the new religious tendencies played no small part in helping to shape the destinies, even as regards temporal things, of Jewish society in the four centuries with which we are concerned.

CHAPTER I

THE RELIGIOUS ATTITUDE OF THE MASSES AT THE TIME OF THE EXILE

THE collapse of the State seems to have reacted somewhat differently on the religious life of the three groups into which the population of the former kingdom of Judah is now divided.[1]

Among the Jews of the Dispersion, especially among those in Egypt, about whom alone we are reliably informed, common opinion did not hesitate to lay the responsibility for the nation's misfortunes at the door of the reformers of Josiah's time, that is to say, the followers of the prophets :—

> " Since we left off to burn incense to the queen of heaven and to pour out drink offerings unto her, we have wanted all things and have been consumed by the sword and by the famine." [2]

The Judæans who took refuge in Egypt in 586 therefore resumed their libations to this goddess on foreign soil, and without any doubt they also returned to the worship of those other deities which the masses of the Jewish population had for centuries venerated alongside of but subordinate to Jahweh. This was exactly the attitude of the Jewish soldiers who composed the colony at Elephantine. Having settled in the country probably before 586, certainly before 525, they had built a temple to Jahu in their new fatherland, and by so doing had shown that they had no particular regard for Josiah's stringent regulations that the Temple at Jerusalem was to have the monopoly of worship. Moreover, even as late as the fifth century, as we shall see,[3] their homage and their gifts were divided between their national god and several co-deities, of which at least one was feminine.

The Jewish settlements in Egypt seem then to have remained impervious to the ideals of the prophets, for they insisted neither on monotheism nor on the necessity for

[1] See pp. 173–180. [2] Jer. xliv, 18.
[3] See pp. 306–7.

repentance on a national scale if Jahweh's wrath was to be appeased. They perpetuated the popular religion of Israel in its lowest forms.

Antonin Causse seems therefore hardly justified in claiming for the Dispersion, and particularly for the Egyptian Dispersion, an influential part in bringing about a new spiritual Judaism by attributing to the diaspora, as he does, though on slight enough evidence, works such as the book of Proverbs, the books of Job and Jonah, or the Psalms which tell of the happiness of the humble (*anâwîm*), because the piety expressed in these writings is more universal and more humane, with less of a specifically Jewish bias.[1] To sub-stantiate that claim it would be necessary to credit the authors of the books in question with quite a different spirit from that which is to be found among the Jews of Tahpanhes and Elephantine in the sixth and fifth centuries.

The large population of Jews left in Palestine, and *even the inhabitants of what had once been the kingdom of Israel*, remained faithful to the Temple of Jerusalem and its worship, in spite of the burning of the sacred edifice by Nebuzaradan in August, 586. A trustworthy document incidentally gives an account of eighty pilgrims, belonging to Shiloh, Samaria and Shechem, who passed through Mizpah in October of the same year, with beards shaven, clothes rent, and bodies slashed, to bring oblations and incense to the house of the Lord.[2] Worship, must, therefore, have continued without interruption on the site of the Temple : the Chaldeans had confined themselves to laying waste the interior and burning the doors, the roofs and everything inflammable. But they had not been able to destroy the sacred rock on which the altar was built, and it was there, no doubt, that offerings were laid. A lamentation, of much later date it is true, contains the suggestion that there were still priests at Jerusalem.[3] The anniversaries of the fateful events which had characterized the destruction of Judah, and in particular the burning of the Temple,[4] were celebrated with fasting ; and the five " Lamentations " of the Biblical book of that name were apparently composed in order that they might be recited at these mournful ceremonies, as were also, perhaps,

[1] **VIII**, 103–130.   [2] Jer. xli, 4.
[3] Lam. i, 4.   [4] Zech. vii, 3, 5 ; viii, 19.

passages such as Psalm 137 ; Deut. 32 ; Is. lxiii, 7–64, 12. As these fasts were doubtless also observed outside Palestine, and were kept up for a long time after the exile,[1] many of these poems may have been composed during the Dispersion [2] or after the return [3] ; such is, however, not the case for the second and fifth Lamentations, which describe the state of affairs in the Holy Land, one in the first, and the other in the second generation. Both of them show that the Jews of Palestine had adopted the interpretation of the nation's misfortunes which Jeremiah had given long before :—

" The Lord hath done that which he devised ; He hath fulfilled his word that he commanded in the days of old ; He hath thrown down and hath not pitied." [4]

The " prophets of Jerusalem ", that is to say, the prophets of the time, the nationalist prophets who did not " discover the iniquity " of the people, had only seen lying visions.[5] " Woe unto us ! for we have sinned." [6]

Nevertheless, this submission to the austere lesson of the great prophets, and to the Deuteronomic law, does not seem to have been either immediate or general as far as the Palestine Jews were concerned. Ezekiel notes [7] that after the destruction of Jerusalem they continued to " eat upon the mountains " [8] and " lift up their eyes to the idols ", that is to say, to celebrate sacrificial meals upon the high places and to worship images, possibly of gods other than Jahweh.

John A. Maynard considers that Jewish Palestine during the exile was a centre of universalist piety and of a spiritual religion continuing the tradition of the great prophets, whereas the colony of exiles in Babylonia, he thinks, showed tendencies inherited from Deuteronomy, and their religion was intellectual and individual, a religion of careful and Utopian scribes. The second Isaiah on the one hand,

---

[1] In the time of Zechariah (518).

[2] E.g. the fourth Lamentation, by a fellow fugitive of King Zedekiah.

[3] As is certainly the case with Ps. cxxxvii, which mentions the captivity in the past tense, and with Deut. xxxii, of which the author seems to be acquainted with the second Isaiah.

[4] Lam. ii, 17 ; cf. ii, 1–8, 21–2.   [5] Lam. ii, 14.

[6] Lam. v, 16 ; cf. 7, 19–22   [7] Ez. xxxiii, 25.

[8] This is probably the correct reading, to judge from xviii, 6, 11, 15 ; xxii, 9 ; instead of " to eat meat with the blood ".

and Ezekiel on the other, seem to him to represent the two types of religion.[1] To assign in this way to the two main Jewish centres the two divergent currents of ideas which can be traced side by side in the literature of the period is an attractive proposition. And there is a certain amount of truth in Maynard's theory, if the second Isaiah, the supreme embodiment of prophetic spirituality, did in reality live in Palestine, as he plausibly maintains. The theory must not be accepted quite unreservedly, however, for it does not seem justifiable to attribute to a whole group the thoughts of this one master-mind. The second Isaiah, like others of his kind, must have been an isolated thinker. The religion of the average Jew in Palestine must have been much the same during the exile as it had been before the Deuteronomic reforms, except that he had learnt to realize that the misfortunes of the nation were the just punishment of the nation's sins.

We know much more about the religious evolution of the third group, the exiles, chiefly thanks to the book of Ezekiel, who for more than twenty years laboured among them. The inner history of the Jewish colony of Babylonia and the prophet's own activities are moreover so closely interwoven that it seems essential to study them together.

[1] **CCXXVI**, xxi, 42–4.

CHAPTER II

TRANSFORMATION OF PROPHECY DURING THE EXILE

I

EZEKIEL

1. *The Prophet and the Exiles before 586.*—As we have seen, a first contingent of Judæans set out for the land of exile in 597, with King Jeconiah. As long as the State, the holy city and the Temple subsisted, these men were convinced that their forced emigration was only for a season ; before long, they thought, the fall of the Babylonian empire would set them free to return in triumph to a fatherland no longer groaning under a foreign yoke. The book of Jeremiah has preserved for us the names of three prophets, Ahab, Zedekiah, and Shemaiah,[1] who encouraged these airy hopes among the captives At one time, the unrest among them assumed such proportions [2] that the authorities were obliged to intervene : the two first-named of these agitators were burnt alive by Nebuchadnezzar's orders.[3] As might be expected, Jeremiah saw nothing in these dreams of glory but dangerous hallucinations, and hastened to undeceive the exiles in unmistakable terms.

> " The captivity is long," [4] he wrote, " build ye houses and plant gardens. . . . Seek the peace of the land [5] whither I have caused you to be carried away captive ; and pray unto the Lord for it, for in the peace thereof shall ye have peace." [6]

A short time afterwards, seized by prophetic inspiration, one of the exiles returned to the same theme. Ezekiel, the

---

[1] Jer. xxix, 21–2, 24, 31–2.
[2] Probably in 594. But see p. 48, n. 1.
[3] Jer. xxix, 21–3. [4] Jer. xxix, 28.
[5] According to the Greek, this is the reading. The Hebrew has " of the city ".
[6] Jer. xxix, 5, 7.

son of Buzi, was a priest, apparently a member of the family
of the Bene Zadok, who ministered in the temple at Jerusalem,
for to them alone he is willing to concede a right to the
priesthood.[1]

He himself relates the way in which he became a prophet.
One day, in June, 593, walking by the " river Chebar ", that
is to say the great canal,[2] he had a vision. He saw the glory
of the Lord, in other words Jahweh himself, coming towards
him in a kind of chariot of marvellous swiftness, borne on
four wheels which seemed alive and by four beings whose
appearance was partly that of a man and partly that of
various animals, an eagle, a lion, and a bull. Jahweh handed
him a roll, written on both sides and filled with lamentation
and mourning, the burden of which was the sinister message
about to be entrusted to him.[3]

Ezekiel went to Tel-Abib, the nearest and perhaps the
most important of the towns in which the exiles of
Judah were ordered to live. And for the six years following
(593–586) he repeated with unwearying insistence his warning
that the Jewish State still existing in Palestine in the reign
of Zedekiah was doomed, and that its fate was inevitable,
just, and in accordance with the will of Jahweh.

It has often been said, for instance by Reuss and Smend,
that unlike his predecessors, who were men of action, and sought
to influence those with whom they came in contact directly
by word of mouth, Ezekiel was a writer, a man of letters,
whose aim was to inspire *by the written word* a distant public,
namely his readers in Palestine.[4] This argument was based on
considerations such as the prophet's preoccupation with the
fate of Jerusalem, his address to the mountains of Israel,
his vision of the Temple, to which he was transported in
the spirit,[5] but it is one which was long ago contradicted
by Lucien Gautier in a book on the Mission of the prophet
Ezekiel,[6] and is now generally discredited. It is not merely
as a figure of speech that Ezekiel represents himself as
inveighing against his companions in exile, or receiving visits

---

[1] Ez. xliv, 10–15.
[2] See p. 177.   [3] Ez. i–iii.
[4] Loisy (**LIX**, 3, 187) shares this opinion up to a point : " Though
his public is still a limited one, he is a prophet whose study is his pulpit."
[5] Vision in cc, viii–xi.   [6] **CCI.**

PLATE VI

[face p. 212

Ezekiel and the Vision of the Valley of Dry Bones. The prophet is successively represented as being carried by the hair into the Valley, commanding the bones to assemble, and entreating the Spirit to restore them to life. From a mural painting in the Synagogue of Dura on the Euphrates, 245 A.D. (From a photograph kindly furnished by M. du Mesnil du Buisson.)

from their elders who come to him for advice. His message was exactly the message which a prophet with Ezekiel's convictions must necessarily desire to bring home with the utmost urgency to men living in feverish expectation of immediate revenge. Jerusalem, the rebellious city, which tolerated heathen practices in its very midst, was denounced and forsaken by Jahweh ; it must succumb and that shortly ; nothing was to be hoped for from Zedekiah, the perjured vassal, nor from his kingdom ; it was the exiles themselves who, some forty years later,[1] would again take possession of the country.[2] This prophecy was indispensable, not only if the exiles were to be kept from despair when the catastrophe occurred, but also if they were to be induced to renounce those evil practices which, according to Ezekiel, brought it about.

The all-important place assigned to the fate of Israel and its capital in most of the book of Ezekiel has, however, been differently explained by certain recent critics, who are of the opinion that these prophecies were originally spoken [3] or even conceived [4] by a prophet whose sphere of activity lay *in Palestine*, whether the prophet was anonymous [5] or Ezekiel himself before he was deported [6] ; an editor would then have gone over the orations, and in the hope of exalting the Diaspora at the expense of Palestinian Judaism, would have presented them as if they had been uttered in the first place in Babylonia.

This theory, which makes it necessary to relegate to the domain of fiction the numerous allusions, all perfectly sober and natural, to those Babylonian surroundings in which the hero of the book lived, does not seem to us convincing. As we have already said, it seems to us quite consistent that a deported prophet, working on much the same lines as

---

[1] Ez. iv, 5–6.
[2] Ez. ii, 1–21.
[3] Torrey, *Pseudo-Ezekiel and the original Prophecy*, 1930.
[4] James Smith, *The Book of the Prophet Ezekiel*, 1931 ; Hernstrich, *Ezechielprobleme*, 1932 ; W. O. E. Oesterley and Theodore H. Robinson, *An Introduction to the Books of the O.T.*, 1934, 326–9.
[5] A supposed contemporary of Manasseh, according to Torrey.
[6] According to James Smith he lived in Northern Israel between 722 and 669 ; according to Hernstrich at Jerusalem, between 593 and 586 ; according to Oesterley and Robinson also at Jerusalem, between 602 and 597.

Jeremiah, and writing between 597 and 586, should have considered it his chief duty to convince his companions in exile that the destruction of Judah and of its capital was imminent and that it was God's will.

Delenda est Jerusalem.—The prophet presents this single theme in the most varied ways—for he is a stylist and likes to diversify his literary effects—retrospective summaries of the history of the nation,[1] allegories and parables,[2] the answer to a question,[3] generally in the form of a *torah*, that is to say one of those points of law about which the priests were consulted,[4] prophetic invective,[5] lyrical outpourings,[6] descriptions of visions[7]—he uses them all to convey his message.

He frequently accompanies the utterance of his prophecies by some symbolic gesture ; sometimes the symbol is unaccompanied by any verbal commentary. For instance, he draws on a tile a picture of a city surrounded by such engines of war as would be used in besieging it, and between the tile and himself he places an iron plate, symbolizing the blockade of Jerusalem by the Chaldeans.[8] He eats rationed and impure food, as the inhabitants of the town will have to do during the siege.[9] He cuts his hair, then burns one-third of it, destroys another third with a sword, and the rest he scatters to the four winds, as a sign of the different calamities which a e to overtake the capital.[10] He starts on a journey by night through a hole which he has pierced in the wall, as Zedekiah will try to do.[11] He traces the plan of a crossroads, that parting of the ways where Nebuchadnezzar will stand, examining the oracle of the arrows and the liver of sacrificial victims so that he may know whether to march first against Rabbah Ammon or Jerusalem.[12]

---

[1] Cc. xvi and xxiii.

[2] Cc. xv (the wood of the vine), xvii (allegory of the eagle and the cedar), xix (the lioness and her cubs, signifying the queen-mother and her sons, the princes), xxiv, 1–4 (Jerusalem besieged, the figure used being a cauldron).

[3] As in ch. xx.   [4] Cc. xiv and xviii.

[5] Ch. xiii, against prophets and prophetesses.

[6] Ch. vi, against the mountains of Israel ; ch. xxi, the song of the sword.

[7] Cc. i–iii ; cc. viii–x and xi, 22–25 ; ch. ii, 1–21.

[8] iv, 1–3.   [9] iv, 9–17.   [10] Ch. v.

[11] Ch. xii.   [12] xxi, 24–5.

This miming of future events, a practice familiar to the Israelite *nabis* of old,[1] may be explained in the case of Ezekiel sometimes as a trance-reflex, the picture which obsessed him translating itself almost involuntarily by the appropriate gestures,[2] sometimes as a legacy of ancient times, when magicians believed that an imitative or sympathetic rite was more efficacious than the spoken word—which in itself was potent—in bringing about the event which they were causing to happen on a small scale [3] : to ill-treat a person's image, or a lock of his hair was a recipe of sympathetic magic universally employed in order to bring him bad luck. This is the method used by Ezekiel—of course at the command of Jahweh—with regard to Jerusalem, which he represents by drawing on the tile,[4] or by himself acting the part of the city.[5]

The prophet may have had a special and personal reason for preferring mimed prophecies. He makes repeated mention of periods of dumbness, when by Jahweh's intervention his tongue cleaved to his palate.[6] It has been thought, and it is a plausible theory, that Ezekiel was subject to attacks which manifested themselves in the paralysis of certain organs, and particularly in fits of aphasia, when gesture was his only means of expression. This theory would also explain his periods of immobility, of varying length, when it seemed to him that Jahweh had bound him with cords to prevent him from moving his limbs.[7] These are thought o have been cataleptic fits.[8] Hölscher thinks that there is a simpler explanation of these phenomena, in so far as he considers them historical, and that they were due to nervous strain resulting from the prophet's ecstatic condition.[9] Ezekiel remained in a dazed condition for seven days after his first vision, it is true [10] ; but it is unlikely that the reaction which would inevitably follow a time of too great tension

---

[1] **LVII**, 242–3.
[2] *Cf.* **XXXVI**, 304.
[3] See pp. 53–5.
[4] Ez. iv, 1–3.
[5] Ez. v, 1–4.
[6] Ez. iii, 26 ; xxiv, 27 ; xxxiii, 22.
[7] Ez. iii, 25 ; iv, 4–8.
[8] **CCXIV** ; **CCI** ; Bertholet, **KHC**, *Hes.*, xix, 27 ; Kraetzschmar, **HK**, *Ez.* 45–6 ; *cf.* D. Buzy (**VII**, 215–16), who, however, will not allow that it was catelepsy, but says that it was only " ordinary infirmities, paralysis, rheumatism, pain in the joints ".
[9] **XXXVI**, 305; *cf.* pp. 58–9.
[10] Ez. iii, 15.

would last 40 or 190 days,[1] which is the length of time
mentioned for these periods of immobility in chapter 4 (vv., 4–8,)
still less that it could have lasted two years, as did the
silence imposed upon Ezekiel at the time of the siege of
Jerusalem.[2] This last-named instance suggests that neither
should the figures 40 and 190 [3] be disallowed in the first-
named instance—and indeed they constitute the chief reason
for relating the episode at all—nor should the whole matter
be regarded as legendary.[4] In any case, Ezekiel's dumbness
is to be taken as a literal fact ; there is no question, as has
often been maintained, of periods during which he abstained
from speaking *in public* [5] or had preached *unsuccessfully*.
The men of God held that all the incidents of their lives,
however personal, were signs and portents bearing on their
mission [6]; Ezekiel would naturally have interpreted in this
way the physical infirmities which might afflict him.

In 588 the Judæan revolt broke out, which was to end
in the destruction of Jerusalem. At about the time when
Nebuchadnezzar began to lay siege to the town,[7] Ezekiel
lost his wife, " the delight of his eyes," but at Jahweh's command he gave no sign of mourning. One must suppose, no
doubt, that the prophet was so overwhelmed by this sudden
blow that he even neglected those traditional rites which
should have been observed at such a time, and that, when in
the course of his night of sorrow he finally remembered his
omission, he saw in it a divine command, and explained it as
such on the morrow : Jahweh had wished his prophet to
abstain from weeping in order to give the exiles a new omen
of symbolic action : the Lord will profane his sanctuary,
your pride, your delight, the object of your love, and you
will be so bewildered with grief that you will not even
remember to show signs of mourning. After this a period

---

[1] This figure, 190, which is given by the Septuagint, is to be preferred
to 390, which appears in the Massoretic text, for only the former fits
in with the symbolic interpretation which follows.
[2] xxiv, 1, 27 ; xxxiii, 21–3, where the Syriac reading should be
adopted, " 11th year " instead of " 12th ".
[3] As D. Rothstein does, for example (**XLVIII,**[4]).
[4] As Hölscher does (**XXXVI,** 305).
[5] Is. viii, 18 ; *cf.* viii, 1–4 ; Hos. i, 3.   [6] Smend, **KEH.**
[7] Not necessarily the same day ; for it is not certain that the date
given at the beginning of the first episode reported in ch. xxiv also
applies to the second (vv., 15–27).

of silence set in for Ezekiel, which was only broken on the day when a fugitive arrived in Babylonia announcing " the city is taken ". The prophet, who had been in trance since the previous evening, then recovered the power of speech, no doubt as a result of his emotion at the news.[1]

2. *Ezekiel and the Exiles after 586.*—It is hard for us to picture the state of spiritual bewilderment and dismay into which the catastrophe of 586 plunged the exiles. Like their co-religionists of Jerusalem, in spite of the warnings of Jeremiah and Ezekiel they had, up till the very last moment, lived in expectation of some miraculous deliverance from the oppressor, whom Jahweh would surely overthrow. Instead of this, the holy city was destroyed ; the very house of God was pillaged and burnt, and he had not made any attempt to defend it.

With more confidence than ever, some drew the conclusion that the misfortunes had been caused by other deities, who were avenging themselves for neglect in worship, resulting from the reforms. For there were syncretists among the exiles in Babylonia, just as there were among the Jews who took refuge in Egypt. Ezekiel accuses some of his hearers of worshipping wood and stone, that is to say graven images, of serving idols, even of immolating children,[2] in fact of trying to become assimilated to the surrounding nations, yet without on that account ceasing to consult the prophet of Jahweh.[3] Herein lies perhaps, at least to some extent, the explanation of those names borne by many of the exiles, which were partly composed of the names of Babylonian gods.

Most of them realized, however, that Jahweh was punishing his people. But they either felt that his wrath was undeserved,[4] or else they admitted that the calamities were a just chastisement for the age-long sins of the nation, as the great prophets had never ceased to tell them, and gave themselves up to despair :

---

[1] Ez. xxiv, 25–7 ; xxxiii, 21–2.

[2] At least according to the Massoretic text of xx, 31.

[3] Ez. xiv, 1–11 ; xx, 30–8. Rothstein and Hölscher reject the authenticity of a part of the second passage, but in our opinion without any really imperative reason.

[4] As is to be inferred from the answer which Ezekiel gives to this question, xiv, 22–3.

" Our transgressions and our sins are upon us, and we pine away in them ; how then should we live ? " [1]

From the religious point of view, the exiles in Babylon were in much worse straits than the refugees in Egypt. It was a recognized principle among all the Israelites, whether they followed the old popular religion, or were disciples of the prophets, that Jahweh would only accept the worship offered up in the Holy Land.[2] Exile therefore necessarily entailed a suspension of sacrifice. Popular Jahwism, as practised by most of the Jews in Egypt, managed to avoid this result by bringing earth from Palestine and building an altar upon it, as Naaman did,[3] or else by asking the gods of the strangers to cede a plot of ground to Jahweh, as Solomon had done for the deities worshipped by his wives,[4] and the Egyptian gods for the Canaanitish gods in the days of the rule of the Pharaohs.[5] It was doubtless in consequence of some such arrangement that the Jewish settlers in Elephantine had built a temple to Jahu near the first cataract. It may be that some of the settlers in Babylonia had a similar plan, which they submitted to the prophet Ezekiel,[6] and that they finally erected a temple at Kasiphia, where in the time of Ezra there lived a great number of Levites and temple servants,[7] and which is twice described as *maqom*, " place," a term which can also mean " holy place ", like the Arabic *maqam*.[8]

Most of the Jews of the Lower Euphrates, however, seem to have been followers of Josiah's reforms, and therefore completely debarred from celebrating the rites of worship outside the temple of Jerusalem. Now these rites were associated with many of the happenings of everyday life, even after worship had been concentrated in one place. Bread and wine were held to be impure if the firstfruits had not been taken to the house of God.[9] It was, therefore, impossible to eat so much as a mouthful of bread in this unclean land

---

[1] Ez. xxxiii, 10 ; *cf.* xxxvii, 11.   [2] *Cf.* **LVII,** 523–4.
[3] 2 Kings v, 17.   [4] 1 Kings xi, 7–8 ; 2 Kings xxiii,13.
[5] *Cf.* **LVII,** 139, 140, 148, 154–5, 161–2.
[6] Several expositors think that this was the gist of the consultation demanded of Ezekiel by some of the elders (ch. xx). *Cf.* Hans Schmidt, **XXVIII,** xi, 2², 425–7 ; Menes, **ZATW,** 50 (1932), 271–3.
[7] Ezr. viii, 15–20.
[8] Gen. xii, 6 ; xxviii, 11 ; Deut. xii, 2, etc.   [9] Hos. ix, 3–5.

of exile without being reminded, to their sorrow and humiliation, that they were being oppressed by the wrath of God.

After 586, Ezekiel therefore found himself confronted
by an entirely new state of affairs. He was no longer faced
with a nation which turned a deaf ear to his appeals, one
which was living in a fool's paradise, whose illusions must
be shattered and whose pride must be brought low ; instead
they turned to him like sheep without a shepherd, willing
to accept his guidance, at least in theory,[1] looking to him
for consolation. His task was no longer to predict the overthrow of the State, but to foretell the future resurrection of
the nation and to pave the way for it.

In order to carry out this work of reconstruction, there
was nothing, in the first part of Ezekiel's career, which had now
to be unsaid or reconsidered. On the contrary, those ideas
on which his preaching had been based, having been
triumphantly vindicated by recent events, formed almost
automatically an integral part of his programme of restoration. The chief aims of this were threefold, having a bearing
on the past, the present and the future.

With regard to the *nation's* past, Ezekiel continued to
maintain—as for the first six years of his activity he had
endeavoured to prove—that it was so saturated with crime
that the calamities of the present were its just and inevitable
sequel. His predecessors among the prophets, however
harshly they may have judged their own times and those
which immediately preceded them, had as a rule conceded
that Israel had loved Jahweh in its earliest days in the desert
(Hosea, Jeremiah), even that, in the time of David, Jerusalem
had been a faithful city (Isaiah) ; the Deuteronomic legislators, although they condemned all worship other than that
which was offered in the one temple chosen by Jahweh, had
not extended their censure to the years previous to the
building of the Temple by Solomon. But Ezekiel, with that
intrepid logic which was characteristic of him, pursued to its
furthest conclusions the law laid down by Josiah. Since
Jahweh abhorred the worship of graven images, the ritual of
high-places, and human sacrifice, the whole history of Israel
from its very beginnings, that is to say, since the sojourn
in Egypt, had been nothing but one long infidelity.[2] Israel

---

[1] Ez. xxxiii, 30–1.   [2] Ez. xvi, xx, xxiii ; *cf.* Jer. iii, 24–5 already.

had always been, and was still, a " rebellious house ". It is hardly necessary to point out the injustice of judging ancient times according to laws which they had never known; but who at that time troubled about the scruples of the historical point of view ? Ezekiel's object was a practical one : he wanted to give the exiles, his hearers, a clear explanation of the destruction of Jerusalem, and one which should satisfy a believer in Jahweh ; above all, with a view to future reconstruction, he wanted to instil in them a horror of past misdemeanours, particularly of " the abomination " which according to him had been the chief cause of the catastrophe, namely the observance of unlawful ritual practices.

With regard to *the present*, it was a matter of urgency that those of his flock, who felt overwhelmed by the burden of divine wrath, should be given a religious motive for making fresh contacts with life if they were to be rescued from their fatalistic despair. " Our transgressions and our sins are upon us . . . how then should we live ? "

With his respect for the nation's past, Ezekiel would have had considerable difficulty in restoring their courage if he had adhered uncompromisingly to the traditional principle of collective punishment, which taught that Jahweh punished the children for the sins of the fathers to the third and fourth generation, or if he had confined himself to declaring that the generation of the exiles was expiating the crimes of Manasseh, as the editors of the book of Kings and of Jeremiah did subsequently.[1]

This principle that punishment could descend from father to son, which all the peoples of antiquity had considered axiomatic, was not allowed to pass unchallenged in Judæa, where in the seventh and eighth centuries it met with lively protests from the public conscience. The individualist movement which had already been outlined in ancient Israel,[2] when once the primitive solidarity of the clan had begun to relax,[3] had been accentuated by the general trend of urban civilization and by the appeals of the prophets for individual repentance.

For some time past, the administration of justice had

[1] 2 Kings xxi, 10–15 ; xxii, 15–20 ; xxiii, 26–7 ; xxiv, 3–4 ; Jer. xv, 4.
[2] LVII, 550–2, 556.   [3] LVII, 453–6. *Cf.* above, p. 161, n. 7.

shown signs of this individualist tendency. No collective punishments figure in the civil laws of the " book of the covenant ". Even the sons of regicides had not been put to death with their fathers since the beginning of the eighth century.[1] And Deuteronomy, although still prescribing mass punishment for a particularly grave religious crime,[2] strictly forbids judges to punish children instead of their fathers, or fathers instead of their children, in civil lawsuits.[3]

Since, therefore, civil law no longer permitted men to visit the crimes of one generation upon another, the practice must necessarily seem equally iniquitous if observed in the divine government of the world. It was the time when the great prophets, especially Jeremiah, were realizing more and more clearly the value in God's eyes of the individual soul.[4] About this time too, the author of Solomon's great prayer declared that Jahweh heard the prayers of all who prayed to him, " spreading forth his hands " towards the Temple.[5]

If the individual had real value in the sight of God, how then could God punish the innocent with the guilty, or even instead of the guilty ? Many minds, troubled by the paradox, accused God of injustice. " The fathers," they said " have eaten sour grapes, and the children's teeth are set on edge ! " [6]

When Jeremiah overheard this rebellious saying, he contented himself with replying that when the restoration took place there would no longer be any grounds for it,[7] a remark which showed that at the moment it was well founded.

One of the commentators of the Deuteronomic code outlines another attempt to solve the problem : God never allows punishment to devolve upon the children, without at the same time punishing the fathers.[8] Which meant that they admitted that God punished the innocent *with* the guilty, though not in their stead.

Others tried to evade the accusation of injustice levelled at Jahweh by declaring that he was ready to pardon a guilty city if it contained a sufficient minority of just men.[9] According to the first decalogue, the principle of solidarity

---

[1] 2 Kings xiv, 5–6a. *Cf.* **LVII**, 556.   [2] Deut. xiii, 16–19.
[3] Deut. xxiv, 16.   [4] See pp. 167–8.   [5] 1 Kings viii, 38–9.
[6] Ez. xviii, 25 ; Jer. xxxi, 29.   [7] Jer. xxxi, 29–30.
[8] Deut. vii, 9–10.
[9] Gen. xviii, 22b–35a ; Jer. v, 1 ; *cf.* Ez. xxii, 30.

in punishment only extended to the third or fourth generation, while God was prepared to show mercy to thousands.[1]

Without rejecting the principle of collective punishment, Jeremiah announced that significant exceptions would be made. He promised that in the chastisement which was to overtake their fellows, Jahweh would spare certain individuals, Baruch, the eunuch Ebed-Melech, and the Jerusalemites who " went forth unto the Chaldean ".[2]

These were only palliatives. Ezekiel went further, and boldly declared that the doctrine of collective punishment was false, that in any case it was contradicted by the facts *of his own day*—he offered no explanation of past happenings.[3] He sought to demonstrate that the present generation was punished for its own sins.[4] He even formulated, under a series of legal headings, a precise theory of individual punishment : a just man was not to be penalized for the crimes of a wicked father ; a wicked man was not to be spared for the sake of his righteous father's righteousness.[5] Ezekiel therefore took the great step of extending to individuals the principle of *absolutely just* retribution [6] which his predecessors among the prophets had declared that God applied to nations. Moreover—and it was no less remarkable—he also affirmed that every individual was the object of God's *love* : Jahweh took no pleasure in the death of a sinner, but desired that he should be converted and live. If a wicked man altered his way of life, Jahweh forgot all his past sins ; and as a corollary, if a just man became evil, no account was kept of his former goodness. The life of each human being had its own religious significance ; every man had a goal before him, and his chief concern was to reach that goal, namely his individual salvation, which might be achieved, to some extent at least, in spite of disasters happening to the nation.

The flaws in this theory, here and there shot through with the gleams of an evangelical hope, are only too evident. How was it possible to maintain that in actual life the evil are always punished and the good spared ? For it was naturally during this life that, according to Ezekiel, everyone was to

---

[1] Ex. xx, 5–6.   [2] Jer. xlv ; xxxix, 15 ; xxi, 9 ; xxxviii, 2.
[3] See for instance xvi, 3.   [4] Ez. viii ; xvii, etc.
[5] Ez. xviii ; *cf.* xiv, 12–23 ; xxxiii, 1–20.   [6] *Cf.* pp. 75–6.

receive his deserts. Usually, when speaking of deserts, the prophet thought of a calamity which should exterminate the wicked and leave the righteous unharmed.[1] Thus he had foretold, before 586, that only the righteous would survive the destruction of Jerusalem.[2] But events sometimes belied his theory in a most embarrassing manner. Nevertheless he did not abandon it, justifying the exceptions as well as he could. If Jahweh, he explained after 586, allowed evil-doers to survive the fall of Jerusalem, it was in order that the exiles might judge for themselves, from such specimens of the inhabitants as remained, how justified God had been in destroying the city.[3]

After Ezekiel, the doctrine of individual retribution became the basic doctrine of morality in Judaism.[4] This doctrine was opposed to the evidence of facts, and lay open to the criticisms of profound or keen intellects such as those of the authors of the books of Job and Ecclesiastes ; but it was in reality something quite different from an experienced truth : it expressed a postulate of the moral and religious conscience. It finally triumphed when, towards the second century, Judaism adopted the belief in retribution *in a future life*.

Ezekiel drew one conclusion of special interest from this theory of his ; it led him to modify the traditional conception of the rôle of the prophet, who was no longer to be merely the sentinel warning the nation of the dangers which threatened it as a whole, but was to be held responsible for the death of every evil-doer who perished without having been warned. The prophet was no longer only a judge—he was also a shepherd.[5]

But after 586, it was *the future*, still more than the present, which absorbed his attention ; and the future, for him, meant the future of the nation. Whatever importance he may have attached to the individual because of the slackening of social ties resulting from the destruction of the State, it is nevertheless the nation which in his eyes was the corner-stone of religion. More forcibly than ever he reiterated the prophecy which he had outlined in the first part of his career, that

---

[1] Ez. xx, 33–8 ; *cf.* iii, 16–21 ; xviii.
[2] Ez. ix, 4–6 ; xiv, 12–20.   [3] Ez. xiv, 21–3.
[4] See pp. 328–31.   [5] Ez. iii, 16–21 ; xxxiii, 1–9.

Israel would return to favour, or, that the exiles would return
to the holy mountain, which, to him, comes to the same
thing. From 593 onwards, it was the little group of exiles
who seemed to him to constitute the true " house of Israel ",
the nucleus of the restored nation of the future.[1] The hope
of return was to sustain the faith of the exiles more than
anything else.

One day he had a vision. Transported by the spirit into
a valley, which he found covered with dry bones, at the
word of God he commanded the bones to come together, to
be covered with flesh, and the bodies thus formed to come
to life. And the miracle was accomplished. Jahweh then
explained to him the meaning of the scene : he would bring
Israel out of the tomb of exile, back to its own land.[2]

For Ezekiel, the restoration was a certainty. His predecessors among the great prophets had declared that
repentance was the nation's only hope of salvation. Several
of them had hoped that the very misfortunes of the nation
would bring about this sincere conversion. But after 597
and 586 Ezekiel became aware that this change of heart
was taking place among a minority at most. Drawing his
conclusions from prophetic principles, he therefore foretold
in certain passages that Jahweh would execute fresh judgment
upon the rebel exiles and would separate them from those who
had repented.[3] Elsewhere, adopting Jeremiah's idea, he
expressed the hope that God would perform a miracle and
give the nation a new heart.[4]

But as a rule he reversed the order of repentance and
salvation preached by his predecessors : according to him,
instead of preceding the restoration, conversion would follow
it. Jahweh would first forgive the sinful nation and reinstate
it in its own country ; and then the nation, humbled by
God's loving kindness, would remember its sins and reject
them with abhorrence.[5] The conception is one of great
spiritual profundity, and already there is about it a suggestion
of St. Paul's " By grace ye have been saved . . . and that

---

[1] Ez. iii, 1, 4, 11 ; ii, in particular vv., 15–21 ; *cf*. pp. 179–180.
[2] Ez. xxxvii, 1–14 ; *cf*. pl. vi. Ezekiel, of course, does not in this
passage either teach or believe in the resurrection of *individuals* : the
resurrection of the dead is a *symbol* of the rebirth of the nation.
[3] Ez. xx, 33–8.   [4] Jer. xxiv, 7 ; xxxi, 32 ; Ez. xxxvi, 26–7.
[5] Ez. xvi, 60–3 ; xxxvi, 28–31.

not of yourselves ". In seeking to establish his hopes on a
secure basis, Ezekiel felt that they must be founded not
on the goodwill of the people, which was bound to be imper-
fect, but on God. What guarantee had he that God would
be willing to restore Israel ? Ezekiel's answer was : Jahweh's
regard for the honour of his holy name. As a result of the
destruction of his people's capital, the burning of his Temple,
and the dispersion of his people, the God of Israel had seen
his holy name profaned among the nations, and his power
declared of no avail. Jahweh could not allow that state of
affairs to continue indefinitely.[1] In spite of the lofty elements
contained in this speculation, it is evident that it was a dis-
guised return to the old traditional religion. Ezekiel's belief
in the continued existence of the nation was founded, like
that of ancient Israel, on the *necessary* bond between Jahweh
and his people, a bond which in Ezekiel's eyes was neither
inevitable nor indissoluble, but created by the free will of
God ; in point of fact, however, Jahweh was inseparable
from Israel, his sole representative in the world. This mixture
of prophetic ideas and previous conceptions is typical of
early Judaism.

Not content with merely stating that a restoration would
take place, and with laying securer foundations for the
nation's hopes, Ezekiel gave details in advance. He foretold
the destruction of certain nations, for instance of Edom,
without which it did not seem to him that Israel could be
restored.[2] In a vision [3] he walks in the restored Temple,
the plan of which he gives with all the precision of an architect;
details of the rites to be celebrated there are revealed to him,
and also instructions as to the constitution of the nation,
and the dividing of the land among the different elements
of the population. We are here confronted by something
more than a prophetic revelation of which some features are
Utopian,[4] namely by a regular project of legislation, which
profoundly influenced the work of codification accomplished
during the exile. We shall return to it later.[5]

---

[1] Ez. xxxvi, 22–4.   [2] Ez. xxxv.
[3] Ez. xl–xlviii. It does not seem to us established that this, the
most important part of the book of Ezekiel is, either wholly or mainly,
the work of one of his disciples.   [4] e.g. Ez. xlvii, 1–12.
[5] See pp. 251–262.

Ezekiel went further still.   He related in advance *the history* of the restored nation.   He foretold that, " after many days," a king of Magog named Gog would march at the head of the nations of the extreme north and the extreme south against the Jews who had returned from exile, and that Jahweh would exterminate this multitude among the hills of Israel : he foretold that it would take seven months to bury such a mass of dead bodies.[1]   This extraordinary pre-diction, which is perhaps not to be attributed to Ezekiel, or not in its entirety,[2] was partly deduced from the study of the prophets who preceded him.   The author, whoever he was, had found in the book of Jeremiah the prophecy of an enemy who was to come from the north [3] which prophecy seemed to him not to have been fulfilled.[4]   The enigmatic names of Magog and Gog may also have been derived from some ancient prediction, if it is true that the former denoted Scythia,[5] and the latter was the general designation of the northern barbarians,[6] or of a legendary people of the extreme north.[7]   A fairly general view is that Gog was none other than Gyges (in Assyrian Gugu), the ruler of Lydia, who was a contemporary of Ashurbanipal, in which case he was another celebrity belonging to the past who was being projected into the future ; `Magog would then be " the country of Gog ", *mat-Gugu*.[8]   On the other hand, the prediction was no doubt partly founded on a theological argument : the holy name of Jahweh must be glorified by a brilliant victory in the very places in which it had been profaned.   Finally, it may perhaps contain a distant echo of the old myth of the struggle of the powers of darkness against the gods of light and the cosmos created by them.   The study of ancient prophecies, dogmatic deduction, the utilization of secular myths : such are already the methods by which the authors of apocalypses in centuries to come will progressively build up the Messianic expectation.

[1] Ez. xxxviii–xxxix.
[2] Herrmann says that it is a much altered version of an authentic prophecy of Ezekiel against Babylon. *Cf.* **XXXVI**, 421.
[3] Jer. i, 13–15 ; iv, 6 ; vi, 1–22 ; x, 22–6 ; xlvi, 24, etc. ; *cf.* Joel ii, 20 ; Am. vii, 1 (LXX).
[4] Ez. xxxviii, 17 ; xxxix, 8.   [5] Josephus, *A.J.*, I, 6, 1.
[6] **XLV**, 147 ; it has been compared with the Gentilic *gagaia* (Tell el Amarna, **KB**, v, 5).   [7] **LXVII**, 257.
[8] Ed. Meyer, *Gesch. des Alt.*, I, § 464 ; **LII**, 133 ; **XXXV**, 137 ; **CCVIII**, 189 ; **LIX**, 223.

3. *The Personality of Ezekiel.*—Ezekiel does not seem to us so attractive a figure as his contemporary Jeremiah, who makes so human an appeal, racked as he is by inward struggles, overwhelmed by pity for his country at the very moment of his sharpest condemnation. Ezekiel has the appearance of a rigid and impassible moralist. No other prophet gives such an impression of absolute single-mindedness. Was he really what he seemed ? A doubt arises when we hear him speak of his love for his wife, and in the same breath show that he understands the affection felt by his opponents for the Temple and for their children left behind in Jerusalem [1] ; when a kind of intercession for Jerusalem escapes him unawares [2] ; when in the name of Jahweh he utters words which are certainly not those of an inexorable lawgiver :—

" Have I any pleasure in the death of the wicked . . . and not rather that he should return from his way and live ? " [3]

Nevertheless, these are only flashes. In his eyes, pity for the guilty was no doubt a reprehensible weakness. When finally Jerusalem falls, he has not a single word of compassion. He takes pleasure in describing the future extermination of Gentile nations.

There is something of the fanatic in him therefore. For the psychologist and the historian, the contrasts of his life and the variety of elements which make up his mental equipment are of too great interest to be thereby impaired.

He was an ecstatic. Of all the prophets of Israel, it was he who experienced, in their most violent form, those pneumatic phenomena which are at times most nearly pathological. At the same time he had excellent reasoning powers, he was a logician who formulated as doctrines and as laws the broad statements of conscience and of faith uttered by his predecessors ; he has been called the first Jewish dogmatist.

He sometimes indulged in strangely Utopian ideas, as, for instance, when he foretold that at the time of the restoration of the exiles to the Holy Land, a stream, gushing out from the Temple, would miraculously grow until its waves

[1] Ez. xxiv, 16, 21, 25.   [2] Ez. ix, 8.
[3] Ez. xviii, 23, 32 ; xxxiii, 11.

purified the Dead Sea. As a general rule, he was a realist of astonishing perspicacity : he saw clearly, for instance, that the nation once restored would adopt the form of a Church rather than that of a regular State.

Ezekiel was a poet, sometimes a great poet [1] ; but his imagination often engendered only complicated figures impossible to represent, or lifeless allegories : his mind is of the fantastic rather than the imaginative type.[2]

In his thoughts there were currents which mingled without always being able to unite in an organic synthesis. Of all the prophets of Israel, he was the most methodical, yet there is less real depth of unity in his teaching than in that of any of the others.[3]

He owed much to the great prophetic movement which began in the eighth century, and was a genuine representative of it himself, as is evident from his constant desire to declare the supreme and absolute will of Jahweh, and the clearness with which he also proclaims the good news of God, who is always ready to forgive the repentant sinner, also from his efforts to give the highest possible idea of the greatness of God, of his transcendence, as it is now called, and of the abyss which separates him from earthly things. He is also in the succession of Amos and Hosea when, from 586 onwards, he ceases to be a prophet of evil and foretells an era of prosperity, finding his text for a powerful moral sermon in these very promises : Israel will repent, no longer from fear of punishment, but from gratitude.

---

[1] See, for instance, Ez. xxxvii, 1–14.   [2] **XXXVI**, 313.

[3] This is the chief reason for Hölscher's view that the contents of the book of Ezekiel should be divided between two people, one of whom is Ezekiel, who, according to him was solely " a poet who wrote brilliant rhetoric, full of imagination and passion ", and the other an interpolator, a priest, a somewhat stilted scholar, who initiated legalist and ritualistic Judaism. This is perhaps logical enough, but reality is not always logical. The co-existence of heterogeneous tendencies in one and the same personality is an everyday occurrence ; and in Ezekiel, as presented by the present form of his book, it does not seem to us to go beyond psychological probabilities. Moreover, there are pages in the book which do not belong entirely to either of the two distinct literary types mentioned by Hölscher, but are midway between the two. The vision of the bones (xxxvii, 1–14), of which this critic does not think Ezekiel was the author, is poetry of a powerful and spacious kind ; and on the other hand, the complicated allegory of the lioness and her cubs (xix), which Hölscher attributes to the prophet, is as meticulous and as artificial as he feels the interpolator to be.

On the other hand, the traditional form of nationalistic Jahwism is given a much more prominent place in his religious conceptions than in those of any of the prophets before him. The care with which he describes what might almost be called the physical aspect of Jahweh is strongly reminiscent of Israelite antiquity. In the complicated picture which he paints (Chapter I), two tendencies common in ancient Israel are noticeable, one ascribing human shape to the national God,[1] the other associating him with the thunder-cloud and representing him as kind of fiery being composed of, or surrounded by, " a glory." [2]

To the old nationalistic Jahwism belongs also the bond, which Ezekiel stresses much more than any prophet before him, between Jahweh and Palestine,[3] and particularly between Jahweh and his Temple. The Temple could only have been destroyed by the Chaldeans because Jahweh had deserted it [4]; the prophet was present in the spirit when the miraculous chariot left it, carrying with it the " glory " of the God of Israel.[5] He also sees, and describes beforehand, the triumphant return of the chariot of the Lord, which ushers in the restoration.[6] Even when for a time Jahweh forsakes his dwelling in Palestine, he carries with him beneath his chariot a fire burning on an ethereal altar.[7]

Another feature of the traditional religion of Israel, in which, it is true, elements of prophetic teaching can also be traced, is Ezekiel's certainty that Jahweh's ruling passion is for his own glory. If, for instance, he leads his people back to Canaan, it is not from love of them, but to further his own interests and enhance the glory of his holy name. His desire to show forth his power sometimes causes Ezekiel's God to forget that strict justice which elsewhere he declares applicable even to individuals, for he announces that he will destroy the innocent with the guilty in the land of Israel.[8] Here we find once more the Jahweh of ancient times, whose purposes are past finding out. Like the Elohim of the earliest Semitic antiquity, the God of Ezekiel avenges even uninten-

---

[1] Ez. i, 26-8 ; ii, 9.
[2] Ez. i, 4, 13, 14, 27, 28 ; cf. LVII, 529-532.   [3] Cf. LVII, 525-5.
[4] Tacitus relates a similar tradition about the ruin of the third temple in A.D. 70 (Hist., v, 13). Cf. Syr. Apoc. of Baruch, 6-7.
[5] Ez. ix–xi.   [6] Ez. xliii, 1-7.   [7] Ez. i, 13 ; x, 6-7.
[8] Ez. xxi, 8-9.

tional offences against his holiness, and the holiness of his Temple or his worship, by the most terrible visitations of calamity. This idea underlies all Ezekiel's plans for the restoration.[1] When he became a prophet, Ezekiel remained essentially a priest, and had preserved intact, without in the least increasing its spirituality, as Isaiah did, the old, almost physical notion of holiness which ancient Israel had inherited from primitive Semitism.[2]

Although prophecy and ancient Jahwism are the two chief elements of Ezekiel's thought, we also meet, not infrequently, with traces of the influence of the art, the myths and the customs of Babylonia, the country in which he lived. When he depicted the figures of the cherubs with the faces of an eagle, a bull, a man and a lion, he doubtless saw in his mind's eye those monstrous hybrids whose forms, sculptured or in colossal bas-relief, guarded the gates of Babylonian cities and palaces. The miraculous stream which he foretold would gush out of the Temple when it was rebuilt, is reminiscent of the myths about the water of life which were current in Mesopotamia.[3] The tradition about the Garden of Eden takes a more mythological form in the writings of Ezekiel than in the Jahwist version.[4] The mountain of God (or the gods), in which Ezekiel locates the Garden, seems identical with that mountain of the extreme north—the northern pole of the sky—where, in Babylonian mythology, Anu dwelt, and which is referred to in another Hebrew text of the period of the exile.[5] That the destroyers whom Jahweh sends to set fire to the Temple are seven in number,[6] may have been connected in Ezekiel's mind with the number of the planets, that is to say, with seven of the great gods of Babylonia, of whom Nebo, the divine scribe, would offer a counterpart to the man with the writer's inkhorn by his side.[7] The spectacle of the pompous and complicated rites of Babylonian worship, many of which were performed with the object of exorcising the malevolent powers which threaten mankind (demons, sorcerers' charms, uncleanness, sin) may

---

[1] *Cf.* pp. 253-7.   [2] *Cf.* **LVII**, 286, 306-7 ; 539-540.
[3] *Mê balâṭi, cf.* **XCV**, 524-5.
[4] Ez. xxviii ; *cf.* xxxi, 8-9, 16, 18 ; xxxvi, 35.
[5] Is. xiv, 13 ; *cf.* Ps. xlviii, 3.   [6] Ez. viii-x.
[7] *Cf.* **XCV**, 400-4 ; **XLV**, 45 ; **XLI**, *passim* (see index, *Nebo, Schreiber*).

have excited the jealousy of the servant of Jahweh, and led him to insist on these sacred acts contained in the religion of his God provided for the " expiation " of sins and uncleanness of every description.

The fusion of these diverse elements in Ezekiel's mind sometimes leads to unexpected results. He, too, by a different path, tends towards monotheism, for Jahweh, he thinks, is able to enforce respect for his honour and his holiness everywhere and at all times [1] ; and to this end he directs the history of every nation. Nevertheless Ezekiel does adhere to, and strongly emphasizes, the idea that God is the God of a certain country and a certain nation. By combining these two divergent statements, he concludes that Jerusalem is the centre of the world and Palestine the navel of the earth.[2] Thus the local and individualistic character attributed to Jahweh does not belittle the God of the prophets, but raises the place with which this God is associated, and the people to whom he is attached, to a higher sphere, one which is above all countries and every nation : Israel is the chosen people of a universal God. The idea that one day Jahweh will be worshipped by all men plays no part in Ezekiel's thought ; the " nations " are fated to be exterminated. This new form of particularism, which is much more radical than that of ancient Israel, whose religion was bounded by the frontiers of the nation, will characterize the new Judaism.

To sum up, Ezekiel appears to us to have been a man of powerful and original personality, possessing much of the purity of moral inspiration and of the boldness of thought which distinguished the earlier prophets, but tending, both as a result of personal idiosyncrasies and the force of circumstances, on the one hand to stereotype by means of theories, regulations and rites, the new life of the spirit which the prophets had wished to create, and on the other to preserve a great number of the institutions, beliefs and customs of ancient Jahwism. In him we witness the transformation of the prophetic principles and of the traditional national religion into something new, namely Judaism. Three of the typical elements of this new form which is about to be adopted by the religion of Israel are directly derived from

[1] Ez. xxviii, 22 ; xxx, 19.
[2] Ez. v, 5; xxxviii, 12.

Ezekiel : the priestly law, apocalyptic eschatology, and individual morality as it appears in the books of " Wisdom ".

II

HABAKKUK

In spite of the oft-repeated assurances of Jeremiah and Ezekiel, it is probable that few Jews were able to share their serene faith in the coming recovery of the nation. They were overwhelmed by the spectacle of the prolonged triumph of the Chaldeans.

At one time it looked as if the oppressors themselves would take the initiative in freeing their victims : this was when Nebuchadnezzar's son released Jeconiah, the deposed King of Judah, from prison (562). But shortly afterwards (560) Amel Marduk was assassinated and the illusion dispelled.[1]

It was during this sombre period, between 555 and 549, to be more precise, that we are inclined to place the short prophecies of Habakkuk.

This is not the place to reopen the puzzling and much-discussed question of the date of the book, the method employed in its composition and its general meaning.[2] We will confine ourselves to indicating and briefly supporting the theory which seems to us to be the most likely one.

It seems necessary, first of all, to set aside a certain number of passages which were apparently added later, such as the whole of chapter three—most critics agree on this point. This is a psalm, somewhat trite, which still retains musical annotations and was given the title of " Habakkuk's prayer ", perhaps because of a general similarity between its subject-matter and that of the prophet's work ; hence its insertion in the book. In the same way, there are several passages in the Psalms which in the Septuagint version are attributed to various prophets, Jeremiah,[3] Haggai, Zechariah.[4]

[1] See pp. 181-3.
[2] **CXXXI** (with an ample bibliography) ; **LXXIX** ; **CCXVI** ; W. W. Cannon (**ZATW**, xliii (1925), 62–90) ; K. Budde (**ZDMG**, lxxxiv (1930), 139–147 ; **OLZ**, xxxiv (1931), 409–411) ; Bevenot (**RB**, xlii (1933), 499–525) ; Staerk (**ZATW**, li (1933), 1–28) ; **XX**, 464–472.
[3] Ps. cxxxvii.   [4] Pss. cxxxviii, cxxxix, cxlvi–cxlviii.

We may also set on one side the first verses of the book (i, 2–4), which seem to us to be an extract from another psalm, which an annotator had first inscribed on the margin of the manuscript thinking they bore some resemblance to the prophet's lament.   For in reality these verses are clearly distinguished from their present context, both by their content—they speak of oppression *by Jews*—and by their rhythm—they are written in asymmetric lines, at least the well-preserved portions of them (v, 2 and 3*a*).

A strophe must also be eliminated (ii, 12–14), for it is composed of quotations from Micah, Jeremiah, and Isaiah, also the phrase ii, 17*b* (a repetition of verse 8) and probably the final couplet against idolatry (ii, 18–20).

What remains seems to us to have been the work of a prophet who was a contemporary of the exile and bore the name or nickname of Habakkuk ; as this strange-sounding word is probably Mesopotamian—in Assyrian it means a culinary herb—there is reason to think that the prophet was one of the Jews who had been deported to Babylonia.

He begins, without acknowledgment—but perhaps the original beginning of the book is lost—by a quotation.   He takes as the text of his reflections a prophecy foretelling the arrival of the Chaldeans, evidently as the instrument of divine vengeance, and therefore uttered before 602 by someone who shared Jeremiah's struggle [1] :

> " For lo, I raise up the Chaldeans, that bitter and hasty nation," etc. [2]

The prophets of the period of the exile—for instance Ezekiel,[3] the second Isaiah,[4] Zechariah,[5] and even Jeremiah already [6]—were inclined to meditate on the preaching of their predecessors : it is an indication of the weakening of prophetic spontaneity which was one of the characteristics of the time.

Habakkuk, then, reproduces an earlier oracle,[7] yet without quoting it word for word ; he cannot resist adapting it to the needs of the moment—just as Jeremiah had done when he repeated the revelations he had already

---

[1] See p. 165.
[2] Hab. i, 6.
[3] Ez. xxxviii, 17 ; xxxix, 8.
[4] Is. xli, 21–2, 26–9, etc.
[5] Zech. i, 4, 5, 12 ; iii, 8.
[6] Jer. xxviii, 8.
[7] Hab. i, 5–10, and perhaps 14–17 in their original form.

uttered about the Scythians when the Babylonians appeared.[1]
To his picture of the power of the Chaldeans, he adds the
details of their greed and pride. Then he lays his grievances
before Jahweh :

> " Then was my spirit heavy and I uttered my complaint ; I laid
> my complaint before my God." [2]

He asks in passionate terms how God could desire the triumph
of so bloodthirsty a nation, whose only god is its weapons
of war :

> " Thou that art of purer eyes than to behold evil, and that canst
> not look on perverseness, wherefore lookest thou upon them that
> deal treacherously . . . and holdest thy peace when the wicked
> swalloweth up the man that is more righteous than he ? " [3]

Like a sentinel on the watch, he lies in wait for the answer
which God will vouchsafe to his agonized questions ; he is
rewarded with the well-known oracle, whose didactic form is
in keeping with the meditative turn of mind of the *nebî'îm* of
the day :

> " Behold as for him who is not upright, his life shall perish in
> him,[4] but the just shall live by his faith." [5]

A few transitional remarks [6] lead up to a series of curses,
which the oppressed nations will one day hurl at the tyrant,
that is to say, the Chaldean.[7] These imprecations must have
been composed, not after the appearance of Cyrus in 549,[8]
but before it ; for the author looks forward to deliverance,
not by the intervention of a foreign ruler, but by a
general insurrection on the part of all the nations conquered
by the Babylonians.[9] A hope of this kind would be easy to
explain if it dated from the beginning of the reign of Nabonidus
(558–539), when the Syrian vassals were preparing to revolt
(554–553), or when the memory of it was still quite fresh.[10]

It is impossible to read without emotion these fervent
and grief-stricken passages. The writer reaches the same
conclusion as Jeremiah and Ezekiel, namely that the oppressed

---

[1] *Cf.* pp. 131–2, 163–4.
[2] Hab. i, 11. We propose to correct as follows: '*áz hâlâh ruḥî
wâ'e'rôk wâ'âsîm hôkîhî lê'lôhay.*
[3] Hab. i, 13.
[4] Read : *hinnêh lô'-yâśâr 'ullephâh naphšô bô.*
[5] Hab. ii, 4.   [6] Hab. ii, 5–6a.
[7] Hab. ii, 6b–11, 15–17a.
[8] As Marti (**LXI**) and Nicolardot (**CCXXXI**) suggest.
[9] Hab. ii, 6b–8, 11.   [10] See p. 181.

will be delivered. But he is without the tranquil assurance of his predecessors, and it is only after a desperate struggle with doubt that he lays hold on faith.

There is another still more characteristic difference. The great prophets since Amos, men of deeply religious mentality, had, in their search for the absolute, judged their people solely by the standard of its relations with its God, the God of perfect righteousness ; and since they found the national life tainted and diseased, they had pronounced it deserving of all the sufferings which the nation had to endure. Habakkuk does not go beyond current, practical and human notions of equity, according to which victory should crown the efforts of the individual or of the nation whose cause is righteous, and whose opponents have not been wronged he takes a more mundane view of retributive justice. While he certainly does not claim that the nation is righteous, in the absolute sense of the word, since he admits that Jahweh had previously, in his wrath, invoked the Chaldeans, his conscience tells him that in the present international conflict, Judah is " more righteous " than the Chaldeans, that Judah is a victim of a tyrannous nation, whose perpetual triumphs are an outrage which a just God cannot tolerate.

Such a view is perhaps hardly on the same plane as the lofty idealism of the great prophets—it is perhaps a reversion to the point of view of the national Jahwism of tradition, with this difference, however : Habakkuk never appeals to that necessary relation which, according to national religions, was supposed to exist between the God and his people,[1] but simply to righteousness.[2]

He has undoubtedly moved a step nearer the ideas which will prevail in Judaism. After the exile, Judæans will have a lively sense of their superiority over heathen nations, in regard to moral values, and will feel aggrieved at having to obey them. In Habakkuk's case, this feeling is still too spontaneous and too amply justified to deserve to be denounced as national pride.

A very remarkable aspect of the prophet's thought is that he seems to expect the reinstatement of the moral order in

[1] *Cf.* Nah. i, 11 ; see pp. 156–8.
[2] Compare the attitude of Isaiah with regard to Asshur, pp. 106–7.

the world, less from any outward punishment at Jahweh's
hands than from a sort of immanent justice : " The man who
does not walk uprightly," he says, " his life withers away."
Injustice, therefore, is a fatal virus, sapping the very life-
blood of the wicked, in spite of his look of triumphant well-
being—but " the just shall live "—that is to say he is henceforth assured of life—" by his faithfulness " (ii, 4).

The same idea is again expressed by the prophet in the
following vengeful words addressed to the tyrant :—

> " Thou hast consulted shame to thy house by cutting off many
> peoples, and hast sinned against thy soul.[1]   For the stone [2] shall
> cry out of the wall, and the beam out of the timber shall answer it." [3]

Here Habakkuk returns to, and amplifies, the ancient
Semitic theme of an organic, natural connection between sin
and misfortune.[4]

III

THE PROPHETS OF THE CLOSE OF THE EXILE. Is. 13–14, Is. 21.
THE SECOND ISAIAH

In 549, rumours of imminent war began to arrive from
the Eastern and Northern frontiers of the empire.   Cyrus,
the Persian leader, whose people were hitherto almost unknown—Ezekiel barely mentions them among the barbarians
of the ends of the earth [5]—had begun his amazingly victorious
career by dethroning Astyages, his suzerain, and proclaiming
himself king of the Medes and Persians. The other powers of
the oriental world, Lydia, Egypt, Sparta, and above all,
Babylonia, whose inhabitants had already crossed swords
with the Medes, their former allies,[6] immediately felt themselves menaced, and made an alliance against him, Among
the Jews, on the other hand, a great hope began to take shape.

An anonymous prophet, the author of the prophesy contained in the thirteenth chapter of Isaiah, foretold that
Babylon would be taken, razed to the ground and reduced
to a desert by the Medes ; the fact that he does not mention

---

[1] This should be corrected as Marti suggests, as follows : *qâṣîthâ ḥêṭ'
lenaphṣekâ.*
[2] i.e. the oppressed nations with which you have built your empire.
[3] Hab. ii, 10–11.   [4] *Cf.* **LXIX**, 430–2.
[5] Ez. xxvii, 10 ; xxxviii, 5.
[6] Great cylinder of Sippar, i, 16–35 (**XLIII**, 268–9) ; *cf.* **XCV**, 111.

the Persians may perhaps indicate that the internal revolution carried out by Cyrus was as yet not well known, and therefore quite recent.[1]

Belonging to the same period, and probably to the same author, is the ironical funeral chant to be found in the following chapter,[2] about a king who will go down into Sheol, where he will lead a miserable existence because he has been deprived of funeral honours. There is no real reason to doubt that this king was the king of Babylon, as we are told in the prose introduction and conclusions which now enclose the poem, or to suppose that originally the threat was directed against a ruler of Assyria, a contemporary of Isaiah, perhaps Sargon or Sennacherib.[3] In any case, there can be no question of its applying to Asshuruballit,[4] the last ruler of the Assyrians, (612–605 ?), a feeble and insignificant prince who would have been quite incapable of stripping Lebanon of its trees or making the earth tremble.[5] The allusions which the satire contains fit in very well with what we know of Nabonidus, on the other hand, for he was the last king of Babylon, a great rebuilder of temples, he visited Lebanon himself, and, because of his repression of the revolt in Syria, might be accused of having " destroyed thy land and slain thy people ".[6]

Another prophet, who probably lived in Palestine, foresaw, it is true, the victory of Cyrus, but seems to have reckoned on nothing more than a change of ruler for the oppressed nations under Babylonian sovereignty.[7] Like the Finnish magicians who send their souls to observe what is happening in distant lands and to act on their behalf, like Ezekiel transported in the spirit to Jerusalem while his body remain at Tel Abib,[8] like Elisha whose " heart goes " with his servant and is present at the latter's interview with Naaman,[9] this prophet felt that there were in him two persons ; a watchman, who could *see* events happening, or about to happen, in Babylonia, and another self who questioned the self who

---

[1] Oesterley dates this prophecy after 546 (**LXVIII**, 259).
[2] Is. xiv, 4b–21.
[3] H. Winckler, *Altorientalische Forschungen*, i, 193–4 ; v, 414 ; **XCV**, 75 ; Cobb (**JBL**, 1896, pp. 18 *ff*.) ; **LXXXIII**, 226 ; **CCXXIV**, 202.
[4] **CCXXXV**, ii, 170 *ff*. See, for the opposite view, **CLXIII**, 194.
[5] Is. xiv, 8, 17.   [6] Is. xiv, 20.
[7] Is. xxi.   [8] Ez. viii–xi.
[9] 2 Kings v, 26. *Cf.* **LV**, 270–2.

watched and was overcome by what was revealed.   This
evidence is of great interest in studying the psychology
of the prophets.   What the watchman saw was the fall of
Babylon beneath the onslaught of Elam (that is to say of
Persia) and of Media.   The mention of the Medes shows that
neither the siege of Babylon by Sargon,[1] nor that of Jerusalem
by Sennacherib [2] is meant, but the capture of the Chaldean
capital by Cyrus : this would have repercussions in the East,
in particular in Edom (Dumah) and the oasis of Teima, the
usual abode of Nabonidus.[3]   But the prophet did not seem to
expect that the collapse of the Chaldean empire would bring
about a final release, for in another oracle the watchman,
when questioned, replies " The morning cometh, and also the
night ".[4]

Other Jews doubtless were of the opinion that even if the
victorious Cyrus would consent to the liberation of their
compatriots, this granting of freedom by a Persian ruler could
not be that miraculous restoration which the prophets of
old had foretold would be accomplished by Jahweh himself.

In the midst of a people divided between hope and
scepticism, there arose, between 546 and 538, a personality
of a very different stamp from the prophets we have just
described, namely the author, also anonymous, whose writings
have been preserved for us in this same book of Isaiah (cc.
40–55), and who is therefore generally known by the con-
ventional title of Second or Deutero-Isaiah.

With infectious enthusiasm he foretold the restoration
of Israel by Cyrus, and acclaimed Jahweh as solely responsible
for this great deed.   It was certainly true that the future
deliverer was a stranger, but was it not convincing proof
of the omnipotence of the Holy One of Israel that he should
have sought the instrument of his will far away in the East ?
Cyrus was " the anointed of the Lord ", as was proved by
the fact that his first victories—evidently the conquest of
Lydia in 546—had been foretold by Jahweh, and by Jahweh
alone.   And now the God of Israel foretold, by the mouth of
his prophet, that Cyrus would overthrow Babylon, and that
the conqueror, convinced of the sovereignty of Jahweh by

---

[1] Kleinert (**TSK**, 1877, pp. 174 *ff.*) ; G. Smith (**TSBA**, 2, 329).
[2] Cobb (**JBL**, 1898, pp. 40–61) ; Barnes (**JTS**, i, 583 *ff.*).
[3] Is. xxi, 11–12 and 13–17.   [4] Is. xxi, 12.

this fulfilment of previous prophecies, would render homage
to the only true God, in common with all the nations of the
world. He would carry out Jahweh's decree, even saying of
Jerusalem " She shall be built ", and of the Temple " Thy
foundation shall be laid ".[1] The exiles would return to Zion,
not by the ordinary route, but straight across the desert ;
as in the olden days, when they left Egypt, Jahweh would
lead them himself ; he would strike the rock and the water
would gush out ; he would even see to it that streams flowed
in the steppes, that there was grazing on the hills, and trees
in barren places.[2] Zion rebuilt would be more glorious than
ever before, the Holy City, into which neither the uncircumcised nor the unclean might enter.[3] All nations would
worship Jahweh. Nature itself would be transformed. Let
Israel then be of good cheer, and having learnt what God's
love could do, repent : " Return unto me, for I have
redeemed thee." [4]

As to the surroundings in which the Second Isaiah lived,
and the conditions under which he worked, conjecture is
our only guide.

It has often been thought that he lived in Babylonia,
because on one occasion he uses the word " here " in speaking
of the country (lii, 5), because he mentions Bel and Nebo
(xlvi, 1), alludes to astrology,[5] and to the wisdom of the
Chaldeans,[6] Babylonian trade,[7] and the rivers of the country,[8]
because he is acquainted with the myth of the first struggle
of God the creator with the dragon,[9] and because, in speaking
of Cyrus as chosen by Jahweh, he uses the same terms which
the king of Persia employs to describe the call he has received
from Marduk. But on the other hand, in speaking elsewhere
of Babylonia, the prophet uses the word " there " [10] ; and
he is wont to represent the exiles as captives who were

---

[1] Is. xliv, 28. The end of this verse should no doubt be transposed
to the end of verse 26 (cf. Budde, **XLVIII**[4], ad loc.).
[2] Is. xli, 18–20 ; xlii, 16 ; xliii, 1–7, 16–20 ; xlviii, 20–2 ; xlix, 9–12.
[3] Is. lii, 1.   [4] Is. xliv, 22 ; cf. lv, 7.
[5] Is. xlvii, 12–13 ; cf. xliv, 25 ; xlvii, 9.
[6] Is. xlvii, 10.   [7] Is. xlvii, 15.
[8] Is. xlvii, 2 ; cf. xliii, 14.
[9] Is. li, 9–10 ; cf. **LIX**, 189–190 ; Gressmann, *Der Ursprung*,
250 ff., 305 ff.
[10] Is. lii, 11 ; cf. xliii, 14 ; xlviii, 20.

ill-treated and imprisoned,[1] which, to say the least of it, was extreme hyperbole.

Abraham Levy has recently put forward the theory that several of the prophets who seem to him to have been responsible between them for chapters xl to lv of the book of Isaiah belonged to the Israelite settlement in Elam,[2] that is, in Persia, because the victories of the young conqueror could not have been celebrated before 539, as they are in these pages outside Cyrus's own country, and because none but subjects of the Persian ruler could at that date have interceded with the king on behalf of their oppressed fellow countrymen in Babylonia.[3] The starting-point of Levy's theory is that the prophecies of the Second Isaiah were from the first proclaimed to all and sundry : a statement which is entirely unsupported. Moreover, Persia seems to be ruled out by the way the prophet has of looking at Cyrus from the standpoint of the inhabitants of the Chaldean empire : Jahweh, he says, has " raised up one from the north . . . and from the rising of the sun ".[4]

Duhm calculated that the Second Isaiah must have lived in Phenicia, chiefly because of the mention of the land of Sinim, which he identified with Sini in northern Phenicia.[5] But the context shows that what was meant was a land in the extreme south, namely Pelusium (Sin), or more probably Syene.[6]

On account of the allusion to this town, and of the fairly frequent mention of Egypt, Kush (Ethiopia) and Sheba, others have supposed that the prophet lived in the land of the Pharaohs.[7] But considering his passionate interest in Babylonian happenings, Cyrus, and the exiles, it is hard to believe that he could have lived beyond the borders of the Chaldean empire ; besides none of his utterances seem to be specially directed against the Jewish Dispersion, whose semi-paganism was so characteristic.

It seems significant that when he wants to portray an idolater, he shows him taking a hatchet and going into the

---

[1] Is. xlii, 7, 22 ; lii, 2.   [2] Is. xi, 11 ; Ezr. ii, 9, 31.
[3] *The Song of Moses* (Deut. xxxii), Paris, 1930, pp. 15, 38.
[4] Is. xli, 25.   [5] Is. xlix, 12; *cf.* Gen. x, 17.
[6] Read *sewênîm* (*cf.* Ez. xxix, 10 ; xxx, 6). *Cf.* Budde (**XLVIII**) ; Hölscher (**XXXVI**, 321–2).
[7] Ewald, Bunsen, Marti, Hölscher, Loisy (*La consolation d'Israel*, 1927, p. 36 ; **LIX**, 187).

forest to fell a tree, from the trunk of which he will carve an image of his god.[1] This would apparently rule out Egypt as well as Chaldæa, for in neither of these countries are there forests, nor any trees whose wood would be fit for carving; in these countries, idols were usually made of clay, stone or metal. The oils to be had from the trees mentioned by the Second Isaiah are those of Western Asia.[2] The landscapes or the climates of Western Asia provide him with most of his metaphors—mountain, forest, sea,[3] snow,[4] land made fertile by rain,[5] and not by the overflow of rivers or by irrigation, drought,[6] which is so common in this part of the world.

It therefore seems extremely likely that the Second Isaiah lived either in Phenicia, as Duhm thinks,[7] because of the frequent mention of Lebanon,[8] the sea and islands—or in Palestine.[9]

Nothing in his work suggests that he tried, like the prophets who went before him, to influence *by word of mouth* a definite circle of *listeners*. He is a man of letters, endowed with magnificent lyrical gifts. There is, however, nothing academic or archaic about his work. He is a true prophet in his eagerness to guide the course of present events by definite and precise prediction. We must think of him, no doubt, as the editor of leaflets or tracts, of which copies were anonymously and secretly circulated among the Jewish settlements scattered about the empire; for, if they had come to the notice of the Babylonian authorities, both the writer and the person in whose possession they were found would have been liable to be charged with high treason.

Written as they were to further a special cause at a particular time, they nevertheless have a scope far wider than that of the conflict between Cyrus and Nabonidus, and the religious and historical philosophy contained in them is not only singularly comprehensive but also in some respects entirely new.

---

[1] Is. xliv, 13–16; *cf.* **CCXXVI**, 30–1.
[2] Is. xli, 19; lv, 13; **CCXXVI**, 31.
[3] Is. xliv, 23; liv, 10; lv, 12.
[4] Is. lv, 10 (it is true that Budde rejects the word).
[5] Is. xliv, 3; lv, 10. [6] Is. xli, 17; lv, 1.
[7] Also Causse, **VIII**, 35. [8] Is. xliv, 16.
[9] Maynard (**CCXXVI**, 25–38); Buttenwieser, **JBL**, 38, pp. 94–112; Mowinckel; Torrey, *The Second Isaiah* (1928).

There is only one God, Jahweh.[1] Monotheism, which the prophets before him had but dimly apprehended, and formulated only indirectly—sometimes with strange and unexpected results, and which seems to mean nothing whatever to some of them—Hosea, for instance—was for the Second Isaiah a definite doctrine, from which he delights to draw every possible corollary. It is the idea of the unity of God, that is to say, a dogmatic statement, which is in his eyes the distinctive feature of the religion of Israel. And though it was no less an innovation to endeavour to establish this doctrinal truth by means of proofs, it was the natural outcome of his views. Therefore he becomes an apologist. He has three main arguments, to which he is never weary of returning.

(1) To Jahweh alone true prophecy belongs, as is shown by the fulfilment of his predictions. The Second Isaiah seems to have in mind especially the predictions of the first successes of Cyrus.

(2) Jahweh is the Creator of heaven and earth.[2] The idea of creation, which had for long been familiar to the Hebrews as a result of their contact with Babylonian mythology,[3] from which the Second Isaiah sometimes borrows some of his illustrations,[4] only became a vital and fruitful element in the religious thought of Israel through his instrumentality.

(3) The gods of other nations are nothing but carved blocks of wood or metal, which can neither see nor hear, nor can they move of their own accord, nor help anyone whatsoever.[5] As an argument against strange gods, or against idolatry, this reasoning, which is already to be found in Deuteronomy,[6] would not be conclusive ; for the worshippers of graven images were generally ready to admit that the god was distinct from the material object in which he had taken up his abode, just as the soul is distinct from the body, or a man from the house in which he lives. But these passages are highly significant because they show that in the sixth century the prophets had reached the stage of denying all

---

[1] Is. xliv, 6, 8 ; xlv, 5, 6, 18, 20 ; xlvi, 9.
[2] Is. xl, 21–2, 26 ; xli, 4 ; xlii, 5 ; xliii, 1, 7, 15 ; xliv, 2, 21, 24 ; xlv, 7, 12, 18 ; xlviii, 13 ; li, 13, 16 ; liv, 5, etc.
[3] **LVII**, 558–9, 564.   [4] Is. li, 9–10.
[5] Is. xli, 22–4, 26, 28–9 ; xlii, 17 ; xliii, 9–10 ; xliv, 7, 9, 10, 12–20 ; xlvi, 1–2 ; xlviii, 14.
[6] Deut. iv, 28 ; *cf.* 1 Kings xix, 18.

reality to any gods but Jahweh, and that they recognized that it was as absurd to worship them as it would be to prostrate themselves before the logs of wood which they used for cooking and at which they warmed themselves.[1] This reasoning had only become possible since the ancient Bedouin aversion to graven images [2] had become transformed, in the minds of the great prophets and their disciples, into the wholesale condemnation of all homage paid to plastic representations of divine beings,[3] and worship without images had become, with the appearance of the first decalogue and the Deuteronomic reforms, one of the *distinctive* features of the religion of Israel.

The triumph of monotheism which is manifested in the writings of the Second Isaiah is partly the result of circumstances. Scattered here and there, from Egypt to Babylonia, the Jewish people became aware of the true proportions of the world which they had long declared to belong to their own God [4]; on the other hand, the more insignificant they felt as a nation, like a drop in the ocean of nations, the greater their need to hold fast to their belief in the real and effective world-dominion of Jahweh, who alone could keep them from despair. But the serene and confident monotheism of the Second Isaiah is primarily the slowly ripened fruit of that revelation of the infinite greatness of God which had first been vouchsafed to Amos and had taken possession of the minds of Isaiah and Jeremiah with ever-increasing clearness.

From the clearly expressed conviction that Jahweh is the only God, the Second Isaiah draws the conclusion that he must be the God of all nations, and the religion of Israel must become the religion of the whole earth.

" Look unto me and be saved, all the ends of earth ; for I am God and there is none else. By myself have I sworn, the word is gone forth from my mouth in righteousness, and shall not return, that unto me every knee shall bow, every tongue shall swear." [5]

The Second Isaiah is a universalist as resolutely as he is a monotheist. Some of the prophets before the exile, Amos,[6]

---

[1] Is. xliv, 16–20.   [2] **LVII**, 304.
[3] Ex. xx, 4–5 ; Deut. iv, 15–18, 23–31 ; v, 8–9.
[4] *Cf.* **LVII**, 528–9.
[5] Is. xlv, 22–4 ; *cf.* xl, 5 ; xli, 20 ; lv, 1–7.
[6] Am. ix, 7.

for instance, and Jeremiah,[1] had shown signs of a similar tendency, but only in stray gleams. And never had even the boldest among them been led by their splendid visions of the future to the conclusion that it was incumbent upon Israel to preach their religion to nations other than their own. So far were they from any thought of converting the heathen that the editors of Deuteronomy, in the seventh century, regretted that all the inhabitants of the land of Canaan had not been massacred. It was hard enough to prevent the encroachments of paganism into the Jewish religion, and the idea of embarking on a conquest of foreign religions occurred to no one ; in practice, religion concerned Jahweh and his people alone. The Second Isaiah has quite a different conception : through all the changes and chances of history he sees Jahweh working out his purpose, which is to establish the reign of " judgment ", that is to say of true religion, on earth. And Jahweh has entrusted this task to Israel, and has destined this nation to be " for a light of the Gentiles ".[2]

This brings us to the third, and most original of the prophet's ruling ideas. Israel has a divine mission to accomplish in the world, namely to be a witness among the Gentiles to the true God ; Israel is " the servant of God ".

The inspiring figure of " the servant of God " is described in four short poems,[3] which many modern critics, in agreement with Duhm,[4] do not consider to be the work of the Second Isaiah in person. Some think he borrowed them from a previous writer, others look upon them as subsequent additions.[5] But the details of style and the various rhythms of these poems are exactly those of the Second Isaiah ; so much so that the above-mentioned critics do not always agree as to the point at which the poem ends and the prophet resumes his writing.

---

[1] Jer. xii, 14–16 ; xvi, 19–21. Most of the analogous passages to be found in the writings of pre-Exilic prophets are, on the contrary, of doubtful authenticity.

[2] Is. xlii, 1–6 ; xlix, 6 ; *cf.* li, 4.

[3] Is. xlii, 1–4 ; xlix, 1–6 ; l, 4–9 ; lii, 13–liii, 12.

[4] **XVI** ; **XV** ; *cf.* Smend, Wellhausen (**LXXXVIII**), Kosters, Bertholet, etc.

[5] e.g. Roy, Laue, Paul Volz (**KAT**, *Jesaia*, ii, 1932, p. 193 ; for Is. liii).

Other recent expositors, not necessarily the same but also followers of Duhm, are of the opinion that in these poems, whether they are by the Second Isaiah or not, the " servant of the Lord " does not mean a nation but a person. Confronted with the task of indicating this person, however, or of describing him, these interpreters are at cross purposes. Duhm thinks he was a doctor of law ; Bertholet a priest, Eleazar by name ; Sellin made him out to be successively Zerubbabel, Jeconiah, and Moses ; lately, he has come round to Mowinckel's view that he was the Second Isaiah himself, a view shared by Gunkel, Hölscher, and Max Haller. Gressmann and Paul Volz [1] look upon him as an eschatological figure—of Babylonian origin, according to the first of these two critics—others see in him the Messiah of the future.[2] Others again see both eschatological and historical elements in the Servant.[3]

These theories are based chiefly on the extraordinarily realistic description of the sufferings of the Servant.[4] But however concrete they may be, these descriptions cannot all be taken literally ; for the hero is represented now as a sick man attacked by a revolting disease,[5] now as a wounded man,[6] now as an outcast,[7] now as a condemned man.[8] Some at least of these statements must therefore be meant as *pictures* of the Servant's sufferings. If one were to accept everything that the poet says literally one would have to admit that he thought his hero had risen from the dead, because he portrays him alive after having described his death and burial.[9] But if this had been his intention, he would certainly have expressed it in so many words, at a time when the Jews did not believe in the resurrection of *individuals*, although the idea of resurrection was familiar enough to them as a symbol for the recovery of a humiliated nation.[10]

Of what personage could it have been said, especially if an

---

[1] *Op. cit.*, pp. 189–193.

[2] Laue, Maecklenburg, Feldmann.

[3] Kittel, Rudolph, In Volz (*op. cit.*, p. 188) will be found a complete account of recent opinions.

[4] Is. l, 6–7, and especially lii, 13–52, 12.

[5] Is. liii, 3–4.   [6] Is. liii, 5–7.

[7] Is. l, 6–7.   [8] Is. liii, 8.

[9] Is. liii, 8, 9, 10.

[10] Ez. xxxvii, 1–14 ; *cf.* Hos. vi, 2.

historical personage was meant, that he never wearies until he has established true religion upon earth, and that the isles shall wait for his law ? [1]

In our opinion,[2] there is no valid reason for rejecting that interpretation of the Servant repeatedly given by the Second Isaiah himself, both in the " poems " themselves [3] and elsewhere.   The " servant of Jahweh " is Israel.

" But thou, Israel, my servant, Jacob whom I have chosen, the seed of Abraham my friend ; thou whom I have taken hold of from the ends of the earth, and called thee from the corners thereof, and said unto thee, Thou art my servant, I have chosen thee and not cast thee away . . ." [4]

It is true that in some passages, the Servant seems distinct from Israel, since he seems called upon to restore the tribes of Jacob [5] and to suffer " for the transgression of my people ".[6] The problem might be solved by supposing, as was commonly done at one time, that the prophet is here contrasting the true Israel, that minority which was conscious of its national mission, with the mass of the people.[7] But it is more probable that in reality the difficulty is non-existent, and that the passages in question have been wrongly interpreted, or else altered, and that the Second Isaiah makes no mention of actions performed by the Servant for the benefit of Israel.[8]

[1] Is. xlii, 4.
[2] This point of view, which was held by the rabbis of the Middle Ages and by most nineteenth-century critics, is still defended by K. Budde (Die sog. Ebed-Jahwe-Lieder . . ., Giessen, 1900 ; **XLVIII**, etc.), O. Eissfeldt (Der Gottesknecht bei Deuterojesaja, Halle, Niemeyer, 1933), G. Hölscher (**XXXV**, 123–4), A. Loisy (La consolation d'Israël, 1927 ; **LIX**, 190–1), etc.
[3] Is. xlix, 3. It does not seem right to reject the word " Israel " on the authority of a single manuscript.
[4] Is. xli, 8–9 ; cf. xlii, 19 ; xliv, 21.
[5] Is. xlix, 5–6.   [6] Is. liii, 8.   [7] Cf. **LIX**, 190–1.
[8] Is. xlix, 5, may be interpreted : " And now saith the Lord, that formed me from the womb to be his servant—i.e. And now the Lord hath decided, promised (cf. 1 Sam. xxx, 16 ; Esth. iv, 7)—to bring Jacob again unto him." In xlix, 6, it is probably necessary, as Duhm himself realized, to reject the words " that thou shouldest be my servant ", and read : " It is too light a thing for me to raise up the tribes of Jacob, etc." Budde (Die sog. Ebed-Jahwe-Lieder, **XLVIII** ; TLZ, 1933, col. 324–6) thinks that an analogous interpretation of the passage is possible even if the Massoretic reading is preserved. In liii, 8, the possessive adjective, 1st person singular, " my," is unjustifiable in the context. The reading should be : " For the transgression of the peoples was he stricken "—mippeša' ammîm (Marti, **KHC**) or " because of our transgressions ", mippeša' enu (Budde, **XLVIII**).

In this idea of a mission entrusted to Israel, the prophet finds the final explanation of the present sufferings of the nation, and the guarantee of its future recovery.

Like his predecessors, the Second Isaiah sometimes interprets Israel's misfortunes as the just chastisement of its sins.[1] But when he remembers the unique dignity of this nation, to which he has entrusted the salvation of the Gentiles, the overwhelming adversities of the " Servant of the Lord " seem an enigma to him : Zion seems to have received double the punishment deserved,[2] or even not to have deserved it at all : " The Assyrian oppressed them without cause." [3] And the upshot of his reflections is that these sufferings were inseparable from Israel's prophetic mission. The true servant of Jahweh, like Jeremiah—whose tragic fate was no doubt present to the author's mind—joyfully accepts every indignity in order that truth may triumph, since he knows that in the end victory is assured.[4] In reality, it is not for his own sins that Israel suffers in exile, but for the sins of many,[5] and for the salvation of the Gentiles.

This is the same pathetic idea of the martyr nation, suffering for the good of the world, which strengthened the patriotic faith of dismembered Poland throughout all the Romantic era. In order to explain how the Second Isaiah came by it, one would no doubt have to take into account those grim and ancient beliefs which were responsible for the practice of mass or vicarious punishment. The prophet was familiar with the idea that one nation may be smitten for the sins of another ; he hoped that one day Egypt, Kush, and Sheba would be given as a ransom for Israel.[6]

But he also thought, it seems, and in this respect his point of view was that of a realist, that Israel must needs be scattered abroad among the Gentiles if the Gentiles were to learn to know the nation, its God, its prophets and their prophesying ; they must also be eye-witnesses of its shame, so that the subsequent spectacle of its miraculous recovery might be brought home to them, and might convince them of the omnipotence of Jahweh.

---

[1] Is. xlii, 24-5 ; xliii, 22-8 ; xlviii, 10.
[2] Is. xl, 2. [3] Is. lii, 4.
[4] Is. xlix, 4 ; l, 4-9. [5] Is. liii, 11.
[6] Is. xliii, 3-4.

Of this recovery the Second Isaiah is absolutely certain. Like Ezekiel, he sometimes bases this certainty on Jahweh's regard for the honour of his name,[1] or, like Jeremiah, on the lovingkindness of the Lord, who freely offers salvation to all who are willing to accept it.[2] But the essential reason for his certainty, the underlying theme which constitutes his originality, is the mission entrusted to Israel : the nation will be restored because it is the servant of Jahweh, because its vocation is to convert all nations. The prophet no doubt looks to believers to help in this conversion. Before it can take place, they must make known the prophecies which Jahweh had inspired [3] ; they must set the standard by means of a *torah*,[4] and we can gather the gist of their instruction from the arguments of the Second Isaiah in favour of monotheism, for their polemic intention is evident. And the Jews of the Exile must, in fact, have been actively engaged in propaganda, and have made many converts, if we may judge, for instance, from the care taken by the prophets and legislators of the time to ensure that the Gentiles " who joined themselves to the Lord " should enjoy absolute religious equality with those who were Jews by birth.

But the chief instrument in winning over the heathen will be the spectacle of the glorious restoration which will be granted to his people. Then the Gentiles, and even Cyrus himself, will worship the God of Israel ; then the rulers of the earth will discover to their amazement, that this people, ill-treated, downtrodden, and despised, had suffered for their sakes.[5]

This outline of the thought of the great anonymous writer of the Exile will have given an idea of the organic unity which is characteristic of him, as far as the broad lines of his teaching are concerned. His point of view may be summed up in these words : Jahweh is the only God ; Israel, his only servant, is entrusted with the task of making him known to all the Gentiles ; therefore let the nation of witnesses willingly accept all suffering, for it is assured of triumph in the end.

This system attaches an importance to the intellectual element in religion which is a sign of the times : Israel shall

---

[1] Is. xliii, 25 ; xlviii, 9–11.   [2] Is. lv, 1–3, 6–7.
[3] Is. xl, 5 ; xliii, 8–13 ; lii, 15.
[4] Is. xlii, 1–4.   [5] Is. lii, 13–liii, 12.

be restored, not as a result of any change in its moral or spiritual nature, as Amos, Hosea, and Isaiah had thought—for the servant of Jahweh is very often blind and deaf [1]—but because Israel alone possesses the true knowledge of God.

On the other hand, the mental outlook of the Second Isaiah is so profoundly spiritual that he falls into line with the most idealistic of its predecessors. Though he adopts the ancient idea of vicarious expiation, he lifts it to a moral plane by his insistence that the victim must deliberately and heroically accept suffering in order that his oppressors may be saved. He has shown us one of the loftiest peaks of religious thought in Israel. It is not difficult to understand why Jesus made this conception his own, and why, applying it to himself rather than to the nation as a whole, he sought therein an explanation of his sufferings and death.

VI

THE DEVELOPMENT OF PROPHECY DURING THE EXILE

It is clear that the attitude of the representatives of the great prophetic movement underwent a profound transformation in the course of the Exile. Seeds previously sown reached their full maturity, individualism with Ezekiel, monotheism and universalism with the Second Isaiah.

On the other hand, few traces were left of the violent clashes between the prophets of the pre-exilic period and the traditional religion of their people. No one now feels it necessary to combat national optimism as Amos, Micah, and Jeremiah had done so ardently : Ezekiel after 586, Habakkuk, and the Second Isaiah prophesy not evil but good. The idea that the nation must, or even can, perish has gone outside their range of thought. There is no longer any opposition to national particularism, for they believe firmly in Israel as a privileged nation, though they attach a different meaning to the term from that which the old Jahwists had understood. No longer is ritual the object of attack : Ezekiel is one of the leaders of the clerical and ritualist

---

[1] Is. xlii, 81–20 ; xliii, 8.

movement. The Second Isaiah himself, however spiritually minded he may be, implicitly takes for granted that the old ideas and the old rites of traditional worship will be kept up ; the priests, when they have been purified, will bring back the sacred vessels [1] ; the Temple will be rebuilt [2] ; Jerusalem will be a Holy City, into which neither the unclean nor the uncircumcised shall enter.[3]

This introduction of a milder note into prophetic preaching during the Exile was no doubt one of the reasons of the success which undeniably attended it, especially in Babylonia, as far as the masses were concerned. It is true that Ezekiel complains that his teaching is not put in practice—which is natural enough in a preacher—but he notes that the people crowd to hear him and sit down on the ground to listen to him.[4] The writings of the period—the interpolations made during the Exile in the books of national history by the Deuteronomic editors, a poem like the canticle which is called the Song of Moses,[5] and the works of the priestly school, then in its infancy—show that some of the prophetic ideas were widely admitted, especially the idea of the unity of God and the conviction that the ills of the present were a punishment for unfaithfulness, above all for compromise with regard to heathenism, and that such sins must at all costs be avoided in future.

[1] Is. lii, 11.   [2] Is. xlviii, 2.
[3] Is. lii, 1. *Cf.* **XXXVI**, 325–6.
[4] Ez. xxxiii, 30–3.   [5] Deut. xxxii.

CHAPTER III

THE RITUALIST MOVEMENT AT THE TIME OF THE EXILE

SOON after the deportation had taken place, a whole group of jurists, that is to say of priests, set to work to define the laws which were to guide the nation when it returned to its native land. There was apparently no contradiction—on the contrary, there was an underlying harmony—between this legislative anticipation of the return and the enthusiastic forecasts of the prophets : the same man, Ezekiel, was both a prophet and the editor, or at least the originator, of a *torah*. And like the editors of the Deuteronomic code, these legislators were anxious to make sure that certain injunctions essential to the teaching of the great prophets should be carried out, for instance, that heathen influences should be carefully eliminated.

In reality, however, we are here concerned with two different outlooks, two opposite conceptions of religion. The existence of a written law which foresaw all possible contingencies made it superfluous to consult a man of God ; its rigidity ruled out all freedom of inspiration ; the magic element in ritual, on which the priestly writers laid great emphasis, was incompatible with the spirituality of the great prophets. A time was coming—not yet, it is true, it would only begin after the return from exile—when the Law would supplant and eliminate prophecy.

I

The Torah of Ezekiel

The book of Ezekiel relates that in 573 the prophet saw himself transported to the land of Israel, to the summit of a very high mountain. There he saw a building which he

was allowed to examine minutely—the Temple of the future.
He saw Jahweh make a solemn entry into it. A mysterious guide,
and then Jahweh himself, gave him precise particulars about
the plan and the measurements of the building, the manner
in which worship was to be celebrated—the altar, the functions of the priests and other ministrants, the part to be played
by the king in ritual, festivals and sacrifices—as well as
about the place where the Temple was to be built, and the
division of the territory among the different elements of the
population (ch. xl to xlviii).

It has lately been debated whether the account of this
revelation should, in fact, be attributed, at least in its entirety,
to Ezekiel.[1] And it is possible that additions were made to
the original text : there is a passage before the middle of the
narrative which looks like a conclusion [2]; there are discrepancies here and there, as in the name given to the future
ruler, who is sometimes called a prince (nâsî), sometimes a
king.[3] On one occasion, the subordinate priests are simply
called " Levites ".[4]

On the other hand, however, this plan of reorganization
must have been drawn up before the priestly law, as it appears
in the Pentateuch, had become, with Nehemiah and Ezra,
the charter of Judaism ; for it differs from it in numerous
respects, and generally speaking its demands are less exacting
than those of the Priestly Code.

To be precise : the legislative project of the book of
Ezekiel was certainly formulated before the return of the exiles
to Palestine : once the unpretentious event of the re-establish-
ment of the Jews in the ruins of Jerusalem had actually
taken place, once they had made their unobtrusive entry
into the small surrounding " province ", it would be impossible
to explain how an editor could have promulgated decrees as
fantastic as that of the alteration of the site of the capital
or the allocation of vast tracts of land to the priests, the
Levites, and the prince, how he could have geometrically
divided the whole of cis-Jordanian Palestine among all the
tribes of Israel, including the tribes of the former kingdom

---

[1] **CCV** ; **CCVI** ; **XXXVI**, 421–3 ; **CCVIII** ; **LIX**, 32–3, 222–3.
[2] Ez. xliii, 1–12.
[3] See, however, **XXXVI**, 423, n. 1.
[4] Ez. xlv, 4–5.

of the north, or how he could have foretold the purification of the Dead Sea and the valley of the Jordan by means of a mighty river whose origin was a miraculous spring welling up in the precincts of the Temple.[1]

It would not be surprising if this " Torah of the Temple " was mainly the work of Ezekiel himself, for the prophet-priest was fond of giving his revelations in the form of priestly instruction,[2] and attached great importance to the observance of ritual, which in his eyes was an essential element of " righteousness ".[3] He himself describes the loathing he would feel if he had to eat unclean food, even at God's command.[4] The personal, as it were almost physical, presence of Jahweh within the walls of the Temple, was for him the *sine qua non* of the nation's prosperity, even of the nation's existence : he saw the " glory of the Lord " depart from the Temple before the destruction of the building in 586 [5]; it would be only natural to expect that, in the spirit, he should behold its return to the holy place when restored, before the restoration had actually taken place.[6]

But in any case, whether it was drawn up chiefly by Ezekiel's own hand, or important additions to the prophet's original version were made by some of his followers, this account of the future institutions of the nation when re-established in Palestine is of the greatest interest : it furnishes us with undeniable proof that a comprehensive work of codification was being carried on in sacerdotal circles during the Exile, and also gives us the date, since it must in any case belong to the years between 573 and 538 ; it shows us the spirit which animated these legislators, their tendencies, their desires, and sometimes the differences between them. We have here an outline of the great legislative structure which was finally to crown their labours, the Priestly Code.

The torah of the book of Ezekiel forms a system of which the leading principles are not explicitly formulated, though they are clearly discernible.

1. *The Idea of Holiness.*—If Israel is to live, Jahweh must be present in the Temple ; now Jahweh is holy. All that

---

[1] Ez. xlv, 1–8 ; xlvii–xlviii.
[2] Ez. iii, 16–21 ; xiv, 3–11, 13–20 ; xviii, 2–18, 20–8 ; xxxiii, 1–20.
[3] Ez. xviii, 5–6, 11–15.   [4] Ez. iv, 14.
[5] Ez. viii–xi.   [6] Ez. xliv, 1–4.

belongs to Jahweh, whatever its nature and purpose may be—his house, his burnt-offerings, the articles used in his service, his priests, the vestments of those who officiate—is also holy, that is, it shares his divinity to some extent, the conception of divinity being that most archaic idea of a kind of awe-inspiring fluid which could be communicated by contact. If one of these sacred beings or objects is touched by a profane being or object, a person or a thing which is not in itself sacred or has not been raised to a level of holiness by the appropriate ceremonies, then profanation takes place, and the profane being or object runs the risk of being consumed by God's anger, which, by contagion, is extended to the whole nation.

The legislator is convinced that one of the principal causes of the divine wrath by which the exiles feel themselves overwhelmed is that hitherto the dividing line between the sacred and the profane, the clean and the unclean, has not been scrupulously observed. And the chief object of his torah is to prohibit in future those ancient practices which seem to him to confuse the sacred and the profane while instituting more efficacious means of protecting holy things, or of restoring to them the holiness they have forfeited.

According to him, the Temple had become unclean before the Exile because only a wall had separated it from the royal palace where so many abominations had been committed, and also because, since the days of Manasseh, there being no longer any room in the ancient necropolis of the kings, in the city of David, the rulers had been buried in the garden of Uzzah, in the immediate vicinity of the house of God.[1] Besides, the mere proximity of the city of Jerusalem meant that the Temple was in constant danger of profanation.

To obviate this danger, Jahweh ordains by the mouth of his prophet that the town of Jerusalem shall be rebuilt about two and a half kilometres to the south of its former site. There is to be neither a palace nor a burial-ground near to the Temple ; it is to stand by itself on the top of the mountain, in the centre of a rectangle 25,000 cubits by 10,000 (8 m. by 3), which is reserved for the priests. On the north side, this holy land is to be protected in its turn by a plot of equal area belonging to the Levites.

[1] Ez. xliii, 7-9.

The Temple was further exposed to the danger of uncleanness by the precincts being open to all ; laymen were allowed
to sacrifice on the altar, and to eat their sacred meals in the
Temple ; the revelations of the prophets were published
abroad in the Temple ; priests and even nobles of the court
had rooms in it ; a kind of platform was reserved for the use
of the king quite near the holy place, and he could sacrifice,
preside over ceremonies,[1] or bless the people as the priests
did.[2]

In the eyes of the legislator, these practices are abuses
which must not be repeated : the new abode of Jahweh
is to be surrounded by two concentric courtyards, of which
the inner one is to be exclusively reserved for the priests.
The only sacerdotal privileges which the prince will retain
will be his obligation to pay the expenses of public sacrifices
and the right to approach the threshold of the inner enclosure,
a right which will be confined to the Sabbath, the feasts of
the new moon, and the days on which he offers up votive or
voluntary sacrifices.   The entire sacrificial rite, from the
immolation of the victim to the burning of the remains,
is to take place out of sight and participation of the person
offering it, except of course in the case of the " sacrifice
of the people ", of which the final ceremony—the cooking
of the flesh and the meal in which the laymen may take
part—will take place in the outer courtyard ; even then the
flesh is to be cooked by the servants of the Temple. Deuteronomy had provided that the priest must perform the sacrifice.
The torah of Ezekiel goes a step further, by theoretically
vindicating the elimination of the layman.   Subsequent
legislation did not dare to go so far : the Priestly Code
reserved to the offerer the right to stand near the altar and
to place a hand on the head of the victim.

A still more scandalous abuse, in the legislator's eyes, was
the presence in the Temple of foreign slaves, who before the
Exile had been employed to carry out the more menial
tasks connected with the Temple, and especially to slaughter
the victims and guard the doors.   The legislator considers
that only the sons of Levi have the right to enter the inner
enclosure, and he makes a distinction among them. Those

---

[1] 2 Sam. vi, 21.
[2] 1 Kings viii, 55 ; *cf.* **CXLIX**, 269–270.

Levites that " went far from " Jahweh, " when Israel went astray, which went astray from him after their idols," that is, the Levites of the high places abolished by Josiah, as a punishment for unfaithfulness, are to replace the strangers who will henceforth be excluded from holding office in the Temple : these ex-priests from the provinces will have to serve the people, and will be degraded from the service of Jahweh, in other words they will not be allowed to officiate as priests any longer. The office is confined to the sons of Zadok, that is to say, the family which had officiated in the Temple of Jerusalem since the days of Solomon.[1] This subordinate position was already occupied in practice by the former priests of the high places, and that, as we have seen, contrary to the rules laid down by Deuteronomy.[2] The departure from the letter of the law, resulting no doubt from the intervention of the family of Zadok, as the interested party, finds its theoretical justification in the torah of Ezekiel. We here perceive the historical origin of the division of the Jewish priesthood into two classes, that of the " priestly Levites "— soon to be known more briefly as " priests ", and that of the Levites deprived of their sacerdotal functions, who will be called simply " Levites ". The Priestly Code widens the gap still further by attributing this distinction to the time of Moses.

Minute regulations are laid down in Ezekiel's legislative scheme to assure the complete purification of the priests and to prevent any contact between holy things, which they alone have the right to touch, and the lay population ; there are to be special rooms in the inner court in which the priests may leave their sacred vestments after officiating, so that, when they go into the outer court, " they sanctify not the people with their garments." [3] We are confronted here with the very material idea of holiness which was held by Semites in ancient times, a conception closely resembling that of the *mana* to be found among many primitive peoples : the profane person who wears or even touches the garment of a chief dies as surely as if he had taken a virulent poison.[4]

---

[1] Ez. xliv, 9–16.
[2] Deut. xviii, 6–8 ; 2 Kings xxiii, 8, 9. *Cf.* pp. 143–4.
[3] Ez. xliv, 19 ; *cf.* xlvi, 20.
[4] *Cf.* **XXI**, i, 248–251.

Such an attitude naturally attaches supreme importance to religious observances, an importance which the most spiritually minded prophets, Amos or Jeremiah, for instance, had expressly denied. And according to Ezekiel's definition, the just man must not only be just and charitable, he must also refrain from eating on the mountains, from consuming flesh containing blood, from intercourse with a woman during the period of her uncleanness, and he must keep the Sabbath etc.[1] To be lacking in equity or in kindness is even, according to him, one way of profaning the land and making it unclean [2] : which shows that he considers injustice to belong to the general category of profanation, as the species belongs to the genus.

There was, then, at the time of the Exile, a revival among Jewish priests of the old materialist, half-magical conception of holiness, which had been current in the earliest Semitic times.[3] It had evidently never quite died out, especially in priestly circles, but it now occupies a central place, and the results which it entails are courageously faced.

2. *The importance of ritual.*—A further characteristic of the legislation of the book of Ezekiel is the emphasis laid on the most minute ceremonial details : not only are there regulations as to the kind, the age, and the sex of the victims to be offered up on the different days of the year, but also about the material of which the priestly clothing is made and the items of which it is to be composed, the days and the hours for the opening of the various gates of the Temple, and the direction to be taken by those walking in the outer court.[4] These regulations are of such importance that they form the subject of a revelation from on high, and are henceforth divine laws.

It is true that there must always have been traditions as to the way in which sacrifice was to be offered and feasts celebrated in Israel. And the deliberate violation of these customs must always have been looked on as a serious crime.[5] But in ancient times, each temple had its own ritual: sacrifices were not offered in Ophrah in the same way as in Jerusalem,[6]

---

[1] Ez. xviii, 6, 11, 15 ; xx, 13, 16, 20, 21 ; xxii, 8, 26 ; xxiii, 38 ; xxxiii, 25.
[2] e.g. Ez. xxxvi, 17.
[3] *Cf.* **LVII**, 286, 306–7, 539–540.   [4] Ez. xlv, 9.
[5] 1 Sam. ii, 12–17, 22–5.   [6] Judg. vi, 19–21.

s

nor in Jerusalem as in Shiloh.[1] Divergences of this kind must almost of necessity have been accompanied by the thought that, after all, ritual was of secondary importance in Jahweh's eyes, and that the chief thing was that the sacrifice was made to him. It was admitted that the God of Israel had accepted sacrifices from Gentiles like Balaam and Naaman, as well as from Gideon or Elijah.

The change of ideas was brought about on the one hand by the concentration of worship enforced by Josiah (622)—henceforth there was only one lawful ceremonial, that of the Temple of Jerusalem—and on the other by the Exile, which obliged the deported priests to perpetuate *in writing* the details of the ceremonial, lest when it was no longer practised it should be forgotten, and also with a view to guarding against heterodox innovations. When defined in written laws which were presented as dictated by God himself, these regulations acquired the prestige of sanctity, and also took on a rigidity which they had not known in the days when they were simply venerable local traditions whose practice was handed down from one generation to another.

3. *The idea of atonement.*—One of the most striking differences between the torah of Ezekiel and both ancient Jahwism and Deuteronomy is the importance attached in the ritual to the idea of expiation.

In ancient Israel, since the beginnings of history, sacrifice was most commonly regarded as a gift to God. It was taken for granted that when Jahweh was angry he might be appeased by presents, and in this way it was possible for sacrifice to take on expiatory significance.[2]

But in the first place this method was considered uncertain and even dangerous, for, by offering up sacrifice, the sinner reminded Jahweh both of his existence and of his sin : in times of calamity, the safest thing was to avoid even uttering the name of Jahweh.[3]

Secondly, it is true that rites whose particular object was expiation must have been in use in ancient Israel. Like all primitive peoples, the Hebrew tribes most probably practised apotropaic rites entailing the expulsion or the sacrifice of an animal, to which the evil which it was desired to banish

---

[1] 1 Sam. ii, 13–16.
[2] 1 Sam. iii, 14 ; xxvi, 19.   [3] Am. vi, 10.

was supposed to have been transferred : some of these rites, preserved in the legislation of Leviticus, have an undeniably archaic air about them.[1] On the other hand, we know that about the year 800, in the Temple of Jerusalem, fines in silver called *âšâm* and *ḥaṭṭâ'th* [2] were paid by the worshippers to the priests, no doubt for some breach of custom. It is also probable that, when a sacrifice was offered up in the hope of appeasing God, certain special regulations were observed, and in particular that the person offering the sacrifice was forbidden to eat the flesh, as is the case with the *dam* of Moslem pilgrims.[3] But the apotropaic sacrifices were doubtless not looked upon as sacrifices intended for Jahweh [4] ; both Deuteronomy and the Priestly Code make a clear distinction between the two.[5] As to sacrifices in the strict sense of the term, those whose purpose was expiation must have been considered merely as a variant of the usual sacrifices. In any case, the terminology current in ancient Israel only distinguished two kinds of ritual immolation, the whole burnt-offering and the peace offering, both of which—and even a simple oblation of cereals or the gift of any other object—might in certain cases appease Jahweh.[6]

Thirdly, before the Exile atonement was far from being the chief motive for the offering of sacrifices. The dominant note of worship was mingled gratitude and joy. Even for the editors of Deuteronomy, to offer a sacrifice was " to rejoice before the Lord ", and they make no mention of sacrifice as expiation.

In the torah of the book of Ezekiel, expiation becomes on the contrary the chief object of worship. In addition to the burnt-offering and the peace offering, two new types of sacrifice make their appearance, the sacrifice of atonement (*'âšâm*) and the sacrifice for sin (*ḥaṭṭâ'th*). They have a special rite : only the blood is poured over the altar—in much the same way as for the peace offering—but the flesh belongs to

---

[1] Lev. xiv, 4–7, 49–53 ; xvi, 20–2.   [2] 2 Kings xii, 17.
[3] *Cf.* **LVII**, 322 ; **XXII**, 262, 278, 290, n. 2.   [4] **LIX**, 236.
[5] The slaughter of a heifer, in the case of murder by someone unknown, does not take place at the altar at Jerusalem (Deut. xxi, 1–9). The he-goat laden with sins is sent to Azazel, and another goat is sacrificed to Jahweh (Lev. xvi).
[6] Gen. viii, 20–5 ; 1 Sam. iii, 14 ; vi, 8.

the priest.[1] These two new kinds of sacrifice entirely eclipsed the peace offering : they are on at least the same footing as the burnt-offering, which was the most solemn of all the sacrifices of ancient Israel. The legislation of the book of Ezekiel mentions two feasts unknown to previous codes : twice a year these are to be celebrated for the atonement of the Temple, on the first day of the first month and the first day of the seventh month. In general, all feasts and all public sacrifices are " for the atonement of the house of Israel ".[2]

From our knowledge of ancient Israel it is clear that neither the idea of ritual atonement, nor the means by which it is here expressed, were pure innovations on the part of the Jewish legislators of the period of the Exile. The torah of Ezekiel mentions the *âšâ'm* and the *ḥaṭṭâ'th* as if they were well known rites. There is an evident connection between these immolations and the fines in silver recorded about the year 800, whether these payments to the priests had been used to provide sacrifices for Jahweh, or as sacrificial dues, or as penalties imposed in addition to sacrifices.[3] The priests of the Exile confined themselves therefore to developing ideas which had already existed in the practices and beliefs of previous ages. But the immense impetus given to the concept of atonement profoundly modified the whole character of traditional ritual.

The explanation of the emphasis laid on deliverance from sin and from uncleanness is to be sought partly in the misfortunes of the times : we have already seen how, since the seventh century, it had become customary to endeavour to win back divine good-will by means of rites over and above the usual, as, for instance, the sacrifice of children.[4] Contact with Babylonian religion may have had a similar effect : in it much more importance was attached to exorcisms, and to practices whose object was to drive away devils and all the powers of evil, than to the hope of obtaining positive

---

[1] At least according to Ez. xliv, 29 ; xlvi, 20. According to the Priestly Code, in certain particularly solemn sacrifices for sin the flesh is consumed, as in the burnt-offering, but not on the altar.

[2] Ez. xlv, 17 ; *cf.* 15.

[3] As was the case among the Carthaginians, according to the Marseilles tariff (CIS, i, 165, ll. 3, 5, 7, 9, 11, 12).

[4] See pp. 123–5.

favours from the gods ; Babylonian myths imply a somewhat pessimistic view of the lot of humanity.

And yet the prominent part given to atonement in worship by the Jewish legislators was no doubt chiefly the logical result of their general outlook. The main object of the torah of Ezekiel is to prevent in future all unnecessary contact between the sacred and the profane, and thus to render possible the beneficent presence of Jahweh in the midst of his people. But it was only to be expected that very often, because they were human, the Israelites of the period of the restoration would, involuntarily, perhaps even unconsciously, be guilty of profanation and of uncleanness, which was sometimes indeed an inevitable factor in life, as, for instance, the uncleanness resulting from contact with a dead body. Was the favour of Jahweh to be forfeited, then, as soon as won ? No : by the grace of Jahweh there was a way of continually making good all involuntary sins against the holiness of the Temple of Israel, namely by ritual. Doubtless these rites might with equal logic have been interpreted as being positive in their effect, they might have been represented as miraculous, supernatural means enabling the nation to avail itself of the benefits to be derived from the presence of God. It is significant that neither the torah of Ezekiel, nor the priestly legislation which followed, emphasized this aspect of worship : a somewhat gloomy austerity—the result of the misfortunes of the time and of the stern preaching of the prophets—was to be one of the distinctive signs of the Jewish religion : the fear of sinning was therefore felt to be a much more pressing reality than mystical aspiration after the presence of God.

There is still another point in which the character of the ritual was modified: instead of being, as hitherto, the naïve and spontaneous expression of the varied emotions and ideas of individuals or small groups, ritual, which had already been to some extent nationalized by Deuteronomy, became a public service, the most indispensable of all public services, since, by assuring the daily purification of the nation, it prevented it from being consumed by the wrath of God. Hence the whole nation lay under a debt which it must discharge in the person of its ruler, assisted by contributions from each individual member.

Such were the main lines of the plan of restoration drawn up in the book of Ezekiel. Utopian, even fantastic as it is in certain respects, it reveals a clear grasp of the conditions which were to prevail at the time of the restoration, by anticipating, not the revival of a State in the usual sense of the word, but the formation of a religious community. And indeed, although the nation is still to be under the leadership of a king—who however usually bears the more modest title of prince—the aim of the new order of things is to be almost exclusively religious, even religious in the restricted sense of being confined to religious observances : it must never lose touch with God.   It was not political acumen which led the priestly legislators thus to ignore the secular side of ordinary national life, nor because they realized that it would be a long time before the Jews were able to shake off the yoke of pagan rule.   It was the result of their general religious outlook.   The secular leader who still, for tradition's sake, retains his place at the head of the nation, will, in fact, have no function to fulfil in the new economy.   He will not have to wage war, for Jahweh himself will defend his people if they are faithful to him.[1]   He will not have to administer justice, for that will be the duty of the priests,[2] nor levy taxes, for his lands will yield enough to support him.[3]   The people who will be entrusted with the really useful work in the new order will be the priests, who alone will be qualified to make atonement for the profanation and uncleanness which otherwise would inevitably compel Jahweh to forsake his people once more.

II

THE HOLINESS CODE

The religious views underlying the torah of Ezekiel, which seemed to reconcile the serious outlook of the prophets with fidelity to ancient customs and long cherished beliefs, had so much in common with the state of mind of a large number of pious Jews, especially among the priesthood, that a school was inevitably founded, the members of which composed various collections of *tôrôth*, all animated by the

---

[1] Ez. xxxviii–xxxix.   [2] Ez. xliv, 24.
[3] Ez. xlv, 7–8 ; xlvi, 16–18.

same spirit. Several fragments of these have been preserved for us in the body of the Priestly Code. The chief of them is the collection to which Klostermann gave the name Holiness Code (P¹) ; it embraces, besides a few scattered passages,[1] chapters xvii to xxvi of Leviticus, with the exception of the alterations made by subsequent priestly editors.[2]

Resemblances to the legislation of the book of Ezekiel are striking. As is shown by the name by which it is known, the predominant idea is one of holiness. It sums up all the commands of Jahweh in one : " Ye shall be holy, for I am holy," [3] that is to say, have no undue intercourse with profane or unclean things, for I will not be approached by anything that is profane or unclean. And like the torah of Ezekiel, it includes under the heading " profane or unclean " ritual shortcomings, participation in heathen practices, and moral transgressions : chapters xviii to xx of Leviticus provide typical examples of this lack of discrimination between the different items, as well as of the subordination of morality to the idea of ritual holiness.

There is the same importance attached to ritual in worship : the code gives a list of the customs to be observed on the different days of the different feasts,[4] and the rules as to uncleanness which the priests and their head are expected to observe.[5]

The idea of atonement occupies the same prominent place : atonement is the chief object of all blood sacrifices.[6]

But if the Holiness Code is closely related in spirit, and even frequently in style, to Ezekiel's legislation, it differs from it : (a) by not having the form of a prophetic revelation but of a priestly canon (torah), possibly not originally attributed to Moses himself ; (b) by devoting much more space to civil and moral laws, it almost looks as if this code were intended, not so much as a supplement to Deuteronomy, like the projected charter of the book of Ezekiel, as a new edition, abridged in some respects, augmented in others, in response to the demands of the time ; (c) the editors of the Holiness Code seem to be of a more conservative turn of mind than those of the legislation in Ezekiel, carefully noting

---

[1] Ex. xxxi, 13–14a ; Lev. xi, 43–5 ; Numb. xv, 37–41.
[2] For details see V.   [3] Lev. xix, 2.
[4] Lev. xxiii.   [5] Lev. xxi.   [6] Lev. xvii, 11.

the customs characteristic of the former Temple, yet not daring to alter them as fundamentally as their new system would logically require : they do not mention the distinction between priest and Levite ; they retain the wine-offerings, which in the book of Ezekiel had been implicitly abolished by invoking the old prejudice against the encroachment of this gift of Baal upon the domain of pure Jahwism.[1] They allow the layman to slaughter his own burnt-offering.[2] In the classification of sacrifices the old nomenclature is retained [3] ; the sacrifices of which the specific object is atonement, 'âšâm and ḥaṭṭâ'th figure only in subsequent additions.[4] As regards the ritual for feast-days, the Holiness Code perpetuates archaic details which show clear signs of the agrarian nature of these ceremonies : at the feast of Unleavened Bread, for instance, a sheaf of corn is to be offered to Jahweh ; and at the Feast of Weeks, two leavened loaves.[5]

On the other hand, the Holiness Code is in some respect in advance of the torah of the book of Ezekiel. At the head of the priesthood is placed a priest who is greater than his brethren, who has been anointed with oil, and who is marked out from the rest by stricter rules of purification.[6] This difference alone would suffice to prove that between Ezekiel's day and the period at which the Holiness Code was drawn up—or at least this particular part of the code—time had not stood still ; the priestly movement had progressed.

The legislators of the Holiness Code show themselves equally radical—utopian even—when they revoke a concession which custom imposed upon the Deuteronomic jurists, and forbid, under pain of death, all profane slaughter of animals for sacrifice : the animals are to be slaughtered in front of the altar in the central sanctuary ; this order could not possibly have been carried out, even in the limited territory occupied by the Jewish community in the early days of the restoration. In subsequent priestly legislation it is therefore tacitly allowed to lapse.[7]

[1] **LVII**, 326, 353–5, 476–7.   [2] Lev. xvii, 5, 8, 9.
[3] Lev. xvii, 8 ; xxii, 14, 18, 21.
[4] Lev. xix, 21–2 ; xxiii, 19.
[5] Lev. xxiii, 9–17.   [6] Lev. xxi, 10–15.
[7] Gen. ix, 2–3 (P²) ; Lev. vii, 22–7 (P³).

CHAPTER IV

THE FIRST CENTURY OF THE RESTORATION. GRADUAL DISAPPEARANCE OF PROPHECY

THE codes drawn up in the priestly circles of Babylonia had no legal validity, however authoritative the names they bore—Ezekiel or Moses—might be. During the whole of the century which succeeded the Exile, "the law," for Palestinian Judaism, seems to have been Deuteronomy, for it is to passages from this book of torah that writers of the period refer.[1]

On the other hand, it is clear that those writers were, if not thoroughly imbued with, at least influenced by the ritualistic and sacerdotal spirit of the priestly codes, for they almost all attach primary importance to the Temple, to ritual sanctity, and to the strict observance of practices such as fasting or the keeping of the Sabbath. Among the prophets, echoes of the lofty spirituality of their predecessors may still be heard. But as a rule they confine themselves to the attempt to equate the outward signs of piety with morality, while inwardly they incline to the view that religion is a system of institutions, the purpose of which is to ensure the salvation of the nation.

Such was the spiritual atmosphere of the period : it provides a sufficient explanation of the decay of prophecy which we are about to record.

I

THE RETURN

As we have seen,[2] there is no reason to doubt that Cyrus allowed the Jews who had been deported, to return to their native land, and that a certain number of them, taking

---

[1] Thus Malachi still identifies priests with members of the house of Levi (ii, 1, 4, 8 ; iii, 3).
[2] pp. 184–190.

immediate advantage of his permission, settled in the
" province of Judah " under the governorship of Sheshbazzar.

These settlers came with the firm intention of rebuilding
the Temple, for not only did they place entire confidence in
the splendid promises of Isaiah—they were also permeated
with the spirit of Ezekiel and the Holiness Code. But for
many a day the hardships they had to endure prevented them
from carrying out their purpose.

When the royal edict was proclaimed, their first
impressions may well have been those described by the poet
who wrote the 126th psalm :

> " When the Lord turned again the captivity of Zion, We were
> like unto them that dream. Then was our mouth filled with laughter,
> And our tongue with singing : Then said they among the nations,
> The Lord hath done great things for them." [1]

When they had to face the hard realities of life, they
ceased to be like unto them that dream. And the first of the
returning exiles no doubt could do no more than continue
to make those sacrifices and offerings which had probably
been brought without intermission during the whole period
of the exile, and laid on the rough, unhewn rock on which the
altar of the former Temple had once stood.[2] And perhaps we
are justified in retaining that part of the Chronicler's narrative [3] which relates that they built a new altar on this rock, one
which should be less unworthy of God's presence than the
bare stone, and that they collected together the ruins of the
Temple as well as they could ; it must have been to this
modest contrivance that the Jews alluded, exaggerating
their achievement in the interests of their cause, when a
little later on they informed a satrap :

> " Then came Sheshbazzar and laid the foundations of the house
> of God which is in Jerusalem : and since that time even until now
> hath it been in building." [4]

In point of fact, the Temple remained in a ruined condition during the eighteen years which succeeded the exile,
and the people said :

> " It is not the time for the Lord's house to be built." [5]

Two fragments of prophecy seem to belong to these first

---

[1] Ps. cxxvi, 1–3.
[2] Jer. xli, 4–5 ; *cf.* perhaps Lam. i, 4. See p. 208.
[3] Ezr. iii.   [4] Ezr. v, 16.   [5] Hagg. i, 2–4.

difficult years. One of them is in the form of a divine declaration :—

> " Thus saith the Lord, The heaven is my throne, and the earth is my footstool : what manner of house will ye build unto me ? and what place shall be my rest ? For all these things hath mine hand made, and so all these things came to be, saith the Lord : but to this man will I look, even to him that is poor and of a contrite spirit, and that trembleth at my word." [1]

In the little colony of ritualists grouped together in the province of Judah, there was therefore at least one man who interpreted the destruction of the Temple as a spiritual lesson given by God himself. True to the spirit of the great prophets of old, and in agreement with Mazdean religion— a coincidence not perhaps entirely fortuitous—he declares that the creator of the heavens and of the earth has no need of a temple, for the worshipper whom Jahweh desires is not the worshipper who brings sacrifices, but the one who is sorry for his sins and hastens to obey the smallest behests of his God.

It is true that some expositors construe this passage merely as an attack against some recusant temple, a rival of Jerusalem,[2] that of the Samaritans on Mount Gerizim,[3] or that of the Jews of Elephantine,[4] or one which it was proposed to erect in Babylonia. But if that were so, the author would seem to have been incredibly clumsy in his choice of expressions, for his argument is obviously directed against all buildings erected by the hand of man to house the Almighty.[5]

The other fragment [6] expresses on the contrary the feelings of the majority of the members of the community when they saw the Temple reduced to ashes :—

> " Be not wroth very sore, O Lord, neither remember iniquity for ever : behold, look, we beseech thee, we are all thy people. Thy holy cities are become a wilderness, Jerusalem a desolation. Our holy and our beautiful house, where our fathers praised thee, is burned with fire . . . Wilt thou refrain thyself for these things, O Lord ? Wilt thou hold thy peace, and afflict us very sore ? " [7]

This touching supplication must have been composed,

[1] Is. lxvi, 1–2.   [2] **XV.**   [3] e.g. **XXXV**, 138–9.
[4] Haller, **XXVIII**, ii, 3², p. 151.
[5] See Acts vii, 48–50 ; xvii, 24–5. Cf. **LX, XLIX**, iii, 2, 482–3 ; **CCXLIX**, 288–9.
[6] Is. lxiii, 7 ; lxiv, 11.   [7] Is. lxiv, 8–11.

as its contents naturally indicate, after the destruction of the Temple in 586, and before it was rebuilt in 520–515. It was perhaps, as Haller thinks,[1] a liturgical prayer : one might well suppose that it was originally intended to be recited at the time of the fast which was kept on each anniversary of the burning of the Temple.[2]

II

Haggai and Zechariah. The Rebuilding of the Temple

In the month of August, 520, a prophet named Haggai, speaking on Jahweh's behalf, called upon the leaders and the people of Judah to undertake at last the rebuilding of the Temple. There can be no doubt that this appeal was connected in the prophet's mind with the course of political events at the time.[3] Since the latter part of the reign of Cambyses, who had died in the spring of 520, the Persian empire had been rent asunder by violent upheavals. In all the provinces of the centre and east, new claimants for power arose, one after the other, their aim being either to seize the reins of government or to carve out for themselves independent kingdoms. These disorders lasted at least until April, 520.[4]

Agitations can hardly have subsided instantaneously ; the western provinces were probably slow in convincing themselves that law and order had again been established even far away in the distant territories of Iran and the Indian frontier. If this was so, it is easy to understand why, even in August, 520, Haggai should look upon the recent conflicts between the nations not only as an omen of the collapse of the Persian empire, but as a sign that the very foundations of the earth were moved, and that it behoved the Jews to rebuild the Temple without further delay. At the very moment when the reign of Jahweh was about to begin, how could they possibly fail to have his dwelling-place ready in his own city ?

[1] **XXVIII**, ii, 3², pp. 144–150.
[2] Zech. vii, 3, 5.
[3] *Cf.* Bentzen, **RHP**, x (1930), 493–503.
[4] See pp. 193–4.

In the prophet's eyes, the explanation of the disappointments and disillusionments which have overtaken the Jews of late must be sought in their neglect of this elementary duty :—

> " Ye looked for much, and lo, it came to little. Why ? saith the Lord of hosts. Because of mine house that lieth waste, while ye run every man to his own house." [1]

Rebuild the Temple, and the fields will once more yield abundant crops. And more than that. By so doing you will give the signal for the reign of the Messiah to begin. It is clear from the titles which Haggai confers on Zerubbabel, the descendant of David whom the Persians had appointed governor in place of Sheshbazzar,[2] that he is prepared to welcome him as the king for whom he hoped : he calls him the chosen of God, the servant of the Lord, the signet carefully guarded by God.[3]

Soon another prophet, the priest Zechariah, joined with Haggai in urging the nation to return to its God, and promised in return a cessation of the Lord's anger, and therefore the salvation longed for by all. " Return unto me . . . and I will return unto you." [4]

The first stone of the new Temple was laid with great solemnity in December, 520.[5]

Events, however, soon proved disconcerting. There was no denying that the strong and capable hand of Darius was coping more and more effectually with the forces of disorder, and that peace was being established in the world on a secure basis—a source of profound disappointment to believers in Jerusalem, as may be gathered from the second great prophecy of Zechariah, the date of which is February, 519. Wishing to counteract the general depression, he relates eight visions which have been vouchsafed to him in one night by Jahweh, their object being to engender among the pious revolutionaries the certainty that the looked-for catastrophe would shortly come to pass.

In the first of these visions, men riding on horses of various hues report that all is quiet on the earth ; but the prophet

[1] Hagg. i, 9.   [2] See p. 189.
[3] Hagg. ii, 23.   [4] Zech. i, 1–6, November, 520.
[5] Hagg. ii, 18 ; Zech. iv, 9.

is told that Jahweh is none the less angry with the nations, and that he will comfort Zion.

In the seven following visions, he contemplates seven scenes depicting the promised deliverance. The different stages of the eschatological forecast are linked together by association of ideas rather than by a strictly chronological plan.[1]

In the second vision the prophet sees four horns, which are beaten down by four blacksmiths : the nations at the four points of the compass will be overthrown.

In the third, a young man is taking measurements with a measuring-line. This means that Jerusalem will be rebuilt and repopulated ; for the population will be too great to be enclosed by a rampart. Besides, Jahweh himself will be for it a wall of fire.

In the fourth, Joshua the high priest appears before the court of heaven. His garments are filthy, no doubt because of the sins of the people, and the public prosecutor, the *sâṭân*, demands that he be condemned. But the angel of the Lord clothes him in clean garments and reproaches the accuser with having misunderstood the Lord's intentions : Jahweh will have mercy ; he has chosen Jerusalem.

In the fifth, two olive-trees and a candlestick with seven lamps appear before the prophet. The two olive-trees represent the two Anointed ones, the two " Messiahs ", Joshua the priest, and Zerubbabel the king, the son of David.

In the sixth, a roll on which curses are written comes flying above the earth : this means that sinners will be expelled from Judah by the curse of God.

In the seventh, a woman is shut up in an ephah, or bushel, and carried through the air by two winged women. The iniquity of Judah will be taken away, and transferred to the country of the enemy, namely Babylonia.

Finally, in the eighth and last revelation, Zechariah hears Jahweh give the signal for this Messianic programme to be carried out : a chariot to which black chargers are harnessed is commanded to bear the wrath of God to the land of the north, that is to say, Babylonia, the centre from which the power of the Persian empire went forth.

On still another occasion, Zechariah proclaimed that final deliverance was imminent. Babylonian Jews had sent an

[1] **LXI,** 400–1 ; **CCXXXVI.**

offering of gold to Jerusalem : the prophet made a crown of it for Zerubbabel.[1]

The two prophets fanned the flame of Messianic hope so diligently that the rebuilding of the Temple was not allowed to lapse.

At one moment, the keenest anxiety was felt. The governor-general of the province beyond the Euphrates got wind of the rebellious intentions underlying the work of reconstruction. He came to Jerusalem and made inquiries. But the Jews pleaded that Cyrus had given them permission. The satrap applied to Darius, who, having respect for his predecessor's decisions, expressed his approval of the enterprise and even gave orders that when the Temple was finished sacrifices and prayers should be offered for the king and his sons.

The Persians took the precaution, however, of depriving the house of David of the right to govern the province of Judah, either by removing Zerubbabel from office, or by refraining from appointing a successor of royal blood when he died. Whichever course they adopted, the last prophecy of Zechariah, the date of which was December, 518, does not mention Zerubbabel. It is a reply to a delegation which came to inquire whether the fasts instituted to commemorate the disasters of 586 were to be continued. Zechariah declares that Jahweh will change the days of mourning into days of rejoicing, but he no longer mentions the Messiah.

The Temple was finished in four and a half years (August, 520, to March, 515).

It may be thought that the prophets Haggai and Zechariah and their contemporaries exaggerated the importance of so material a work as the erection of a temple. But it must be remembered that, for a generation so deeply imbued with the ritualistic spirit of Ezekiel, to desist from the building of the Temple would have been to declare both faith and hope bankrupt.

Nor should we forget that the two prophets, and particularly Zechariah, took the hopes which they kindled in the breasts of their people as the text of a moral exhortation

---

[1] Such was the original meaning of the passage (vi, 9-15). According to the text as it now stands, having been altered to fit subsequent events, the crown was meant for Joshua the priest.

which in some respects is reminiscent of the preaching of the great prophets before the Exile. Their argument is two-fold. Sometimes they say : " Repent, for the kingdom of God shall shortly be established," [1] sometimes : " Repent, or the kingdom of God cannot come." [2] It is true that the two lines of thought are somewhat contradictory, and that the censure of Haggai and Zechariah is far from being either as scathing or as spontaneous as that of their predecessors.

III

FROM THE REBUILDING OF THE TEMPLE TO THAT OF THE WALLS. ISAIAH 56–66. MALACHI

After the completion of the Temple, there is a period of at least sixty years about which our only narrative source, the book of Ezra, is silent [3] ; of the events which may have marked the lives of the Jews at this time, we therefore know nothing. Thanks to some prophecies which apparently belong to this time, we do, however, know something about their state of mind.

It is generally recognized to-day, chiefly as a result of the researches of Bernhard Duhm,[4] that chapters lvi to lxvi of the book of Isaiah, which had previously been attributed to the Second Isaiah, in reality belong to the century after the return. Duhm regarded them as the work of a disciple of the unnamed prophet of the Exile, a man who echoed, though he was far from equalling, his master's teaching, and was saturated with the theocratic and ritualistic ideas of his day. He proposed to call him the Trito-Isaiah.

It seems to us, and to a good many recent critics as well,[5] that the path opened up by the Basle scholar should be followed a step further, and that these passages should cease

[1] As in Hagg. ii, 4–7 ; Zech. viii, 14–17.
[2] As in Hagg. i, 5–11 ; ii, 15–19 ; Zech. i, 3.
[3] Except for the brief mention of an accusation brought against the inhabitants of Judaea under Xerxes, Ezr. iv, 6 ; cf. pp. 194–5.
[4] **XV.**
[5] Cheyne (1895), Kittel (1898), Gressmann (1898), Cramer (1905), Budde (**VI**, 1906 ; **XLVIII**, 1908, 1922), Sellin (**LXXVII**), Skinner (1917), Jacques Marty (**CCXXV**), Abramowski (1925), Volz (**CCXLIX**), Eissfeldt (**XX**).

to be considered as the work of a single author. For in spite of their appearance of being related—a similarity due to their having been written in the language and with the mentality of one and the same period—it seems to us that there are distinct differences, both of inspiration and of emphasis, and that these differences can be better explained if the chapters are attributed to several authors and several generations.

We have already mentioned two of these passages,[1] which must date from before 520 ; their most distinctive feature is their deep spirituality. This applies particularly to the second.

Others, on the contrary, show that somewhat pedestrian mixture of ritualism and morality which we have already noted in Haggai and Zechariah. To this class belongs the prophecy which explains the delay in the coming of deliverance by saying that the duty of fasting has been observed in too formal a manner, unaccompanied by righteous dealing.[2] According to another, salvation depends on strict observance of the Sabbath, but at the same time is inspired by a generous spirit of hospitality towards converts from heathenism, which is reminiscent of that which characterized Babylonian Judaism[3]; it may have been a torah proclaimed in Babylonia in the hope of persuading converts, or even eunuchs, to join a party about to leave for Palestine.[4]

There is one group of prophecies hardly less buoyantly hopeful than those of the Second Isaiah, chapters lx to lxii, for instance, which might almost pass for the work of the master himself, if they did not assume that the Temple was already rebuilt, since all that it requires is to be adorned.[5]

In other adjacent passages, on the other hand, the religous and moral condition of the Jewish community is judged with a severity which recalls the fundamental pessimism of Ezekiel. The leaders, or watchmen, as the prophet calls them, are all blind and foolish. They are like dumb dogs which cannot bark. What is more, they are greedy,

---

[1] Is. lxiii, 7–lxiv, 11 and lxvi, 1–2.
[2] Is. lviii, 1–15a. There is the same idea in Zech. vii–viii.
[3] Cf. p. 248.
[4] Is. lvi, 1–8.   [5] Is. lx, 13 ; cf. lxii, 8–9.

T

insatiable dogs ; they are shepherds incapable of understanding, whose one thought is drink.   The righteous
perisheth, and no man layeth it to heart.[1] This unsparing
critic is especially incensed against those whom he calls
" the sons of the sorceress, the seed of the adulterer and the
whore ",[2] that is to say, the descendants of the Judæans and
the Israelites who remained behind, when the rest were sent
into exile.   In spite of Deuteronomy, these continued to
worship as of old " among the oaks, under every green tree ",
in caves or on the smooth stones of rivers—an allusion to
the worship of water-springs and stones—setting up a table
to Gad,[3] and filling a goblet with aromatic wine for Meni,
making mystical meals of the flesh of animals which the Law
had declared unclean,[4] even sacrificing—such is the charge
brought by the prophet—children in the valleys, under the
clefts of the rocks.[5]   " Therefore is judgment far from us,
neither doth righteousness overtake us." [6]

From these passages full of reproach and invective, we
learn that the Israelites in Palestine, who, like their fellow-
countrymen in Elephantine at the same period, continued to
observe the customs of ancient Jahwism, closely connected
as it was with pagan practices inherited from primitive
Semitism, were still looked upon as part of the Jewish community grouped round the temple at Jerusalem, and that
there was as yet no cleavage between the Jews who have
returned from exile—they were still called the *gôlâh*, " the
deportation "—and " the people of the land " (*'am hâ'âreṣ*),
who later on were to be known as the Samaritans.

These passages also show that there was already a definite
breach between the leaders, whom the prophets accuse of
greed, and of a lack of understanding (of religious things),
and the " righteous ", the " merciful men ",[7] that is to say,
the strict observers of the Law : here we already have the

---

[1] Is. lvi, 9 ; lvii, 1.

[2] Is. lvii, 3–13 ; lxv, 1–7, 11–15.

[3] The God of Fortune.   Even in the fourth and fifth centuries of our
era Jewish families made ready a table for the presiding genius of the
house, called *'arsâ de Gaddâ*, " bed of Gad " (*talm. bab. Sanh.* 20a ;
Ned. 56a) ; cf. **XXXII**, 183 ; **LVI**, i, 235–6.

[4] Is. lxv, 4 ; lvi, 17 ; cf. Deut. xiv, 20 (LXX F[lmg.]) ; Ex. xxiii,
19 (Sam.).   Revival of ancient totemic cults.

[5] Is. lvii, 5.

[6] Is. lix, 9 ; cf. vv. 9–15.   [7] Is. lvii, 1.

antithesis between the " wicked " and the " righteous "
which is to be found in so many of the psalms, the prototype
of the subsequent divisions between the Hellenists and the
Hasidim, the Sadducees and the Pharisees.

Another anonymous prophet of the time, commonly called
Malachi, makes it possible to add a few supplementary touches
to the general picture. In reality, *Mal'âkî* is a common noun
meaning " my messenger ", " my angel ". A passage in the
book [1] was misinterpreted by a scribe, who thought himself
justified in applying this title to the author and in inscribing
it at the head of his writings (i, 1).

It is evident from this short document that even the
" righteous " of the community at Jerusalem gave way to
depression and discontent. Disappointed at finding no
improvement in the humiliating lot of the chosen people,
many of them said :—

> " Wherein hath the Lord loved us ? " In other words : " Has
> the Lord shown that he loves us ? " [2] " Where is the God of judg-
> ment ? " [3] " It is vain to serve God : and what profit is it that we
> have kept his charge, and that we have walked mournfully before
> the Lord of hosts ? And now we call the proud happy, yea, they
> that work wickedness are built up ; yea, they tempt God and are
> delivered." [4]

The result is that faith in the efficacy of sacrifice is undermined. The priests carry out their duties with extreme
reluctance, while laymen avoid their obligations whenever
they can.[5] Gain is everyone's chief preoccupation, in the
hope of obtaining a less precarious footing in the country.
There is an increase in the number of marriages between
the Jews who have returned from exile and the influential
families of the neighbourhood, even if heathen.[6]

The task which the writer of the book of Malachi sets
himself is to prove, one by one, that these grievances are
unfounded, and to struggle against tendencies which, if
unchecked, will prove fatal. As a rule he sets about it from a

---

[1] Mal. iii, 1. The angel of Jahweh is meant, and not the prophet
Elijah, as a gloss, added to the book by way of an appendix, explains
(iii, 22–4).

[2] Mal. i, 2.   [3] Mal. ii, 17.
[4] Mal. iii, 14–15.   [5] Mal. i, 6–ii, 9 ; iii, 7–12.
[6] Mal. ii, 11–22. In their present context these verses are an inter-
polation but they may have been simply transposed. In any case they
certainly belong to the time.

ritualistic standpoint, as might be expected from a religious writer of his day.

On one condition will the prosperity of the nation be restored, and on one only. Sacrifices must be regularly offered to Jahweh and accepted by him ; but they cannot be accepted if a blemished animal is brought to the altar, if the priests are lacking in zeal, or if the tithe offerings are not paid.[1] And God also turns away his face from the Jew who rejects the wife of his youth,[2] and from the nation where sorcerers and perjurers are tolerated, and unjust practices condoned.[3] In this way, as in Ezekiel and the Holiness Code, morality is not only regarded as inseparable from the ritualistic element in religion, but subordinated to it.

There is, however, in Malachi such a keen moral sense, that he sometimes breaks through the cramping restrictions of the narrow-minded outlook of the day, and regains the freedom of thought, and even the audacity, of the older prophets.

Although it was authorized by law, he pronounces on principle a condemnation of divorce which is as uncompromising as that of Jesus : " I hate putting away, saith the Lord." [4]

In an indignant outburst against negligent priests, he boldly declares that Jahweh is more willing to accept the worship offered anywhere in the whole universe than the homage paid to him in the Temple at Jerusalem :—

> " O that there were one among you that would shut the doors, that ye might not kindle fire on mine altar in vain ! I have no pleasure in you . . . neither will I accept an offering at your hand. For from the rising of the sun even unto the going down of the same my name is great among the Gentiles ; and in every place incense is offered unto my name, and a pure offering [5] ; for my name is great among the Gentiles, saith the Lord of hosts. But ye profane it. . . ." [6]

The implication that the offerings brought by the heathen to their gods are in reality intended for Jahweh—the only true God—is scarcely meant to be taken seriously, any more than those sayings of Amos, Ezekiel, the author of the

---

[1] Mal. i, 6–8, 12–14 ; iii, 7–12.   [2] Mal. ii, 10, 13–14.
[3] Mal. iii, 1–5.   [4] Mal. ii, 10, 13–16.
[5] Probably *muggâš* (explanatory gloss) should be rejected, and *u* before *minḥâh*.
[6] Mal. i, 10–12.

book of Jonah, or Jesus, which exalt the most despised of
the Gentiles at the expense of the Israelites.[1] The paradox
nevertheless reveals a broadmindedness towards non-Jewish
religions—and not only to non-Jews—more generous than
any which is to be found in ancient Hebrew literature [2] :
though pagans believe they are worshipping Marduk, Ammon
or Ahura Mazda, they are in fact worshipping the only true
God.[3]

Such an idea is not as impossible as it might at first appear,
in a Jew of the fifth century. In ancient times it was
universally held that the deities worshipped by different nations
under different names were really one and the same. In the
Baal of the Canaanites the Egyptians recognized their god
Sutku, and in Astarte their goddess Hathor ; the Greeks
found Zeus, Hermes and Helios in many a barbarian deity,
and so did the Romans with Jupiter, Mars, Juno, and Minerva.
The Persians, by speaking of the god of the Jews as " God
of the heavens ", seem to have identified him with Ahura
Mazda,[4] and the Jews, on their side, by their preferential use
of this title to denote Jahweh, in their relations with the
Persians,[5] must naturally have been inclined to make this
identification themselves. In Manasseh's time, there may
have been an intentional and conscious amalgamation of the
national god with Anu.[6]

Certain Babylonians had even arrived at the idea that all
personifications of divinity were but names, different aspects
of one and the same god. In a Neo-Babylonian text we
read :—

> Enlil is Marduk as the god who rules and counsels.
> Nebo is Marduk as the god of fortune.
> Sin is Marduk as the god who illumines the night,
> Shamash is Marduk as the god of justice, etc.[7]

[1] Am. iii, 9–11 ; Ez. iii, 4–7 ; xvi, 46–58 ; Jon. i ; iii ; iv ; Matt.
xi, 21–4.
[2] Including Deut. iv, 19.
[3] According to Oesterley and Robinson (*Introd.*, 1934, p. 428)
the prophet meant only to include those pagans who, because they
inclined towards monotheism, venerated " the most high God " ; but
the general phrase " in every place " seems to make such a limitation
impossible.
[4] **CXCVI**, iii, 5–6.
[5] Ezr. v, 11 ; *cf.* i, 2 ; vi, 9 ; Elephantine Papyrus.
[6] See pp. 128–9.   [7] **CCXXXIII** ; **XXVII**, 329 ; **XIV**, 99.

In the inscription of Eshmunazar, the Sidonian Astarte bears the title of " Name of Baal ".   In Punic inscriptions Tanit is called " The Face of Baal ".[1] Some of the semi-pagan Jews may have made use of speculations of this kind to justify the homage paid by them to Gad, Meni, Anat-Jahu, and Ašam-Bethel.

A species of syncretistic monotheism was in the air. It would hardly be surprising that it should have left its mark even on a Jew who was a staunch upholder of prophetic ideals.

Other critics think that in " Malachi's " mind, the pure sacrifices everywhere offered to Jahweh mean the sacrifices offered to the national God in the temples built by the Jews of the Dispersion, at Elephantine, for instance, and perhaps at Kasiphia in Babylonia.[2] But even if this interpretation were correct, it would show a curious degree of independence on the part of " Malachi " with regard to Deuteronomic orthodoxy, of which the first essential was that the Temple at Jerusalem should have a monopoly of worship.

His reply to the malcontents who said " Where is the God of judgment ? " is also noteworthy.   He tells them that the judgment for which they clamour will descend upon them without warning, and that it will *not be in their favour*.[3] It is like an echo of the terrible question of Amos :—

" Wherefore would ye have the day of the Lord ?   It is darkness and not light." [4]

It is clear that the personality of the writer whom we call Malachi was both vigorous and orginal.   It is nevertheless true that indications of the decline and fall of prophecy are to be found in him.   He is in fact hardly a prophet, in the strict sense of one who reveals the will of Jahweh for his own times.   He is above all a preacher, a moralist who is trying to instil God's will into minds already familiar with it, an advocate of a written law and an eschatology already defined.

The manner of his preaching differentiates him still further from former prophets.   He does not proceed from revelation to revelation, he develops an argument.   His book is composed of a series of debates, with statement, counter-

---

[1] *Cf.* **CXCVI**, 33.   [2] Ezr. viii, 17–20. See pp. 218–19.
[3] Mal. ii, 17–iii, 5.   [4] Am. v, 18.

statement, and reply.[1] Even though these discussions have
nothing in common with the controversies of the schools
as regards their subject-matter, but grapple directly with
the practical difficulties of life, " Malachi " is a forerunner
of the scribes and of the Talmudists.

The scribe is the new " representative man ", and in
days to come he will succeed the prophet as a leader of men's
minds. He it is who by his interpretation of the Law and
by his books of moral apophthegms (Proverbs, Wisdom of
Jesus, son of Sirach) will provide rules of conduct, who will
discuss the problem of theodicy (Proverbs, Job, Ecclesiastes,
Wisdom), and by studying past history and ancient prophecies will endeavour to explain the future and penetrate
the mysteries of the world to come (Apocalypses).

As to pneumatic phenomena, there was doubtless no
abrupt cessation of their appearance, for there were prophets
at Jerusalem in the time of Nehemiah,[2] and others arose
intermittently, such as the peasant who for seven years
would not desist from crying " Woe to Jerusalem " in spite
of the blows with which he was received.[3] Priests were
looked upon as the recipients of divine revelation, especially
when officiating in the Temple.[4] Inspiration was perhaps
never so frequently mentioned as in the first six centuries
of Judaism : not only the writers of Apocalypses, but
moralists like Eliphaz and Elihu in the book of Job,[5] Solomon
in the book of Wisdom,[6] the pious rabbis,[7] Philo,[8] all describe
themselves, or are described, as inspired ; even morality
was presented as a fruit of the Spirit.[9]

But the very fact that the terminology of the religious
ecstatics of bygone times had become so widespread shows
that they must have almost disappeared from the everyday

---

[1] *Cf.* Hagg. ii, 10–13 ; Zech. vii and viii.
[2] Neh. vi, 7, 10–14.   [3] Jos., *B.J.*, VI, v, 3, §§ 300–8.
[4] John Hyrkanus (Jos., *B.J.*, I, ii, 8, § 69 ; *A.J.*, XIII, x, 3, §§ 282–3,
and 7, §§ 299–300 ; *talm. bab. Sota,* 33*a*, *jer. Sota* 24*b* ; *midr. rabb.
Cant.* viii, 10, 35*a*), Zacharias (Luke i, 8–22), Caiaphas (John xi, 49- 52 ;
xviii ,14), Josephus (*B.J.*, III, viii, §§ 351–3, and 9, §§ 399–408 ; IV, x, 7,
§§ 623–5), Simeon the Just (*talm. bab. Sota* 33*a* ; *Yoma* 39*b* ; *midr.
R. Cant.* viii, 10). *Cf.* **LXXXVI**, 133–5.
[5] Job iv, 12–16 ; xxxii, 8.   [6] Wisd. vii, 7, 27.
[7] *Cf.* **LXXXVI**, 115–19.
[8] **LXXXVI**, 130–3.   [9] **LXXXVI**, 104–9.

life of religious society. At the time of the Maccabeans, the Jews felt that they were living in days when prophets were no more.[1] Those who thought that they had been entrusted with revelations published them under some well-known name of a bygone age, an age of prophets, as if they belonged to Daniel, Enoch, Moses, Abraham or Adam. A writer of the day even goes so far as to foretell, as a blessing from Jahweh, the final abolition of prophetic inspiration, since he sees in such inspiration nothing but a spirit of defilement.[2]

[1] Ps. lxxiv, 9.   [2] Zech. xiii, 2–6.

CHAPTER V

COMPLETION OF THE REDACTION OF THE PRIESTLY
LEGISLATION. ITS ADOPTION BY THE JUDAISM
OF THE SECOND CENTURY OF THE RESTORATION

I

THE PRIESTLY REDACTION AND SACRED HISTORY

THE work of codifying and revising ancient rites and
customs, which had been begun by Ezekiel and continued in the Jewish colonies in Babylonia in the time
of the Exile, was zealously continued during the century
which followed the return. Of the products of this activity,
there is one document [1] which is more extensive than
any of the others, and is distinguished from them by the
manner of its presentation, for it is written in historical
form.

Overwhelmed like Ezekiel by the majestic sublimity of
God, the author of this work considers it superfluous, and
even unworthy of God's greatness, to accompany his
enumeration of the laws of Jahweh by any exhortations to
Israel to obey them, as the editors of Deuteronomy and the
Holiness Code had done. Divine commands are in no need of
justification : he therefore confines himself to relating the
time and circumstances of their inception. He writes a
History of the setting up by God of those sacred institutions,
which in his eyes form the very corner-stone of the religion
of his people.

Like the writers J and E, he looks to national tradition
to furnish him with details about this distant past, being
familiar with it both in the pages of his predecessors and by
means of a living oral tradition. Nevertheless, he is, as
a rule, either indifferent to, or suspicious of, tradition,

---

[1] Denoted by the siglum P[2] to distinguish it from older priestly
laws, e.g. the Holiness Code (P[1]).

for tradition cannot provide that in which he is chiefly interested.

Tradition provided him with stories, pathetic or ironical, picturesque, colourful, natural, instinct with delicate or profound psychological observation, as well as ingenious myths explaining local customs, or poetic legends ; and the authors J and E, kindred spirits of those who had of old created or transmitted these tales, had reproduced them faithfully. But to a legal mind like his, all this folklore apparently seemed futile, unedifying, even tainted with heresy—did it not glorify the high-places ?—for he omitted it almost entirely.

What he wanted was exact chronology, like that of the Assyro-Babylonian annals, unbroken genealogies, and precise information about the state of law in ancient times, none of which tradition could provide. He was therefore reduced to supplying the deficiency himself.

That is why he presents the greater part of history, the history of the patriarchs Isaac, Jacob, and Joseph for instance, in the form of a dry list of names and dates. There are some narratives, however, which he delights to elaborate ; these are almost exclusively such as seem to end with the enunciation of some divine law.

To begin with, there is the account of the creation,[1] which he bases on an old Israelite tradition, derived from a myth very popular in Babylonia, and also among Hebrew poets, the myth representing the struggle between the God of light and the Sea of primitive chaos, the Abyss.[2] This narrative interests him, both because as told by him it expresses with incomparable grandeur the power of God over nature and because, when he has divided the eight or nine acts of creation among six days, he finds therein an explanation of the divine origin of the law of the Sabbath.

Then there is the story of the Flood, which he relates because its conclusion is that Noah and his descendants are forbidden to eat flesh with the blood.

The prophecy of the birth of Isaac is also recorded in detail, because on that occasion God instituted the rite of

---

[1] Gen. i, 1–2, 4a.

[2] The goddess Tiamat in Babylonia ; in Hebrew, Tehôm, Rahab, " the Serpent," Leviathan, etc.

circumcision as a sign of the covenant established between himself and Abraham.

Another episode which is related at great length is the purchase of the burial cave at Machpelah by Abraham.[1] It is often thought that here the centre of interest was the claim of the Israelites to the possession of the land of Canaan, on the grounds that their forefathers had been buried there.[2] To us it seems that the author's interest in this scene was inspired by the veneration felt by every Judæan for the sacred sepulchres at Hebron. Their claim to the ownership of this cave must have been espoused by him all the more ardently that the whole district in which it lay had been in the hands of the Edomites since 586 : another juridical motive, but of a rather specialized kind.

The priestly historiographer records with considerable wealth of detail the way in which Esau, having married wives who were not of the pure race of Abraham, became separated from the family of the elect, and how Jacob was forbidden by his father to take a wife from among the Canaanites.[3] The importance of this question of mixed marriages at the time of Malachi, Nehemiah and Ezra is well known.

The narrative element is more strongly developed in that part of the priestly history which is devoted to the Mosaic period. But here, too, most of the stories consist of legislation in the guise of history. There is first of all the institution of the Passover, destined to save the lives of the first-born of the Israelites at the time of the tenth plague, and there is the law about the first-born.[4] Then there is the main body of the legislation given on Sinai.

Finally, after the conquest, there is the division of the territory among the various tribes, which had also formed part of the charter of reconstruction as conceived by Ezekiel.

In tracing his majestic picture of the progressive revelation of God, the author may have been guided by certain historical motives. He adopts the Elohist tradition, according to which God revealed his name, Jahweh, only to Moses, which meant that Jahwism proper only dated from the time of the Exodus.[5] He also knows that the religious institutions of his

---

[1] Gen. xxiii.
[2] *Cf.* Neh. ii, 3.
[3] Gen. xxvi, 34–5 ; xxvii, 46–xxviii, 9.
[4] Ex. xii, 1–13 ; xiii, 1–2.
[5] *Cf.* **LVII,** 239–240.

people do not all come from Moses, that some are more recent,[1] above all that there are others which are older, and shared by other nations : it is probably because he is acquainted with the extent of the diffusion of blood taboos that he places the origin of the Jewish restrictions as far back as the days of Noah, father of all humanity since the Flood. In the same way, it may be because he knows that circumcision was to be met with among various Semitic peoples, that he attributes its origin to the time of Abraham, the father of the Arabs, the Edomites, the Midianites, and others, as well as of the Israelites, contrary to the J and E traditions, of which the first attributed its introduction to the wife of Moses [2] and the second to Joshua.[3]

Historical considerations, however, play but a minor part in the historico-legal scheme which the priestly narrator develops : they are far outweighed by dogmatic preoccupations, and the care for their immediate practical application.

The institutions which the author traces back to days before the revelation on Sinai—the observance of the Sabbath, abstention from blood, circumcision, and the Passover—are to be honoured by the Jews even when they are unable to take part in the worship of the Temple, when they are in exile, or among the Diaspora.

Those which, in his view, date from the days of sojourn beneath the Holy Mountain are all connected with the Temple of Jerusalem, such as the regulations concerning the classes of priests, sacrifices, feast-days, etc. By an ingenious theory he even credits Moses with the creation of the Temple. The E tradition mentioned a tent erected by the liberator of Israel for the purpose of receiving oracles from Jahweh, and, probably, of sheltering the Ark ; this " tent of meeting " (with God) was guarded by Joshua, the Ephraimite servant of Moses.[4] Taking this as his starting-point, the priestly historian portrays the tent as a luxurious temple, served by a number of priests, its plan being an exact replica of that of the Temple. In other words, the " tent of meeting " described by the priestly historian is a portable edition of the Temple of Jerusalem. At times the author forgets himself, and speaks of the south, the east, the

---

[1] Josh. xiii–xxi (P parts).   [2] Ex. iv, 24–6.
[3] Josh. v, 2–3, 8–9.   [4] Ex. xxxiii, 7–11.

north, and the west of the tent, without indicating that it
was to be given any special orientation : he is thinking of the
Temple in the Holy City.[1] For him, the worship of Jahweh
has existed, immutable, with all its details carefully regulated,
ever since religion in Israel began, and it will undergo no
change when it is celebrated in Jerusalem after the return
from exile.

He goes still further, by implying that Jahweh has never
desired, and never received, any other form of worship.
That is why he never mentions a single sacrifice before
Israel came to the foot of Mount Sinai. Neither Noah, after
the Flood, nor the patriarchs in Canaan, ever raised an altar
nor burnt an offering. This shows how unhistorical the
theoretic evolutionism of the priestly narrator really is. It also
shows that the historiographer meant not only to complete
the JED collection of traditions, but to take its place :
because this collection seemed to him to speak evil of the
fathers, by representing their actions as almost wholly illegal.

It is evident that the attempt made by the school of
Deuteronomy to edit the ancient collection (JE) had been
timid indeed in comparison with the arbitrary treatment of
the history of origins by the Priestly school.

II

FURTHER RITUAL LEGISLATION OF THE RESTORATION PERIOD.
THE PRIESTLY CODE

Other legislative texts, dating from about the same time
as the priestly history, have been preserved for us, for
instance a collection of laws regulating the distinction between
the clean and the unclean (Lev. xi, 15), in which the work of
several hands can be recognized.[2] Some of them must have
been written after the priestly history,[3] such as the laws
extending to all priests the right to be anointed which the
priestly history, in agreement with the Holiness Code, had
reserved to the high priest ; the law lowering the age at
which the Levites were to begin their functions, from thirty

---

[1] Ex. xxvi, 18–27, 35 ; xxvii, 9–13 ; Numb. ii and iii.
[2] P^P and P^{P2} in the Century Bible (V).
[3] And are therefore usually indicated by the siglum P^3.

to twenty-five [1] ; those which order, or take for granted, the erection of a golden altar of incense,[2] the priestly narrative having related that censers were used for this purpose. To these must be added the legislation about sacrifices,[3] which is itself formed by the amalgamation of two collections.[4]

These laws, as well as the Priestly Code, were inserted in different places in the main body of sacred history. In this way that vast whole which we call the Priestly Code was built up, forming a charter of ideal legislation for the Jewish community, as conceived by the group of ritualist priests whose centre was in Babylonia, and as they hoped to see it carried out.

The ruling ideas of the more recent of the priestly legislators [5] are the same as those of the torah of Ezekiel and the Holiness Code : they attach the same importance to holiness, to details of ritual, and to atonement. In some respects, however, they break fresh ground.

To begin with, in regard to the *holy places*, they no longer fulminate against the multiplicity of places of sacrifice, as did their predecessors, the Deuteronomic reformers, Ezekiel, and the editors of the Holiness Code. They take for granted that the centralization of worship is already established, that unity has existed since the days of Moses.

Holy Persons.—The person whom they place at the head of the hierarchy which constitutes the nation in their eyes is no longer simply a priest greater than his brethren (Holiness Code), he is " the High Priest ", or " the Anointed Priest ", who alone has the right to wear the urim and thummim, the ephod and the robe, and to enter once a year into the Holy of Holies. His death is the occasion of an amnesty for those who have committed homicide unintentionally.[6] The chief of the civil power, if there is one, must take instructions from the high priest : according to the priestly historian, it was on the order of Eleazar that Joshua and all the children of Israel went in and out.[7] In thus investing

---

[1] Numb. viii, 24 ; on the other hand, see iv, 3, 35–47.
[2] e.g. Ex. xxx, 1–10 ; *cf.* on the other hand, Lev. x, 1 ; Numb. xvi 6, 17–18, 37–46 ; and even Lev. xvi, 12–13.
[3] Lev. i–vii.
[4] Po¹ and Po² in **V.**
[5] P², Po, Pp, P³.
[6] Numb. xxxv, 28.
[7] Numb. xxvii, 21.

the head of the priesthood with supreme power, the priestly lawgivers were doubtless inspired by the events which had taken place in the community at Jerusalem : since, after the death or the deposition of Zerubbabel, the Persians had ceased to entrust the government of the province to a ruler of the house of David, the high priest had been the sole official representative of the Jewish population in their dealings with the pagan authorities : he became in fact the head of the nation, and even of all the Jews of the empire.

Next to the high priests come the priests. Ezekiel had demanded that *in future* the priesthood should be confined to the sons of Zadok. The priestly historian, true to his usual practice, attributed the inauguration of this privilege to Moses himself, who, according to him, had given to members of the house of Aaron alone the right to become priests. But the priestly legislators were prepared to admit the lawfulness of priests descended from Aaron by Ithamar, as well as those who were descended from Aaron by Eleazar, these latter being none other than the sons of Zadok. This concession was no doubt the result of the actual situation in Palestine : some priestly families not belonging to Jerusalem had succeeded after the return in obtaining recognition, along with those whose ancestors had officiated in the Temple before the Exile.

As we have seen, the torah of Ezekiel admitted that all the descendants of Levi had been priests, but prescribed degradation to the rank of Temple servants to those among them who had officiated in high-places, that is to say, in temples other than the Temple of Jerusalem.[1] According to the Priestly Code, the distinction between Levite-priests and ordinary Levites goes back to Moses. It is not in the nature of a measure adopted to suit a special occasion in history, but part of the original constitution of Israel. Among the Levites, only the descendants of Aaron are priests—the others never have been priests. Aaron and his sons had been at their task long before the Israelites, at Jahweh's command, offered the Levites to the priests as a substitute for their first-born, whom they ought to have given to the Temple.[2]

[1] Ez. xliv, 10–15.   [2] Numb. iii and viii.

Only the descendants of Aaron have the right to place the sacrificial victims upon the altar, to bless, and to enter the Holy of Holies. The Levites must confine themselves to slaying and washing the victims, guarding the Sanctuary, and carrying the sacred vessels after the priests had wrapped them round. Woe to those who presumed to encroach on the functions of the priests ! Let them remember what happened to Korah and his accomplices, when, as mere Levites, they took upon themselves to offer incense, and were consumed by fire from Jahweh.[1]

It may be added that the status of the Levites improved in the course of the centuries following, especially when their number, which for long had been strictly limited,[2] was increased by the granting of the title of Levite to the Temple singers, who formed guilds of considerable importance. But this improvement did not take place until after the completion of the Priestly Code : the compilers of these laws breathe no word of Levitical music ; also the author of the Chronicles attributes its introduction to David and not to Moses.

Sacred Acts.—The legislators of the Priestly Code adopt the classification and nomenclature of offerings which appear in the torah of Ezekiel. Naturally, they give many more details about the ritual of the different kinds of sacrifices and their use. They also show themselves more exacting with regard to their nature. Cereals, for instance, must as a rule be brought in the form of flour (*sôleth*), and not of ordinary meal (*qemah*) as hitherto. The offerings of incense are increased to such an extent that a late law insists on the erection of a separate altar from that used for the burnt-offerings.

The priests' incomes are considerably increased. Hence the firstlings of the flock, and the tenth part of the produce of the soil, which in ancient Israel had been consumed *by the offerers* as a sacred repast,[3] are now handed over to the priests as dues.[4]

---

[1] Numb. xvi (P parts).
[2] Hence the necessity of lowering the age at which they became eligible for service, from 30 to 25, then to 20 years (Numb. iv, 3 ; viii, 23–5 ; 1 Chron. xxiii, 24–7 ; 2 Chron. xxxi, 17 ; Ezr. iii, 8).
[3] Deut. xv, 19–23 ; xiv, 22–7.   [4] Numb. xviii, 15–19, 20–32.

Sacred Seasons.—In addition to the Sabbath, which, with minute attention to detail, is prescribed under pain of death [1] as a day of rest, and the Sabbatical year, which is to be observed every seventh year, a late law [2] requires that a Jubilee shall be celebrated after seven times seven years. On the tenth day of the seventh month of the forty-ninth year—and therefore at the beginning of the fiftieth, according to the old calendar, which began in autumn—to the sound of the trumpet made from the horn of a ram (*yôbêl*), the year of *yôbêl* (jubilee) is to be ushered in, the year when Hebrew slaves are to be freed, when sowing and reaping alike will be forbidden (as in the Sabbatical year), and when all landed property will revert to the first owners (Israelites). This last regulation was no doubt a further development of an ancient tradition, a survival from nomadic times, necessitating the periodical re-allotment of certain communal land.[3] It may be added that the law about the jubilee, inspired by a generous desire for social betterment, seems to have never been observed, and scarcely could have been observed : one result of it would have been, for instance, that for two years in succession the Jews would have had no harvest—the forty-ninth year (the Sabbatical year) and the fiftieth year (the jubilee year).

The three great feasts—the Passover and Unleavened Bread, the Feast of Weeks, and the Feast of Tabernacles—are to be celebrated on a fixed day of the month, as the torah of Ezekiel had prescribed, whereas, according to Deuteronomy,[4] and doubtless also the Holiness Code,[5] the date depended on the state of the harvest. The Feast of Tabernacles lasts eight days instead of seven.[6] There are to be two new occasions of solemnity, " New Year's Day," and " the Day of Atonement ". To these we shall return later, for the second of the two in any case was only introduced after Ezra's time, at least in the form described in the text.[7]

[1] Numb. xv, 32–6 ; *cf.* Neh. xiii, 15–22.
[2] Lev. xxv, 8–13, 15–16, 26–34.
[3] *Cf.* **LVII**, 460.
[4] Deut. xvi, 9.
[5] *Cf.* Lev. xxiii, 11, and note in **V**, *ad loc.*
[6] Lev. xxiii, 36*b* ; Numb. xxix, 35–8. *Cf.* Ez. xlv, 25 ; 1 Kings viii, 66 ; Lev. xxiii, 31, 36*a*.
[7] See pp. 312–16.

III

VALUE AND PURPOSE OF RITUAL ACCORDING TO THE PRIESTLY LEGISLATORS

The nature of ritual in Israel underwent a profound change as a result of the innovations of the priestly legislators, the additions they made to existing institutions, the importance they attached to certain elements which had previously been subordinate, as for instance the rites of atonement,[1] and, conversely, their lesser emphasis on other features previously regarded as essential, such as the " peace offering ", once the chief of all the sacrifices, and the sad number of gaps they seem to have made, by simply allowing many of the old customs to lapse.[2]

It is none the less true that the imposing construction erected by priestly exertions was chiefly composed of ancient, even of very ancient, stones. The rites ordained by the Priestly Code were for the most part, without any doubt, those which had been observed in the Temple of Jerusalem just before the exile. The Code even sanctioned many customs which reeked of idolatry, of religious materialism, and of belief in magic of the most primitive kind, as for instance the ordeal of drinking holy water,[3] the making of the " water of separation " with the ashes of a red heifer,[4] or the ceremony by which the leper's uncleanness was transferred to a bird which was then allowed to fly away.[5]

These old rites, when first initiated, had been but the logical application of current ideas. The question now arises : by making them lawful, did the priestly lawgivers preserve— or restore—their original significance, or did they give them a new meaning ? Or again, did they merely sanction them without trying to explain them ?

In certain respects they undoubtedly interpreted the ancient customs in their archaic sense : as we have pointed out, they regarded holiness as a kind of fluid which could be conveyed from one person to another. The blowing of trumpets was to them a means of attracting Jahweh's attention [6] to any cause which Israel might have in hand, and they

---

[1] Cf. pp. 258–262.　　　　　　[2] Cf. **LVII**, 325 ; **CCXVIII,** 141.
[3] Numb. v, 11–31.　　　　　　[4] Numb. xix.
[5] Lev. xiv, 1–7.　　　　　　　[6] Numb. x, 9–10.

recognized " an offering of memorial, bringing iniquity to remembrance ".[1] Sacrifices were for them so many sacred acts and, provided that they were correctly carried out, sure to be effectual : this was a return to a very early magical conception, for in Israel before the Exile sacrifices had as a rule been interpreted in a more moral sense, as presents which God might accept or refuse at will.

In other cases, the legislators gave to ancient observances a new meaning. No longer was the Sabbath to be kept as a day of sacrifice,[2] or in order to give rest to slaves and beasts of burden,[3] but because, in the beginning, the Creator rested on the seventh day. The observance of the Sabbath had ceased to be a traditional or humanitarian regulation, and had become one of those sacred, mystic rites, so often to be found in ancient religions, which the worshipper must perform in imitation of some gesture made by his God.[4] Circumcision which, in the time immediately preceding the Exile had been regarded chiefly as a mark of civilization,[5] was now interpreted as a sign of the covenant between Jahweh and his people.[6]

But, as a rule, those responsible for the laws made no attempt to justify them by any commentary, and did not seem to care greatly whether one sense more than another was attached to the prescribed action. This is true about the laws with regard to defilement, which occupy so important a place in their code. Although our information on this point is very scanty, it is highly probable that most of them were already observed in ancient Jahwism, as in many other archaic religions, and that they went back to the earliest days of Semitic animism, the original explanation of the uncleanness of the dead, and of everything that came in contact with them, being the terror inspired by the spirit of the dead,[7] the uncleanness of the leper being due to fear of the demon which possessed him,[8] sexual uncleanness being the result of the dread inspired by the supernatural powers presiding over generation,[9] and the uncleanness of

---

[1] Numb. v, 15.
[2] 2 Kings xi, 5–8 ; cf. iv, 23.
[3] Ex. xxiii, 12 ; Deut. v, 14.
[4] Gen. ii, 1–3.
[5] Josh. v, 2–3, 8–9 ; Jer. iv, 4.
Cf. LVII, 225–9.
[6] Gen. xvii.
[7] Cf. LVI, i, 175–183 ; LVII, 258.
[8] Cf. LVII, 277.
[9] Cf. LVII, 277.

certain kinds of animals being attributable to the belief in the supernatural capacities or knowledge of that particular species.[1] It is unlikely that the Jewish priests of the fifth century had any clear idea of the original meaning of these practices. Nevertheless, they required that they should be strictly observed, *not because of their precise meaning*, which seemed to them a matter of indifference, but because, since they formed a part of national custom, they constituted so many signs that the nation belonged to God and God to the nation : to obey these laws, to practice circumcision and keep the Sabbath, was for the layman the best hope of that " holiness " which was as essential as the priest's, if the presence of Jahweh in the midst of his people was to continue.

It was obviously the Exile which revealed the supreme value of these observances as a bond between the members of a nation bereft of its fatherland, and as a barrier between them and the Gentiles.[2] The importance attached to ideas of cleanness and uncleanness by the Mazdeans may have had some influence on the esteem in which these regulations were held [3] ; but there is no indication that their compilers justified them by an appeal to a dualist theory akin to Zoroastrianism. Their interest in these rites seems to have been connected *with their utility*—both mystical and national —rather than with their intrinsic significance.

Sacrifices constituted a still more important group of rites. In ancient Israel, sacrifice had been employed for a variety of ends, and with effects diversely interpreted according to the particular kind : there was the communal sacrifice, the gift sacrifice, the sacrifice of the sacred meal, the covenant sacrifice, and others whose object was apotropaic, preservation, divination, imprecation, and so on.[4] The priestly legislators kept a certain number of these different types of sacrifice, and made room for several of the ideas originally inherent in them, but seem to have had no general doctrine as to the nature of sacrifice, and, in particular, atonement through sacrifice. They show certain main lines of thought, and here and there a tentative interpretation, but these interpretations vary, if they do not contradict each

---

[1] *Cf.* **LVII**, 281–8.
[2] **LXVII**, 243–7.
[3] **LIX**, 235.
[4] *Cf.* **LVII**, 321–4 ; **LVIII**, *passim.*

other, and there is no general system.[1] This no doubt was
because they did not feel it imperative to explain the existence
of the traditional rites. Atonement through ritual was for
them essentially a mystery, of which the only solution was
that God had seen fit to ordain it. And this very mystery
enhanced its value—the rites of atonement were of the nature
of sacraments.[2]

o

APPENDIX

THE NATURE AND FUNCTION OF SACRIFICE, ACCORDING TO THE PRIESTLY CODE

An attempt has often been made to collect and co-ordinate
Biblical references to sacrifice, in the hope that a systematic body
of doctrine could be deduced from the whole mass of evidence,
particularly in its bearing on the redemptive aspect of the death
of Christ. Hubert and Mauss thought they had found in the Bible,
that is to say, in the Priestly Code, a learned and intricate body
of doctrine relating to sacrifice, which was identical with that
which they thought they had found in the Vedas.[3] In the same way
René Dussaud declared that all the rites of Israelite sacrifice—he
meant the Levitical sacrifices—were logically derived from a few
fundamental and coherent ideas, that there was a definite " Israelite
doctrine of sacrifice ",[4] and that this doctrine even provided the
original idea of sacrifice, whether it was maintained intact by the
Jewish priests of the time of the Exile, or rediscovered by them.[5]
With regard to certain points, the views of the priestly legislators
are certainly clear-cut enough. They consider that the chief object
of sacrifice is to atone for, strictly speaking to " cover ", sins and
defilements—for they must have attached to the verb *kapper* the
Hebrew,[6] rather than the Assyrian meaning, which was " to blot
out ".[7]
They therefore posit—as Christianity did after them—a
close and organic relation between religion and removal of
sin. This no doubt was a result of the preaching of the prophets
and the misfortunes of the Exile.
As regards another question their thought is also clear : they
hold that sacrificial rites have an active value in themselves, *ex
opere operato*. It has often been supposed that they looked upon
these sacred acts simply as symbols, representing the repentance of
man and the forgiveness of God. Such is not the case : the texts

[1] See appendix, pp. 293–6.
[2] *Cf.* **LXVII**, 298.
[3] **XXXVIII.**
[4] **XVIII**, 2–29, particularly pp. 27–9.
[5] **XVIII**, 12.
[6] Gen. vi, 14 ; xxxii, 21 ; Prov. xvi, 14.
[7] **XCV**, 601–2, 650 ; Lagrange, *Études sur les rel. sémitiques* [2], Paris, Lecoffre, 1905, p. 232.

concerned expressly state that when the ceremony is over the atonement has been made.[1] There is no mention of the spiritual attitude
of the offerer. Even the confession of sins committed, which doubtless
accompanied sacrifices of atonement, in the form of a psalm or
liturgical statement, is only rarely included in the Law.[2] The reason
was partly that, according to priestly theory, only involuntary
transgressions could be expiated by sacrifices—that is to say, acts
which are not sins in the moral sense, and cannot therefore be
followed by true repentance—while the harm done by voluntary
sins could only be " taken away from Israel " by punishment or
by banishment, or by putting the culprit to death. Nevertheless,
certain passages in the Law itself show that, in practice there were
included in the category of involuntary sins all sorts of witting sins
which had been committed through fear or carelessness—false
witness, deliberate defilement, falsehood for personal gain, theft
—provided that the culprit admitted his fault and, if necessary,
made amends.[3] We even read that Aaron atoned for a rebellion
of the people against himself and Moses by an offering of incense.[4]
The priestly legislators, therefore, had an objective, almost magical
conception of the efficacy of sacrifice, as Hubert and Mauss have
clearly shown.

But how is atonement achieved by the act of sacrifice ? This is
a question about which the priestly texts give us only the barest
hints, and their attempts to explain agree neither with each other
nor with the details of the rites. The most explicit is that which is
given incidentally in the Holiness Code in connection with the
prohibition against eating meat containing blood : " For the life
of the flesh is in the blood, and I have given it to you upon the altar
to make atonement for your souls : for it is the blood that maketh
atonement by reason of the life (that is in it)." [5] It would seem
from this passage that the life (" the soul ") of the sinner is
threatened by the holiness of God : he must give, as an equivalent,
blood, that is a soul, a life. There is a ransom, a redemption,
a death by proxy.

This interpretation of sacrifice, at least of certain sacrifices, is
widespread enough. In a Babylonian text we read : " Give the
sucking-pig in his stead,[6] flesh for his flesh, blood for his blood,
and may the gods accept it ! " [7] Many temple traditions told of the
acceptance of an animal by the deity in place of a human victim.[8]
The idea of substitutional death was familiar to the ancient
Israelites : it was thought that if Jahweh was deprived of the
enemies which were his due as the result of a curse (ḥerem), he
would take in their stead some of his own people.[9] At the present
time the inhabitants of Syria and Palestine give the name fêdu

[1] Lev. iv, 20, 26, 35b ; v, 13 ; etc.
[2] Lev. xvi, 21 ; Numb. v, 7 (P³).
[3] Lev. v, 1–4, 21–6 ; Numb. v, 5–10.
[4] Numb. xvii, 9–15 (xvi, 46–50 E.V.).
[5] Lev. xvii, 11.   [6] For a sick person.
[7] Zimmern, *Keilinschriften und Bibel*, 27 ; **XLV**, 230.
[8] As in the Hebrew story of the sacrifice of Isaac (Gen. xxii).
[9] 1 Kings xx, 42 ; *cf.* Gen. xlii, 37 ; 1 Sam. xiv, 45 ; Is. xliii, 4 ;
liii, 4–6, 8.

" ransom " to the sacrifices which they offer to the *welis*, the saints, or to local spirits.[1]

But this interpretation does not take account in a natural way either of the totality of sacrificial rites—sacrifices which were eaten, for instance—nor of certain very important points in the ceremonial of the Levitical expiatory sacrifices themselves.

If the death of the victim was a substitute for that of the culprit, how was it that sacrifices were powerless to atone for mortal sin ?

If the victim was the sinner's ransom, it would seem as if a victim should have been slain for each culprit. But the sacrifices of atonement, even when offered for the whole nation, *never exceeded a single victim.*[2]

The idea of substitution was therefore certainly not the only one involved.

Another explanation of atonement by sacrifice is not expressly formulated in the Levitical ceremonial, but it is suggested. The act in the ritual which was evidently regarded as the culminating point of the sacred drama and invested with the greatest degree of sanctity was the sprinkling of the blood. As Benzinger has pointed out,[3] successive additions to priestly legislation attribute more and more importance to this act ; it was therefore a rite which was deliberately adopted, and not merely inherited by the priests of the fifth century. The blood of the victims, being a very holy thing, had the effect of conferring sanctity on the objects or beings touched by it, or of restoring holiness which had been forfeited ; in other words, it had the power of consecrating them or making atonement for them. If such was the guiding principle, it is easy to understand why sacrifices of atonement consisted of but one victim, and why the blood was all-important : for the sole object of the slaying was to provide the blood necessary to give strength to sacred things and persons, and specially to the temple which is defiled, and therefore deprived of virtue, by any uncleanness on the part of the people among which it is situated. The idea that blood could impart new vigour to beings and to things was extensively held : Ulysses had recourse to this method in order to revive the shades in Hades [4] ; the Dyaks use it to render their weapons more effective.[5]

There were other interpretations of the sacrifice of atonement in priestly circles besides the ideas of redemption and reconsecration : some of the writings of this school include it with the other sacrifices in the category of *qorban*,[6] or present. It was still sometimes considered, therefore, as a " present " capable if necessary of appeasing a wrathful God, a conception dating from pre-Exilic days. The ritual required, moreover, that the fat of the victim should be placed on the altar as well as the blood ; and the term " to offer " was used to describe this act.[7] The sacrifice for sin might, in quite

---

[1] *Cf.* **XI**, 256–8 ; **XLII**, 357–363 ; **XVIII**, 27 ; **LVIII**, 339.

[2] Lev. iii, 13–21.

[3] **I**, 1st edn., Freiburg, Mohr, 455.

[4] *Od.*, XI, 96–7 ; *cf.* **LVII**, 120 ; Duhm, *Rot und Tot*, **AR**, 1906, pp. 1–34.

[5] **AR**, 1913, p. 209 ; *cf.* Alfred Bertholet, *Zum Verständnis des alttest. Opfergedank.*, JBL, 49 (1930), pp. 223, 225.

[6] Numb. vii, 12, 16, 17 ; vii, 19, 22, 23, etc.   [7] Lev. vii, 3.

exceptional cases, it is true, consist of a *minḥâh*, properly speaking
" a present ", that is an oblation of cereals.[1]

On the other hand, priestly legislation sanctioned certain rites
of a very archaic, almost savage, nature, according to which the
evil—whether defilement, sickness, or sin—was transferred to an
animal, which was then hunted away or put to death.[2] According
to the dominant priestly idea, however, this could not explain
sacrifices of atonement, for the animal to which the sins
had been transferred was not sacrificed. Nevertheless, a late
text seems to indicate that certain legislators of a subsequent period
themselves interpreted sacrifices of atonement by analogy with
these rites of transference and expulsion. Moses asks the priests :
" Wherefore have ye not eaten the sin-offering in the place of the
sanctuary, seeing it is most holy, and Jahweh hath given it you
to bear the iniquity of the congregation, to make atonement for them
before the Lord ? " [3] If the priests can " bear the iniquity " by
devouring the victim of the *ḥaṭṭâ'th*, it would seem to be because the
sin is in the flesh.

On the other hand the rite which consisted in the culprit's laying
his hand on the head of the victim, thereby, it is thought, implying
that his sin was also laid on the animal's head, must not be quoted
as evidence of the antiquity of the above-mentioned interpretation
of the sacrifice of atonement, as has often been done. For this
act was required also in non-expiatory sacrifices, which suggests
that, originally at least, it had another meaning : it might express
the surrender (*manu missio*) of the animal to God, or it might be
held to establish communion between God and the offerer by the
mediation of the victim.

Let us add in conclusion that, although the priestly legislators
laid special emphasis on the expiatory value of sacrifice, they also
left room for many of the other conceptions current in ancient
Israel ; as we have seen, they often include all sacrificial slaughter
in the category of *qorban*, a gift. They allow special liturgies for
the thank-offering (*tôdâh*) and the votive offering (*neder*).

Elsewhere sacrifice is represented as the sacred meal, " the
bread of Jahweh," and the altar as his table.[4]

The idea of communion persists : they speak of the " salt of the
covenant " which is to accompany every offering.[5]

To sum up : the work of the priestly writers affords a large
number of tentative explanations, more or less contradictory, but
no proof that they ever made any serious attempt to construct a
coherent doctrine of sacrifice from these beginnings.

IV

NEHEMIAH AND EZRA

As we have seen,[6] the ritualist and separatist tendency,
which was apparently prevalent among the Jews of Babylonia,

---

[1] Lev. v, 11–13.   [2] Lev. xiv, 4–7, 49–53 ; xvi, 21–3.
[3] Lev. x, 17.
[4] Lev. iii, 11 ; xxi, 6 ; Numb. xxviii, 2 ; *cf.* Mal. i, 7, 12.
[5] Lev. ii, 13.   [6] pp. 268–280.

had also its representatives in Palestine, particularly among
the repatriated exiles. But they must have been only a
minority. The mass of the Jewish population, especially in
the northern provinces, remained attached to the ancient
customs of traditional Jahwism, with its greater freedom
and its tolerance of syncretism : it felt no need of reform,
and had no fanatical dislike of strangers. About the middle
of the fifth century, the leaders of this latitudinarian party
were Sanballat, of Horonaim in the land of Moab, a
certain Tobias, whom Nehemiah calls an Ammonite slave,
and a man with the Arab name of Gashmu, all doubtless
worshippers of Jahweh,[1] but having foreign connections.

Among the stricter minority, there were also many who
were discontented and discouraged. The leaders at Jerusalem,
and in particular the priests, were lukewarm, their chief
object being to maintain an understanding between the
two parties, such an understanding seeming to them no
doubt indispensable to the welfare of the " nation " ; many
of them had intermarried with the influential families of the
country.

This stricter minority might in the end have been obliged
to give in, if it had not been strongly reinforced by
Jewish settlers from Babylonia, who in their turn were
supported by the Persian government.

We have a good deal of detailed information about the
decisive events of this particular time, drawn from two
documents which seem trustworthy, the autobiographies of
the chief actors in the drama, Ezra and Nehemiah. Unfortunately the order of events is somewhat uncertain. One
cannot in fact be sure that the editor of the books of Ezra
and Nehemiah as they now stand arranged the extracts,
which he made from his sources, in the right order. As we
have seen from another example,[2] he was capable of making
grave mistakes with regard to the chronology of the period
of the restoration.

Here is the sequence of events as given by him : (1)
Ezra arrives in Jerusalem in the seventh year of the reign

---

[1] e.g. the names of Tobiah and the sons of Sanballat, Delaiah and
Shelemiah.
[2] pp. 188–9.

of Artaxerxes (let us say in 458, if Artaxerxes the First is meant, as the present context would suggest), he demands that mixed marriages should be annulled (Ezr. vii–x) ; (2) Nehemiah rebuilds the walls of Jerusalem in the twentieth year of the reign of Artaxerxes, i.e. 445 (Neh. i–vii) ; (3) Ezra proclaims the Law (Neh. viii) ; (4) the leaders of the people bind themselves in writing to observe various ordinances (Neh. x) ; (5) Nehemiah and Ezra dedicate the walls (Neh. xii, 27–43) ; (6) in the thirty-second year of the reign of Artaxerxes (432), Nehemiah makes a second sojourn in Jerusalem (Neh. 13).

The above order presents serious difficulties. Why does Nehemiah, in his account of his arrival in Judæa in 445, make no allusion to Ezra, who must have held a position in the forefront of the community ? Why do neither Ezra nor any of the Jews who had returned with him from Babylonia figure in the list of men working at the rebuilding of the walls, whereas after this Ezra plays the chief part in the promulgation of the Law ? Why does Nehemiah not insist that the Jews who have married Gentile women in the interval before his second return to the country should fulfil the obligation laid by Ezra upon all the members of the community, to put away their non-Jewish wives (Ezr. x), and why does he content himself with making them promise not to allow mixed marriages among *their sons and their daughters* (Neh. xiii, 23–7) ?

Maurice Vernes, and more recently Gustav Hölscher,[1] followed by Alfred Loisy,[2] have found a way out of the difficulty which is both simple and thoroughgoing : they reject everything that is said about Ezra. Hölscher, returning to Torrey's view, holds that the so-called memoirs of Ezra are the work of the editor of the Chronicles himself.[3] According to him, the priestly scribe himself is in reality a doublet of Nehemiah, adapted to a different epoch : the redactor wished to attribute to priestly initiative the great work in which a layman had taken the most active part. And so Ezra's labours are " a legendary echo of the reform of Judaism which had been carried out since the second half of the fifth century ".[4] The passage in which the Son

[1] **XXXIV**, 491–502 ; **XXXV**, 140–1.   [2] **LIX**, 228.
[3] **XXXV**, 141.   [4] **XXXV**, 140.

of Sirach, reviewing the glories of Israel, mentions Nehemiah but omits Ezra, may be quoted in support of this view.

We cannot ourselves agree with it, for Ezra's auto-biography contains a number of statements so concrete, sober, precise and probable that it is impossible to regard them as pure fiction. There are, for instance, the unflattering details about the attitude of certain Levites and singers, which the editor of the Chronicles, himself a Levite singer and always eager to praise the guild to which he belonged, would certainly not have invented. Their reluctance to return to the Holy Land is noted,[1] as well as the marriages which many of them contracted with non-Jews.[2] As to the omission made by the Son of Sirach, it is possible that a lack of sympathy between a writer of Sadducean tendencies and one of Ezra's strict views [3] may account for it, as also the fact that the great work which was chiefly responsible for the scribe's reputation (Chronicles–Ezra–Nehemiah) was probably non-existent in his day.[4]

Most of the difficulties can be solved by assuming that the editor of the books of Ezra and Nehemiah has once more mistaken the chronology of events, and that Ezra's activities took place in reality after Nehemiah's work was ended, and not partly before and partly at the same time. This solution is borne out by several passages : a short time after his arrival in Palestine, Ezra thanks God not only for having allowed the Temple to be rebuilt, but also for having " given " the Jews " *a wall* in Judah and in Jerusalem ".[5] On the other hand, Nehemiah lived in the days of the high priest Eliashib,[6] while Ezra was a contemporary of one " Jehohanan, the son of Eliashib ",[7] who can scarcely be other than the person of this name, a grandson of Eliashib,[8] who was high priest in 408 in the time of Darius II.[9] It is true that some passages give the impression that Ezra and Nehemiah collaborated ; but either the text is doubtful,[10] or else

---

[1] Ezr. viii, 15–20.

[2] Ezr. x, 23–4.

[3] *Cf.* **LXVIII**, ii, 139 ; **CCXLI.**

[4] See pp. 6–7.

[5] Ezr. ix, 9.

[6] Neh. iii, 1.

[7] Ezr. x, 6.

[8] Neh. xii, 11, 22.

[9] Elephantine Papyri 1 and 2.

[10] Neh. viii, 9 : in the Greek Esdras, the name of Nehemiah is not mentioned.

they are clearly written by the " chronicler ", who thought
the two men were contemporaries.[1] It has also been objected [2]
that two of the men who helped Nehemiah to rebuild the
ramparts also figure in Ezra's memoirs.[3] But there is no
reason why Nehemiah's contemporaries should all have been
dead seventeen or forty-seven years later.

Here is a possible explanation of what took place. In the
reign of Artaxerxes the First, the orthodox Jews of Judæa,
seeking a rupture with " the people of the land ", undertook the rebuilding of the walls of their capital, which had
been destroyed by the Chaldeans in 586. It was indeed
the first precaution which must be taken, if the colony at
Jerusalem wished to live in isolation. The plan had already
reached a fairly advanced stage of completion when it was
denounced to the king by the local authorities [4] as an act
of rebellion. Artaxerxes ordered that the work should be
suspended until his express permission to resume it was
received. The Palestinian officials, making the most of the
opportunity of showing their zeal, apparently wrecked the
workshops [5] : the doors were burnt and part of the walls
broken down.

The news of this humiliation spread consternation among
the Jews of Babylonia. One of them, Nehemiah, who occupied
a high position at court—he was the king's cup-bearer and
probably one of the eunuchs of his harem [6]—took advantage
of the favour he enjoyed, and obtained permission from the
changeable sovereign to go and rebuild the walls of the city
of his fathers. He arrived in Jerusalem in 445 with the title of
satrap of Judah. In spite of the intrigues of the opposition,
and the ill-will of the influential families of the capital itself,
he energetically resumed the work which had been interrupted, and finished it in fifty-two days.[7] The rapidity with
which the work was done [8] is explained if, as we have supposed,

---

[1] Neh. xii, 26, 36.
[2] **XXXV**, 141.
[3] Meremoth (Ezr. viii, 33, and Neh. iii, 4, 21) and Malchijah
(Ezr. x, 31, and Neh. iii, 11).
[4] Rehum was probably a lieutenant-governor residing in Samaria.
[5] Ezr. iv, 8–23.
[6] Cf. **XXXV**, 138, note 1 ; **LIX**, 225.   [7] Neh. vi, 15.
[8] Josephus, whose chronology is very different, extends it to two
years and four months (*A.J.*, XI, v, 8, § 179).

it was only a matter of putting the final touches to a work of reconstruction which was already far advanced, and not, as is usually supposed, of undertaking from the beginning the rebuilding of the ramparts demolished by the Chaldeans.

The dedication of the walls was marked by a solemn ceremony.[1] But as they had been rebuilt on the site which they had previously occupied, the space enclosed was now too vast for a city as sparsely populated as Jerusalem was at the time. Nehemiah therefore gave orders that all the leaders were to make their abode in the capital, and that the rest of the population was to send one-tenth of its members, such members to be chosen by lot if volunteers were lacking.[2]

Actuated entirely by strictly orthodox ideas, like most of his co-religionists in Babylonia, Nehemiah made use of his official authority to wage war against irregularity in the payment of tithe, neglect of the Sabbath, and mixed marriages.[3] He seems, however, to have relied chiefly on persuasion, for at the time when his campaign was launched it does not seem as if he had any officially recognized code which would have enabled him to punish defaulters, as the present sequence of chapters would now seem to indicate.

Nehemiah's contribution to the organization of a Jewish church was still more considerable, if it was he who was responsible for two important measures described in the book which bears his name : the decision to exclude from the community all who were not of Jewish race,[4] and the requirement in writing of a formal promise to observe a certain number of rules, this promise to be made by representatives of the community, both priests and laymen.[5] Some of these rules were aimed at precisely those abuses which Nehemiah had attacked [6]—and it is easy to understand that he should

---

[1] Neh. xii, 27–42 (narrative much amplified by the Chronicler).
[2] Neh. vii, 4–5 ; xi, 1–2.   [3] Neh. xiii, 4–31.
[4] Neh. xiii, 1–2.
[5] Neh. x. It is generally held that this promise was exacted by Ezra, either before or after the reading of the law, as described in ch. viii. With Bertholet (**CXCV**) we should be inclined to attribute the initiative to Nehemiah. Verses 29–30 (E.V. 28–9) mention a general promise, made in advance, that *the whole law* would be observed ; but these sentences were no doubt added by the compiler, who thought that the scene in ch. x was a sequel to that in ch. viii : in these verses the contracting parties are spoken of in the third person, while in the rest of the story they themselves use the first person.
[6] Neh. x, 31–2 (E.V. 30–1).

have desired the support of laws expressly designed to compass the removal of such abuses—others to ensure a regular supply of the funds necessary for the maintenance of the cult.   Several of the financial measures undertaken in this way by the community at Jerusalem were the same which had been advocated by the priestly legislators in Babylonia : the payment of a third of a shekel to defray the expenses of the sacrifices, in particular the sin offering,[1] and the tithe of the tithe paid by the Levites to the priests.[2] We are told that Nehemiah signed the first of these.[3] This seems a typical example of the way in which certain laws of a ritual nature were gradually introduced among the community at Jerusalem, even before the main body of the Priestly Code was accepted in its entirety, as the law of Moses.

It was, in our opinion, after Nehemiah's term of office, that there arrived in Jerusalem a band of Babylonian Jews, including many priests and some Levites, under the leadership of the priestly scribe Ezra. As was the custom, they brought generous contributions towards the Temple funds. According to the book of Ezra, this event took place in the seventh year of the reign of Artaxerxes ; the compiler evidently thought that the reference was to the seventh year of the reign of the sovereign who is also mentioned in the memoirs of Nehemiah, Artaxerxes the First, which would make the date 458. But it seems probable to us, for reasons already stated, that he made an error in chronology, and that he may have mistaken either the identity of the king—for it is possible that Artaxerxes II was meant, in which case Ezra's journey would have taken place in 398—if this is the correct date ; according to some critics, the correct reading would be " thirty-seventh year " and not " seventh year ", in which case the event would have taken place in 428. Like Nehemiah, Ezra was supported by the Persian government ; but it is characteristic of the mentality of the two men that the idealistic scribe, counting on " the good hand of his God " to protect him,[4]

---

[1] Neh. x, 34 (E.V. 33).

[2] Neh. x, 39 (E.V. 38). This may, however, have been added afterwards ; cf. **XXXIV**, ad loc.

[3] Neh. x, 2 (E.V. 1). The list of signatories (x, 2–26) may, however, have been added by the editor, since it is written in the third person ; cf. **XXXIV**.

[4] Ezr. viii, 22–3.

had deliberately abstained from requesting the escort of horse-men which the realistic and practical layman had accepted.[1]

Ezra was entrusted with a definite mission, the terms of which were set forth in a royal warrant. The version of this, which we now have, has been considerably amplified,[2] but it seems possible to deduce from it what the original was like :—

> Ezra, " a ready scribe in the law of Moses," was sent by the king, " to inquire concerning Judah and Jerusalem, after this law that was in his hand, to teach those that knew it not." [3]

The scribe first attacked the abuse which Nehemiah had also combated, that of marriages between Jews and foreigners. But his methods were much more radical than those of the satrap, for not only did he demand that unions of this kind should be forbidden *in future*—he insisted that those already existent should be annulled. He obtained from an assembly of the people approval of the principle of this severe measure, but it is not certain that he succeeded in applying it *in toto*, for the end of the story is missing. All that we know is that a commission was appointed to see that the measure voted by the assembly was carried out, but commissions are not always successful.[4]

Later on, Ezra won a victory which was still more decisive and more lasting. At a date which is unfortunately unknown to us—we only know that it was the first day of the seventh month—a general assembly of the nation was held at the Water Gate ; and Ezra read aloud from a platform the " Book of the Law ", the same book, apparently, which he had brought with him to Jerusalem. Tears were shed, and everyone was profoundly moved. Two weeks later, the Feast of Tabernacles was celebrated in conformity with the law. Nothing like it had been done since the days of Joshua.[5]

The extraordinary excitement aroused by this reading of the law would be incomprehensible if, as Hölscher thinks,[6] it took place at an ordinary service of the synagogue. The emotion can only be explained if the law which Ezra read

---

[1] Neh. ii, 9.   [2] Ezr. vii, 12–26.
[3] Ezr. vii, 6, 14, 25.   [4] Ezr. ix–x.
[5] Neh. viii.
[6] **XXXV**, 141 ; **XXXIV**, *ad loc. Cf.* **LXVIII**, ii, 137.

was—at least the greater part of it—unknown to the people, as Deuteronomy had been in 622. Moreover, the details of the ceremonial of the Feast of Tabernacles[1]—which ceremonial, we are told, had not been used since the days of Joshua—are in keeping with the requirements of the Holiness Code,[2] and the period mentioned for the duration of the Feast agrees with that prescribed in the priestly narrative.[3]

Everything therefore seems to indicate that this is an account of the official proclamation, in Jerusalem, of a group of priestly laws brought from Babylonia, probably the whole of the collection which we call the " Priestly Code ".

It is hardly necessary to call attention to the importance of the events which we have briefly summarized : the formation of a community of purely Jewish race, segregated by the erection of walls from all who did not wish to make a complete break with the religious mistakes of the past, and the adoption of the priestly code of laws as the official standard of Judaism.

V

THE JEWISH COLONY AT ELEPHANTINE

The chance exhumation of a number of papyri in an island of the Nile has made it possible for us to follow to some extent the way in which a small Jewish group belonging to the Egyptian diaspora reacted to the decisive changes which were taking place in Jerusalem.[4]

These documents, many of them dated during the reigns of Xerxes, Artaxerxes (the First), and Darius (the Second), belonged to a military colony settled in Elephantine, a frontier post which had become of great importance since

---

[1] Neh. viii, 13–18.   [2] Lev. xxiii, 39–43.

[3] Lev. xxiii, 36.

[4] These papyri, of which the first were known in 1901, were published in 1903 (Euting, *Notice sur un papyrus égypto-araméen de la bibliothèque impériale de Strasbourg*, **MAI**, 1ᵉ s., xi, 2, Paris, 1904), 1906 (**CCXL**), 1907 (**CCXXXVII** and **CCXLVI**), 1909 (**CCXXXVIII**), and 1911 (**CXXXIX**). They have been studied by Israel Lévy (**REJ**, 1907), Ad. Lods (**CCXX**), Ed. Meyer (**CCXXVIII**), A. van Hoonacker (*Une communauté judéo-araméenne à Éléphantine*, The Schweich Lectures, 1914), A. Causse (**VIII**, 78–95), Rud. Kittel (**XLIX**, iii, 2, 501–6), Oesterley (**LXVIII**, ii, 159–163), etc.

PLATE VII

1. A Papyrus from Elephantine rolled up and sealed (after RICCIOTTI, *Storia d'Israele*, II, p. 186)

2. Papyrus from Elephantine : abstract of the letter from the satrap Bagohi (from SACHAU, **CCXXXVII,** Berlin, Reimer, 1908)

Egypt and Ethiopia had ceased to be united under one king
(about 645). It was probably the Pharaohs of the national
Saite dynasty, the twenty-sixth (645–525), who garrisoned
it with Jewish troops [1] ; in any case it was one of them who
allowed the Jews to build a temple to their God. " In the
days of the kings of Egypt " (and therefore before the Persian
conquest and after the Assyrian domination) " our fathers had
built a temple to Jahu." [2]   The letter of Aristeas mentions
a Jewish immigration under Psammetichus.[3] In 590, in his
expedition against Ethiopia, Psammetichus II had Semitic
mercenaries.[4]

It has often been thought that these soldiers must have
been Israelites from the north,[5] because of their Aramaic
speech, the extremely heterodox nature of their worship
of Jahweh, the names of the deities which they associated
with the God of Israel, and the term Bethel which forms
part of many of these names. Oesterley [6] thought himself
justified in stating that they were troops recruited by
Asshurbanipal from the " ten tribes " deported into Mesopotamia and Media, with a view to his campaign against Egypt,
these troops having remained on the banks of the Nile.
According to S. Spinner, they were mercenaries levied from
among the Israelites who had been exiled in the Taurus.[7]
These theories are discounted by the fact that the garrison
at Elephantine was called the " Jewish army " (the Judæan
army), because it was formed, the greater part, at least, of
men from Judah. Moreover, when they required assistance
from their co-religionists in Palestine, it was to Jerusalem
that they first turned, as we shall see, and only when all else
failed did they have recourse to the authorities in Samaria.

The original language of these settlers had certainly been
Hebrew, for genuinely Hebraic proper names continued to
predominate among them, even at the end of the fifth century,
But they had adopted Aramaic, a kind of international

---

[1] The Second Isaiah (546–538) seems to have known of the existence
of a Jewish colony at Syene (Is. xlix, 12, original text ; cf. p. 240, n. 6).

[2] Pap. 1, l. 13 ; 2, l. 11.   [3] § 13.

[4] See above p. 42.   [5] e.g. Van Hoonacker.

[6] **LVXIII**, ii, 162. Cf. Oesterley and Robinson, Introduction
(1934), 59.

[7] **LXXX**, 197. The new arguments adduced by this author are
usually extremely precarious.

dialect in use throughout the Levant, as early as the eighth century,[1] either because it had already invaded Palestine, the south[2] as well as the north, before they had left the country, or because soldiers in Persian services were obliged to speak and understand Aramaic, as the official language of administration and of the army in all the western half of the empire.[3]

The Jewish population of Elephantine was divided into " standards ". These " standards " each bore the name of a person who was probably the first organizer rather than the commanding officer of the regiment at the time ; for one of these names appears for sixty consecutive years.[4] To judge from their names, these organizers, like the other superior officers mentioned in the documents, must all have been Persians or Babylonians.

The men of the " Jewish army " owned houses and lands ; unlike the military colonists of the Ptolemaic period, who only had a life-interest in their plots of ground and were not allowed to bequeath them—in theory at least[5] ; they were at liberty to leave their land to their sons[6] *and to their daughters*,[7] even to more distant relations,[8] and they could sell them or give them away.[9] That being so, one wonders if the military character of the group was not more or less discarded in the course of time. If the descendants of the first settlers had remained soldiers, like the " epigones " of the time of the Ptolemies,[10] how is it that in the papyri and ostraca there is no allusion to details of the military profession, that the Jews of Elephantine apparently maintained a passive attitude when their temple was sacked, and that in their petitions to the Persian authorities they never made use of the argument that they had rendered the empire any services of a military nature ?

The Jews of Elephantine worshipped Jahu (Jahweh). But their Jahwism was very different from the Jahwism whose

---

[1] 2 Kings xviii, 26.   [2] *Cf.* Neh. xiii, 24.
[3] Concerning the question, of which little is yet known, of the progress of the diffusion of Aramean, *cf.* **XLIX**, iii, 2, pp. 519–531.
[4] *Cf.* Isr. Lévi, **REJ**, 1907, pp. 43–4.
[5] **CCXI**, 382–3, 385.
[6] Assouan Pap. (ed. Staerk), A, 9 ; C, 6 ; E, 7 ; J, 16.
[7] D, 2–3, 8–9.   [8] B, 12–13.
[9] E, 4–6, J, 10–11.   [10] **CCXI**, 382.

ascendancy Nehemiah and Ezra were striving to establish
at about the same time in Jerusalem. They had built themselves a temple, which had its priests, its burnt-offerings,[1]
oblations, peace-offerings,[2] and incense,[3] for which tithe
was paid, and which was therefore one of those " high-
places " of which Deuteronomist orthodoxy disapproved.

With regard to " other gods ", their latitude would have
scandalized a disciple of the prophets. One of the documents
discovered was sealed in the name of Amon Rā.[4] A Jewess,
on oath in the lawcourts, did not refuse to swear by the
Egyptian goddess Seti.[5] One of her co-religionists swore
by the Mesged [6] and by Anat-Jahu, the Canaanite goddess
Anat, associated with Jahweh.[7]

Mixed marriages—the abomination denounced by
Nehemiah and Ezra—were allowed. There is the marriage
contract between a Jewess named Mibtaḥiah (confidence in
Jahweh) and her second husband, an Egyptian called Ashor.[8]
As must also have been the case in Palestine on occasion
—we can see it in the story of Ruth—this union constituted
a gain to Judaism, for in subsequent documents Ashor
figures under the Jewish name of Nathan, and it is evident
that he gave to his sons names compounded with the name of
Jahweh [9]; he had apparently been converted to his wife's
religion.

But there is a still more significant feature. One of the
papyri contains a list of which the heading reads :—

" These are the names of (the members of) the Jewish army who
gave money for the God Jahu, two shekels of silver each."

Now at the end of the document we are informed that
the sums collected were divided between Jahu and two
other deities, Asam-Bethel and Anat-Bethel, the latter being
given almost as much as Jahu.[10] It is clear that these two
deities were closely associated with Jahu, and that consequently Anat-Bethel must be another name for the goddess
elsewhere known as Anat-Jahu. There were, therefore,

[1] Pap. 1, ll. 21, 25, 28 (**CCXXXIX**).
[2] Pap. 1, l. 28.   [3] Pap. 1, l. 28 ; 3, l. 9.
[4] *Cf.* Pl. vii, 1.   [5] F 5.
[6] i.e. " the place of worship ". This is the word from which
" mosque " is derived.
[7] Pap. 32, l. 3.   [8] Pap. G.
[9] H 3 ; J 3 ; K 2.   [10] Pap. 18, col. 7, l. 6.

consorts of Jahweh at Elephantine, one of them at least
being feminine.

The peculiarities of the Judaism of the colonists at
Elephantine cannot be explained as the effect of the surroundings in which they lived. The deities associated with
Jahu are not Egyptian but Palestinian : that is certainly
true of Anat,[1] and probably true of Ašam.[2] Bethel, the real
meaning of which was " holy stone "—as a " house of
God "—had become a divine appellation, even the name
of a particular god, in Semitic lands. Like their ancestors,
the Jews of Elephantine identified it more or less with
Jahweh.[3] They also used the word Ḥaram (sacred enclosure),
as a kind of synonym for " god ", as is seen from the name
Ḥaram-Nathan, " the sacred enclosure has given ".[4]   One
Jew swears by Haram-Bethel, " the enclosure of the sacred
stone ",[5] another, as we have seen, by the Mesged, " the
place of worship."

The Jewish settlers at Elephantine, who must all have
belonged to the working class, to judge by what may have been
their original trade, evidently remained, right on into the fifth
century, at the same religious level as had been reached by the
mass of the people in Palestine at the time when they had left
their country. It is this fact which makes them exceptionally
interesting.   There are, moreover, many indications of the
survival of this syncretistic Jahwism in Judah among the
lower strata of the population, and it is evident that the
movement which had triumphed under Manasseh and Amon,
had persisted, in spite of the official reaction marked by
Josiah's reforms, throughout the reigns of Jehoiakim and
Zedekiah and at the period of the Exile, among the women
who worshipped the Queen of Heaven and Tammuz.[6]   It
was still predominant among the Palestinian peasants of
the fifth century, who combined the worship of Jahweh
with homage paid to Gad and to Meni.[7]

Two interesting episodes of the internal history of the
Jewish community at Elephantine were revealed by the
papyri.

[1] Cf. LVII, 153–6, 161–2. 469.   [2] LVII, 469, 586.
[3] LVII, 142.   [4] Pap. 34, 1. 4.
[5] Pap. 27.   Cf. CCXXVIII, 63–4.
[6] Jer. vii, 18 ; xliv, 15–25 ; Ez. viii, 14 ; cf. pp. 128–9, 167.
[7] Is. lxv, 11 ; cf. p. 274.

In 419–418 the priest of the temple of Jahu, Jedoniah by name, received from a certain Hananiah a letter informing him that an order—evidently from the government—had reached Arsham, the satrap of Egypt, as to the way in which the Jews were to celebrate the Feast of Unleavened Bread.[1]

The care shown by the Persian authorities in issuing detailed regulations as to the religious practices of their subjects is quite in accordance with the policy of the Achaemenides. Darius the First commissioned an Egyptian doctor named Uzahor

"To go into Egypt . . . and restore the number of sacred scribes in the temples, and rebuild that which had fallen into ruin " so as to " preserve the names of all gods, their temples, their revenues, and the order of their feasts in perpetuity."[2]

The Elephantine papyri confirm what we are told in the book of Ezra about the full powers granted to this scribe by Artaxerxes to make the law of Jahweh known and observed by all the Jews of Transeuphrates.

Here, as in Ezra's case, it seems that the official circular had been drawn up at the instigation of the orthodox Jews of Babylonia or Palestine. As far as it is possible to judge, in spite of the gaps in the text, it seems that the chief aim of the decree was to fix the days on which the Feast was to take place (from the 15th to the 21st Nisan). Now it is precisely with regard to this point that the priestly laws about the Feast of Unleavened Bread differ from previous texts : they require that the ceremony shall be celebrated *at a fixed date*—from the 15th to the 21st Nisan, instead of at a time reckoned from the day on which the sickle was first put to the harvest,[3] which day varied according to the year and the locality.

It is therefore possible that the Hananiah whose business it was to see that the royal decree was carried out, was either Nehemiah's brother,[4] or in his confidence.[5] In any case, his views can hardly have been more sympathetic towards the Jews of Elephantine, for we learn from another document that they suspected both him and his followers

---

[1] Pap. 6.
[2] Brugsch, *Gesch. Aegyptens*, 1877, pp. 748–751 ; **CXCV**, 26–7.
[3] Deut. xvi, 9.   [4] Hanani (Neh. i, 2).
[5] Hananiah, governor of Jerusalem (Neh. vii, 2). According to some commentators, these were one and the same person.

of intriguing against them with the Egyptian priest of their town.[1]

Unfortunately, the text does not enable us to decide whether the decree of Darius was intended to ensure the observance of the Priestly Code, which would then have been promulgated before 419, or whether it was a measure calculated to prepare the way for Ezra's reforms, whose date would in that case be later than 419.

The second episode was much more serious. The priests of Chnum, the ram-god who was the patron of Elephantine, looked with great disfavour on the blood-sacrifices, in particular the sacrifices of rams, with which the Jews sought to honour

FIG. 5.—Chnum, the ram-god of Elephantine (after Ricciotti, *Storia d'Israele*, ii, p. 198, S.E.I., Turin).

Jahweh in their temple. Such a practice was to them equivalent to deicide. In 410, taking advantage of the absence of Arsham, the satrap of Egypt, they bribed one of the Persian magistrates of the town, Widarnag (Hydarnes), to give orders that the Jewish temple should be sacked by the troops from Syene, the neighbouring city.

There is reason to suppose that these disturbances were not devoid of political motives. The Jews formally accused the Egyptians of revolt.[2] According to Diodorus of Sicily,[3] the country was governed, precisely in 410, by a national king, who was evidently in rebellion against the Persians; moreover, one of the Elephantine papyri is dated the fifth

[1] Pap. 11.   [2] Pap. Euting, l. 1.   [3] **XIII**, xlvi, 6.

year of the native Pharaoh Amyrtæus,[1] the year which
Wiedemann, long before the discovery of the papyri, had
calculated exactly as 410–409. That would explain the
severity of the punishment inflicted by the Persians, the least
of which was to dismiss Widarnag and put to death those
responsible for the disturbance. They did not, however,
allow the Jews to rebuild their temple, a fact which seems
to indicate that the desire to repair the damage done to the
worshippers of Jahu was neither the sole, nor even the principal, motive for the energetic intervention of the authorities.

In the hope of obtaining an authorization to rebuild
their temple, the Jews of Elephantine applied to their brethren
in Jerusalem. They wrote letters to Bagôhi (Bagoas)—a
Persian, to judge by his name—then satrap of Judæa, to
the high priest and his colleagues, and finally to the nobles,
that is to say, the lay " elders ", of whom the chief was a
certain Ostan. They received no reply. Reformist tendencies
were evidently uppermost in the councils at Jerusalem at
the time : to Jews, animated by the spirit of Nehemiah and
Ezra, the destruction of the schismatic temple of Upper
Egypt could only seem like chastisement well-deserved and
heaven-sent.

Three years later, in 407, the colonists at Elephantine
reiterated their request. They again wrote to Bagôhi—the
rough copy of this letter has been preserved in duplicate [2]
—and at the same time applied, not to the priests and elders
of Jerusalem, but to Delaiah and Shelemiah, the sons of
Sanballat, to whom they give the title of satrap of Samaria.
Sanballat had been Nehemiah's bitterest opponent, and the
most prominent supporter of the old syncretistic Jahwism in
Palestine ; he and those nearest him were, therefore, in
complete sympathy with the views of the petitioners. Their
appeal was well received both in Samaria and by Bagôhi,
whether because the latter had in the meantime quarrelled
with the high priest Johanan,[3] or whether the gold [4] which
accompanied the request was convincing proof that it was
just and reasonable. Delaiah and Bagôhi made a joint
appeal to Arsham. They did not dare, however, to ask that

---

[1] **CCXXXVIII.**   [2] Pap. 1 (see pl. vii, 2) and 2.
[3] Jos., *A.J.*, XI, vi, 1, §§ 297–301 ; *cf.* p. 198 above.
[4] Pap. 1, ll. 28–9.

the *status quo* should be in every respect restored ; all that they petitioned, on behalf of the Jews of Elephantine, was that they should be permitted once more to offer oblations (cereal) and incense to their God.[1] What it amounted to seems to have been that Arsham should authorize the petitioners to rebuild their temple but forbid them to sacrifice those animals which the inhabitants of the country regarded as divine.

We still have the remains of a letter which five notables of Elephantine sent to Arsham to protest ; they offer a sum of money if their request for the *total* restoration of their temple and their worship [2] is conceded.

We do not know whether they were successful and the authorization was granted.   But, if so, they did not enjoy the fruits of it for long.   For three years later, in 404, a general insurrection delivered Egypt from Persian rule for the space of about sixty years.   This explosion of national feeling must have brought about the destruction of the temple of the foreign god, even if it had been rebuilt.   A fragment of papyrus may perhaps have preserved for us an echo of a catastrophe which befell the Jewish colony : it tells of women put in prison, men found at the gate and put to death, and the first on the list is Jedoniah, the chief priest of Jahu at Elephantine.[3]

It is evident that these curious documents shed an interesting light on the conditions of life and thought among the members of the Dispersion in the fifth century, on the policy of the Persian government, and indirectly on the state of the parties in Jerusalem ; they make it possible to fix the date of the government of Nehemiah, and show that the community at Jerusalem dominated the other Jewish settlements of the empire to an extent which was no doubt recognized, either tacitly or openly, by the ruling power.

VI

The Completion of the Pentateuch. The Samaritan Schism

After the reforms of Nehemiah and Ezra, various steps were taken to consolidate or extend their work.   Several

---

[1] Pap. 3.   [2] Pap. 5.   [3] Pap. 15.

of the laws sanctioning these developments also found a place
in the final charter of the Jewish community, in addition
to those which Ezra had enforced. e.g., the law we have
which fixed the contribution due for the expenses of the cult
at half a shekel, whereas in Nehemiah's day the inhabitants
of Jerusalem had only undertaken to pay a third of a shekel.[1]
Another added the tithe of the cattle to that of the products
of the soil, which was the only one known to the contemporaries of the cup-bearer satrap.[2] The daily sacrifice
was increased from one burnt-offering in the morning and
one oblation of cereals in the afternoon—which had been
customary before the Exile and was still usual in the time
of Nehemiah and Ezra [3]—to two burnt-offerings a day, one
in the morning, and the other in the evening.[4] Possibly in
imitation of a practice observed in Iranian temples,[5] the fire
on the altar was always to be kept burning.[6]

But the most important of the new laws was that which
prescribed a definite ritual for use on the Day of Atonement,[7]
celebrated on the tenth day of the seventh month. This law
was non-existent in the time of Ezra, for when, on the first
of this same month, the torah was solemnly read, the Feast
of the New Year was celebrated, in accordance with the
regulations laid down in the code, on the first day, and that
of Tabernacles on the fifteenth, but there is no mention whatever of a feast to be observed on the tenth.[8] The Day of
Atonement must, therefore, either not have been instituted
as yet, or else it had not yet been given a definite date :
and the second of these two alternatives is more likely to
be correct, chiefly because the law seems to be composed of
the fusion of three successive editions,[9] and it is only in

[1] Ex. xxx, 11–16 ; cf. Neh. x, 33–4 (E.V. 32–3). In the second of
these two passages, however, it may be a question of a third of a
Persian shekel, equivalent to half a Jewish shekel.
[2] Lev. xxvii, 32 ; cf. Neh. x, 38 (E.V. 37).
[3] 2 Kings xvi, 15 ; Ez. xlvi, 13–15 ; Neh. x, 34 (E.V. 32) ; Ezr.
ix, 4–5.
[4] Ex. xxix, 38–42 ; Numb. xxviii, 3–8 ; cf. Lev. vi, 2, 5 (E.V.
9, 12).
[5] Cf. **XXXV**, 145–6.
[6] Lev. vi, 5 (12) ; on the other hand, see Numb. iv, 13.
[7] Lev. xvi.
[8] It is quite improbable that the editor omitted it intentionally,
because " he wished to end his work on a note of joy " (**XXXV**, 146).
[9] Lev. xvi, 5–10, 11–28 and 29–34a. See notes in **V.**

the most recent that mention of the above date is to be found.

In any case, the fixing of the date fulfilled a need which the ritualistic school had long felt : the torah of Ezekiel ordained that two such ceremonies were to be observed, on the first day of the first month and on the first day of the seventh.[1] This was the logical outcome of sacerdotal tenets. Worshippers were not always conscious of sins which they had committed involuntarily, and consequently the idea of atonement did not occur to them. But sins, if not expiated, defiled the temple ; they might even rob the cult of its entire efficacy, and be the cause of Jahweh's leaving the Temple once more. Ceremonies were therefore required which should periodically cleanse both temple and people of all defilement. Hence we understand why the Day of Atonement quickly became the chief solemnity in the Jewish year : in the time of the Mishna it came to be called " the day " *par excellence—yômâ.*

The ceremonial included a fast, as a sign of contrition, the only fast prescribed in the Law. Two he-goats were to be brought to the high priest ; one was assigned by lot to Jahweh and one to Azazel. The former was to be " sacrificed for sin " on the nation's behalf, after the high priest had offered up a bull for himself and his house (the priests). With the blood of the bull and the goat he was to sprinkle the mercy-seat, the holy place, and the altar. Then he was to lay both hands on the head of the goat which belonged to Azazel, and confess over it all the sins of the children of Israel :

> " He shall put them upon the head of the goat . . . and the goat shall bear upon him all their iniquities unto a solitary land ; and he shall let go the goat in the wilderness." [2]

It is clear that the actions of which the above ritual is composed form two groups of ceremonies having the same object and, therefore, strictly speaking, each made to serve two ends, but profoundly different in character : one of these is a ceremony of atonement of the ordinary Levitical type—supplemented by a few extra details—and the other

---

[1] Ez. xlv, 18–20.   [2] Lev. xvi, 21-2.

is an apotropaic rite of transference of a picturesque and popular kind, such as are to be found in great numbers among so-called primitive peoples.

Opinions are divided as to the precise meaning and origin of the second of these two. It is generally recognized, and rightly so, that the mysterious Azazel, whose name Jerome translated as *caper emissarius*, " scape-goat," because he thought it was made up of *'êz*, " goat," and *'âzal*, " to go away," was in reality a person, since the word is used as a pendant to Jahweh—no doubt some demon of the wilderness. But was the ceremony itself invented by the priests of the time of the restoration, or derived from the Babylonians, who certainly had very similar rites,[1] or was it an ancient popular practice among the Israelites ? And in the latter alternative, was it perhaps a survival of some ancient sacrifice to a satyr god,[2] one of those demons of the wilderness which were supposed to resemble goats, and were called *se'îrîm*,[3] or an ancient nomadic ceremony which is still said to survive in the *jamârât* or " lapidation ", the rite forming part of the pilgrimage to Mecca, which is observed on the tenth of the month of *ḥajj*, and in fulfilment of which the Moslems throw stones against a pillar called the great demon ? [4]

The most probable explanation seems to us to be that the beginning of the new year,[5] at Jerusalem, as in many other places, had long been marked by a popular ceremony, in the course of which the evils of the past year (sins, defilements, bad luck), were dispelled by transferring them to an animal, which was then driven away.[6] The original idea may have been either that the goat itself was supposed to be the embodiment of the evil which was to be expelled, or the evil spirit which was responsible for it. The demon having later been clearly distinguished from the animal, the ceremony then was no doubt interpreted as a means whereby

---

[1] *Cf.*, for instance, **XL**, 324, note 2.
[2] Holzinger, **XLVIII**[4], *ad loc.*   [3] *Cf.* **LVII**, 276, 285.
[4] **XL**, 324 ; *cf.* **XC**, 80, and, with numerous details, **XXII**, 268–276.
[5] Before adopting the Babylonian calendar shortly before the Exile, the Israelites began the year in autumn, with the month which was afterwards called the seventh.
[6] See numerous examples in **XXI**, ii, 233–393 ; **LVIII**, 312 ff., 353–5.

the sin of the people could be sent back to the spirit with whom it had originated,[1] or else the disastrous consequences thereof diverted to Azazel.[2]

This popular custom, which had nothing Jahwist or even religious about it, which also had nothing to do, and apparently never had had anything to do, with any sacrificial rite, but was essentially of a magical nature, was sanctioned by the ritualist priests at the time of the restoration, and related to the national religion, because it seemed to them to express in a striking way one of the fundamental ideas of that religion, as understood by them—the necessity for a thorough and complete expulsion of all impurity. It may be that they simply paid no heed to the part played by Azazel in the matter, and that they regarded the rite merely as a symbolic act, signifying that the sin of Israel was banished from Palestine and would never return. This explanation, often upheld,[3] can only have arisen late, and cannot be taken to interpret the original meaning of the rite.

After some hesitation,[4] the date was fixed for the tenth of the month Tishri, because at one time this day was considered to be the real beginning of the year.[5]

The ceremony of Atonement was thus separated by a few days from the " Day of the blowing of the Horn ", afterwards the " New Year's Day "—rô's hassânâh (head of the year)—of Judaism, which fell on the first of the same month.

There is reason to think that this festival, which also does not figure in the older codes, likewise had its roots in pre-Exilic customs, when, apparently, rites of enthronement of Jahweh were celebrated at the beginning of the year, with acclamations and trumpet-blowing as for the accession of a king [6] ; but these rites were part of the rejoicings at the Feast of the Harvest or Tabernacles, which took place at the full moon in the month of Tishri, the original beginning of the year.[7] It, therefore, seems that the priestly legislators transferred to the beginning of the month some of the ceremonies of the Feast of Tabernacles.

---

[1] **XVII**, 56.
[2] **I**, 1st ed., 478.
[3] e.g. by Dillmann (**KEH**, *Ex.-Lev.*[3] 580), Marti (**LXII**, 257), Holzinger (**XLVIII**[4]).
[4] *Cf.* Ez. xlv, 18–20.
[5] Ez. xl, 1 ; Lev. xxv, 9.
[6] *Cf.* **LVII**, 506–7, 587.
[7] Ex. xxiii, 16 ; xxxiv, 22.

PLATE VIII

Synagogue of Capernaum
1. Present state (photo 1927)
2. Reconstruction (after BENZINGER, *Heb. Arch.*, 3rd ed., fig. 425, p. 340)

The two feasts, that of New Year's Day and that of the Day of Atonement, apparently new, prescribed by the Priestly Code, would then in reality be two ancient *rites de passage* for the new year, which after the Exile had been separated and more or less adapted to the ritualist conception of the cult.

Some at least of the priestly writers were confident that their work would take the place of the semi-historical, semi-legislative document which had hitherto reigned supreme (JED). Their hopes were not to be realized, for the old traditions were too well known, the veneration and esteem in which they were held was too great for the nation to surrender them without a struggle. All that happened was that the new sacred history was added to the old, the priestly element becoming, it is true, the dominant element.[1] According to several critics, it was Ezra who was responsible for the union of the two. This seems unlikely. The compiler preserved even the most heterodox parts of the older collection with a scrupulous respect, a fidelity and a piety which a party-man and a fighter like Ezra would scarcely have shown.

In this way the Pentateuch was formed, almost as we have it to-day. It is thought that the work must have been finished before the Macedonian conquest, for in order to ensure its acceptance in every quarter, whether in Samaria or at Jerusalem, the support of the government must have been needed, and it is unlikely that any government other that the Persian would have undertaken the task.

Since the Pentateuch was looked upon as a sacred book both by the Samaritans and by the Jews of Judæa, it goes without saying that the collection must not only have been finished, but already regarded as canonical when the schism between the two communities took place. But the date of this event is too uncertain for it to shed much light on the question as to when the Law was completed.

It is true that, between the orthodox Jews of Jerusalem and the majority of the descendants of those Israelites who had remained in the central provinces of Palestine, there was a distinct lack of sympathy, which was at times very marked, especially after the middle of the fifth century.

[1] *Cf.* Gunkel, **XXVIII**, i, 1², p. 13.

It was a survival of inherited feuds between the north and the south, and of the struggle between the Deuteronomist orthodoxy which often held sway in Jerusalem and age-long traditions of religious liberty in the country. But even in the days of Nehemiah, it was only a question of party differences, clashes between divergent tendencies *in one and the same religious community.* Tobiah, one of the leaders of the Israelites in Samaria who were most hostile to Nehemiah, had a room in the Temple at Jerusalem which had been given him by the high priest Eliashib. Nehemiah, it must be confessed, deprived him of it,[1] but the fact of his having it proves that even as late as the second sojourn of the satrap in Palestine (after 432), the " Samaritans " considered themselves, and were considered by the religious authorities in office at Jerusalem, legitimate members of the assembly of Jahweh.

The conflict must have become sharper when the more rigidly orthodox undertook to exclude from the assembly all who were not of pure Israelite blood. On account of the establishment of a number of Gentile colonies by Assyrian kings in what had once been the northern kingdom, the strict Jews of Jerusalem looked upon the northern Jews as half-castes, or even as descendants of those Babylonian or Aramæan settlers who had only embraced the faith of Jahweh after their arrival in Palestine : this is the meaning of the story in the book of Kings.[2] But the facts in this story have obviously been manipulated to suit the author's point of view ; it implies that the country had been laid waste by the Assyrians until it was nothing better than a desert haunted by wild beasts, and that not a single worshipper of Jahweh remained, since one of the deported priests had to be brought back to teach the rites of his religion to the newcomers. Nevertheless, although as regards racial purity the Israelites of the north lived under a cloud, they were not necessarily excluded from the cult : they were at least allowed to take part in it as proselytes.

It is often held that the schism took place as the result of the dismissal by Nehemiah of a grandson of the high priest Eliashib, for having married a daughter of Sanballat.[3] The

---

[1] Neh. xiii, 6–9.
[2] 2 Kings xvii, 24–41.   [3] Neh. xiii, 28.

record of this episode is associated with a story told by Josephus, which relates how Sanballat obtained from Alexander the Great—who only arrived in Palestine a hundred years later—leave to build a temple on Mount Gerizim, in which his son-in-law was to officiate.[1] But the gross anachronisms with which Josephus embellished his tale make it impossible to attach much faith to it.[2]

It may be true that the temple on Mount Gerizim was built in Alexander's time. But neither its construction, nor its demolition by John Hyrkanus in 128, necessarily indicates that the rupture was henceforth final. The schism only began when the Samaritans claimed that their mountain was *the only place* where sacrifice should be allowed, and their body of priests the only legitimate Aaronic priesthood, as the Jews said of their temple and its ministrants. Josephus does state that in Egypt under the Ptolemies there were disputes between Samaritans and Judæans as to where their offspring were to be sent, to Gerizim or to Jerusalem[3]; but he does not give the date. And Hölscher has recently maintained that " the sect of the Samaritans of Shechem only became a separate religious community, detached from Jerusalem ", at the time when Pompey (63) and Gabinius (57) separated Samaria from the territory which they left to the Hasmonean Jewish prince Hyrkanus II. Although conclusive proof is not forthcoming, this date gives the impression of being too recent : as early as 590, Jesus, son of Sirach, already looked upon the Samaritans as a separate " nation ", as foreign to the people of Israel as the Edomites and the Philistines, and still more detestable :

> " With two nations is my soul vexed, And the third is no nation :
> They that sit upon the mountains of Samaria, and the Philistines,
> And that foolish people that dwelleth in Shechem." [4]

It is at least possible from these words to gauge the depths of hatred which divided the two communities at the beginning of the second century.

[1] *A.J.*, XI, viii, 2 (§§ 306–312) and 4 (§§ 321–4).
[2] *Cf.* **XXXV**, 172.
[3] *A.J.*, XII, i, 1, § 10.   [4] Sir. 1, 25–6.

BOOK III

RELIGION (Conclusion)

GENERAL CHARACTERISTICS OF RELIGIOUS LIFE IN EARLY JUDAISM

CHAPTER I

RELIGIOUS THOUGHT

GROWTH OF SYSTEMATIC THEOLOGY

THE special task which Judaism undertook was to preserve and bring within everyone's reach those higher religious values which the prophets had bequeathed, by enclosing them in rigid receptacles which cramped or even, at times, distorted them, because they had been made for quite a different purpose.

The Law was such a protective covering. We have seen how it evolved and the various elements of which it was composed. Those who created it no doubt had other objects in view as well : they wanted to ensure that the mystical presence of God would remain in the midst of the nation, to prevent the faithful from mingling with the pagan world by isolating them with the help of a system of distinctive practices ; but they also aimed at defining the religious and moral demands of the God of the prophets—whose scope and magnitude seemed infinite—by reducing them to items in a code.

At the same time and in the same spirit, an effort was made to give doctrinal shape to the moral intuitions, to the soaring faith and hope of the prophets, independently both of the personal piety and historical circumstances of those who held the doctrines. Not only had Judaism, like ancient Israel, more or less implicit beliefs—it had also clearly defined teaching on certain points.

I

THE DOCTRINE OF GOD

Monotheism, clearly formulated as a doctrine by the Second Isaiah and by the Deuteronomic writers, finally became an integral part of the common patrimony of all Jews. Some held that the gods of the Gentiles were beings subordinate to Jahweh, and given by him to the nations [1] as objects of their worship ; others regarded them as devils.[2] More often they were denied any real existence.[3] Malachi, as we have seen, went still further, and declared that when the heathen served their gods they were in reality invoking and worshipping Jahweh.[4] Such a pronouncement seems to imply that those to whom the words were addressed stood in no great danger of becoming polytheists.

And, in fact, this rigorous monotheism, far from being conducive to any broad-minded universalism, gave rise to a much more exclusive particularism than the national pride of ancient Israel had ever known. For the average Jew, a Gentile was not merely a rival, but a being whom God had made inferior.[5] According to most of the authors of the period of ancient Judaism, the nations apparently only existed to provide victims for the miracles by which Jahweh showed forth his power and glory : that is how the priestly historian wrote of the plagues of Egypt. Almost all the prophets of the time [6] held that not only those nations which were unjust or had done harm to Israel should be judged—that is to say, horribly massacred, but all nations, for the simple reason that they were not Israel. Some persisted in foretelling that the heathen would finally be converted to the worship of Jahweh,[7] but in that case they would be subject to the chosen people, they would bring tribute and also offerings to the Temple, they would become the builders, the ploughmen and the vinedressers of the

---

[1] Deut. iv, 19 ; xxix, 25 ; *cf*. Ps. xcvii, 7, 9.

[2] Deut. xxxii, 17 ; Ps. cvi, 37.

[3] Deut. iv, 28 ; Is. xliv, 9–20 ; xlvi, 6–8 ; Jer. x, 1–10, 12–16 ; Ps. cxv, 4–8 ; cxxxv, 15–18.

[4] Mal. i, 10–12.   [5] *Cf*. p. 231.

[6] Ezekiel, Zechariah, Is. lvi–lxvi, Obadiah, Malachi, Joel, Isaiah xxiv–xxvii, etc.

[7] e.g. Is. xix, 16–25.

Jews.[1] The nation which refused to serve them would perish.[2] Israel was to form a caste of priests in the commonwealth of humanity, and even the lowliest of the utensils to be found in Jerusalem would take on the sacred character of Temple vessels.[3]

Another feature of the " theology " of ancient Judaism, which has often been noted, was what is known as the " transcendence " which it attributed to God. The term cannot here be taken in its strictly philosophical sense, or it will give rise to false conclusions : the Jews of this period did not think that because God was a spirit he could have no relation to the world of matter, or that he was outside the visible universe.[4] Ezekiel and the priestly historian tell of the appearances of God to man, and sometimes make use of distinctly anthropomorphic expressions to describe divine activity. But Jahweh is now regarded as endowed with infinite and overwhelming might, wisdom, and holiness, incommeasurable with the might, wisdom, and holiness of man. Ancient Israel drew naïve pictures of God intervening in human affairs in the likeness of man, coming down to earth and eating with Abraham, but these old ideas seemed grossly irreverent after the period of the Exile. Ezekiel, relating his first vision, says only that he saw on " the likeness of the throne " a " likeness as the appearance of a man upon it above ".[5] The author of the priestly history takes care never to describe the manner of the divine appearances.

From the time of the Exile onwards, the idea of the creation of the heavens and the earth becomes a frequent subject of pious reflection, because it bears witness more impressively than any other to the omnipotence of God. The Second Isaiah makes frequent allusion to it.[6] The priestly account of the origin of the world [7] expresses, in terms which have rightly become classic, the idea of God's sovereignty over the universe—" God said : Let there be light, and there was light "—and of a supreme wisdom, of a spirit of reason and order presiding over the work of creation, beginning with the shaping of the elements, followed by that

---

[1] Is. lxi, 5–7.
[2] Is. lx, 12 ; Zech. xiv, 12–15.
[3] Zech. xiv, 20–1.
[4] *Cf.* CCXXVI, 54–8.
[5] Ez. i, 26.
[6] See p. 242.
[7] Gen. i, 1–ii, 4a.

of the beings which inhabit them, and crowned by the appearance of mankind, whose mission was to make all things subject unto him. The majestic character of the narrative and the quasi-scientific regard for logic are all the more remarkable because the account is adapted from an old cosmogonic myth, of which traces are still visible in their new and nobler setting. As the question of the creation of chaos does not arise, there is, properly speaking, no creation at all, but rather the systematic ordering of pre-existent matter. Objects are shaped *successively*, as if by an effort. The idea of the world-egg is apparent in what is said about the spirit of God *brooding* over the waters. The earth *of its own accord* produces plants, as the sea produces fish. The plural " *Let us* make man in *our* image " presupposes a plurality of Elohim as creators.

The question of the origin of the world is one which many other Jewish thinkers of the same period were revolving in their minds. Some of them had recourse to traditions somewhat different from those utilized in the story in Genesis, keeping more closely to the mythological background.[1] Others freely expressed their own thought, and reached a more absolute conception of the sovereignty of the Creator ; to this class belongs the author of the thirty-third psalm :

> " By the word of the Lord were the heavens made ; and all the host of them, by the breath of his mouth . . . For he spake and it was done ; he commanded and it stood fast." [2]

The price paid for this majestic conception of God is that Jahweh henceforth is removed much farther from the worshipper. " God is in heaven, and thou upon earth." [3] As they were now understood, both worship and the Law ceaselessly reminded the Jew of the distance which separated him from his God. In ancient Israel, those who wished to know the will of God consulted him in person, but, according to the Jewish idea, He was represented by His book, the Law. And every ritual act, aimed at preserving the temple from the defilement with which it was ceaselessly

---

[1] Job xxvi, 7–14 ; xxxviii, 4–11 ; Ps. xxiv, 2 ; civ ; Prov. viii, 24–31. Cf. Ps. lxxxix, 10–11 ; lxxiv, 13 ; Is. li, 9–10 ; Job vii, 12.
[2] Ps. xxxiii, 6, 9.　　　　　　　　　　　　　　　[3] Eccl. v, 2.

threatened, proclaimed unceasingly the awe-inspiring, inaccessible holiness of the Almighty.

Hence the growing reluctance to call Jahweh by his real name—for did it not presuppose a familiarity, now deemed presumptuous, between man and God ? Preference was shown for such expressions as Elohim,[1] the God of Heaven, the Most High God (*'El 'elyon*), the Lord, Heaven, the Name.[2] As we know, the Jews even went so far as to forbid that the name of Jahweh should be uttered, and this prohibition was inserted at an early date into the original text of the Law ; in a passage in Leviticus, in which it was forbidden under pain of death to *curse* " the name ", not only the Massoretes, but before them the Greek translators, interpreted or corrected the parts of the verb *qâbab* " to curse ", as derivatives of the root *nâqab*, " to pronounce distinctly." [3]

As usually happens when God is thought to be afar off, religious feeling tried to find satisfaction in intermediary beings which were more within man's reach. Hence the increasing importance, at this time, and still more in the periods which followed, of angels [4] and other " sons of Elohim ",[5] including the Adversary, the *Sâtân*,[6]—or of personifications of divine attributes, of " hypostases ", such as Wisdom, the Spirit, the Word of God.[7]

II

THE DOCTRINE OF RETRIBUTION

The prophets had proclaimed that Jahweh valued righteousness above all other considerations, and that, in spite of his love for His people, He would visit the nation's sins upon it without pity. Judaism adopted this statement, borne out as it was by the disasters of the Exile ; but, as with the monotheism of the prophets, it took the form of an axiom

---

[1] Chronicles, 2nd and 3rd books of the Psalms (Pss. xlii–lxxii and lxxiii–lxxxix), Ecclesiastes.

[2] Lev. xxiv, 11.　　　　　[3] Lev. xxiv, 11, 16.

[4] Ez. ix, 1–7, 11 ; xl–xlii ; Zech. i, 12–13 ; ii, 2, 5–9 ; iii, 1–6 ; iv, 1, 4–5 ; v, 2–3, 5–11 ; vi, 4, 7 ; Job v, 1 ; xxxiii, 23 ; Is. lxii, 6, etc.

[5] Job i, 6 ; ii 1.

[6] Zech. iii, 1–2 ; Job i–ii ; 1 Chron. xxi, 1.

[7] With regard to these intermediaries, see vol. xxviii, pt. ii, cc. vii and viii.

in their hands, a soulless mathematical abstraction, according to which chastisement followed so closely on the heels of crime that a kind of mechanism might almost have been said to have been set in motion.

The Deuteronomic editors who, shortly before or during the Exile, were revising the books of Judges and Kings, had already begun to revise systematically the ancient history of Israel with the object of discovering the punishment which must have followed every past fault, and the fault which was responsible for every national misfortune. They did, however, practise a certain amount of discretion in this work of interpreting history from a moral point of view. Thus, in their version of the reign of Solomon, they contented themselves with inverting the order of events, relating first his glorious acts, then his sins, and finally his failures, thus giving the impression that the disasters encountered by the king—some of which really went back to the beginning of his reign [1]—were so many punishments for his later infidelity.

The editors of the book of Chronicles pursue this path much further.[2] We are able to arrive at an exact estimate of the changes made by them by comparing their work with the books of Samuel and Kings, which were almost their only sources.

Sometimes they, too, confined themselves to a free juxtaposition of sins and disasters, introducing a prophet, if necessary, to explain cause and effect. For instance, the book of Kings relates that Jehoshaphat could not send a fleet to Ophir, as he wished, because the ships were dashed in pieces,[3] and elsewhere,[4] that this king allied himself with various kings of Israel. The book of Chronicles represents the shipwreck as the punishment of this alliance with sinful men, a punishment which the prophet Eliezer had foretold.[5]

---

[1] 1 Kings xi, 14–22 (in particular v. 21), 23–5 (esp. v. 25).

[2] There seem to have been at least two, for the writer of the book in its present form seems to have been following a previous version written from the same point of view, to which he repeatedly refers, and the title of which may have been *Midrash of the book of Kings* (2 Chron. xxiv, 27).

[3] 1 Kings xxii, 49.

[4] 1 Kings xxii, 2 ; 2 Kings iii.   [5] 2 Chron. xx, 35–7.

Elsewhere, the editors of the Chronicles are still more zealous in their adaptation of history to meet the needs of dogma : when their sources provide them with a king of exemplary piety who is overtaken by misfortune, they supplement his biography with some fault which will explain his adversity. Azariah was smitten with leprosy and died [1] ; this was because he, a layman, had burnt incense in the Temple.[2] The pious king Josiah was killed by Neco, king of Egypt, at Megiddo. The authors of the Chronicles make short work of explaining this disaster, which had been a grievous stone of offence for Josiah's contemporaries : their explanation is that the king had refused to obey the order delivered to him *on God's behalf* by the Pharaoh, that he should refrain from opposing his advance.[3]

Conversely, when a wicked monarch has been fortunate, it is because he became converted. This, according to the book of the Chronicles, is the explanation of the un-precedented length of Manasseh's reign ; he was first punished for his sins by being exiled to Babylon, but adversity made him repent of his evil ways.[4]

When history only provides the fault, the editors of the Chronicles supply the chastisement, which to their mind, cannot have been lacking : wicked kings are not buried in the royal sepulchre ; Manasseh and Jehoiakim are deported.[5]

And, conversely, they see to it that those rulers whose record is entirely blameless do not go unrewarded. Hence, no doubt, the brilliant victory which they attribute to Asa over Zerah the Ethiopian [6] : Egypt was not then governed by an Ethiopian dynasty. There is a slight possibility that the name Zerah was a corruption of Osorkon, the Egyptian Pharaoh who was a contemporary of Asa, but it is somewhat risky to regard this confused and biased narrative as evidence of a defeat inflicted on this Osorkon in Palestine.[7]

---

[1] 2 Kings xv, 5. [2] 2 Chron. xxvi, 16–21.
[3] 2 Chron. xxxv, 21–2. [4] 2 Chron. xxxiii.
[5] The historicity of the exile of Jehoiakim has been defended, however, e.g. by Klamroth (*Die wirtschaftl. Lage . . .*, 17–20) : he believes it to be attested by Ezekiel (xix, 5–9).
[6] 2 Chron. xiv, 8–14.
[7] Champollion's theory, supported by G. Jéquier (*Hist. de la civilis. égypt.*, 249) and Dussaud (**SY**, VI (1925)), 114–15.

Early Judaism does not only apply the law of strict reward and punishment to nations, and to kings as the representatives of nations, but also, and with the utmost rigour, to individuals. It is an axiom, and it underlies every line of the book of Proverbs, and also of the Wisdom of Jesus, son of Sirach. Nehemiah calls upon God to keep account of each of his good works and to visit upon his enemies each of their misdeeds.[1]

It was doubtless a very old idea among the Jews that there is an organic connection, a kind of fundamental identity, between moral evil and misfortune, and that sin entails a decrease in vital strength.[2] It had also long been a principle universally enshrined in ancient morality, that the deity favours the good and punishes the wicked. And it might be thought that the authors of the maxims collected in the book of Proverbs, in foretelling prosperity to the just and calamity to the unjust, were merely inspired by the principles of their predecessors, the Oriental moralists, with whose works they were familiar, having imitated them occasionally,[3] and that, consequently, the aphorisms of the book of Proverbs may have been composed long before early Judaism came into being. This may certainly be true of many of them. But the chief reason for believing that even the earliest of the collections of maxims in the Bible were assembled after the Exile is that in 'them the misfortunes of the individual are never attributed to any cause other than the personal shortcomings of that individual, and that it is never implied that he may be suffering for the sins or his fathers or his country, a possibility always present to the mind of ancient Israel, nor as a result of the machinations of any enemy, sorcerer, or demon. Evidently the theory of strictly individual rewards and punishments, which Ezekiel had formulated in such categorical terms,[4] had become an article of faith for the scribes who wrote the maxims. A two-fold heritage from the prophets was theirs, although in a somewhat narrow and rigid guise : on the one hand, the great belief in the justice of God, and on the other, the principle, discovered

---

[1] Neh. v, 19 ; xiii, 14, 22, 31 ; iii, 36–7 ; vi, 14 ; xiii, 29.
[2] *Cf.* **LXIX**, particularly pp. 428–437.
[3] See pp. 13–14, 72–6.
[4] Ez. xviii and xxxiii. See pp. 220–3.

at the cost of so much suffering and expressed in so heart-rending a way by Jeremiah, that human personality had its own religious value.

As is shown by the book of Proverbs and by the book of Ecclesiasticus, the good things which God has in store as a reward for the righteous are of an exclusively terrestrial order : a long and peaceful life, riches, honour, numerous off-spring, a name to be gratefully remembered after death ; and the punishments which await the wicked are of the same order : poverty, shame, sickness, violent or premature death.[1] There could naturally be no question of recompense or penalties beyond the grave, such as Egyptian sages foretold. For early Judaism, doubtless because of the agelong attitude of hostility adopted by Jahwism towards ancestor-worship, has a still more sombre conception of the life after death than had ancient Israel.[2] None ever leave Sheol, man's " eternal abode ". Complete equality reigns among those upon whom the doors have closed for ever, and an almost complete annihilation.[3] Sheol is the realm of silence, darkness, and oblivion ; a place where the praises of Jahweh never sound. The dead know nothing, not even that they are dead.[4] The synonym of Sheol is Abaddôn, destruction. Therefore, if everyone is to reap the reward of his deeds, he must do so during his lifetime.

The theory often seemed contradicted by facts, but it was not hard to persuade oneself that exceptions were only apparent. The authors of the Proverbs rarely resort to such arguments, however[5] ; they do not seem to be aware of the difficulties, and do not embark on any explanation of discrepancies between theory and reality, such as were a source of profound perplexity to many contemporary believers, if we may judge from certain of the psalms, the book of Job, and the book of Ecclesiastes.

The mentality of the Jewish moralists was so saturated with the belief in individual retribution that they made it the basis of their teaching. As represented by the books of Proverbs and of Ecclesiasticus, this teaching was essentially

---

[1] Prov. x, 3 ; xiii, 18 ; etc.   [2] *Cf.* **LVII**, 249–264, esp. 252–4.
[3] Job iii, 13–15, 17–19 ; xiv, 21–2 ; Eccl. ix, 4–6 ; Ps. lxxxviii, 6, 11–13.
[4] Eccl. ix, 5.   [5] Prov. xxiv, 1, 19–22.

utilitarian. It may, of course, be urged, in explanation of this characteristic, that the sages were endeavouring to make sure that their wisdom should be such that youth could understand ; it may also be urged that all religious moral teaching appeals to some extent to self-interest, since it makes salvation the object of righteousness. The fact remains that the Proverbs put the emphasis on the prospect of reward or of punishment, while the prophets, for instance, had laid chief stress on the feelings of gratitude, piety, or love, which should fill the hearts of the people, and that for the rest they trusted in God with a whole-hearted faith which, in men like Jeremiah, or the Servant of Jahweh, was ready to accept undeserved suffering and death for the sake of others. Moreover, when they promise happiness, it is usually the happiness of the nation.

The utilitarian point of view of Jewish morality is particularly evident in the term used by its exponents to indicate their cherished ideal, the term " wisdom ", *hokmâh*. It does not convey to them the idea of a spiritual knowledge of God, still less of a philosophical speculation ; it stands for the practical means of attaining a wished-for object, here the object and aim of life, which is happiness. Wisdom means cleverness and prudence. It is true that this wisdom is not mere worldliness, for its first precept is : " Fear Jahweh." [1] Wisdom founded on the fear of God is even regarded as the only wisdom worth the name.[2] Statements of this kind show better than anything else that to the moralists of ancient Judaism, the practice of righteousness and piety appear as the first rule of enlightened self-interest : the really wise man is the man who tries to please the Master of the universe, the impious man is a madman.[3]

With this in mind, it is easy to understand why, in the collections of maxims in the books of Proverbs and of Ecclesiasticus, side by side with the loftiest precepts enjoining pity, forgiveness of injury, charity, even towards an enemy,[4] are others appealing to the most primitive selfishness :

" He that is surety for a stranger shall smart for it : But he that hateth suretyship is sure." [5] " He that hath pity upon the poor

[1] Prov. iii, 7.   [2] Prov. i, 7 ; ix, 10.
[3] *Cf.* Ps. xiv, liii.
[4] Prov. x, 12 ; xxiv, 11 ; Ecc. iii, 30–iv, 10 ; xxviii, 1–7.
[5] Prov. xi, 15.

lendeth unto the Lord, And his good deed will he pay him again." [1]
Rejoice not when thine enemy falleth . . . Lest the Lord see it and it
displease him, And he turn away his wrath from him." [2]

Adultery is to be eschewed lest the outraged husband
avenge himself,[3] and a vow should not be made in haste,
for fear it may be repented of at leisure.[4]

III

ESCHATOLOGY

However confidently the Jew might expect the immediate
reward of his fidelity, he nevertheless continued to believe,
as his fathers before the Exile had believed, that the individual
can only realize his whole destiny if that of the nation is
realized, that is, if with the coming of the " day of the Lord "
he can see dawning on the horizon that era of grandeur and
prosperity eagerly awaited since the days of Amos.[5] At
first the great prophets had endeavoured to quench this
hope,[6] but in the end they had made it their own, subject
to the fulfilment of moral conditions which were more or
less exacting. The happiness to which the individual can
attain in the present is but relative and partial. When the
day of the Messiah dawns, the span of life itself will be
changed: " He who dies at the age of a hundred will be young,
and the sinner being an hundred years old (i.e. dying at that
age) shall be accursed." [7]

The fulfilment of the promises made *to the nation* by Jahweh
is the goal to which all the religious life of Judaism tends.
Even the Law draws its inspiration from the national
hope. Those responsible for the written torah—whether
Deuteronomy or the Priestly Code—those who struggled
to establish it or strove to follow it, all laboured towards
the same end, all longed to bring about that glorious restoration which God had in store for the nation when it returned
to his allegiance.

There are three characteristics of the Jewish views of
the future belonging to this period.

---

[1] Prov. xix, 17 ; *cf.* Sir. vii, 32–6.
[2] Prov. xxiv, 17–18 ; *cf.* xxv, 21–2.
[3] Prov. v, 8–14 ; vi, 32–4.
[4] Prov. xx, 25.
[5] Am. v, 18.
[6] Am. v, 18–19.
[7] Is. lxv, 20–2.

1. Promises tend completely to eclipse threats. The Jew is persuaded that the dire chastisement foretold of old by the prophets has already been accomplished : the nation has paid the penalty of bygone sins. It now awaits from day to day the fulfilment of the promises made to it. It is, moreover, entitled by more than its past sufferings to a splendid restitution, for of all the nations upon earth it alone knows the true God, the Ruler of the Universe. The honour of the name of Jahweh demands that the chosen people shall be exalted, and as a necessary corollary, that the other nations shall be brought low, either by mass conversion of the heathen to the worship of the God of Israel—as the Second Isaiah generally interprets the idea—or by wholesale extermination, the last judgment—a more usual view.[1] The " day of the Lord " no longer means, as it did to Amos, Isaiah, or Zephaniah, the day of *Israel's* discomfiture, it is the day on which vengeance shall overtake *the nations*. Prophecy has become almost synonymous with promises. It now becomes clear why, in the period which followed the Exile, a number of Messianic passages were interpolated in the old collections of prophecies, and those already existing expanded. The question which the prophets of the Jewish period seek to solve is not : will salvation come ? it is almost exclusively : when and in what form will it come ?

2. The answer to these questions is often sought in the books of the older prophets. No longer is direct revelation from Jahweh the only source of knowledge. Even Jeremiah already invoked the authority of his predecessors.[2] Ezekiel constructed a history of future times which he combined with old predictions.[3] The Second Isaiah ceaselessly referred to previous prophecies and their fulfilment. In the days of Zechariah it was calculated that the Messianic era was about to begin because the seventy years foretold by Jeremiah had passed.[4] Another indication of the widespread influence of the book of Jeremiah is the use of the word " Branch " as a kind of proper name meaning the Messianic king. " Behold," (says Jahweh), " I will bring forth my servant the Branch." [5] Elsewhere the Messiah is called " The man

---

[1] Joel iii and iv ; Is. xxiv ; xxvi, 20–xxvii, 1 ; Zech. xii, 14.
[2] Jer. xxviii, 8.   [3] Ez. xxxviii, 17 ; xxxix, 8.
[4] Zech. i, 12.   [5] Zech. iii, 8.

whose name is the Branch ".[1] This is an allusion to a passage in Jeremiah : " I will raise up unto David a righteous Branch." [2]

There is a tendency to form a body of eschatological doctrine, a programme of the great final drama drawn up in advance, and based—sometimes rather artificially—on ancient texts. These glimpses of the future no longer had any close connection with contemporary events, as those of the older prophets had had, and therefore assumed proportions and a colouring increasingly foreign to the ordinary course of everyday happenings. In addition to that expectation of a last judgment which we have already mentioned, there was also a belief that Elijah would return,[3] and ideas about Gehenna.[4] In an apocalyptic passage possibly written at the time of the conquests of Alexander,[5] the hope that death will be abolished becomes apparent,[6] entailing no doubt also the hope of resurrection [7] which, nevertheless, was not to take root in Palestinian Judaism until the second century B.C. with the appearance of the apocalypses of Daniel and Enoch.

The extraordinary expansion and development of Jewish eschatology will be studied as a whole in its relation to the period which followed that of the Maccabees ; particular attention will be paid to the study of the question of how far it was influenced by Babylonian myths and Iranian speculations.[8]

---

[1] Zech. vi, 12.
[2] Jer. xxiii, 5.
[3] Mal. iii, 23–4 (E.V. iv, 5–6).
[4] Is. lxvi, 24.
[5] Is. xxiv–xxvii.
[6] Is. xxv, 7–8.
[7] Is. xxvi, 19.
[8] See vol. xxviii, pt. ii, ch. ix, x, and xi, 2.

CHAPTER II

RELIGIOUS THOUGHT (*Conclusion*)

DISCUSSION OF THE PREVALENT DOCTRINES

I

RUTH AND JONAH

IT would be wrong to regard the four centuries of Early
Judaism as a period during which religious thought
lay benumbed and benighted in blind submission to the
dictates of conformity; it is no longer possible to speak
as Renan did of the great sleep of Israel during this period,
for it is now known that some of the most important books
of Hebrew literature belong to it. It was, in fact, in the days
of early Judaism that, as Wellhausen has observed, nearly
everything which can be read and understood to-day without
special historical preparation, was written, that is everything
which the religious mind of to-day most readily welcomes,
in particular the Psalms and the book of Job.

There were among the Jews men of eager and independent
minds, who did not shrink from re-examining problems
or from solving them in a manner diametrically opposite
to that recommended by the doctrines in vogue. These
independent thinkers no longer presented their protest in
the form of inspired oracles : in conformity with their time
they dealt with such problems on the plane of the discussion
of ideas or of practical piety.

The author of the little book of Ruth discreetly criticizes
the narrow-minded views of those orthodox followers of
Nehemiah and Ezra who mercilessly condemned every
marriage with a Gentile : he tells the story of a Moabite
woman whose first husband had converted her to the worship
of Jahweh and who, after having given evidence of the
finest feelings, receives the signal honour of becoming the
ancestress of the king, David.

The book of Jonah is an amusing satire directed against

334

those who desired the annihilation, rather than the conversion, of heathen nations, and were annoyed by God's patience with their accursed cities—the author speaks of Nineveh, but doubtless is thinking of Babylon, spared by Cyrus, Darius, Xerxes, and Alexander successively. He asks his ruthless fellow-believers how the Lord could refrain from showing mercy to towns where there are thousands of little children and harmless animals. And the heathen might even repent before it is too late, who knows ?

But the prevalent idea most open to objection was the doctrine of immediate individual retribution ; for it was obvious that the world contained righteous men who endured suffering, and wicked men who prospered. This was the problem which the book of Job attempted to solve.

II

THE BOOK OF JOB

Job was the name of a man who in ancient times was famed for his righteousness.[1] There was a curious tradition about him. One day, when Jahweh had boasted of the uprightness of his servant Job before the assembly of divine beings—the sons of Elohim—one of them, the Adversary (the *Sâtân*),[2] replied : " Doth Job fear God for nought ? . . . Thou has blessed the work of his hands . . . But put forth thine hand now, and touch all that he hath, and he will curse thee to thy face." Jahweh allowed the Adversary to take away from Job all that belonged to him, so that disaster after disaster befell him, and he lost all his flocks, his sons, and his daughters. But all he said was :

" The Lord gave and the Lord hath taken away ; blessed be the name of the Lord ! "

As the Adversary was still unconvinced, Jahweh allowed him to afflict Job with a terrible disease, apparently leprosy. The unhappy man's wife adjured him to renounce his piety, which had been of no advantage to him. He replied: "What ? Shall we receive good at the hand of God, and shall we not receive evil ? " And in spite of all his sufferings, Job uttered no sinful word. And so in the end Jahweh restored to him

---

[1] Ez. xiv, 14, 20.　　　[2] *Cf.* p. 325 above.

his first estate, even granting him double of all he had previously possessed.[1]

This tale was probably a version of a theme to be met with
in folklore throughout the world, describing, as in the Indian
variant,[2] the fate of a just man who became involved in
the rivalry of two divine beings. It was in the nature of a
popular and easily understood tale, and was intended
to be both moving and edifying,[3] but not to solve a problem
of theodicy. Nevertheless it was possible to gather from it a
clear explanation of the sufferings of the righteous. Disinterested and persevering piety is ultimately rewarded—in this the
story maintains the point of view universally held in ancient
times—but there are afflictions which may, for a time, befall
those who are entirely innocent, not as punishments or
warnings, but solely as *trials*—the word being used in its
strict sense—in order that God, who is not credited with
omniscience, may be convinced, or may convince another
Elohim, that his servant is really devout. This truly archaic
idea is also to be found among the stories collected by the
Elohist, such as that of the sacrifice of Abraham (Gen. xxii).

The moral of the tale, which was the chief reason for the
telling of it, is not the only idea underlying this popular
narrative. Other thoughts suggested by the way are : (1) that
there are invisible powers of evil in the world which take
delight in tormenting mankind. God, however, only tolerates
their misdeeds up to a point ; (2) that a distinction must be
drawn between those evils which God *allows*, in order to
accomplish his own inscrutable purpose, and those *willed*
by him—a distinction foreign to primitive Semitic thought ;
(3) that true piety is disinterested, and that man must serve
God " for naught ", even if God send him nothing but misfortune : a fertile idea which might have revolutionized the
whole of traditional Jewish morality, fundamentally
eudæmonist as it was.

In ancient times, Oriental moralists were quite familiar
with the literary method which consists in embodying teaching
in a dialogue interpolated in the course of an account of
some adventure, real or fictitious : it is only necessary to
quote in this connection in Egyptian literature the dialogue

---

[1] Job. i, 1–ii, 10 ; xlii, 11–17.   [2] See pp. 13–14.
[3] See the excellent remarks of Paul Volz (**XXVIII**, iii, 2², pp. 13–14).

between the Weary of Life and his Soul,[1] or the Lament of the Eloquent Peasant,[2] the Assyro-Babylonian discourse between a master and his servant,[3] or the romance of Ahiqar, and in Hebrew literature the intercession of Abraham on behalf of Sodom [4] or the book of Jonah. In the same way a Jewish poet took for his framework the popular tale of which Job was the hero, not because he agreed with any of those solutions which the ancient story suggested—none of them is advocated *or even discussed* in the course of the poem [5]— but simply because the problem which obsessed him was there stated in the clearest possible way : if a just and all-powerful God really exists, how is it that there are innocent people who suffer ? And in Job's case it was impossible to adopt the usual course of denying the righteousness of the sufferer, for God himself admitted it ; his wrongs, therefore, were not punishments.

The poet accordingly brings in three friends,[6] who overwhelm Job with explanations and " consolations " more unkind than his fate, such as a pious Jew who had fallen on evil days might receive from those who shared his faith. All three defend the orthodox view, the " pure doctrine ",[7] that he who has done wrong suffers, and he who suffers has done wrong, the extent of his misfortune being an infallible indication of the gravity of his sin.

There are only shades of difference between the three champions of orthodoxy. Eliphaz loves to invoke the traditions of the fathers [8] or the revelations which he has received.[9]

[1] Adolf Erman, **ABA,** 1896, pp. 1 *ff.* ; transl. XXVII, i, 25–8.
[2] F. Vogelgesang and A. H. Gardiner, *Hieratische Papyrus der königl. Museen zu Berlin,* iv, 1, 1908 ; partly transl. **XXVII,** i, 34.
[3] **XXVII,** i, 284-7.   [4] Gen. xviii, 18–33a.
[5] In our opinion this and other indications make it impossible to regard the prologue and epilogue as the personal work of the poet, as has again recently been held by Karl Kautzsch (**CCXII**), Meinhold (**LXIV,** 277–9), P. Paul Dhorme (**CXCVII,** pp. l–lxviii), Emil Kautzsch (**XLVIII,** ii, 326).
[6] By reason of Jahweh's approval of Job's words (xlii, 7) that the three friends already appeared in the folkstory. But it seems more likely that they were put in afterwards by the poet, because there are traces of joins in the epilogue (xlii, 10, is a doublet of xlii, 11–16), and because the gloomy depression in which Job's friends find him on their arrival (ii, 13) agrees better with the tragic despair attributed to the hero by the poem than the serene resignation attributed to him by the prologue (i, 21 ; ii, 10). *Cf.* **CCXVII.**
[7] xi, 4   [8] xv, 7–10 ; xxii, 15–20.   [9] iv, 12–16.

z

He emphasizes the fact that man, because of his natural weakness, man in his " house of clay ", is always sinful, so that the Almighty is justified in crushing him.[1] By following the path of virtue, the upright man creates no rights before God.[2] Eliphaz is older and less hard-hearted than the others. He reminds Job that the misfortunes with which God has seen fit to afflict him are not mere punishments—they are also a means of educating him.

> " Happy is the man whom God correcteth : Therefore despise not thou the chastening of the Almighty." [3]

Bildad is more trenchant, Zophar more hot-tempered : if Job only knew the secrets of divine wisdom, he would see that God had let him off lightly.[4]

And the conclusion at which they all arrive, a conclusion which is brought home to their friend first tactfully, then bluntly, is that in the past his piety was only hypocrisy, and his sins more in number than the sand.[5] There is only one thing for him to do—to repent without delay ; when he has done that, God will not fail to deliver him.[6]

Job opposes these explanations of traditional piety by asserting the fact of his innocence. Not that he can claim to be without sin : like every being that is fashioned of clay, he is not without blemish in the sight of God[7] ; in his youth he may have sinned,[8] but how could God punish by torture, such as he is called upon to undergo, those imperfections from which no one is free ? Should he not have patience with so frail a creature ? [9] Job knows himself guiltless of the exceptional crimes of which his misfortunes accuse him. But—and this shows the tyranny exercised by established doctrine over the mind of the Jews—in thus protesting his innocence in the face of his adversity, Job believes himself to be uttering an unheard-of blasphemy, and expects to be struck dead on the spot.[10] Even so, he adheres to his statement. He even declares that his case is far from being an isolated one : there is no end to the oppression on earth which is never avenged.[11] And whether a man be righteous or wicked, he is born to perpetual sorrow.

---

[1] iv, 17–19 ; xv, 14–16. [2] xxii, 2–3.
[3] v, 17–19 ; cf. xxii, 22–3.   [4] xi, 6.   [5] xxii, 5–11.
[6] iv, 17 ; xxii, 29–30.   [7] xiv, 3.   [8] xiii, 26.
[9] vii, 17–21.   [10] ix, 21–4 ; xiii, 13–15   [11] xxiv, 1–12 ; iii, 20.

Job's point of view does not alter in the course of the discussion, any more than that of his opponents : from beginning to end the same points are urged. But the poet is extraordinarily skilful in depicting the ebb and flow of feeling, and the conflicting moods through which an unhappy man, tortured by doubt and by physical suffering, must pass. Now he sends up agonized appeals to the justice of God, now he utters fervent protestations of his faith (for he is sure that God knows him to be an upright man, and that his innocence will be proven, if not before, then after, his death); sometimes, however, he is bowed down by the thought of God's power, and it seems to him that even an innocent man will never be able to establish his uprightness before a judge whose very greatness will strike him dumb.[1] Occasionally, there is something very like hatred in Job's complaints, and he accuses God of being a cruel persecutor, or a tyrant spying on the beings whom He has created.[2]

In the end it is Job who has the last word. After a magnificent monologue, in which he swears a solemn oath that he is innocent,[3] he calls upon the Almighty to appear and do him justice.[4]

From the heart of the storm, Jahweh replies. By asking Job a number of questions which he is incapable of answering, he shows him that man is surrounded by phenomena which he can neither understand nor dominate—the two forms of incapacity were closely connected in the minds of the ancients, for it seemed to them that if man but knew, he would have the power. Some critics have thought that Jahweh's words constitute a defence of the orthodox thesis, and have concluded that this discourse, in spite of a poetic splendour equalling, if not surpassing, that of the rest of the book, was the work of another hand, added with the intention of correcting the original. To us it seems that, except for certain interpolations here and there,[5] it forms the normal climax of the poem. The lesson which it teaches is not the *justice* of God's rule over the world, but the mystery of everything beneath the heavens, a mystery infinitely greater than the meagre official philosophy defended by the three friends would lead one to

---

[1] ix, 2–21.   [2] vii, 20 ; x.   [3] Ch. xxix–xxxi.   [4] xxxi, 35-7.
[5] xxxix, 13–18 ;   xl, 1 (E.V. xxxix, 31) ;   xl, 15–xli, 26 (E.V. xl, 10–xli, 25).

suppose, or than Job, with his narrow anthropocentric outlook, can conceive. God has many other things to attend to beside human interests—he guides the stars, sends rain to fertilize regions of the earth uninhabited by man, looks after the prosperity of animals which man can never tame, and even feeds the beasts of prey.[1] Man is surrounded by the unknown. Therefore, though Jahweh does not require Job to cease proclaiming his innocence, he must admit that to demand a reckoning from God was to reveal the depths of his ignorance.

Job makes the admission. Whereupon Jahweh severely blames his three friends for not having " spoken of me the thing that is right, as my servant Job hath ". The poet therefore attaches much greater importance to absolute sincerity of thought, and to intellectual courage, even when they are a source of error or even of blasphemy, than to the mechanical repetition of pious formulas.

The poem offers no solution to the problem which it states : it does not explain the suffering of the righteous. Negatively, however, there is a clear moral to be drawn from it, namely, that there are sufferings which are not punishments, and that it is, therefore, unjust to measure a man's guilt by the evils he endures.

It also inculcates the recognition of man's ignorance, in face of the might and terror and wisdom to be found in the wonders of the universe.

A protest of the conscience, a confidence, implied, though not avowed, in spite of all, in the God who rules the world ; further than this, perhaps a religious thinker of complete honesty of mind could hardly go, determined as he was not to take refuge in illusion, unless he had dared to believe in the possibility of a readjustment of the moral order beyond the grave, a hope of which he caught a glimpse, but rejected as an impossible dream.[2]

It is scarcely necessary to add that the average Jewish mind did not aspire to any such free treatment of established doctrine, and it is not surprising that the book as it now stands

---

[1] xxxviii, 39–40 ; xxxix, 26–30. *Cf.* **CCX**, 76, 191–2 ; **LXVII**, 316.

[2] xiv, 13–15, 18–20. On the contrary, the obscure and corrupt passage, xix, 25–7, evidently refers to a reparation which Job was expecting *during his life*, not after his death.

shows signs of numerous attempts to mitigate the author's audacity. Between Job's appeal to Jahweh and Jahweh's reply, a fourth friend suddenly intervenes, and under cover of teaching both Job and his three opponents a lesson, delivers a fresh vindication of the orthodox thesis only slightly modified.[1] An emendator attributes to Job a part of Bildad's third speech, and the whole of Zophar's,[2] so that in the end the hero appears to have embraced the " pure doctrine ". In several places the text has been modified, or interpolations made, with the same purpose in view.[3] Let us not waste too much regret on these well-intentioned alterations : it is thanks to them that the great poet's work, uneasy, perplexed, sometimes bitter, always admirably sincere, could be admitted to the Biblical canon and be handed down to us.

III

ECCLESIASTES

It is certainly to corrections of a similar kind that we owe the preservation of another work, much more radically opposed to the prevailing trend of Jewish thought than the poem of Job—the little book of *Qoheleth* or Ecclesiastes.

And, in fact, to explain some of the manifest contradictions to be found in this short work, it is not enough to admit that the author now and then reproduces the statements of an opponent, or that he stages a contest between two or three voices speaking in his own soul, or even that he intended to write a real dialogue, but that the allocation of the parts has been confused ; it is not enough to suppose that sheets of manuscript have been transposed, or think, as Renan did, that we are here confronted with the confessions of sincere mind relating in good faith the diverse and sometimes contradictory experiences encountered in the search for truth. There are passages affording undeniable evidence that additions have been made to the original work [4] and that it has been corrected.[5] It is also probable that we must

---

[1] Elihu's speech, cc. xxxiii–xxxvii. [2] xxvi, 5–14 ; xxvii, 7–23.
[3] ix, 8–10 ; xii, 7–10, 13 ; xiii, 15 ; xiv, 4 ; xxi, 16 ; *cf.* **CCX**, 109–135.
[4] e.g. xii, 9–12. [5] e.g. xii, 13–14.

allow for at least three interpolators, as suggested by Podechard [1] : (1) an enthusiastic disciple of Qoheleth, who
inserted, among other matter, the eulogy of his master [2];
(2) a " sage " (ḥâkâm), who inserted here and there rhythmical maxims with the object of defending the wisdom for
which the original author had shown scant consideration [3];
(3) a " pious man " (ḥâsîd), who interpolated here and there
the affirmation of the traditional doctrine of retribution, in
order to anticipate the dangerous conclusions which some
readers might draw from the original work.

To the master's exhortation :—

> " Rejoice, O young man in thy youth," he adds the corrective:
> " But know thou that for all these things God will bring thee into
> judgment," [4] and later : " Remember also thy creator in the days
> of thy youth." [5]

At the end of the book he adds a few sentences which, he
says, sum up its teaching :—

> " God shall bring every work into judgment, with every hidden
> thing, whether it be good, or whether it be evil." [6]

When once these various modifications have been removed,
instead of a philosophical treatise logically constructing
a coherent system, we are left with a collection of thoughts
animated by the same spirit, and a most unusual one.

The fundamental problem itself must have been new to
Israel. Hitherto the question of the manner in which God
had distributed worldly goods to mankind had been the subject
of many a passionate debate—how passionate, the book of
Job shows. For Ecclesiastes, the question is settled :—

> " All things come alike to all. There is one event to the righteous
> and to the wicked ; to the good and to the clean and to the unclean ;
> to him that sacrificeth and to him that sacrificeth not." [7]

The statement is not tinged with rebellion : it is a fact.
But he puts forward another problem : however much they
may be desired, can riches, pleasure, wisdom, a long life,
a numerous posterity, really bring happiness ? Can lasting
profit be derived from any one of them ? When he has
reviewed them all, he replies : " All is vanity," a mournful
refrain which he justifies in the most heterogeneous fashion

[1] CCXXXIV.　　[2] xii, 9–12.
[3] e.g. vii, 1–12.　　[4] xi, 9.
[5] xii, 1a.　　[6] xii, 13–14.　　[7] ix, 2.

by reasons drawn from the simplest of everyday experiences or from the subtlest and most penetrating psychology, but all burdened with the thought that for the man in quest of " that which endureth ", life holds nothing but disillusion.

> " Wherefore I praised the dead which are already dead more than the living which are yet alive : yet, better than them both did I esteem him which hath not been, who hath not seen the evil work that is done under the sun." [1]

Not that the author has the slightest hope of any happiness in a future life ; on the contrary, he is so completely convinced that death is followed by annihilation that he declares elsewhere, with no fear of contradiction, that " a living dog is better than a dead lion ",[2] and rejects as chimerical the theory that there is any difference between the fate that awaits the spirit of man after death and what happens to the life-principle in animals.[3]

His general conception of the universe agrees with his pessimistic views about human happiness. All is determined beforehand, all is immutable, good as well as evil, the fate, as well as the most secret thoughts, of every individual.[4] Qoheleth pushes his theory of predestination so far as to affirm a perpetual cycle of existence.

> " That which hath been is that which shall be ; and that which hath been done is that which shall be done ; and there is no new thing under the sun. Is there a thing whereof men say, See, this is new ? it hath been already, in the ages which were before us." [5]

" God brings back the past " [6]—an idea which reminds one of the " great year " of the philosophers of ancient Greece, in particular of Heraclitus, and the " endless cycle " of which many modern thinkers tell us.[7] But to the Jewish sage, this rigid law by which all things are ruled is indistinguishable from the will of God. On the other hand, he declares with repeated insistence that man is incapable of understanding, and consequently of foreseeing, the links in the chain of contradictory phenomena which make up the life of the world and of himself, and the reason for his blindness and lack of understanding is that in his heart he longs for the permanent, the eternal, the absolute, while

[1] iv, 2–3.　　　　　[2] ix, 4.
[3] iii, 21.　　　　　[4] iii, 14 ; ix, 1.
[5] i, 9–10 ; cf. i, 4–11 ; vi, 10.　[6] iii, 15.
[7] Spencer, Heine, Blanqui, Guyau, Le Bon, Nietzsche.

reality offers him nothing but the ephemeral, the transitory, the relative.

> " God hath made everything beautiful in its time ; also he hath set eternity in their heart, yet so that man cannot find out the work that God hath done from the beginning even to the end." [1]

Hence for man, destiny has the appearance of chance. The moral which Ecclesiastes draws is in harmony with his utilitarian and pessimistic point of view : the best that man can do is to eat and drink and enjoy life in the midst of all his troubles, although that, too, is but vanity. He does not, of course, mean to advise men to indulge in any excesses, he wants them to enjoy, calmly and honestly, the small joys which each day brings in its train.

He also proffers religious advice, chiefly remarkable for its negative character. Make no long prayers nor rash vows, " for God is in heaven, and thou upon earth." [2] He can scarcely be called fervent :—

> " Be not righteous over much," [3] he says, " neither make thyself over wise : why shouldest thou destroy thyself ? "

But neither does he advocate declared irreligion :—

> " Be not over wicked, neither be thou foolish : why shouldest thou die before thy time ? " [4]

Elsewhere he expresses regret that the righteous do not rule.[5] He adheres to a belief in God, His omnipotence, and His wisdom. But his piety has neither warmth nor vitality ; nor has it any intimate association with his outlook on life, an outlook which would square as well, perhaps better, with atheism. Ecclesiastes offers another example of the hold which doctrine already, divorced from life, had over the minds of men in Judaism.

The attempt has been made to explain the attitude of Qoheleth in terms of Greek philosophical systems—from which he is supposed to have borrowed his ideas—especially those of Heraclitus,[6] Zeno, Epicurus, and Pyrrho.[7] These attempts have not been very convincing,[8] for the Jewish

[1] iii, 11 ; cf. iii, 1–10 ; vii, 14.   [2] v, 1–6.
[3] vii, 16.   [4] vii, 17.   [5] viii, 10.
[6] E. Pfleiderer, *Die Philosophie des Heraklit von Ephesus in Lichte der Mysterien*, Berlin, 1886, pp. 255–287.
[7] CCXLVIII ; C. Siegfried, ZWT, xviii (1875), 284–291, 469–471 ; CXXXIII.
[8] Cf. CCXIX.

sage does not move in a world of abstract principles, but in the world of everyday occurrences. His disillusioned utterances, and his exhortations to make the most of the small pleasures of life are in a vein common enough among many Oriental moralists of ancient times,[1] and are to be met with later on in the pages of the Son of Sirach. It is none the less true that the audacity of his scepticism, and the almost philosophical way in which he states the problem of happiness, would be difficult to understand if they belonged to a time before Israel came in contact with Greek thought. Influence there must have been, but not of any particular system. It was due rather to the new atmosphere created in the East by the spread of Hellenic civilization.

It even seems as if, in one passage,[2] the author avowedly has in mind the Greek doctrine of the personal survival of the human soul, which appears to him unreasonable, and which he more or less travesties. If it is indeed the idea of the immortality of the soul which he thus rejects, the fact would be significant enough ; for that same belief in personal survival which Qoheleth refused to entertain was to be the solution which, with the books of Daniel, Enoch, and of the Wisdom of Solomon, the teaching of the Pharisees and of the Christians, was to extricate Jewish thought from the blind alley in which it had been trapped ever since it had made an axiom of the belief in individual retribution.

[1] **XXXIX**, 106–124, esp. 110–12, 114–15 ; **XXXV**, 182.
[2] iii, 19–21.

CHAPTER III

PIETY

IF the main tendencies of Judaism, like the doctrines on
which they were based, sometimes met with resistance
and protest on the part of the thinking minority, the general
run of believers welcomed them with wholehearted sincerity,
and even enthusiasm. There are, however, various indications
that among the more simple-minded, those who were more
concerned to be devout than intellectual, aspirations existed
which were either inherited from the past or portents of
future change, and these did not find complete satisfaction
in the established religion. The religious life of the Jewish
community was too intense and too varied to remain within
the dykes built for it by the dogmatists without at times
overflowing them.

To begin with, the masses of the people, side by side
with the official religion enjoined upon them by the Law,
had also a lower type of religion made up of ancient beliefs
and practices such as the worship of the dead, or of ideas
borrowed from foreign folk-lore, as for instance the story
of Asmodeus (the Aešma Dæva of the Persians), the demon
who was in love with a young Jewess and killed all other
suitors for her hand.[1] The book of Tobit, which is a monotheistic adaptation of the international folk-story of the
grateful dead, sheds a curious light on this undercurrent
of popular religion, and shows that it was not felt to be in
the slightest degree contrary to official religion : Tobit,
who bids his son offer food and pour wine upon the graves
of the righteous,[2] and risks his life to render to the dead the
honours due to them, is represented as a model of fidelity
to the law of Moses.

But the piety of the faithful found its best expression
within the framework of the beliefs and institutions which
the legislators of the restoration had approved. This side
of the religious life of ancient Judaism is illuminated for

[1] Tob. iii, 7–8, 16 ; vi, 14–18 ; viii, 1–3.   [2] Tob. iv, 17.

us by a document of inexhaustible richness and variety—
the book of Psalms. It is in fact generally recognized that,
though some of the poems contained in this collection date
back to the times before the Exile, and others belong to the
age of the Syrian persecutions or the Maccabees, the great
majority were either composed in the time of the Persian
domination or that of the Diadochi, or else adapted to suit
the needs of this period.

Before considering these psalms as historical documents,
it is important to have a clear idea as to the use to which they
were put, and to know why and in what surroundings they
were composed. Were they poems written for special
occasions, in which the poet had expressed his personal
feelings and recorded his experiences, or was their purpose
liturgical ? Did they embody the collective piety of the
Jewish community, or the sentiments, desires, and hopes
of the individual ? Were they used in the worship of the
Temple, or in the synagogue, or in small gatherings of pietists,
the " poor of Israel " ? Or again, were they largely " spiritual
songs ", not intended for use in public worship, but for the
private edification of the believer ? [1] Or did they form a
kind of manual of religion for the instruction of the nation ? [2]
Opinions are still very much divided on these various points, and
this is not the place to discuss them. Let us confine ourselves
to indicating briefly that solution of the problem which seems
to us the most probable.

Mowinckel's important contribution to the study of the
question [3] seems to us to have established the conclusion
that the psalms had not only been originally, as their
Babylonian and Egyptian prototypes are generally considered
to have been, *canticles intended to be sung or recited in the
course of certain ceremonies of Temple worship*, but that the
great majority were still used for this purpose in the time
of early Judaism.

There were hymns for the various feasts—the Passover,
the New Year, and the Harvest—*Te Deums* for days of
victory, and national intercessions for periods of public
calamity. There were processional chants and pilgrim
songs.

[1] Willy Staerk, **XXVIII**, iii, 1², 17*, 25*, 5–6, and *passim*.
[2] **CXCIX**, pp. xxiv–xxx.   [3] **LXVI**.

On the other hand, there were psalms for individual use,
for instance, psalms of gratitude to be sung by, or for, those
who had been delivered from some misfortune, at the time
when the thankoffering (*tôdâh*) was made which had been
vowed in the hour of distress ; the song was sung while the
person making the offering walked round the altar,[1] or took
in his hand the " cup of salvation ",[2] either to offer a libation,
or in the course of the sacrificial repast.[3] In this way he gave
his meed of praise in the sight of " the great congregation ".[4]
The Biblical collection also contains a great number of psalms
of supplication, intended to accompany the sacrifice offered in
case of sickness,[5] or in any misfortune ; in particular there
were those which were to be said by an accused man under
oath, who, by washing his hands [6] before the altar, and sub-
mitting to the ordeal prescribed by the law,[7] called upon God
to show forth his innocence by a sign.[8]

Other psalms were instructions (*tôrôth*) given by a priest
in the course of a ritual [9] ; others again were oracles uttered
in response to the prayers of the worshippers by one of
the prophets attached to the Temple.[10]

Parts of the Biblical collection show psalms of different
kinds combined together so as to form a liturgy for a single
ritual.[11]

The psalms were therefore not only the expression of the
collective piety of the Jewish community ; like the sacrifices
with which they were connected, they left ample room for
the display of the religious feelings and needs of the
individual.[12]

They were composed *for* worshippers who found themselves
in special situations,[13] but not necessarily *by* a man in such

[1] Ps. xxvi, 6 ; *cf.* cxviii, 27.   [2] Ps. cxvi, 13.
[3] *Cf.* **XXXV**, 145, n. 10.
[4] Ps. xxii, 22, 25 ; xxxv, 18 ; xl, 10–11.
[5] Sir. xxxviii, 11.   [6] Ps. xxvi, 6 ; lxxiii, 13.
[7] *Cf.* Numb. v, 11–31.
[8] 1 Kings viii, 31–2 ; Ps. vii ; xxvii, 7–14 ; xxxv, etc.   *Cf.*
CCXLII ; CCXLIII.
[9] Ps. xv, 2–5 ; xxiv, 4–6 ; cxviii, 20.
[10] Ps. lx, 8–10 ; lxviii, 23–4 ; lxxxv, 9–14 ; xcv, 8–11. *Cf.* **LXVI**, iii.
[11] Ps. xv ; xxiv ; cviii ; cxviii ; cxxxiv.
[12] Consequently the psalms written in the 1st person singular are
doubtless to be interpreted personally, except when it is expressly stated
that they are meant to personify Israel.
[13] Ps. cii, 1.

a situation, although a worshipper might compose a psalm testifying to his personal joy or sorrow.[1] If heaven had bestowed quite exceptional favours, it was seemly to sing a " new song ",[2] but that very fact shows that as a rule one of the psalms already in existence was used ; and that is why various attempts were made, in particular by the guilds of Temple singers—those of Asaph, the sons of Korah, Ethan or Heman—to compose collections of psalms, and why, later, these incomplete collections were united in a single book.

If this conception of the place of the psalms in Jewish life is correct, it follows that they are to be regarded neither as the reflection of the attitude towards religion of any particular sect, or of a few men of more than ordinary spirituality, nor, on the other hand, as a kind of realistic panorama of the piety of the masses, but rather, like church hymns to-day, as an image of that piety to which the average man aspired.

We will confine ourselves to a definition of the attitude adopted by the psalmists with regard to four of the fundamental institutions or beliefs of the official religion of the day : Temple worship, the Law, the doctrine of God, and that of retribution.

A number of psalms bear witness to the ardent and profound affection which embraced the Temple, the dwelling-place of Jahweh,[3] the impregnable abode of the Almighty,[4] and Jerusalem, the City of the Great King,[5] whose ramparts and gates were the haunt of pilgrims listening to the story of the wonders which had been enacted there in days gone by.[6] The processions and the majestic ceremonial of the ritual were dear to the hearts of all.[7] The Jews of the Dispersion turned in the direction of the Temple to pray,[8] and rejoiced when they could make the pilgrimage to the Holy

---

[1] In the historical books, Hannah, David, Hezekiah, and Jonah are said to have composed them. Ben Sira wrote them (xxxix, 12–35 ; li, 1–12).

[2] Ps. xxxiii, 3 ; xl, 4 ; xcvi, 2 ; cxlix, 1 ; Is. xlii, 10.

[3] Ps. xliii, 3 ; lxxxiv, 2.　　　　　[4] xlvi, 5 ; lxv, 5.

[5] xlviii, 3 ; cf. lxxxvii ; cxxii.　　　[6] xlviii, 4–9, 13–15.

[7] Ps. xlii, 5 ; Sir. l, 5–21.

[8] Ps. cxxi, 1 ; 1 Kings viii, 44, 48 ; Dan. vi, 11 ; Tob. iii, 11; Esdras iv, 58.

City,[1] Nevertheless, it is significant that belief in the efficacy of the rite as such, and in the magical effect of ritual, plays hardly any part in the piety which is reflected in the psalms. It was not, needless to say, because there was any doubt of the efficacy of the sacred act : the penitent who recited Psalm li called upon God to " Purge me with hyssop [2] and I shall be clean ". But his cry for inward cleansing is more insistent still : " Create in me a clean heart, O God." [3]

Among the observances connected with Temple ritual, the psalmists show a marked preference for the thankoffering, the votive offering, and above all for the song of praise to God, for those, in fact, which expressed the personal feelings of the worshipper.[4] Some even go so far as to discount the worship consisting of the sacrifice of bulls and goats in favour of the homage rendered to God by the hearts and lives of the faithful.[5] It is this fact which has led so many critics to regard most of the psalms as " spiritual canticles ", and to speak of their tendency to disparage ritual. That is going too far, but it is true that average Jewish piety paid more regard to moral life than to mysterious rites, and found its greatest satisfaction less in sacred acts, however venerated, than in original channels of expression which it had either considerably extended, like the religious hymn, or else created, like the worship of the synagogue. The latter, which included prayers, the reading and expounding of the Law and the prophetic books, and a blessing, is for the first time reliably attested in the reign of Ptolemy III (247–222) in Egypt.[6] We subsequently find mention of synagogues at Alexandronesus [7]—also in Egypt—Antioch,[8] and Ptolemais.[9] The new institution probably first saw the light among the Jews of the Diaspora.[10]

It is evident that the Jewish piety which is reflected in

---

[1] Ps. lxxxiv ; cxxii.
[2] Shrub used as a sprinkler.
[3] Ps. li, 7, 10.   [4] e.g. Ps. l, 14, 15 ; cxvi, 17–18.
[5] xl, 7–12 ; l, 7–15 ; li, 18–19 ; lxix, 31–2 ; cxli, 2.
[6] Inscription of the synagogue of Schedia about 14 m. from Alexandria (Theodore Reinach, REJ, 45 (1902), 62 ; cf. E. Schürer, TLZ, 1903, col. 156 ; 1910, col. 99 ; LXXV, ii[4], 500 ; iii, 41).
[7] Papyrus of 217.   [8] Josephus, B.J., VII, iii, 3, § 44.
[9] 3 Macc. vii, 20.
[10] See vol. xxviii, pt. ii, ch. vi, 3, and cf. pl. viii.

the Psalms had not really assimilated the ritualism of
Ezekiel and the Priestly Code ; it had preserved something
of the spirituality of the great prophets.

The truth, beauty, and supreme utility of the Law are
themes of which the psalmists love to sing.[1] Its demands
never weigh heavily upon them—they are obeyed with joy.
Here we may point out that they never mention those
refinements and subtleties in the observance of the regulations regarding the clean and the unclean, or the keeping
of the Sabbath, which in ages to come were to be considered
essential. All the emphasis is on the moral demands of the
Law.[2] No others are declared by the priest, when he recites
to the procession of the faithful who are about to enter the
Temple the conditions on which Jahweh will allow them
to approach him.[3] The moral teaching of the Psalms bears,
moreover, the stamp of the times ; like that of the Proverbs
it wears a legal air, it appeals to the fear of God as the chief
motive, and recommends above all the everyday virtues of
uprightness, simplicity and truth. Nevertheless it has one
heroic feature : it implies that death is preferable to a
renunciation of the religion of the fathers,[4] though the texts
in which this conviction is stated belong for the most part
to the following period, that of the Syrian persecutions.

The teaching about God which we have found in the
other writings of early Judaism is also that of the Psalms :
as a rule, strict monotheism is either inculcated or taken
for granted. There are hardly any signs of the survival
of the old " polytheism ", of which, however, an example
is to be found in certain traditional phrases, such as
" There is none like unto thee among the gods, O Lord ",[5]
" Thou art exalted far above all gods ",[6] or in the title of
" god " which is sometimes given to kings.[7] The Psalms
abound in striking descriptions of the " transcendence " of
Jahweh, his creative power, his rule over the universe. That

---

[1] Ps. i ; xix, 8–14 ; xxxvii, 30–1 ; xl, 9 ; cxix.
[2] xxxiv, 13–15.
[3] xv, 1–5 ; xxiv, 3–6 ; cxviii, 19–20.
[4] xliv, esp. vv. 18–23 ; lxxiv, 19–21 ; *cf.* Sir. iv, 28.
[5] Ps. lxxxvi, 8 ; *cf.* lxxxix, 7.
[6] Ps. xcvii, 9 ; *cf.* xcv, 3 ; xcvi, 4.
[7] lviii, 2 ; lxxxii ; cx ; *cf.* 2 Sam. xiv, 17, 20 ; Zech. xii, 8. The
interpretation of these passages has been much disputed.

does not mean that the notion of God has assumed the abstract character which is noticeable in other writings of the period. The gulf between God and man had grown ever deeper, but Jewish piety was able to bridge it. The God of the Psalms is as living, as near, and is invoked with as great an intimacy as ever the Jahweh of ancient times had been.

When a psalmist depicts the awe-inspiring grandeur of God and the nothingness of man, the conclusion he reaches is :—

" Put not your trust . . . in the son of man, in whom there is no help. . . . Happy is he that hath the God of Jacob for his help." [1]

And, when one of these poets sings of the marvels of creation, it is to render thanks to God for having given into the hands of man power over all created things,[2] or for having ordered it all for the welfare of each inhabitant of the earth.[3] When he proclaims that Jahweh is the one God, and that other gods are as nothing, it is that he may rejoice in the closeness of the bond uniting the ruler of the universe with the people of Israel,[4] and that he may summon all dwellers upon earth to give him glory and honour.[5] The omnipotence of Jahweh is the truth in which the psalmists trust [6] because he is omniscient and everywhere present they know that he will punish the wicked and ensure the triumph of the righteous,[7] and that he will deliver those who trust in his mercy.[8] And so what might have widened the chasm between God and the worshipper has narrowed it.

With regard to the practical importance attached to the doctrine of retribution, and to its repercussions in the lives of the faithful, the Psalms give us first-hand information.

First of all, we learn from them that the explanation which this doctrine affords of the evils of life was not the only one. There was another, much more archaic and still of great potency, which attributed suffering, and especially sickness, to the evil influence of an enemy. This is of course the commonest explanation to be met with among

---

[1] Ps. cxlvi, 3, 5. [2] viii, 3–10.
[3] civ, 10–24. [4] xcv, 3–7 ; cviii, 5.
[5] xcvi, 1–10. [6] xxxiii, 6–12 ; xlvi, 9–12 ; xlvii, 3–4.
[7] xi, 5 ; cxxxix, 7–12, 19–24. [8] xxxiii, 18–19.

non-civilized races to-day ; it was one of the most important elements in the official religion of the Assyro-Babylonians, the search for the sorcerer or sorceress who had cast a spell upon the patient, and the discovery of a rite capable of counteracting its fell power, being one of the principal occupations of the exorcizing priest (*ašipu*). The same idea persisted among the masses of the Jewish population : hence, the, to us, surprising frequency with which " enemies " are mentioned in the supplicating psalms [1] ; the first thought of a man overtaken by misfortune or sickness, especially the latter,[2] is that evil-intentioned men have " devised to take away his life ",[3] privily laid a net for him,[4] cursed him,[5] or at least foretold that evil would befall him,[6] or if they have not injured him with their tongues,[7] they have done it by some ill-omened gesture of the foot,[8] or the fingers,[9] or by some sinister look.[10] And like the Babylonian exorcist, the unhappy man often retaliates with similar weapons, and indulges in terrible curses against those responsible for these occult machinations.[11]

At times, but very rarely, the explanation given was the same which had been proffered of old—the sufferings of the present were a punishment for the sins of the fathers.[12]

But the conception which predominates in the thoughts of the psalmists is undoubtedly that of immediate individual retribution. It was moreover quite consistent with the attitude of the simple-minded which, in the presence of any evil, could evoke the comment : " An enemy hath done this." If a man came within the circle in which his adversary could harm him with magic, it was because Jahweh had delivered him into his opponent's hands in punishment for sin.[13]

The righteous always prosper ; they escape from their enemies, and if they fall they can rise up. The wicked, on the contrary, when they fall a prey to calamity,

---

[1] See Ad. Lods, **RHR, LXXVIII** (1918), 276–7 ; **LXVI**, 1.
[2] e.g. Ps. xxii, 15–16 ; xxxi, 10–11 ; xli, 4, 8–9 ; cix, 22–4.
[3] xxxi, 13 ; xxxv, 4, 7 ; xl, 15 ; lxiii, 10 ; lxxi, 10–13, 24, etc.
[4] xxxi, 4, etc.   [5] cix, 17, 18, 28.   [6] xli, 6–9.
[7] x, 7 ; xxxvi, 4 ; xli, 6–9 ; lii, 4–6 ; lvii, 5 ; lix, 8, 13 ; lxiv, 4–6, 9 ; xciv, 4 ; cxx, 2–3 ; cxl, 2–6, 12.
[8] Prov. vi, 13.   [9] Prov. vi, 13 ; Is. lviii, 9.
[10] Prov. vi, 13 ; x, 10.
[11] e.g. Ps. xxxv, 4–8, 26 ; lviii, 7–10 ; cix, 2–20.
[12] lxxix, 8 ; cix, 14.   [13] xxvii, 12 ; xli, 3–4.

AA

succumb, being destined to misfortune, shame, and a premature end.[1] In many of the psalms, this idea is developed in a
didactic form similar to that used in the wisdom literature.[2]
Everywhere it is taken for granted. When a believer is
overtaken by misfortune, and particularly when he is falsely
accused, he may try to protest his innocence before Jahweh
and implore God to prove it by delivering him.[3] But his
safest course is to confess himself guilty,[4] to acknowledge that
a sin, committed perhaps in his youth or even unconsciously,[5]
has brought punishment upon him, and to accept divine
chastening [6] : touched by his repentance, it was thought,
Jahweh would not fail to deliver him.

But if, instead of lifting, the clouds grew still more
lowering, if the believer was made aware that he was about
to die a death of violence or wretchedness before his time,
it was a proof that he had committed unforgivable sins;
his neighbours, even his relations, looked askance at him and
left him, as did the friends of Job, for had not God condemned him ? [7] This explains the anguished supplications of
the pious Jew that Jahweh would keep him from Sheol [8] :
for it was possible to interpret the other sufferings which the
righteous might be called upon to undergo as trials, or
warnings, or salutary chastisement, but to die before his time
was a sign that his most precious possession had been
forfeited—the name of a righteous man. Or else—and the
alternative was fraught with still greater terror—it was a
sign that the evil-doers were right in their denunciation of
the folly of piety, and that the scoffers were justified in
asking " Where is thy God ? ".[9] Hence the suffering of
the " righteous ", and the immunity and lasting prosperity
of the wicked, was a riddle so tormenting and so bewildering
that faith hung in the balance. Hence the feeling of instability,
the total lack of inward security, which inevitably resulted
from the belief inculcated by early Judaism, that the

[1] xxxiv, 20–3. [2] Ps. i ; xxxiv ; xxxvii ; cxii, etc.
[3] v ; xvii ; xxvi ; xxxv, etc. [4] xxv, 11 ; xxxii ; li.
[5] xix, 13 ; xxv, 7 ; xliv, 22 ; xc, 8.
[6] xxv, 5 ; xxvii, 11 ; lxxxvi, 4.
[7] xxxi, 12 ; xli, 10 ; lxxxviii, 9.
[8] Ps. lxxxviii ; cf. vi, 5–6 ; xxx, 10 ; Is. xxxviii, 18–19.
[9] Ps. x, 3 ; xiv, 1 ; xlii, 4, 11.

happiness or unhappiness of man's earthly lot provided the only reliable sign of God's response to man's piety.

Nevertheless some of the psalmists show a tendency to escape from the narrow confines of established doctrine. Since the men whose chief aim was strict obedience to the Law, the orthodox and the zealous, formed a party of idealists who were not usually in power, while the leaders of the community were politicians willing to flatter their pagan masters with every sort of compromise, the terms " rich " and " powerful " had become synonymous with " unrighteous "—by which term the pious referred to their enemies—and the term " poor " almost an equivalent for " righteous ".   It would be exaggeration to conclude that the zealous followers of religion idealized and glorified poverty in the way that Saint Francis of Assisi did, or that they regarded it as eminently conducive to a holy life.   They endured it with a temporary resignation.   Nevertheless, they affirmed their conviction that however humble their present state might be, it was more enviable than that of men who, in spite of their prosperity, could not count on help from Jahweh.

> " Thou hast put gladness in my heart, More than they have whose corn and wine are increased." [1]

The author of Psalm lxxiii shows a more enlightened spirituality.   At the sight of the prosperity of the wicked, he tells us, he had almost lost faith, but his serenity returned when " he went into the sanctuary of God " ;

> " Nevertheless I am continually with thee : Thou hast holden my right hand . . . Whom have I in heaven but thee ?   And there is none upon earth that I desire beside thee. My flesh and my heart faileth, But God is the strength of my heart and my portion for ever." [2]

This passage and two or three others [3] contain perhaps a hint, a foreshadowing, of belief in a fellowship between God and the believer which shall outlast death.   Whether this is so or not, without definitely breaking with the prevalent idea—for he looks forward to the visible downfall of unbelievers [4]—he finds in some inner experience, in his

---

[1] Ps. iv, 7.
[2] lxxiii, 17, 23, 25–6.
[3] xvi, 9–11 (unlikely) ; xlix, 16.
[4] lxxiii, 17, 27.

consciousness of God's nearness, a witness capable of withstanding even the most overwhelming of outward happenings.

In this way much of the richness, intensity, and deep spirituality of that religious life which the prophets had engendered was projected into the new forms inaugurated by Judaism.

BIBLIOGRAPHY

PERIODICALS, DICTIONARIES, AND COLLECTIONS

Abhandlungen der Berliner Akad. der Wiss., phil.-hist. Klasse	ABA
Académie des Inscriptions et Belles-Lettres, comptes rendus des séances	AI
The American Journal of Semitic Languages and Literatures	AJSL
Archiv für Religionswissenschaft	AR
Beihefte zur Zeitschrift für die alttestamentliche Wissenschaft, Giessen, Töpelmann	BZAW
Bulletin de correspondance hellénique . . .	BCH
The Cambridge Ancient History, Cambridge, Univ. Press, Press, vol. ii, 1924	CAH
Corpus inscriptionum semiticarum	CIS
Dict. d'Archéologie chrétienne et de Liturgie (Dom F. Cabrol et Dom H. Leclerq, Paris, 1903 *ff*. The publication has reached part cxxv and the syllable Mon)	DACL
Dict. of the Bible (J. Hastings, 5 vols., Edin., 1897–1904)	DB
Encyclopedia Biblica (Cheyne and Black, 4 vols., Lond., 1899–1903)	EB
Encyclopædia judaica, Das Judentum in Geschichte und Gegenwart (Klatzkin et J. Elbogen, Berlin, 9 vols. have appeared out of 15 (1934))	EJ
Expository Times	ET
Handkommentar zum A. T. (Nowack), Göttingen, Vandenhoeck and Ruprecht	HK
The Harvard Theological Review	HTR
The Jewish Encyclopedia, New York, 1901 *ff*, 12 vols.	JE
Journal of Biblical Literature	JBL
The Journal of Egyptian Archaeology, Lond. . .	JEA
Journal of Theological Studies	JTS
Keilschriftliche Bibliothek	KB
Kommentar zum A. T. (Sellin), Leipzig, Deichert .	KAT
Kurzer Hand-Commentar zum A T. (Marti), Tubingen, Mohr	KHC
Kurzgefasstes exegetisches Handbuch zum A. T., Leipzig, Hirzel	KEH
Mémoires présentés par divers savants à l'Académie des Inscriptions et Belles Lettres	MAI
Mitt. der Vorderasiatischen Gesellschaft . .	MVAG
Museon	MUS
Orientalistische Literaturzeitung	OLZ
Palaestinajahrbuch	PJ
Palestine Exploration Fund	PEF
Real-Encyklopaedie für prot. Theologie und Kirche, 3rd ed. (Alb. Hauck, 22 vols., Leipzig, 1896–1909) .	HRE

Recherches de science religieuse	RSR
Recueil de travaux relatifs à la philologie et à l'archéologie égyptienne et assyrienne	RTEA
Die Religion in Geschichte und Gegenwart, Tubingen, Mohr.	RGG
Revue d'Assyriologie	RA
Revue Biblique, Paris, Gabalda	RB
Revue des Études anciennes	REA
Revue des Études grecques	REG
Revue des Études juives	REJ
Revue des Études sémitiques	RES
Revue d'histoire et de philosophie religieuses, Strasburg-Paris, Alcan	RHP
Revue de l'histoire des Religions	RHR
Revue de théologie et de philosophie, Lausanne . .	RTP
Sitzungsberichte der Preussischen Akademie der Wissenschaften, phil.-hist. Klasse	SBA
Syria, Revue d'art oriental et d'archéologie, Paris, Geuthner	SY
Theologische Blätter, Leipzig, Hinrichs . . .	TB
Theologische Literaturzeitung, Leipzig, Hinrichs . .	TLZ
Theologische Quartalschrift	TQS
Theologische Rundschau	TR
Theologische Studien und Kritiken, Gotha, Perthes .	TSK
Theologisch Tijdschrift	TT
Transactions of the Society for Biblical Archaeology .	TSBA
Zeitschrift der Deutschen Morgenlaendischen Gesellschaft, Leipzig, Brockhaus	ZDMG
Zeitschrift des Deutschen Palästinavereins, Leipzig, Baedeker	ZDPV
Zeitschrift für Assyriologie	ZA
Zeitschrift für die alttestamentliche Wissenschaft, Giessen, Töpelmann	ZATW
Zeitschrift für wissenschaftliche Theologie (Hilgenfeld) .	ZW

GENERAL WORKS

I. BENZINGER, *Hebraeische Archaelogie*, 3rd ed., Leipzig, Pfeiffer, 1927	I
PHILIPPE BERGER, *Histoire de l'écriture dans l'Antiquité*, Paris, Imprimerie nationale, 1891	II
ALFRED BERTHOLET, *Histoire de la civilisation d'Israël*, tr. by JACQUES MARTY, Paris, Payot, 1929 . .	III
R. BEVAN and CH. SINGER, *The Legacy of Israel*, Oxford, 1928	IV
La sainte Bible, traduction nouvelle d'après les meilleurs textes, avec introductions et notes (Bible du Centenaire), Paris, Société biblique protestante de Paris, 1916 *ff*	V
KARL BUDDE, *Geschichte der althebraeischen Literatur*, Leipzig, Amelang, 1906	VI
D. BUZY, *Les symboles de l'Ancien Testament*, Paris, Gabalda, 1923	VII

ANTONIN CAUSSE, *Les dispersés d'Israël*, Paris, Alcan, 1929   VIII

A. CAUSSE, *Les " Pauvres " d'Israël (prophètes, psalmistes, messianistes)*, Strasburg-Paris, Istra, 1922 . . IX

KARL HEINRICH CORNILL, *Einleitung in die kanonischen Bücher des Alten Testaments*, Tubingen, Mohr, 5th ed., 1905 X

SAMUEL IVES CURTISS, German tr. by H. STOKES, *Ursemitische Religion im Volksleben des heutigen Orients*, Leipzig, Hinrichs, 1903 . . . XI

LOUIS DELAPORTE, *La Mésopotamie. Les civilisations babylonienne et assyrienne*, Paris, Renaissance du livre, 1923 XII

JOSEPH DERENBOURG, *Essai sur l'histoire et la géographie de la Palestine, d'après les Talmuds et les autres sources rabbiniques*, Paris, 1867 XIII

P. PAUL DHORME, *Choix de textes religieux assyro-babyloniens*, Paris, Lecoffre, 1907 XIV

BERNHARD DUHM, *Das Buch Jesaia*, Handkommentar zum Alten Testament, iii, 1, Göttingen, Vandenhoeck and Ruprecht, 1892 XV

B. DUHM, *Die Theologie der Propheten*, Bonn, 1875 . XVI

HANS DUHM, *Die bösen Geister im Alten Testament*, Tubingen, Leipzig, Mohr, 1904 XVII

RENÉ DUSSAUD, *Les origines cananéennes du sacrifice israélite*, Paris, Leroux, 1921 XVIII

R. DUSSAUD, *Topographie historique de la Syrie antique et médiévale*, Paris, Geuthner, 1927 . . . XIX

OTTO EISSFELDT, *Einleitung in das Alte Testament* Tubingen, Mohr, 1934 XX

JAMES FRAZER, *The Golden Bough* . . . XXI

GAUDEFROY-DEMOMBYNES, *Contribution à l'étude du pèlerinage de la Mekke*, Paris, Geuthner, 1923 . XXII

LUCIEN GAUTIER, *Introduction à l'Ancien Testament*, 2 vols., Lausanne, Bridel, 1st ed., 1906 ; 2nd, 1914 . XXIII

GEIGER, *Urschrift und Uebersetzungen der Bibel*, Breslau, 1857 XXIV

GRAETZ, *Histoire des Juifs*, tr. by WOGUE, vol. ii, Paris, 1884 XXV

GEORGE BUCHANAN GRAY, *Sacrifice in the Old Testament. Its Theory and Practice*, Oxford, Clarendon Press, 1925 XXVI

HUGO GRESSMANN, *Altorientalische Texte und Bilder zum Alten Testament*, 2 vols. (I Texte, II Bilder), 2nd ed., Berlin-Leipzig, de Gruyter, 1926 . . . XXVII

HUGO GRESSMANN, HERMANN GUNKEL, MAX HALLER, HANS SCHMIDT, WILLY STAERK, PAUL VOLZ, *Die Schriften des Alten Testaments in Auswahl übersetzt*, Göttingen, Vandenhoeck and Ruprecht, 1st ed., 1910 *ff.* ; 2nd, 1921 *ff.* XXVIII

HERMANN GUNKEL, *Genesis*, Handkommentar zum A. T., 3rd ed., Göttingen, Vandenhoeck and Ruprecht, 1910 XXIX

HERMANN GUTHE, *Geschichte des Volkes Israel*, Tubingen, Mohr, 2nd ed., 1904 ; 3rd, 1914 XXX

H. GUTHE, *Kurzes Bibelwörterbuch*, 1905 . . . XXXI

JOSEPH HALÉVY, *Mélanges de critique et d'histoire*, Paris, Maisonneuve, 1883 XXXII

360 BIBLIOGRAPHY

R. T. Herford, *Judaism in the New Testament Period*,
London, 1928 . . . .   **XXXIII**

Gustav Hölscher, *Die Bücher Esra und Nehemia*, in
Emil Kautzsch, *Die Heilige Schrift des Alten
Testaments*, 4th ed., Tubingen, Mohr, 1923, vol. ii,
pp. 491–562 . . . .   **XXXIV**

G. Hölscher, *Geschichte der israelitischen und jüdischen
Religion*, Giessen, Töpelmann, 1922 . . .   **XXXV**

G. Hölscher, *Die Profeten, Untersuchung zur Religionsgeschichte Israels*, Leipzig, Hinrichs, 1914. . .   **XXXVI**

A. van Hoonacker, *Les douze petits Prophètes traduits
et commentés*, Études bibliques, Paris, Gabalda,
1908 . . . .   **XXXVII**

Henri Hubert et Marcel Mauss, *Essai sur la nature et
la fonction du sacrifice*, Paris, Alcan, 1899 . .   **XXXVIII**

Paul Humbert, *Recherches sur les sources égyptiennes de
la littérature sapientiale des Hébreux*, Neuchâtel,
secrétariat de l'Université, 1929 . . . .   **XXXIX**

Morris Jastrow, jun., *Aspects of Religious Belief and
Practice in Babylonia and Assyria* (American Lectures
on the History of Religions, 9th series, 1910), New
York and London, Putnam, 1911 . . . .   **XL**

Morris Jastrow, jun., *Die Religion Babyloniens und
Assyriens*, 2 vols., Giessen, Töpelmann, 1912 . .   **XLI**

J. A. Jaussen, *Coutumes des Arabes au pays de Moab*,
Paris, Gabalda, 1908 . . . . . .   **XLII**

Charles F. Jean, *La littérature des Babyloniens et des
Assyriens*, Paris, Geuthner, 1924 . . . .   **XLIII**

Charles F. Jean, *Le milieu biblique avant Jésus-Christ*,
Paris, Geuthner, 1st vol., 1922 ; 2nd, 1923 . .   **XLIV**

Alfred Jeremias, *Das Alte Testament im Lichte des
Alten Orients*, Leipzig, Hinrichs, 1904 ; 2nd ed., 1906 ;
3rd, 1916 ; 4th, 1930 . . . . . .   **XLV**

Josephus, *Œuvres complètes de Flavius Josèphe*, traduites
en français sous la direction de Théodore Reinach,
Paris, Leroux, 1900 *ff.* . . . . . .   **XLVI**

Jean Juster, *Les Juifs dans l'Empire romain, leur
condition juridique, économique et sociale*, 2 vols.,
Paris, Geuthner, 1914 . . . . . .   **XLVII**

Emil Kautzsch, *Die Heilige Schrift des Alten Testaments*, 2 vols., Tubingen, Mohr, 3rd ed., 1908 ; 4th,
1922–3 . . . .   **XLVIII**

Rudolf Kittel, *Geschichte des Volkes Israel*, 6th ed.,
vol. ii, 1925, Gotha ; vol. iii, 1929, Stuttgart, Kohl-
hammer . . . .   **XLIX**

J. A. Knudtzon, *Die El-Amarna Tafeln mit Einleitung
und Erlaeuterungen*, 2 vols., Leipzig, Hinrichs, 1915 .   **L**

M. J. Lagrange, *Le Judaïsme avant Jésus-Christ*, Paris,
1931 . . . .   **LI**

C. F. Lehmann-Haupt, *Israel, Seine Entwicklung im
Rahmen der Weltgeschichte*, Tubingen, Mohr, 1911 .   **LII**

Lucien Lévy-Bruhl, *La mentalité primitive*, Paris,
Alcan, 1922 . . . .   **LIII**

Mark Lidzbarski, *Handbuch der nordsemitischen
Epigraphik*, Weimar, Felber, 1898 . . . .   **LIV**

ADOLPHE LODS, *L'ange de Yahvé et l' " âme extérieure "* (Wellhausen-Festschrift, pp. 263–278), Giessen, Töpelmann, 1914 LV

AD. LODS, *La croyance à la vie future et le culte des morts dans l'antiquité israélite*, 2 vols., Paris, Fischbascher, 1906 LVI

AD. LODS, *Israël, des origines au milieu du* VIIIᵉ *siècle*, Paris, Renaissance du livre, 1930 ; 9th thousand (with additions), 1932 LVII

ALFRED LOISY, *Essai historique sur le sacrifice*, Paris, Nourry, 1920 LVIII

A. LOISY, *La religion d'Israël*, 2nd ed., Ceffonds, 1908 ; 3rd, Paris, Nourry, 1933 LIX

KARL MARTI, *Das Buch Jesaja*, Kurzer Hand-Commentar zum Alten Testament, x, Tubingen-Friburg-Leipzig, Mohr, 1900 LX

K. MARTI, *Das Dodekapropheton*, Kurzer Hand-Commentar zum Alten Testament, xiii, Tubingen, Mohr, 1904 LXI

K. MARTI, *Geschichte der israelitischen Religion*, 5th ed., Strasburg, F. Bull, 1907 LXII

S. MATHEW, *The History of New Testament Times in Palestine*, New York, 1910 LXIII

JOHANNES MEINHOLD, *Einführung in das Alte Testament*, Giessen, Töpelmann, 1919 LXIV

MOMMSEN, *Histoire romaine*, tr. by CAGNAT et TOUTAIN, vol. xi, Paris, 1889 LXV

SIGMUND MOWINCKEL, *Psalmenstudien*, 6 vols., Kristiania, Dybwad, 1921–4 LXVI

W. O. E. OESTERLEY and THEODORE H. ROBINSON, *Hebrew Religion. Its origin and development*, London, S.P.C.K., 1930 LXVII

W. O. E. OESTERLEY and TH. H. ROBINSON, *A History of Israel*, 2 vols., Oxford, Clarendon Press, 1932 . LXVIII

JOHS. PEDERSEN, *Israel, its Life and Culture*, i–ii, London, Milford, 1926 LXIX

C. PIEPENBRING, *Histoire du Peuple d'Israël*, Paris, 1898 LXX

ERNEST RENAN, *Histoire du Peuple d'Israël*, Paris, Lévy, 1887 *ff.* LXXI

GIUSEPPE RICCIOTTI, *Storia d'Israele*, 2 vols., Turin, Soc. editrice internaz., 1932 LXXII

C. W. ROGERS, *Cuneiform Parallels to the Old Testament*, Oxford, University Press, 1912 . . . LXXIII

A. SCHLATTER, *Geschichte Israels von Alexander dem Grossen bis Hadrian*, 1906 LXXIV

EMIL SCHÜRER, *Geschichte des jüdischen Volkes im Zeitalter Jesu Christi*, Leipzig, Hinrichs, 2nd ed., 1886–1890 ; 3rd–4th, 1909 . . . LXXV

R. P. SCHWALM, *La vie privée du peuple juif à l'époque de Jésus-Christ*, Paris, Gabalda, 1910 . . LXXVI

ERNST SELLIN, *Einleitung in das Alte Testament*, Leipzig, Quelle and Meyer, 1st ed., 1910 ; 2nd, 1914 . LXXVII

E. SELLIN, *Geschichte des israelitisch-jüdischen Volkes*, 1932 LXXVIII

E. Sellin, *Das Zwölfprophetenbuch* (Kommentar zum A. T., xii), 2nd and 3rd eds., Leipzig, Deichert, 1929–1930 . . . . **LXXIX**

S. Spinner, *Herkunft, Entstehung and antike Umwelt des hebraeischen Volkes*, Vienna, Vernay, 1933 . . **LXXX**

Willy Staerk, *Das assyrische Weltreich im Urteil der Propheten*, 1908 . . . . **LXXXI**

Bernhard Stade, *Geschichte des Volkes Israel*, 2 vols., Berlin, Grote, 2nd ed., 1889 . . . . . **LXXXII**

B. Stade, *Biblische Theologie des Alten Testaments*, 2 vols., Tubingen, Mohr, 1905 . . . . **LXXXIII**

Edmond Stapfer, *La Palestine au temps de Jésus-Christ*, Paris, 1897 . . . . **LXXXIV**

Tiele, *Kompendium der Religionsgeschichte*, tr. by F. W. T. Weber, 3rd ed. revised by Nathan Söderblom, Breslau, Biller, 1903 . . . . **LXXXV**

Paul Volz, *Der Geist Gottes und die verwandten Erscheinungen im Alten Testament und im anschliessenden Judentum*, Tubingen, Mohr, 1910 . . . . **LXXXVI**

Julius Wellhausen, Bleek's *Einleitung in die Heilige Schrift*, 1st pt., *Einl. in das A. T.*, 4th ed., Berlin, Reimer, 1878 . . . . **LXXXVII**

J. Wellhausen, *Israelitische und jüdische Geschichte*, Berlin, Reimer, 2nd ed., 1895 ; 6th, 1907 ; 7th, 1914 **LXXXVIII**

J. Wellhausen, *Die Composition des Hexateuchs und der histor. Bücher des A.T.*, 2nd ed., Berlin, Reimer, 1889 **LXXXIX**

J. Wellhausen, *Reste arabischen Heidentums gesammelt und erlaeutert*, 2nd ed., Berlin, Reimer, 1897 . . **XC**

Alexandre Westphal, *Les sources du Pentateuque*, 2 vols., Paris, Fischbacher, 1888–1892 . . **XCI**

A. Westphal, *Les prophètes*, 2 vols., Paris–Lausanne, 1924 . . . . **XCII**

Hugo Winckler, *Alittestamentliche Untersuchungen* . **XCIII**

H. Winckler, *Untersuchungen zur altorientalischen Geschichte*, Leipzig, 1889 . . . . . **XCIV**

Heinrich Zimmern et Hugo Winckler, *Die Keilinschriften und das Alte Testament*, 3rd ed., Berlin, Reuther et Reichard, 1902 . . . . . **XCV**

SPECIALIST WORKS

1. The Pre-Exilic Prophets and their Times

G. Ch. Aalders, *De Profeten de Ouden Verbonds*, Kampen, Kok, 1918 . . . . . . **XCVI**

A. Allwohn, *Die Ehe des Propheten Hosea in psychoanalytischer Beleuchtung*, Giessen, Töpelmann, 1926 . **XCVII**

Albrecht Alt, *Israel und Aegypten*, 1908 . . . **XCVIII**

Hedwig Anneler, *Zur Geschichte der Juden in Elephantine*, Berne, 1912 . . . . . **XCIX**

William Frederic Badè, *Der Monojahwismus des Deuteronomiums*, ZATW, 25 (1910), pp. 81–90 . . **C**

Walter Baumgartner, *Ein Kapitel vom hebraeischen Erzaehlungsstil, Eucharisterion*, Gunkel-Festschrift . **CI**

A. BENTZEN, *Die josianische Reform*, Copenhagen, 1926 .   CII

BINNS, *The Book of the Prophet Jeremiah* (Westminster Commentary), London, 1919   CIII

BUDDE-FESTSCHRIFT, BZAW, 34 (1920), Giessen, Töpelmann   CIV

KARL BUDDE, *Auf dem Wege zum Monotheismus*, Rektoratsrede, Marburger akademische Reden, Marburg, Elwert, 1916   CV

WALLIS BUDGE, *Egyptian Hieratic Papyri*, British Museum, 2nd series, 1923   CVI

ANTONIN CAUSSE, *Les prophètes contre la civilisation* (Christian. social), Alençon-Cahors, Coueslant, 1913 .   CVII

A. CAUSSE, *Les plus vieux chants de la Bible*, Paris, Alcan, 1926   CVIII

CHAINE, *Introduction à la lecture des prophètes*, Paris, Gabalda, 1932   CIX

STANLEY ARTHUR COOK, *The Religion of Ancient Palestine in the second millenium B.C. in the Light of Archœology and the Inscriptions*, London, Constable, 1908 . .   CX

J. CULLEN, *The book of the Covenant in Moab*, Glasgow, 1903   CXI

RENÉ DUSSAUD, *Observations en faveur de l'authenticité de la lettre adressée par Sennachérib à Ézéchias et rapportée dans 2 Rois* xix, 10–13 (*Isaïe* xxxvii, 10–13). Actes du Congrès international d'Histoire des Religions tenu à Paris en octobre 1923, Paris, Champion, 1925, vol. ii, pp. 5–6   CXII

OTTO EISSFELDT, *Die Bücher der Könige*, in EMIL KAUTZSCH, *die Heilige Schrift des A.T.*, 4th ed., Tubingen, Mohr, 1923, i, 492–585   CXIII

ADOLF ERMAN, *Eine ägyptische Quelle der Sprüche Salom.*, Sitzungsberichte der Preussischen Akademie der Wissenschaften, P. H. Kl., 1924, xv–xvi, 86 *ff.* . .   CXIV

C. J. GADD, *The Fall of Nineveh, the newly discovered Babylonian Chronicle*, no. 21901 in the British Museum, London, Brit. Mus., 1923   CXV

ALAN GARDINER, *Admonitions of an Egyptian Sage*, Leipzig, 1909   CXVI

GOTZEL, *Hizkia und Sanherib*, B.Z., 1908, pp. 133 *ff.* .   CXVII

GRENFELL and HUNT, *The Hibeh Papyri*, i, 1906 . .   CXVIII

HUGO GRESSMANN, *Die neugefundene Lehre des Amenemope und die vorexilische Spruchdichtung Israels*, ZATW, 42 (N.F. 1), 1924, pp. 272–296   CXIX

F. L. GRIFFITH, *Catalogue of the Demotic Papyri in the John Rylands Library*, Manchester, 1909 . . .   CXX

JOHANNES HEMPEL, *Die Schichten des Deuteronomiums*, Leipzig, 1914   CXXI

H. W. HERZBERG, *Prophet und Gott*, Gütersloh, Bertelsmann, 1928   CXXII

H. V. HILPRECHT, *Explorations in Bible Lands* . .   CXXIII

GUSTAV HÖLSCHER, *Das Buch der Könige, seine Quelle und seine Redaktion*, Eucharisterion, pp. 158–213, Göttingen, 1923   CXXIV

G. HÖLSCHER, *Komposition und Ursprung des Deuteronomiums*, ZATW, 40 (1922), pp. 161–255 . .   CXXV

F. Horst, *Die Anfänge des Propheten Jeremias*, ZATW, 41 (1923), 94 *ff.* CXXVI

F. Horst, *Die Kultusreform des Königs Josias*, ZDMG, 77 (1923), 220–238 CXXVII

L. P. Horst, *L'extase chez les Prophètes d'Israël d'après les travaux de Hölscher et Gunkel*, RHP, 1922, pp. 337–348 CXXVIII

Frédéric Hrozny, *Code hittite provenant de l'Asie Mineure (vers 1350 avant J.-C.)*, Paris, Geuthner, 1922 CXXIX

Paul Humbert, *Essai d'analyse de Nahoum* i, 2–ii, 3 (offprint from ZATW, 1926), Giessen, Töpelmann . CXXX

P. Humbert, *Un héraut de la justice : Amos* (inaugural lecture), Lausanne, La Concorde, 1917 . . . CXXXI

P. Humbert, *La logique de la perspective nomade chez Osée et l'unité d'Osée* 2, 4–22 (Vom Alten Testament, Karl Marti . . . gewidmet, Giessen, Töpelmann, 1925, pp. 158–166) CXXXII

P. Humbert, *Le problème du livre de Nahoum* RHP, 12 (1932), pp. 1–15 CXXXIII

P. Humbert, *Quelques aspects de la religion d'Amos* (RTP, lxxiii, 1929), 1930 CXXXIV

P. Humbert, *La vision de Nahoum* 2, 4–11 (offprint from *Archiv für Orientforschung*, Bd v, Heft i, 1928) . . CXXXV

W. Jacobi, *Die Extase der alttestamentlichen Propheten* (Grenzfragen des Nerven- und Seelenlebens), Munich, Bergmann, 1923 CXXXVI

Johns, *Assyrian Deeds* CXXXVII

H. Junker, *Prophet und Seher in Israel*, Trêves, Paulinus, 1927 CXXXVIII

R. H. Kennett, *The Date of Deuteronomy*, JTS, 1906, 481–500 CXXXIX

R. H. Kennett, *Deuteronomy and the Decalogue*, Cambridge, 1920 CXL

Rudolf Kittel, *Die Bücher der Könige*, Handkommentar zum A. T., i, 5, Göttingen, Vandenhoeck and Ruprecht, 1900 CXLI

August Klostermann, *Der Pentateuch, neue Folge*, Leipzig, Deichert, 1907 CXLII

Abraham Kuenen, *De Propheten en de prophetie ouder Israel*, 2 vols., 1875 CXLIII

Stephen Langdon, *Die neubabylonischen Königsinschriften*, 1912 CXLIV

Julius Lewy, *Forschungen zur Geschichte Vorderasiens* (MVAG, 1924, 2), Leipzig, Hinrichs, 1925 . . CXLV

Joh. Lindblom, *Hosea literarisch untersucht*, Helsingfors, 1927 CXLVI

J. Lindblom, *Die literarische Gattung der prophetischen Literatur*, Upsala, 1924 CXLVII

J. Lindblom, *Micha literarisch untersucht*, Åbo, 1929 CXLVIII

Adolphe Lods, *La divinisation du roi dans l'Orient méditerranéen et ses répercussions dans l'ancien Israël*, 2e congrès national des sciences historiques, Alger, 1932, pp. 261–275 CXLIX

Ad. Lods, L' " *étang supérieur* " *et l'approvisionnement en eau de la Jérusalem antique*. 5e Congrès int. d'Archéologie (Alger, 1930), Alger, 1933, pp. 183–204 ... CL

Max Löhr, *Das Deuteronomium*, Berlin, 1925 . . CLI

Luckenbill, *Ancient Records of Assyria and Babylonia* CLII

Luckenbill, *Annals of Sennacherib*, 1924 . . . CLIII

Johannes Meinhold, *Die Jesaiaerzählungen*, 1898 . CLIV

Adalbert Merx, *Die Bücher Moses und Josua*, Rel.-gesch. Volksbücher, Tubingen, Mohr, 1907 . . CLV

Sigmund Mowinckel, *Die Chronologie der israelitischen und jüdischen Könige*, Leyden, Brill, 1932 . . CLVI

S. Mowinckel, *Le Décalogue*, Paris, Alcan, 1927 . . CLVII

Nagel, *Der Zug des Sanherib*, 1902 CLVIII

Édouard Naville, *La découverte de la loi. Une interprétation égyptienne d'un livre biblique* (offprint from *Mémoires de l'Acad. des Inscriptions et Belles-Lettres*, vol. xxxviii, 2), Paris, Imp. Nat., 1910 . . . CLIX

É. Naville, *Le Deutéronome, un livre mosaïque*, Fontenay-sous-Bois, 1924 CLX

T. Oestreicher, *Das deuteronomische Grundgesetz*, Gütersloh, Bertelsmann, 1923 CLXI

Orr, *Le problème de l'Ancien Testament*, Geneva, 1908 . CLXII

Otto Procksch, *Jesaia I übersezt und erklärt* (Kommentar zum A. T. von Ernst Sellin, ix), Leipzig, Deichert, 1930 CLXIII

A. F. Puukko, *Das Deuteronomium*, Beiträge zur Wiss. vom A. T. (Kittel), 5, Leipzig-Stuttgart, 1910 . . CLXIV

George A. Reisner, *Recent Discoveries in Ethiopia*, The *Harvard Theological Review*, xiii (1920), 23–44 . . CLXV

G. L. Robinson, art. " Deuteronomy " in the *International Standard Bible Encyclopedia*, 1915 . . CLXVI

Theodore H. Robinson, *Baal in Hellas*, Classical Quarterly, 1917 CLXVII

T. H. Robinson, *The Ecstatic Elements in Hebrew Prophecy*, Expositor, 1921, pp. 217 *ff*. . . . CLXVIII

T. H. Robinson, *Prophecy and the Prophets in Ancient Israel*, London, Duckworth, 1923 . . . CLXIX

H. Wheeler Robinson, *Prophetic Symbolism* (*Old Testament Essays*), London, Griffin, 1927, pp. 1–17 . CLXX

R. W. Rogers, *Sennacherib and Judah* (Studien zur Semitischen Philologie und Religionsgeschichte, pp. 319–328) CLXXI

Hans Schmidt, *Das deuteronomische Problem*, Theologische Blätter, 37 (1927), pp. 40–8 . . CLXXII

H. Schmidt, *Geschichte Judas unter König Josia*, Schriften des A. T. in Auswahl, 2nd ed., ii, 2, pp. 177–202, Göttingen, 1923 CLXXIII

H. Schmidt, *Die Herkunft des Propheten Amos*, BZAW, 34 (1920), pp. 158–171 CLXXIV

Kurt Sethe, *Die Aechtung feindlicher Fürsten Völker und Dinge auf altägyptischen Tongefässscherben des mittleren Reiches* (Abhandlungen der preuss. Akad der Wiss., 1926, ph.-hist. Klasse, no. 5), Berlin, 1926 . . CLXXV

Arthur Robert Siebens, *L'origine du code deutéronomique*, Paris, Leroux, 1929 . . . CLXXVI

366 BIBLIOGRAPHY

J. Skinner, *Prophecy and Religion*, 2nd ed., Cambridge, University Press, 1926 . . . . . **CLXXVII**
Sidney Smith, *Bab. Hist. Texts*, 1924 . . . **CLXXVIII**
W. Spiegelberg, *Zur Datierung des Deuteronomiums*, OLZ, 26 (1923), 481–2 . . . . . . **CLXXIX**
C. Steuernagel, *Das Deuteronomium und Josua*, Handkommentar zum A. T., Göttingen, Vandenhoeck and Ruprecht, 1898, 2nd ed., 1923 . . . . **CLXXX**
C. Steuernagel, *Die Entstehung des deut. Gesetzes*, Halle, 2nd ed., 1901 . . . . . . **CLXXXI**
Vater, *Commentar über d. Pentateuch*, 1805 . . . **CLXXXII**
Vatke, *Die biblische Theologie*, 1835 . . . **CLXXXIII**
Paul Volz, *Der Prophet Jeremia* (KAT), Leipzig, Deichert, 2nd ed., 1928 . . . . . **CLXXXIV**
A. C. Welch, *The Code of Deuteronomy*, London, 1924 **CLXXXV**
A. C. Welch, *Jeremiah* . . . . . . **CLXXXVI**
W. M. L. De Wette, *Dissertatio critico-exegetica*, Jena, 1805 . . . . **CLXXXVII**
Harold Wiener, *Das Hauptproblem des Deuteronomiums*, Gütersloh, Bertelsmann, 1924 . . **CLXXXVIII**
H. Wiener, *The Altars of the Old Testament*, Leipzig, Hinrichs, 1927 . . . . **CLXXXIX**
Wilke, *Das Skythenproblem im Jeremiabuch* (Alttestamentliche Studien für Rudolf Kittel, pp. 222–254) . **CXC**
Wilke, *Jesaia und Assur*, 1905 . . . . . **CXCI**
Hugo Winckler, *Die Keilschrifttexte Sargons*, 1889 . **CXCII**

2. Early Judaism

H. J. Bells, *Jews and Christians in Egypt*, Brit. Mus., 1924 . . . . **CXCIII**
Alfred Bertholet, *Das Buch Hesekiel*, Kurzer Hand-Commentar zum A. T., xii, Friburg-Leipzig-Tubingen, Mohr, 1897 . . . . **CXCIV**
A. Bertholet, *Die Bücher Esra und Nehemia*, Kurzer Hand-Commentar zum A. T., xix, Tubingen, Leipzig, Mohr, 1902 . . . . **CXCV**
Antonin Causse, *Israël et la vision de l'Humanité*, Strasburg, Paris, Istra, 1924 . . . . . **CXCVI**
Paul Dhorme, *Le livre de Job* (Études bibliques), Paris, Gabalda, 1926 . . . . **CXCVII**
August Dillmann, *Die Bücher Exodus und Leviticus*, Kurzgefasstes exegetisches Handbuch, xii, Leipzig, Hirzel, 3rd ed., 1897 . . . . . . **CXCVIII**
Bernhard Duhm, *Die Psalmen*, Kurzer Hand-Commentar zum A. T., xiv, Friburg-Leipzig-Tubingen, Mohr, 1899 . . . . **CXCIX**
Gadd and Legrain, *Ur Excavations, Royal Inscriptions*, 1928 . . . . **CC**
Lucien Gautier, *La mission du prophète Ézéchiel*, 1891 . **CCI**
Hermann Gunkel, *Ausgewählte Psalmen*, 4th ed., 1917 . . . . **CCII**
H. Gunkel, *Die Psalmen*, Handkommentar zum A. T., Göttingen, Vandenhoeck and Ruprecht, 4th ed., 1926, ii, 2 . . . . **CCIII**

O. E. Hagen, *Keilschrifturkunden zur Geschichte des
König Kyrus*, 1891   CCIV

J. Hermann, *Ezechielstudien*, Beiträge zur Wissenschaft
vom Alten Testament (Kittel), 2, Leipzig-Stuttgart,
1908   CCV

J. Herrmann, *Ezechiel*, Kommentar zum A. T. (Sellin),
Leipzig, Deichert, 1924   CCVI

Hilprecht and Clay, *Bab. Exped.*, vol. ix, x, 1898,
1904, 1912   CCVII

Gustav Hölscher, *Hesekiel, der Dichter und das Buch*,
1924   CCVIII

Clement Huart, *La Perse antique et la civilisation
iranienne*, Renaissance du livre, 1925 . . .   CCIX

Morris Jastrow, jun., *The Book of Job. Its Origin,
Growth, and Interpretation*, Philadelphia and London,
Lippincott, 1920   CCX

Pierre Jouguet, *L'impérialisme macédonien et
l'hellénisation de l'Orient*, Paris, Renaissance du livre,
1926   CCXI

Karl Kautzsch, *Das sogenannte Volksbuch von Hiob*, 1906   CCXII

King and Thompson, *The Sculptures and Inscription of
Darius the Great on the Rock of Behistûn in Persia*,
London, British Museum, 1907, pp. xxxvi–xxxviii .   CCXIII

Klostermann, *Ezechiel. Ein Beitrag zur besseren
Würdigung seiner Person und Schrift*, TSK, 1 (1877),
391–439   CCXIV

Richard Kraetzschmar, *Das Buch Ezechiel*, Handkommentar zum A. T., iii, 3, 1, Göttingen, Vandenhoeck and Ruprecht, 1900   CCXV

Lachmann, *Das Buch Habakkuk. Eine textkritische
Studie*, Aussig, 1932   CCXVI

Adolphe Lods, *Recherches récentes sur le livre de Job*,
RHP, 1934, pp. 501–533   CCXVII

Ad. Lods, *Éléments anciens et éléments modernes dans le
rituel du sacrifice israélite* (RHP, 1928, pp. 399–411),
Paris-Strasburg   CCXVIII

Ad. Lods, *L'Ecclésiaste. et la philosophie grecque*, Paris,
Jouve, 1890   CCXIX

Ad. Lods, *Les découvertes d'Éléphantine et l'Ancien
Testament*, Revue Chrétienne, Montbéliard, 1910 .   CCXX

Ad. Lods, *Le monothéisme israélite a-t-il eu des precurseurs
parmi les " sages " de l'ancien Orient ?* RHP, 1934,
pp. 198–205   CCXXI

William Lods, *Les Juifs en Égypte à l'époque ptolémaïque
et romaine d'après les textes papyrologiques et épi-
graphiques* (unpublished thesis for the Fac. de Théol.
prot. de Paris), 1925   CCXXII

Alfred Loisy, *La consolation d'Israël*, 1927 . .   CCXXIII

A. Loisy, *Les mythes babyloniens et les premiers chapitres
de la Genèse*, Paris, Picard, 1901 . . .   CCXXIV

Jacques Marty, *Les chapitres 56–66 du livre d'Ésaïe*,
Nancy, Berger-Levrault, 1924 . . .   CCXXV

John A. Maynard, *The Birth of Judaism, a Study of
Hebrew Religion during the Exile*, London, Luzac,
1928   CCXXVI

EDUARD MEYER, *Die Entstehung des Judentums, eine historische Untersuchung*, Halle, Niemeyer, 1896 . CCXXVII

E. MEYER, *Der Papyrusfund von Elephantine*, Leipzig, Hinrichs, 1912 CCXXVIII

ALDO NEPPI MODONA, *La vita pubblica e privata degli Ebrei in Egitto nell' età ellenistica e romana*, Aegyptus, ii (1921), pp. 253–275 ; iii (1922), pp. 19–43 . . CCXXIX

SIGMUND MOWINCKEL, *Statholderen Nehemia*, 1916. *Ezra den Skriftlærde*, 1916 CCXXX

FIRMIN NICOLARDOT, *La composition du livre d'Habacuc* (thesis for the Fac. des Lettres de Paris), Paris, Fischbacher, 1908 CCXXXI

G. PINCHES, *Journal of the Victoria Inst.*, 1896, pp. 8 ff. . CCXXXII

E. H. PLUMPTRE, *Ecclesiastes*, Cambridge, 1881 . . CCXXXIII

E. PODECHARD, *L'Ecclésiaste*, Études Bibliques, Paris, Gabalda, 1912 CCXXXIV

ROST, *Altorientalische Studien*, f. B. Meissner . CCXXXV

J. W. ROTHSTEIN, *Die Nachtgesichte des Sacharja*, Beiträge zur Wissenschaft vom A. T. (R. Kittel), 8, Leipzig, Hinrichs CCXXXVI

EDUARD SACHAU, ABA *vom Jahre* 1907, Berlin, 1908 . CCXXXVII

E. SACHAU, *Ein altaramäischer Papyrus aus der Zeit des ägyptischen Königs Amyrtaeus*, Florilegium Melchior de Vogüé, 1909 CCXXXVIII

E. SACHAU, *Aramäische Papyrus und Ostraka aus einer jüdischen Militärkolonie zu Elephantine*, Leipzig, 1911 CCXXXIX

SAYCE and Cowley, *Aramaic Papyri discovered at Asouan*, London, Morning, 1906 CCXL

H. H. SCHAEDER, *Ezra der Schreiber*, Beiträge zur hist. Theol., 1930 CCXLI

HANS SCHMIDT, *Das Gebet der Angeklagten im Alten Testament*, Old Testament Essays, London, Griffin, 1927, pp. 143–155 CCXLII

H. SCHMIDT, *Das Gebet der Angeklagten im A. T.*, BZAW, 49 (1928), Giessen, Töpelmann CCXLIII

RUDOLF SMEND, *Der Prophet Ezechiel*, Kurzgefasstes exegetisches Handbuch, viii, 2nd ed., Leipzig, Hirzel, 1880 CCXLIV

SIDNEY SMITH, *Babylonian Historical Texts relating to the Capture and Downfall of Babylon*, London, 1924 . CCXLV

W. STAERK, *Die jüdisch-aramäischen Papyri von Assuan, sprachlich und sachlich erklärt*, Bonn, Marcus Weber, 1907 CCXLVI

CHARLES C. TORREY, *The Composition and Historical Value of Ezra-Neh.*, 1896 CCXLVII

TH. TYLER, *Ecclesiastes*, London, 1874 . . . CCXLVIII

PAUL VOLZ, *Jesaia II* (KAT), Leipzig, Deichert, 1932 . CCXLIX

INDEX

Aaron, 287–8, 294
Abraham, 117, 280, 283–4, 323, 336–7
Adadnirari III, 73 ; IV, 20
Adonis, 129
Adrammelech, 124
Æsop, 16
Agrarian Rites, 67, 264
Agriculture, 63–6, 174–5, 177–8, 196
Ahab (King), 20, 58, 64, 129 ; prophet, 211
Ahasuerus (Xerxes), 194
Ahaz, 6, 22–3, 28, 53, 63, 103, 105, 109, 128, 131
Ahiqam, 26
Aḥiqar, 5, 13, 16, 337
Ahura Mazda, 277
Albright, 3
Alexander, 5, 6, 9, 13, 187, 199–201, 319, 333, 335
Alexandria, 202 (n. 4, n. 5), 350 ; Covenant, 60, 73, 117, 135, 138, 162, 170, 283, 291, 296 ; of blood, 160
Alliance, 326 ; foreign, 63, 92, 105, 109
Allwohn, 91
'*Almâh*, 104
Altaqu, 33, 35
Altar, 95, 99, 127, 138, 144, 159, 208, 218, 229, 252, 255, 264, 266, 285, 288, 313–14, 348 ; raised, 67, 136, 151 ; horned, 136 ; of sweet savour, 12, 286, 288 ; Assyrian, 23, 138
Amasis, 181
Amaziah, 80–1
Amel Marduk (Evil-merodach), 181, 232
Amen-em-Ope, 13, 74–5
Amenophis IV, 73
'*Am hâ'âreṣ*, 274, 300
Ammon, Ammonites, 23, 47–50, 165, 180
Amon (King), 40, 42, 118, 308
Amon Râ (God), 69, 71, 73, 128, 277, 307
Amos, 51–2, 60–1, 65, 72, 76, 77, 79–87, 88, 89, 90, 92, 95, 99, 100, 102, 109–113, 126, 169, 170, 228, 235, 243, 257, 276, 278, 332 ; Book of, 8, 85–7
Amyrtæus, 311
Anammelech, 124
Anat(h) (Goddess), 124, 151, 307–8 ;

Anat-Bethel, 278, 307–8 ; Anat-Jahu, 167, 278, 307
Anathoth, 142, 170
Anâwîm (see Poor), 208
Ancestor Worship, 66, 329
Angel of Jahweh, 36, 122, 270, 275 ; angels, 325
Animals (unclean), 274, 291–2 ; victims, 294 ; objects of God's care, 340
Animistic customs, 150, 291
Anointed, 264, 270, 286
Anointing, 12, 285
Antioch, 201–2, 350
Antiochus III, 202
Anu (God), 129, 230, 277
Apocalypses, 70, 226, 232, 279
Apotropaic rites, 258–9, 292, 314–16
Arabs, 20–1, 25, 31, 36–7, 39, 74, 179, 297 ; religion, 53, 284
Aramæans (Syrians), 20, 21, 22, 47, 79, 85, 87, 104, 318 ; language, 35, 305–6
Aristæus (letter from), 42
Armaments, 92, 109
Armenia (see Urartu), 193
Arpad, 21, 29
Arrows (in divination), 214
Arsham, 309–312
Artaxerxes I, 4, 5, 187, 194–5, 198, 298, 300, 302, 304 ; II, 197–8, 302, 309 ; III, 198–9
Arvad, 18, 33
'*Âšâm (see* Sacrifice of Atonement), 259–260, 264
Ašam-Bethel, 308
Ascalon (Ashkelon), 23, 33, 41, 130
Ashdod, 30, 34, 40
Asherah (Goddess), 126
Asherah (sacred pole), 67, 114–16, 138, 143
Ashima, 84
Ashkenaz (see Scythians)
Asmodeus, 346
Asshur (God), 17
Asshur (town), 157
Asshurbanipal, 25, 38–41, 123, 130, 226, 305
Asshurdân, 21
Aššur-etil-ilani, 41
Aššuruballit, 44, 237
Assyria, Assyrians, history, 2–5, 16, 17–25, 28–46, 53, 60, 62, 63, 80,

87–8, 92, 103–7, 109, 112, 113, 115–16, 122–3, 129–131, 142, 156–9, 184–5, 201, 237, 247, 318 ; country, 94, 157, 176 ; speech and writing, 3, 146, 178 ? ; texts, 4–5 ; literature, 13, 130, 336–7 ; religion, 115, 124, 127 ; gods, 127–130, 143 ; customs, 84

Astarte, 277–8

Astrology, 239

Astyages, 182, 236

Atôn (God), 73, 128

Atonement (*see* Expiation)

Atonement, Day of, 12, 260, 289, 313–17

AU (God), 26

Awwa, 24

Azariah (Uzziah), 99, 327

Azazel, 314–315

Azriyahu, Azariah, 21–22

Baal, 67, 92, 94, 124, 126, 129, 131, 264, 277

Baalis, 49–50

Babel, 65, 163

Babylon, Babylonia, 2, 18, 20, 23, 25, 29–31, 36–7, 38–41, 42–4, 46–50, 60, 62, 105, 122, 131, 162, 164–7, 178–183, 184, 188, 191, 193–5, 236–241, 226, 270, 306, 318, 335 ; country, 239–241, 270 ; Babylonian Jews (*see* Captivity), 6, 26, 173, 177, 185, 189, 190–2, 195–7, 210, 213, 233, 240, 243, 270–1, 273, 296–7, 301–2, 309 ; texts, 4–5, 181 (n. 1) ; literature, 39, 120 ; psalms, 13 ; Job, 14–15 ; religion, 75, 124, 159, 230–1, 245, 260–1, 294, 315, 353 ; Gods, 217, 230, 239 ; monotheism, 72–3, 277 ; myths, 230, 239, 242, 261, 333 ; art, 230

Badé, 3

Bagôhi (Bagoas, Bagoses) satrap, 198, 311 ; eunuch, 199

Baruch, 8, 164, 222

Beersheba, 79, 151

Bel, 239

Bel-Ibni, 31

Bel-šar-uṣur (Belshazzar), 181–2

Benjamin, 26, 87, 187

Benzinger, 3, 295

Bertholet, 245, 301

Bethel (town), 42, 79–81, 94, 148, 305

Bethel (God), 308

Bigwai (Bagôhi), 192

Bisutun (Behistun), 193

Blood (taboo), 160, 209 (n. 8), 257, 282–4, 294 ; life-giving power, 295

Book of the Covenant, 9, 64, 135, 151, 221 ; name for Deuteronomy, 145

Budde, 86, 98, 246

Burial, 47, 106, 254, 283

Burnt offering, 12, 68, 89, 125, 150, 259, 307, 313

Byblos, 33

Cæsar, 203 (n. 5)

Caiaphas, 279 (n. 4)

Calebites, 175

Calendar, 315

Cambyses, 190, 193, 268

Canaanites, population, 119, 124–5, 244, 283 ; civilization, 65–6 ; rites, 67, 94, 114–15, 124–5, 151–2 ; gods, 117–18, 126, 143, 218

" Canaanization," Reaction against, 63–4, 67, 151–2

Carkemish, 44, 46, 48, 168

Causse, 66, 208

Centralization of the Cult, regional, 146–7 ; at Bethel, 148 ; in the Temple at Jerusalem, 122, 138–9, 141–5, 146–8, 150–2, 218, 258, 286 ;

Chaldeans (*see* Babylon), 20, 29–31, 41, 43, 163–7, 170, 174–6, 185, 208, 214, 222, 229, 232–5, 239–240, 300 ; empire, 46–50, 201, 238 ; country, 196, 241

Champollion, 327

Chariot of the Sun, 127, 138 ; of Jahweh, 212, 229

Cherub, 230

Chiun (Kêvân), 84

Chnum, 310

Chosen people, 153

Chronicles, 5–6, 32, 38, 45, 47 (n. 2), 140, 187, 189, 298–9, 326–7

Chronicler, 190, 192, 288, 298–300, 301 (n. 1)

Chronology, 4–5, 28 (n. 1), 193 (n. 1), 282, 298, 302

Cimmerians, 20, 41, 130

Circumcision, 282–4, 291–2 ; spiritual 66, 170

Cities of Refuge, 146 (n. 3.)

Civilization, 291 ; value, 63–6

Claudius, 203 (n. 5)

Communion with God, through sacrifices, 296 ; beyond the grave, 355

Confession, 294

Conversion, of the heathen, 197, 238–9, 248, 273, 322, 332, 334–5

Converts, 248, 273

Corban, 295–6

Covetousness, 121

Creation, 73, 242, 267, 323–4, 352 ; story, 282, 291

Crœsus, 182

Crowfoot, 3

Cult, value and efficacy, 61, 66–9, 75–7, 84–5, 94–5, 100–1, 109,

119–120, 150–1, 170, 249–250 ; nature, 154, 260–1, 290, 324–5 ; origin, 284–5 ; purpose, 261
Cuneiform (texts), 3–5, 195
Curse, 54, 135, 145, 164, 234, 270, 325, 353
Custom (tradition), 134–5, 147, 257
Cyaxares, 41, 43, 157
Cyprus, 198
Cyrus, 27, 182–190, 192–4, 234, 236–242, 248, 265, 271, 335 ; his edict, 184–8 ; the younger, 197

Damascus, 21–3, 29, 79–80, 84 (n. 2), 103–5
Daniel, 6, 182, 280, 333, 345
Darius I, 186–7, 188, 193–4, 269, 271, 309, 335 ; II, 4, 5, 195, 197–8, 299, 304 ; III, 6, 187 (n. 3), 199–220
David, 66, 72, 82 (n. 5), 86, 93–4, 111, 135, 152, 189, 219, 269–271, 287–8, 333, 334 ; city of, 254
Day of Jahweh, 9, 70, 72, 109, 278, 331–2
Dead Sea, 227–8, 253
Dead, the (in Sheol), 329 ; unclean-ness, 291 ; honourable burial, 18 ; worship of, 126, 346
Death (abolition of), 333
Debts, 64, 84
Decalogue, the first, 9–10, 119–121, 135, 137, 221–2, 243 ; the second, 9, 67, 119, 135, 151 ; of the first Elohist, 67, 120
Delaiah, 297 (n. 1), 311
Demetrius I, 202
Demons, 230, 291, 328, 336, 346
Deportation (*see* Captivity), General procedure, 20, 34, 80, 178–9 ; of Israelites, 23–7, 179 ; into Israel, 24–5, 38, 179, 318 ; into Hyrcania, 199 ; from Ashdod, 30 ; from Akko, 39
Determinism, 343–4
Deuteronomy, 9–11, 41, 126, 139, 142–154, 159, 170–1, 191, 209, 219–221, 242–4, 255–6, 258–9, 260, 263, 265, 274, 281, 285–6, 289, 303–4, 307, 318, 331
Deuteronomic school, 118, 120, 250, 285, 322, 326
Diaspora, 173–4, 202–3, 209, 284, 350 ; in Egypt, 4, 173–4, 180, 202–3, 207–8, 218, 240, 243, 304, 312, 350
Diodorus of Sicily, 310
Disillusioned man (dialogue), 14, 336–7
Division of land, 252–3, 283
Divorce, 96, 276

Doctrine, 205, 227, 242–3, 249, 322–333, 337–8, 340–1, 342, 343, 351, 352–5
Dreams, 58
Duhm, 240–1, 244, 246 (n. 8), 272
Dumah, 37
Dussaud, 293, 327 (n. 7)

Ebed-Melech, 167, 222
Ecbatana, 188
Ecclesiastes, 15, 223, 279, 329, 341–5
Ecclesiasticus (*see* Sirach, son of)
Ecstasy, 55–9, 91, 165, 215, 217, 227
Eden, 230
Edom, Edomites, 14, 22–3, 30–1, 33, 48–9, 74, 86, 165, 175–6, 225, 238, 283–4, 319 ; country, 181
Egypt, history, 15, 18, 20, 29–30, 33, 35, 37, 39–46, 48–50, 55, 73, 85, 88, 92, 103, 105–6, 130–1, 163, 167, 181–2, 185, 190, 194–5, 197–9, 201–3, 236, 240, 247, 304–5, 311–2 ; Hebrew sojourn in, 92, 219, 239, 322 ; refuge for Judæans, 167, 173–4, 207 ; discoveries, 3–4 ; literature, 13, 120, 336–7 ; legends, 32–3, 36 ; prophecies, 69–70 ; religion, 72–3, 75, 148, 159, 277, 329 ; gods, 73, 218 ; magic, 164
Eissfeldt, 81 (n. 2)
Ekron, 31, 33–4
Elam, Elamites, 20, 25, 29, 31, 39–40, 47–8, 179, 238 ; Jewish settlers, 240
Elath, 22
Elders, 64, 117, 134, 159, 163, 166, 175, 177, 213, 218
Eleazar, 245, 286
Elephantine, 4, 16, 26, 42, 167, 173–4, 195, 198, 207–8, 218, 274, 278, 304–312
Eliashib, 299, 318
Elihu, 15, 279
Elijah, 64, 67, 119, 258, 333
Eliphaz, 279, 337–8
Elisha, 52, 58, 59, 67, 81, 119, 237
Elkosh, 157–8
Elohist (school), 9, 65, 117–121, 148, 151, 274, 283–5
Elulæus, 24, 31
En-Nasbeh, 3
Enoch, 280, 333, 345
Ephod, 93, 286
Ephraim, 21, 23, 88, 100
Epicurus, 344
Epigones, 306
Epigraphy, 2, 4–5
Eponyms, 4–5
Esarhaddon, 25, 38–9, 123
Eschatology, oriental, 69–71 ; popu-lar in Israel, 69–71, 72, 331 ;

prophetic, 71–2, 331 ; Jewish, 278, 331–2
Eshmunazar, 278
Esther, 194
Ethiopia, Ethiopians, 61, 167, 170 ; nation, 20, 30, 42, 55, 87, 105 ; dynasty (Egypt), 4, 30, 35, 37, 38, 40, 105, 327
Eunuch, 222, 273, 300
Evil-Merodach (*see* Amel Marduk)
Exile (*see* Deportation), 284 ; Babylonian, 6, 26, 47–50, 78, 144, 147, 166, 173–4, 176–180, 211, 236, 249 ; number of exiles, 174 ; return, 189–192, 224–5, 238–9, 265–6
Expiation (Atonement), 249, 258–262, 289, 292–6 ; explanation, 294–6 ; rites, 101, 160, 230–1, 258–9, 289
Eye, evil, 121, 353 ; "King's eye," 184
Ezekiel, 11, 14–15, 26, 47, 56, 67, 77, 101, 129, 139–140, 159, 174, 176, 180, 209–210, 211–232, 233–4, 236–7, 248–250, 265–6, 271, 273, 276, 286–7, 323, 328, 332, 351 ; life, 177–8 ; pathological states, 215–17, 227 ; trance gestures, 55, Book of, 8, 210, 226 ; Torah, 11, 161, 191, 225, 251–264, 265–6, 276, 281, 283, 286–7, 289, 314
Ezra, 6–7, 9, 12, 77, 135, 180, 191–2, 198, 252, 283, 289, 296–300, 301 (n. 5), 302–3, 306–7, 310–13, 317 ; followers, 12, 334 ; Book of, 5–7, 185–192, 195, 198, 272 ; Greek, 190 (n. 3) ; memoirs, 7, 297

Faith, 103, 110–11, 120, 122, 126, 340–1
Feasts, 84, 94, 149, 188, 257, 260, 264, 284, 289
Fêdu, 294–5
First born, 135, 283, 287
First Day of the Year (*see* New Year), 289, 316
First fruits, 245
Flood, 130, 282
Folk-lore, 14, 336, 346
Foods (unclean), 253
Foreigners, laws protecting, 149–150
Freedom of the City, 202

Gad (God), 274, 278, 308
Gadd, 43
Galilee, 23–4
Gautier, 212
Gaza, 23, 29, 34, 45 (n. 7), 200–1
Gedaliah, 50, 167, 175
Gehenna, 125, 333
Gerizim, Mount, 267, 319
Gestures, prophetic, 53–6, 90–2, 95–8, 105, 108, 163–4, 165, 167, 214, 216

Gezer, Assyrian tablets, 3, 39 ; calendar, 3
Gideon, 101, 136, 258
Gihon, 31
Gilgal, 89, 94
Glory (" brightness "), 229, 253
Glossolaly, 56, 108 (n. 1)
Gnomic literature, 13–15, 74–6, 354
Gobrias, 182, 226
God (conceptions of), judge, 88 ; father, 88–9, 109 ; bridegroom, 89, 92 ; king, 99–100, 110 ; name given to kings, 351
Gôlâh, 274
Gomer, 90, 95–8
Goodness (of God), 85, 222, 228
Gozan, 24, 26
Greeks, 41, 184, 194–5, 200–3 ; language, 13 ; religion, 53, 75, 119, 124, 277 ; philosophy, 343–4
Gressmann, 71, 75 (n. 1), 245
Gunkel, 245
Gutium, 27, 182, 185
Gyges, 226

Habakkuk, 8–9, 164–5, 232–6, 249
Ḥabur, 24
Hadad, 124
Hadrach, 21
Haggada, 15–16
Haggai (prophet), 77, 186, 193, 260, 268–9, 272–3 ; Book of, 9
Hakkoz, 191–2
Halah, 24–5
Haller, 245, 268
Hamath, 24, 29, 79
Hammurabi, 18, 145
Hananiah, prophet, 59, 162, 165, 168 ; papyrus from Elephantine, 309
Hanun, 29
Haram-Bethel, 308
Haram-Natan, 308
Hariscandra, 14
Harran, 24, 44
Ḥâṭṭâ'th (*see* Sacrifice for Sin), 259–260, 264, 296
Hebron, 151, 175, 192, 283
Hellenization, 201–2, 345
Heraclitus, 343–4
Ḥerem, 294
Herodotus, 32, 36, 41–2, 45, 48, 189
Ḥesed, 89, 95, 126
Hezekiah, 2, 4, 6, 29–38, 63, 105–6, 112, 117, 118–19, 131 ; reforms, 77, 114–16, 147
High places, 67–8, 94, 114–16, 138–142, 144, 146–7, 151–2, 160, 219, 256, 282, 287, 307
High priest, 200, 264, 286–7
Hilkiah, 137, 146, 148

Hittites, 20 ; religion, 128, 164
Holiness, 265, 286, 291–2, 295 ; of God, 99, 109, 111, 117, 230–1, 253–7, 263, 294, 324
Holiness Code, 11, 145, 161, 262–4, 266, 276, 281, 285–6, 289, 294, 304
Hölscher, 12, 139–141, 215–16, 228 (n. 1), 245, 298, 303, 319
Hope, 86–7, 96–8, 110–11, 170–1, 223–6, 247–8, 332–3
Hophra, 48, 197
Horses, 191 ; warhorses, 35, 41, 63, 92 ; of the Sun Chariot, 127, 138
Hosea, prophet, 53–5, 59, 61, 65–9, 72, 77, 86–102, 109–112, 116, 118, 121, 126, 136, 148, 152, 170, 219, 228, 242 ; life, 90–1, 95–8, 101 ; Book of, 8, 96–7 ; king of Israel (also Hoshea), 23–4, 88, 105 ; exile, 26
Hosts of heaven (cult), 42, 127–8, 138, 143, 147
Hubert, 293–4
Huldah, 137, 14—1
Humanitarian Laws, 149–150, 291
Humbert, 65, 91
Hyrcania, 199
Hyrcanus, John, 279 (n. 4), 319 ; II, 319
Hyssop, 350

Idolatry (*see* Images), 242–3
Ilubi'di, 29
Images (worship of), 67, 94, 109, 115, 120, 121, 136, 143, 147, 153, 209, 217, 219, 240–3
Immanuel, 103–4
Immortality of the Soul, 343, 345
Inarus, 194
Incense, 123, 159–160, 208, 288, 307, 312
Incisions, 94
India, 14, 36, 336 ; religion, 124
Individualism in religion, 102, 117, 168–170, 221, 223, 249, 329–330
Inspiration, 53, 58, 205, 279–280
Ipsambul, 4, 41
Ipuwer, 70
Isaiah, 6, 21–2, 30–3, 52–6, 61, 63, 65–6, 67–8, 72, 77, 86, 99–111, 112–14, 115–17, 118–19, 121, 122, 125–6, 129, 136–7, 147, 152, 219, 230, 332 ; life, 99–108, 129 ; Book of, 8, 32, 107–8, 125–6, 233 ; Is. xiii–xiv, 9 ; Is. xv–xvi, 9 ; Is. xxi, 9, 237 (n. 7) ; Is. xxiv–xxvii, 9
Isaiah (Second), 9, 60, 76–7, 209–210 and 209 (n. 3), 238–250, 266, 273, 305 (n. 1), 322–3, 332 ; his abode, 210, 239–241
Isaiah (Trito), 9, 267–8, 272–5

Ishmael, 49–50, 167
Ishtar, 128, 151
Ithobaal, 33

Jaazaniahu, 3
Jahwism (ancient), 274, 291–2, 297, 323, 352
Jahwist, 9, 65, 117, 147, 151, 230, 281, 284–5
Jamârât, 315
Jeconiah (Jehoiakin), 47, 159, 161–2, 176, 181, 189, 211, 232, 245
Jehoiakim, 6, 46–7, 128, 159, 162, 164, 308, 327
Jehu, 20, 81, 119
Jeremiah, 13, 26, 46–7, 52–5, 59, 61, 63, 65–8, 76–7, 101, 122–3, 126, 128, 131–3, 139, 143, 145, 153–5, 158, 161–171, 177, 209, 211, 213–14, 217, 219, 221–2, 224, 227, 232–3, 234, 243, 247, 257, 329–330, 332–3 ; life, 106 (n. 4), 112, 122, 142, 175, 248 ; Book of, 7–8, 57, 211, 220, 233
Jericho, 49, 199
Jeroboam I, 81, 136 ; II, 21, 79, 81, 87
Jesus, 170, 249, 276–7 ; son of Sirach (*see* Ecclesiasticus)
Jezreel, 87
Joaz, Jehoahaz, 45, 159
Job, Book of, 14–15, 208, 223, 279, 329, 334–342, 354 ; Jahweh's harangue, 339–340 ; Elihu's speech 15, 341
Joel, 9
Johanan, 198, 299, 311
Jonadab (*see* Rechabites), 64–6, 110
Jonah, 15–16, 208, 276–7, 334–5, 337
Jonathan, 202
Josephus, 44 (n. 2), 185, 189, 198, 200, 202, 279 (n. 4), 300 (n. 8), 319
Joshua, 117, 135, 284, 286, 304 ; high priest, 186 (Jeshua), 190, 270 (Joshua) ; priest, 198 (Jeshua)
Josiah, 40–3, 44–6, 159, 327 ; minority, 42 ; reform of the twelfth year, 140 ; of the eighteenth year, 6, 10, 32 (n. 3), 42, 66, 68, 77, 115–16, [?119], 127, 131, 137–156, 158–9, 161–2, 170, 207, 210, 218, 256
Jubilee, 140, 289
Judges, 118, 138 ; Book of, 118, 326
Judgment of God, 134 ; Last Judgment, 332–3
Justice, 85, 89–90, 109, 111, 118, 120, 126, 149, 273, 330 ; divine justice, 74–5, 222, 228–9, 235, 325, 329, 339–340 ; immanent, 236 ; the true religion, 244 ; administration of justice, 64, 84, 129, 153, 136–7, 149, 220–1, 262

Kadytis, 45
Kahal, 192
Kannu, 25
Kapper, 293
Karnaim, 79
Kasiphia, 177, 218, 278
Kawwân, Kâmanu, 128
Kebar, Chebar (Canal), 177, 212
Kennett, 139
King, institution of royalty, 64, 66, 110–11, 147, 178, 252, 255, 262, 271, 316; divine nature, 69–71, 93, 111, 351; anti-royalist tendency, 93, 118–19
Kings, Books of, 5–6, 10, 29, 32, 37–8, 44, 106, 123, 137–143, 159, 181, 220, 318, 369
Kir, 85
Kittim, 24
Kittel, 192
Klamroth, 50 (n. 2), 327 (n. 5)
Knowledge of God, 89, 95, 136
Korah, 288, 349
Kosters, 180, 185
Kuenen, 56
Kush (see Ethiopia), 85, 240, 247
Kutha, 25

Labašimarduk, 181
Lachish, 33–5
Laity, 255, 327
Lamentations, 12–13, 176, 208–9
Law, 170, 258, 278, 321, 324, 331, 350–1, 355; books of laws, 9–12, 135–9, 143–8, 198, 205, 225, 251–264, 303–346; priestly law, 232, 302
Laying on of hands, 296
Lebanon, 237, 241
Leprosy, 290, 327, 335
Levites, 67, 149–150, 153, 191, 218, 252, 254–6, 264, 285–6, 287–8, 299, 302; monopoly, 147, 255–6
Levy (Abraham), 26 (n. 10), 240
Libations, 94, 207, 264, 348
Libnah, 35
Lindblom, 97–8
Liver (as omen), 214
Livy, 186
Lo-ammi, 87, 91
Loisy, 63, 212 (n. 4), 298
Lo-Ruhamah, 87, 91
Love of God, 89, 92, 93–5, 153, 219
Lydia, 182, 202, 226, 236, 238

Maccabees, 2, 13, 16, 347; 1st Book of, 201 (n. 1)
MacCown, 71
Macedonians, 203
Machpelah, 283

Magic, 120, 135, 150, 215, 290, 316; imitative, 54; connected with the cult, 69, 75, 95, 251, 294, 350
Magicians, 52, 193
Maher-Shalal-Hash-Baz, 104
Mahommed, 151
Malachi, 77, 275–9, 322; book of, 9
Malevolence, 15, 164, 230, 260, 328, 352–3
Mana, 55, 256
Manasseh, King, 3, 38–40, 42, 78, 116, 118, 125–9, 148–9, 159–162, 220, 254, 277, 308, 327; tribe of, 21
Marduk, 14–15, 73, 183, 194, 239, 277
Marduk-aplu-iddina (Merodach Baladan), 29, 31, 105
Marriage, 178; mixed, 275, 283, 297–8, 301, 303, 307, 334; Hosea's 90–1, 95–8
Maṣṣebah, 146
Mauss, 293–4
Maynard, 209–210
Mazdeism, 267, 292
Mecca, 151, 315
Medes, Media, 20–2, 24–5, 40–1, 43, 46, 130, 179, 182, 188, 193, 238, 305
Medînâh, 175, 191–2, 252, 266
Megabyzus, 194
Megiddo, 43, 45, 141, 158, 162, 327
Melek, Moloch, 124
Menahem, king, 21–2; an exile, 26
Meni (God), 274, 278, 308
Mercenaries, 41, 197
Merikere, 74, 76
Mesged, 307, 308
Messiah, Messianism, 104, 111, 245, 270–1; in Egypt, 69–71; in ancient Israel, 70–1; references in Isaiah, 72; in Haggai and Zachariah, 193, 332
Mibtahiah, 307
Micah, 61, 86, 111–14, 116–18, 126, 163; Book of, 8, 114, 233; VI, 1–8, 125–6; son of Imlah, 67
Midianites, 284
Milcom, 131
Mission of Israel, 60, 76, 244–8
Mitanni, 18
Mizpah, 3, 49, 167, 208
Moab, 23, 30–1, 33, 47–8, 79, 165, 180, 334
Mohar, 96
Monojahwism, 151–2
Monolatry, 120
Monotheism, 2, 16, 60, 72–5, 77, 88, 152–3, 171, 207, 231, 242–3, 248, 249–250, 276–8, 321–2, 325, 346, 351–2
Moralists (see Gnomic literature), 336–7, 345
Morality, 120–1, 223, 329–331, 351

Moresheth, 113, 126
Moses, 10, 52, 60, 67, 100–1, 114, 119, 135–7, 142–3, 145–8, 245, 263, 265, 283–4, 286–8, 294, 346
Mountains, holy, 139, 147, 209 ; of God, 230
Mourning, 271 ; rites, 90, 135, 168, 216 ; dirge, 13, 80, 237
Mowinckel, 103 (n. 3), 245, 347
Muraḫu, 5, 195
Music, 84, 288
Mystics, 57–8
Myth, 230, 282, 324 ; struggle against powers of darkness, 226, 239, 282

Naaman, 218, 237, 258
Naaman (God), 129
Nâbî' (*see* Prophet), 51–3
Nabonassar, 5
Nabonidus, 44 (n. 1), 181–3, 193, 234, 238, 241
Nabopolassar, 41, 43, 46, 156
Nahum, 131, 156–8 ; Book of, 8, 158 (n. 5)
Names, prophetic, 54, 82–3, 87, 91, 102, 104, 108 ; altered, 46–7 ; individual, 196–7 ; for Jahweh, 195, 276, 283, 325 ; honour of his name, 225–6, 229, 332
Napata, 4
Nâsî (prince), 178, 252, 261–2
National religion, 73–4, 85, 157–8, 205, 207, 225, 229–232, 235, 249–250
Naville, 146
Nebo (God), 73, 239
Nebuchadnezzar, 46–8, 50, 55, 163, 165–7, 174, 179–181, 188, 192, 211, 214, 216, 232 ; III, 198
Nebuzaradan, 49–50
Necho, 39, 40 ; II, 44–5, 48, 197, 327
Necromancy, 126, 139, 143
Neferrehu, 70
Negeb, 175, 192
Nehemiah, 9, 191–2, 195, 252, 279, 283, 296–303, 307, 309, 311–13, 318, 328, 335 ; Book of, 6–7, 187, 190–2, 198 ; memoirs, 297 ; Neh. viii–ix, 12
Nehushtan, 114
Nergal-šar-uṣur, 181
New Moon, 94, 255
New Year (*see* First Day of the Year), in Babylonia, 182, 184 ; in Israel, 70, 314, 347
Nineveh, 5, 34–5, 38–9, 41, 43, 130, 141, 156–8, 335
Nippur, 5, 177, 179, 195
Nisibis, 27
Noah, 282, 284–5

Nomads, 182 ; nomadic ideal, 63–6, 93, 110
North, divine abode, 230 ; northern foes, 132, 163, 226

Oath, 134, 276 ?, 339, 348
Obadiah, 9
Oblation, 208, 259, 296, 307, 312
Œsterley, 148, 277 (n. 3), 305
Oil, offering, 123–5 ; anointing, 264
Olives (Mount of), 138
Omri, 67, 119
Ophra, 257
Ordeal, 134, 290, 348
Organization (social and political), 2, 63–6, 84, 161, 174–5, 177–8, 205–6, 225, 228, 252, 262, 289, 205–6
Osorkon, 327

Padi, 31, 34
Palestine (Jews left in), 173–6, 179, 185, 190, 209, 274, 317
Panammu, 20
Particularism, 77, 152, 209, 231, 249, 322
Passhur, 54, 164
Passover, 135, 138, 143, 283–4, 289, 347
Pathros, 50
Pehâh, 178, 188–9, 198
Pekah, 22–3, 103
Pekahiah, 22
Pelusium, 240
Pentateuch, 143, 317
Perfumes (offerings), 123, 288
Persians, 4, 184–199, 201, 236–240, 271, 297, 302, 306, 310–12, 317, 347 ; religion, 127, 185, 277, 333, 346
Pessimism, 342–3
Pharisees, 275, 345
Phenicia, 18, 24, 33, 41, 198, 240–1
Philistines, 23, 30–1, 49, 86 (n. 1), 87, 105–6, 319
Philo, 279
Phrygia, 202
Piety (*see* Ḥesed), 120
Pilgrimages, 347, 349–350
Place (holy), 286, 288, 296, 314
Plague, 35–7, 80, 122
Pneumatic phenomena, 57, 205, 279
Podechard, 342
Poetry, 12–15
Poor People (*see* Anawim), 347, 355
Predictions, 54–5, 90–1, 168, 216
Priestly Code, 11–12, 161, 251–3, 255–6, 261, 263–4, 265, 286, 290–6, 302, 304, 310, 331, 351 ; P¹, 11, 263 (*see* Holiness Code); P², 11–12, 281–6, 304, 323 ; P⁰, 12, 286 ; PP, 12, 285 ; P³, 12, 285–9, 312–17

Priests, 49, 64, 80–1, 90, 95, 112, 116, 119–120, 134–8, 141–2, 144, 149, 156, 161–4, 175, 179, 191–2, 200, 208, 212, 230, 250–2, 254–7, 259, 262–3, 275–6, 288, 296–8, 312, 315–16, 318–19, 323, 351 ; distinguished from Levites, 158, 254–6, 264, 284, 287–8, 302 ; prophet priests, 279 ; supervisor of prophets, 59, 164 ; Babylonian, 181 ; Egyptian, 310 ; Prayer, 76, 169, 268, 344, 350 ; facing the Temple, 349

Primitive mentality, 62, 127

Prophets 255 ; sons of the Prophets 51–2, 59, 81 ; attached to the Temple, 348 ; nationalist, 48, 51, 59, 80, 102, 111–12, 156, 158, 161–3, 165–6, 209 ; Montanist, 57 ; of the Cevennes, 57 ; great prophets, 2, 10, 51–78, 162, 205–6, 228, 321, 325, 330, 332 ; vocation, 51–2, 82–3, 99–102, 212 ; psychology, 55–9, 237–8 ; attitude to social questions, 63–6, 84–5, 88–90, 101, 109, 111–14 ; in exile, 162, 166, 211–12 ; role, 223 ; influence of the great prophets, 114–121, 149–151, 154, 205, 207–210, 219, 249–250, 351, 356 ; prophetic books, 7–9, 56–7, 164–5, 169, 244–6, 350

Prostitution, sacred, 67, 83, 94, 97 (n. 4), 138, 143 ; metaphorical, 69, 88–95

Proverbs, Book of, 13–14, 74, 208, 279, 328–331, 351

Psalms, 13, 275, 329, 334, 347–355 ; Babylonian, 167, 347 ; Egyptian, 347 ; supplicatory, 167, 294, 348, 353 ; for the accused, 348 ; of the *anâwîm*, 208 ; thank offering, 167, 348 ; kinds and uses, 347–9 ; Ps. cxxxvii, 209 (n. 3) ; Hab. i and iii, 232–3

Psammetichus I, 40–4 ; II, 4, 42, 48, 304

Psychoanalysis, 91–2

Ptolemais, 350

Ptolemy, geographer, 5 ; kings of Egypt, 201–2, 306, 319 ; I, 201–2 ; II, 350

Pul, Pulu, 23

Purification (by fire), 124

Purity, 256, 291–2, 351

Pyrrho, 344

Qarqar, 20, 29

Queen of heaven, 128, 159–160, 167, 207, 308

Rabbath Ammon, 214

Rabshakeh, 34–5

Raphia, 29

Ras Shamra, 74, 129 (n. 1)

Rats, 36

Reallotment (of land), 289

Rechabites, 64, 67, 151, 175

Recurrence, perpetual, 343

Rehum, 300 (n. 4)

" Remnant," 102, 106, 108, 110

Renan, 56, 334, 341

Reson (Resîn), 22–3, 103

Resurrection, 224, 245, 333

Reuss, 56, 212

Reward and punishment, 325–331 ; collective (*see* Vicarious punishment) ; individual, 14–15, 117, 219–223, 228–330, 335–341, 391, 353–4 ; after death, 223, 329, 340

Rhodians, 127

Riblah, 45, 49, 162

Rich, 355

" Righteous " (party), 274–5

Ritual, importance, 253, 257–8, 263, 286, 350 ; purpose, 290–3 ; of transference, 290, 296, 314–6

Robinson, 50 (n. 2), 97 (n. 4), 148, 277 (n. 3)

Romans, 41 ; religion, 53, 124, 277

Ruth, 15, 307, 334

Sabbath, 94, 120–1, 150, 202, 255, 257, 265, 273, 282, 284, 289, 291–2, 301, 351

Sabbatical Year, 200, 289

Sacrifice, 79, 94, 149, 188, 255, 257–8, 266, 271, 275, 284, 302, 315–16, 348 ; peace offerings, 255, 259, 290, 307 ; thank-offerings, 296, 350 ; sacrificial meal, 94, 209, 255, 288, 295, 348 ; votive and voluntary, 255, 296 ; for sin, 11, 258–260, 296, 302, 314 ; of atonement, 11, 259–260 ; in memory of sin, 291 ; for the sick, 348 ; of infants, 68, 123–5, 143, 217, 219, 260, 274 ; origin, 285 ; character and function, 292–6 ; of gifts, 258, 291, 292, 295–6 ; of expiation, 258, 294 ; of the covenant, 292 ; divine repast, 292, 296 ; in divination, 292 ; of imprecation, 292 ; impossible outside Palestine, 218–19 ; value and efficacy 68–9, 75–6, 84–5, 89, 94–5, 291, 350

Sadducees, 275, 299

Sais, 40–1, 305

Salt, 179, 296

Samaria, 3, 21–2, 24, 26, 28–9, 38, 42, 82, 84, 94, 104–5, 112–13, 202, 208, 300 (n. 4), 305, 311, 317–18

Samaritans, 187, 274, 317–19
Samuel, 52, 57 ; Book of, 326
Sanballat, 297, 311, 318–319
Sargon II, 3, 24, 29–30, 105, 112, 237–8
Sâṭân, 270, 325, 335
Satrap (Governor, viceroy), 178, 184, 195, 197–9, 271, 300, 309–311
Satyrs (*se'îrîm*), 138, 315
Saul, 52, 58, 93
Schiffer, 25–6
Schmidt (Hans), 81 (n. 2), 114 (n. 1)
Scribe, 13, 74, 146, 209, 279, 328
Scythians, 20, 41, 63, 130, 142, 163
Seleucia, 201
Seleucids, 201–2 ; era, 201 ; persecutions, 13
Seleucus I, 201
Sellin, 245
Sendjirli, 41 (n. 2)
Sennacherib, 6, 28 (n. 1), 30–7, 46, 122, 157, 237–8
Sepharvaim, 24
Seraphim, 99–101
Serpent, 164 ; bronze, 100, 114
" Servant of Jahweh," 76, 244–9, 269, 330
Seven, 230
Seti (goddess), 307
Shabako, 30–1
Shamash, 127, 277
Shallum, 21–2
Shalmanezer III, 20 ; IV, 21 ; V, 24
Shaphan, 137, 148, 163, 164, 167
Shear-Jashub, 102–3
Sheba, 240, 247
Shebna, 106
Shechem, 28, 117, 208, 319
Shelemiah, prophet, 211 ; son of Sanballat, 297, 311
Sheol, 237, 329, 354
Shepherd, 81–3, 1 03, 110
Sheshbazzar, 178, 186, 188–9, 266, 269
Shiloh, 28, 163, 208, 258
Sibi', 23, 30
Siccuth, 84
Sidon, 31, 33, 38, 48, 165, 198
Siebens, 144, 146 (n. 3)
Siloam, 2, 31, 104
Simeon the Just, 279 (n. 4)
Simirra, 29
Simon (Richard), 101
Sinai, 283–5
Singers, Temple, 288, 299, 349
Sinim, 240
Sinšariškun, 41
Sippar, 182
Sirach, son of (Ben Sirach), 6, 13, 279, 298–9, 319, 328–9, 330, 345
Slaves, 149, 190–2, 289, 291, 297
Smend, 212

Smerdis, 193
Sô (*see* Sibi')
Solomon, 10, 116, 138, 147, 152, 218–19, 221, 256, 326 ; wisdom of, 279, 345
Song of Moses, 12, 209, 250
Song of praise, 350
Song of Songs, 13
Sorcerers, 276, 353
Sparta, 127, 182, 236
Spinner, 305
Spirit, 325
Sprinkling (ritual), 350 ; with blood, 295, 314
Statues, 136, 139, 151 ; bull, 94
Steles, 67, 95, 114–16, 138, 143, 147
Stone (sacred), 208, 266, 274
Suffering (causes), 14, 169–170, 328–9, 335–345, 352–4
Sun (God), 127, 138, 159
Susa, 25, 39, 184, 188, 193, 196
Syene, 240, 305 (n. 1), 310
Sympathetic magic, 215, 353
Synagogue, 154, 303, 347, 350
Syncretism, 38–9, 129, 148, 159–160, 196, 217, 278, 297, 308, 311
Syria, 201, 351

Tabernacles (Feast of), 289, 303–4, 313, 316, 317
Tacitus, 229 (n. 4)
Tahpanhes, 55, 167, 208
Talent, 22, 34, 46
Talmud, 279
Tammuz (god), 129, 159, 308
Tanis, 37
Tappuah, 22
Teima, 181, 238
Tekoa, 52, 72, 82–3, 86, 175
Tel Abib, 177, 196, 212, 237
Tel Harsa, 177
Tell Ahmar, 19, 38 (n. 2), 41 (n. 1)
Tell El-Amarna, 3, 18, 33 (n. 1), 74
Tell El-Fûl, 3
Tel Melaḥ, 177, 196
Temple of Jerusalem, 23, 28, 36, 38, 42, 46, 49, 68, 77, 99–101, 111–12, 114, 122, 127, 137–8, 143, 146–8, 151–2, 159, 163–4, 180, 185–8, 190, 193, 198, 208, 212, 219, 221, 225, 227, 229, 239, 250, 252–3, 258–9, 264, 265, 278, 284–5, 290, 327 ; of the Torah of Ezekiel, 225, 251–2, 257 ; second Temple of Jerusalem, 266–271, 273, 276, 278, 284, 299, 318, 322–3, 348–350 ; worship, 247–9 ; at Elephantine, 26, 174, 207, 218, 267, 278, 307, 310–12 ; of the Babylonian Jews, 218, 267, 278 ; Babylonian Temples, 181, 184, 194

Temple Servants, 218, 255–6
Tent of Meeting, 284
Teraphim, 93, 139
Thebes, 39
Theocracy, 73, 276–8
Theodicy, 336–341
Theriomorphic deities, worship of, 159–160
Thoth, 75
Tiglath Pileser I, 18 ; III, 20–4, 28, 80, 88, 128
Tirhaqah, 4, 35, 37–8
Tirzah, 22
Tithes, 276, 288, 301, 307, 313
Tobiah, 297, 318
Tobit, 16, 346
Tophet, 125
Torah (*see* Law and Ezekiel), 10, 134–6, 140–8, 154–5, 161, 205, 214, 248, 253, 263
Torrey, 298
Trade, 84, 189, 195–6, 239
Transcendence of Jahweh, 228, 323–4, 351
Transjordan, 21–3, 49
Trees, sacred, 94, 147, 274
Trumpets, 291
Tyre, 24, 31, 33, 39, 48, 50, 165, 180–1, 200

Umman Manda, 44
Uncleanness, 115, 257, 261, 263, 290–2
Universalism, 1–2, 60, 73, 88–9, 100, 109, 209, 231, 243–4, 249, 322
Unleavened Bread, 135, 264, 289, 309
Unqi, 21

Urartu, 20–1, 30
Uriah, 163, 165
Urim and Thummim, 134, 286
Usu, 39
Uzahor, 309

Vedas, 293
Vernes, 298
Vicarious Suffering, 15, 161, 219–222, 247, 249, 328, 353
Vines, 66, 170, 178
Volz, 245, 336 (n. 3)
Vow, 331, 344

Wahabis, 152
Walls of Jerusalem, 298–300, 349
War, 150, 262
Water of life, 230, 253 ; holy, 274, 290 ; of separation, 290
Weeks (Feast of), 264, 289
Welch, 44, 146
Welis, 152, 295
Wellhausen, 334
de Wette, 10, 144
Widarnag, 310
Winckler, 37, 56
Wine, 64, 66, 95, 178, 218, 264, 274, 346
Wisdom, 325, 330, 342
Word, efficacy of, 54, 215 ; of God, 325

Xerxes I, 4, 187, 194–5, 272 (n. 3), 304, 335 ; II, 195

Yamani, 30
Yaudi, 21, 30
Yedoniah, 4, 16, 309, 312

Printed in Great Britain by Stephen Austin & Sons, Ltd., Hertford.